EMPLOYEE SELECTION: LEGAL AND PRACTICAL ALTERNATIVES TO COMPLIANCE AND LITIGATION

Edited by

Edward E. Potter

EQUAL EMPLOYMENT ADVISORY COUNCIL
MONOGRAPH SERIES NO. 2

EMPLOYEE SELECTION: LEGAL AND PRACTICAL ALTERNATIVES TO COMPLIANCE AND LITIGATION

Edited By

Edward E. Potter

EQUAL EMPLOYMENT ADVISORY COUNCIL
Washington, D.C.

Copyright 1983 by the Equal Employment Advisory Council
  1015 15th Street, N.W.
  Washington, D.C. 20005

Library of Congress Catalog Card Number 83-80033
International Standard Book Number 0-937856-07-X

All rights reserved. No part of this work may be reproduced or copied in any form or by any means without written permission of the publisher.

EEAC and the Monograph Series

The Equal Employment Advisory Council is a voluntary nonprofit association organized to promote the common interest of employers and the general public in the development and implementation of sound government policies and procedures pertaining to nondiscriminatory employment practices. The Council's membership comprises a broad segment of the employer community in the United States including both individual employers and trade associations. The members of EEAC are firmly committed to the principle of equal employment opportunity and to the goals of our nation's equal ememployment laws.

With the rapidly increasing volume of court and administrative rulings interpreting these laws, it is essential that those responsible for decisions in precedent-setting cases understand as fully as possible the practical impact of their decisions. It is the function of the Council to explain this impact and to suggest useful solutions through the filing of amicus curiae briefs in significant court proceedings and through submitting appropriate comments to administrative agencies.

In order to deal with particularly significant issues in greater depth, from time to time EEAC has also published resource books on compliance with EEO requirements. Occasionally, however, legal and policy issues arise that need immediate discussion but are neither ripe for direct EEAC amicus participation nor sufficiently developed to warrant book-length treatment. To provide our members and the public with timely analysis and discussion of such issues, the Council has established an EEAC Monograph Series.

Each title in the Monograph Series is devoted to a topic that is of current concern to EEO practitioners. In keeping with EEAC's longstanding emphasis on program content and utility, the monographs are designed to impart a maximum amount of information and analysis in a comparatively brief and readable form useful to both lawyers and non-lawyers responsible for dealing with equal employment matters. Like other EEAC publications, the underlying purpose of the series is to provide the employer community with resources that will assist compliance with the civil rights laws and enhance the quality of employer representation in the EEO area. More generally, we hope this and future monographs will assist EEAC member companies and others to better understand and prepare for changes in EEO law and policy.

FOREWORD

Nondiscriminatory employee selection procedures might well be characterized as the cornerstone to the achievement of equal employment opportunity. Although tensions are bound to exist between employer desires to select qualified employees and government policies which emphasize numerical proportions of minorities and women in the workforce, there are few who would disagree with the premise that employment tests provide valuable information about prospective employees. Certainly no workable alternatives presently exist to validated tests that are as informative, fair-in-form, and technically adequate.

Unfortunately, since the enactment of Title VII of the 1964 Civil Rights Act, the federal enforcement agencies have promulgated increasingly complex, technical and rigid guidelines for the validation of employment tests rather than focusing on whether tests are in fact discriminatory. The first guidelines on employee selection were issued by the Equal Employment Opportunity Commission (EEOC) in 1966. They provided that any test or other selection procedure which resulted in proportionately lower selection rates for minorities or females than for white males would be considered to be discriminatory and unlawful unless the employer could validate the test or selection procedure in accordance with their general validation requirements. Between 1966 and 1970, two other enforcement agencies—the Office of Federal Contract Compliance of the Department of Labor and the U.S. Civil Service Commission—issued regulations on testing and validation that varied from those of the EEOC. 33 Fed. Reg. 14392 (September 24, 1968); FPM Supp. 335.1 (1969).

In 1970, the EEOC established more detailed selection guidelines, 35 Fed. Reg. 12333 (August 1, 1970), and the following year, the U.S. Supreme Court issued its decision in *Griggs v. Duke Power Co.*, 401 U.S. 424 (1971). *Griggs*, which held that selection procedures that are fair-in-form but discriminatory in result must be shown to be job related, placed added emphasis on demonstrating the job relatedness or validity of tests or other selection procedures.

Following the decision in *Griggs* and the 1972 amendments to Title VII, the federal enforcement agencies attempted to develop a single uniform set of guidelines that would be applied by the EEOC, the Departments of Justice and Labor, and the Civil Service Commission in carrying out their enforcement functions. The result of this effort was the issuance in 1976 of the Federal Executive Agency (FEA) Guidelines on Employee Selection Procedures. 41 Fed. Reg.

51734 (November 23, 1976). EEOC, however, declined to adopt them and, instead, reissued its 1970 Guidelines. Finally, in 1978 as a result of renewed efforts to achieve a single set of guidelines, the Uniform Guidelines on Employee Selection Procedures, 43 Fed. Reg. 38290 (August 25, 1978), were issued by EEOC, the Departments of Justice and Labor and the Civil Service Commission (now the Office of Personnel Management), which established complex and rigorous validation and documentation requirements.

Since their publication on August 25, 1978, growing numbers of employers, industrial psychologists and others involved in employee selection have expressed concern about the difficulties of complying with the Uniform Guidelines. They maintain that the Guidelines are inconsistent in a number of important respects with established Title VII case law and the accepted practices of the psychological profession. Also, many employers and industrial psychologists are convinced that certain provisions of the Guidelines serve neither to increase equal employment opportunities nor to foster a more productive workforce.

Over the course of the last two years, the need to review and revise the Uniform Guidelines and to appraise their underlying premises has become increasingly apparent. Thus, as part of the Reagan Administration's regulatory reform program, the Guidelines were targeted for review by Vice President Bush's Task Force on Regulatory Relief. The initial focus of the Task Force was on the recordkeeping provisions, but many observers looked upon this as incidental to a broader, overall review of the Guidelines. This conclusion was reinforced by the July 30, 1982, report of the General Accounting Office (GAO), entitled "Uniform Guidelines on Employee Selection Procedures Should Be Reviewed and Revised." Citing difficulties with the technical and policy provisions of the Guidelines and with their overall clarity, the GAO concluded that the Guidelines should be reviewed and revised. Among the problems cited in the GAO report were those associated with collecting and maintaining adverse impact data, searching for alternatives during validation and the relationship of merit laws. The report also cited the complexity and high reading level demanded by the Guidelines, as well as the fact that a number of groups from the psychological and personnel professions had recommended substantial changes.

The need for revision also was supported by the issuance in February 1982 of the report of the National Academy of Sciences entitled *Ability Testing: Uses, Consequences, and Controversies*, Washington, D.C., National Academy Press, 1982. This report was the result of over three years work by a distinguished, multidisciplinary group established under the auspices of the National Research Council and charged with the responsibility of conducting a broad examination of the role of testing in American society. After identifying many of the same concerns which employers have expressed regarding the use of tests under the Uniform Guidelines, the report concluded that "[i]t is disingenuous to impose test validation requirements that employers, even with the best will and a sizable monetary investment, cannot meet."

Another important consideration has been the Supreme Court's decision in *Connecticut v. Teal*, 102 S. Ct. 2525 (U.S. June 21, 1982). As a result of *Teal*, any facially neutral selection procedure—such as a written test—which disproportionately precludes persons protected by Title VII from the opportunity to be considered at the next step of the selection process, will be subject to challenge, whether or not the number of persons actually selected shows an adverse impact. Consequently, *Teal* has placed a renewed emphasis on demonstrating the job relatedness or validity of facially neutral components which have an adverse effect on persons covered by Title VII. Because substantial research evidence has demonstrated that even validated tests result in adverse impact against some groups covered by Title VII, the standards by which a showing of job relatedness or validity may be demonstrated have become even more critical.

Finally, from the inception of the Uniform Guidelines employers have been concerned about the conflict between the Guidelines, the requirements of Title VII, and accepted professional practices. This concern led to the establishment of an Ad Hoc Committee on Employee Selection within the Equal Employment Advisory Council (EEAC), composed of recognized experts on employee selection and test validation. During the past two years the Ad Hoc Committee has conducted a professional study of the Uniform Guidelines. The result of their work has been a revised set of guidelines with a supporting professional and legal analysis.

Based on the above factors and the collective experiences of employers, industrial psychologists, equal employment lawyers and personnel specialists, EEAC believes that a comprehensive review of the Uniform Guidelines is imperative. This monograph contains a number of studies and articles which are designed to contribute to the overall discussion of the current Guidelines, to offer suggestions for revisions, and to supply insight on other related issues regarding employee selection. The publication will also be useful to parties involved in employee selection lawsuits, practitioners engaged in compliance with the requirements of the Uniform Guidelines, and professionals, academics and students interested in the field of personnel selection.

Part I consists of EEAC's position statement on the Uniform Guidelines. The position statement has identified certain general principles which EEAC suggests should govern any review of the Guidelines. The principles emphasize the need to re-examine the assumptions on which the current Guidelines are based and offers a basic practical framework on which new guidelines could rest. The position statement also outlines problem areas of the current Guidelines which have proved to be most troublesome. Such problem areas include the overall difficulty of compliance, lack of conformity with Title VII precedent and the accepted practices of the psychological profession, burdensome and costly recordkeeping and validation requirements, the standard for adverse impact, and the uncertainty as to whether the agencies will continue to adhere to a "bottom line" approach in their enforcement activities.

The studies and papers that follow the EEAC position statement suggest alternative approaches to the Uniform Guidelines and to compliance with the legal requirements of TitleVII. The positions expressed by the authors of these papers and studies are their own and do not necessarily represent the views of EEAC, its member companies and trade associations, or any other employers or their associations.

Part II contains the professional study of the Ad Hoc Committee on Employee Selection. Included in the study are the Committee's recommendations for revision of the Uniform Guidelines and the professional and legal reasons supporting their revision.

Part III contains an article by Bruce Nelson of the law firm of Morrison & Foerster, San Francisco, California, on the potential use of opinion letters from the EEOC as a means of demonstrating the job relatedness or validity of a selection procedure. Section 713(b) of Title VII, 42 U.S.C. § 2000e-12(b), permits a defense to a Title VII lawsuit based on actions taken "in good faith, in conformity with, and in reliance on any written interpretation or opinion of the Commission." This article suggests that section 713(b) opinion letters should be available to demonstrate the lawfulness of a selection procedure.

Part IV contains an article by Val H. Markos, U.S. Steel Corporation, and John M. Rauschenberger, Armco, Inc., on the proposed revisions of the 1974 *Standards For Educational & Psychological Tests* by the American Psychological Society (APA), the American Educational Research Association and the National Council on Measurement in Education. Both authors serve as the principal testing and personnel research supervisors for their respective corporations. Because the APA *Standards* provide one source of the accepted practices of the psychological profession, the authors discuss the potential effect of the proposed revisions on equal employment, the Uniform Guidelines, and employment testing.

Part V contains an article by Edward E. Potter and Thomas R. Bagby of the law firm of McGuiness & Williams, Washington, D.C., on the impact of the Supreme Court's decision in *Teal* on employee selection. The article summarizes its factual background, discusses the Supreme Court's majority and minority opinions, and analyzes the effect of the decision on Title VII litigation and compliance. The paper also suggests alternative selection procedures strategies that employers should consider.

The Appendix consists of a summary of an EEAC survey concerning the Uniform Guidelines; a complete text of the Ad Hoc Committee's Revised Employee Selection Guidelines; the text of the Uniform Guidelines; the Questions and Answers clarifying the Uniform Guidelines; and a selected bibliography on the Uniform Guidelines.

The development of workable and job related employee selection procedures is a fundamental requirement for implementing the nondiscrimination mandate of Title VII. However, the field of industrial psychology and testing is one which is in a constant process of evolution and development. As demonstrated by the continual but unsuccessful revisions that the Selection Guidelines have gone through since 1966, it is not realistic at this time to expect to adopt a single standard by which validity of selection procedures should be evaluated. Instead, as indicated in EEAC's statement of principles, it should be possible to demonstrate validity by any method consistent with Title VII law.

The Council is publishing this book with the hope that it will be useful to all who are responsible for or merely interested in assuring that discrimination is eliminated from the job selection process. EEAC's primary objective in all its activities is to assist in developing practical and effective solutions to the many problems involved in making certain that equal employment opportunity is a reality, not just a policy.

Washington, D.C.
March 1983

Kenneth C. McGuiness
President
Equal Employment Advisory Council

TABLE OF CONTENTS

Page

FOREWORD v

POSITION STATEMENT OF THE EQUAL EMPLOYMENT ADVISORY COUNCIL ON GUIDELINES ON EMPLOYEE SELECTION PROCEDURES 1

    Principles Governing Guidelines on Employee Selection Procedures 4

    Problem Areas in the Current Guidelines 9

    Conclusion 17

REVISION OF THE UNIFORM GUIDELINES ON EMPLOYEE SELECTION PROCEDURES—A PROPOSED ALTERNATIVE
    by Ad Hoc Committee on Employee Selection 19

    Introduction 21

    Section-by-Section Comparison and Professional and Legal Analysis 23

    Section 1. Statement of Purpose 24

    Section 2. Scope 27

    Section 3. Relationship Between Use of Selection Procedures and Job Relatedness 31

    Section 4. Information on Impact 35

    Section 5. General Recommendations for Validity Evidence 41

    Section 6. Use of Selection Procedures Which Have Not Been Validated 52

    Section 7. Use of Other Validity Evidence 54

    Section 8. Cooperative Validation Efforts 59

Section 9. No Assumption of Validity 60
Section 10. Employment Agencies and Employment Services 62
Section 11. Disparate Treatment 63
Section 12. Retesting of Applicants 65
Section 13. Affirmative Action 66
Section 14. Technical Recommendations for Validity Evidence 67
Section 15. Documentation of Impact and Validity Evidence 89
Section 16. Definitions 117
Section 17. Policy Statement on Affirmative Action 125
Conclusion 125

DETERMINING THE VALIDITY OF TESTS THROUGH THE EEOC OPINION LETTER PROCESS
by Bruce A. Nelson 127

EEOC Opinion Letter Process 130
Development of Agency Expertise 132
Confidentiality of Accompanying Documentation 132
    The Freedom of Information Act 134
    Suggestions for Safeguarding Confidential Information 137
Proposal for a Pilot Program 142
Conclusion 142

THE IMPACT OF PROFESSIONAL STANDARDS ON EMPLOYEE TESTING AND EQUAL EMPLOYMENT
by Val H. Markos and John M. Rauschenberger 145

Introduction 147
Revision of the 1974 *Standards* 149

Protection of Individual Rights 152
Burdensome Nature of Requirements 153
References or Documentation of Standards 156
Technical Standards 157
Conclusion 159

THE IMPACT OF *CONNECTICUT v. TEAL* ON EMPLOYEE SELECTION, EEO COMPLIANCE AND LITIGATION
by Edward E. Potter and Thomas R. Bagby................... 161

Introduction 163
Connecticut v. Teal 166
    Facts and Lower Court Decisions 166
    The Majority Opinion 168
    The Dissenting Opinion 171
Title VII Litigation Standards After *Teal* 173
    Burdens of Proof 175
    Business Necessity and Other Defenses 177
    Determinination of the Plaintiff's Entitlement to Relief 183
Effect of *Teal* on Affirmative Action 185
    Affirmative Action as a Defense 186
    Judicial Remedies 189
    Employment of Protected Classes and Maintaining the Bottom Line 190
Revision of the Uniform Guidelines 192
    The Bottom Line 192
    The Search for Alternatives 193
    The Eighty Percent Rule 194
Selection Alternatives After *Teal* 195

Multiple Hurdle Selection Processes 196
Cumulatively-Scored Selection Processes 198
Public Sector Considerations 201
Recent Legal Developments 201
Conclusion 206

Appendix A—Summary of EEAC Survey Concerning the Uniform Guidelines on Employee Selection Procedures 207

Appendix B—Ad Hoc Committee's Revision of the Uniform Guidelines on Employee Selection Procedures 213

Appendix C—Uniform Guidelines on Employee Selection Procedures 237

Appendix D—Questions and Answers Clarifying the Uniform Guidelines on Employee Selection Procedures 285

Appendix E—Selected Bibliography on the Uniform Guidelines on Employee Selection Procedures 319

POSITION STATEMENT OF THE EQUAL EMPLOYMENT ADVISORY COUNCIL ON GUIDELINES ON EMPLOYEE SELECTION PROCEDURES

The Equal Employment Advisory Council believes that a comprehensive review of the 1978 Uniform Guidelines on Employee Selection Procedures is imperative at this time because their complexity and inconsistency with professional practice and the requirements of Title VII of the 1964 Civil Rights Act have caused a substantial number of employers to eliminate testing. The resulting use of less job-related and objective selection procedures and criteria has adverse implications for equal employment opportunity and this nation's productivity.

The Position Statement sets forth the underlying principles that are most significant in effectively eliminating the discriminatory aspects of selection procedures. The principles emphasize that tests provide valuable information about prospective employees and that job-related tests should be encouraged by the enforcement agencies. In order to encourage the use of job-related tests, the principles stress that Guidelines should be flexible recommendations that are clear and understandable, and not complex legal rules. Moreover, they should not contain provisions that are inconsistent with, or in excess of, the requirements of Title VII or the accepted practices of the psychological profession. Because testing and the field of industrial psychology are not precise sciences and are in the process of development, alternative sources of accepted professional practices, in addition to the Guidelines, should be available to employers to demonstrate the job relatedness of a selection procedure. Furthermore, the costs of compliance with the Guidelines should be reduced to the minimum level necessary to accomplish their objectives. Finally, the principles encourage the enforcement agencies to continue to adhere to a "bottom line" approach for enforcement actions. In suggesting these principles, the Position Statement also discusses the areas of the Guidelines that have proved most troublesome. They include: the overall difficulty of compliance; lack of conformity with Title VII precedent and the accepted practices of the psychological profession; burdensome recordkeeping requirements; excessive costs of validation; the standard for adverse impact; and uncertainty regarding the weight to be given to a nondiscriminatory "bottom line."

The Equal Employment Advisory Council is a voluntary nonprofit association organized to promote the common interest of employers and the general public in sound government policies, procedures and requirements pertaining to nondiscriminatory employment practices. Its membership comprises a broad segment of the employer community in the United States, including both individual employers and trade and industry associations. Its governing body is a board of directors composed primarily of lawyers and specialists with broad practical experience in the field of equal employment opportunity which provides the Council a unique depth of understanding of the practical and legal considerations relevant to the proper interpretation and application of EEO policies and requirements. The members of the Council are firmly committed to the principles of nondiscrimination and equal employment opportunity.

POSITION STATEMENT OF THE EQUAL EMPLOYMENT ADVISORY COUNCIL ON GUIDELINES ON EMPLOYEE SELECTION PROCEDURES

The practical difficulties encountered in complying with the Uniform Guidelines on Employee Selection Procedures since their publication on August 25, 1978, has been a matter of growing concern to employers. The Equal Employment Advisory Council (EEAC) has been closely monitoring this experience and has found that, while there is widespread agreement that equal employment opportunity is furthered by the use of nondiscriminatory selection procedures which are as "job related" as possible, attempts to comply with the Guidelines are more frustrating than fruitful. The practical problems facing employers as they deal with these requirements are confirmed by the July 30, 1982, report of the General Accounting Office (GAO), entitled "Uniform Guidelines On Employee Selection Procedures Should be Reviewed and Revised." After citing problems with the Guidelines' technical and policy provisions and with their overall clarity, the report concluded that they should be reviewed and revised.

For the past year and a half, the members of an EEAC committee of industrial psychologists, lawyers and company equal employment officers have been examining their experiences under the Guidelines to see if improvements can be made. At first, emphasis was placed on a technical revision of the current provisions but, as the study continued, it became apparent that it would be useful to identify the underlying principles that are most significant in effectively eliminating the discriminatory aspects of selection procedures. In dealing with complex issues such as these, basic objectives are sometimes overshadowed by the technicalities of achieving them.

The principles set forth below were developed by EEAC's Board of Directors, which is composed of lawyers and specialists with broad practical experience in the field of equal employment opportunity, in consultation with the chair and vice-chair of the technical committee studying the Uniform Guidelines. They are followed by a brief summary of specific employer concerns with respect to the current Uniform Guidelines. These concerns were reflected in a survey of EEAC's members, a summary of which is included in the Appendix. EEAC expects to continue its efforts to develop specific recommendations for implementing these principles. In the meantime, it is hoped that the statement of principles will be helpful to others who are searching for practical methods of developing and maintaining nondiscriminatory selection procedures.

PRINCIPLES GOVERNING GUIDELINES ON EMPLOYEE SELECTION PROCEDURES

The objective of any guidelines on employee selection procedures must be to assure that such procedures are nondiscriminatory and further the broader goal of equal employment opportunity. This means that the selection procedures an employer uses should be job related, focusing on the job's requirements. They must not be influenced by factors such as race, color, sex, and national origin, unless those factors are job related.

Also it is important to recognize that selection guidelines are used in the context of compliance or enforcement proceedings. They are neither statutes, nor agency rules or regulations. They are instead technical recommendations as to appropriate measures of employer conduct, used both by government officials responsible for investigating allegations of discriminatory practices and by the courts who determine the validity of such allegations.

Viewed in the light of these considerations and the problems which have arisen under the current Guidelines (see pp. 9–17, *infra*) EEAC recommends that the principles set forth below govern needed revisions.

1. Selection Guidelines are flexible recommendations and not legal rules

The courts have held that the Guidelines are "useful as a source of guidance, but they need not be adhered to in every detail as if they were substantive regulations." *Guardians Ass'n of New York City v. Civil Service*, 630 F.2d 79, 110 (2d Cir. 1980), *cert. denied*, 101 S. Ct. 3083 (1981). The federal enforcement agencies should clearly accept this rule of law and acknowledge that the Guidelines are intended to be flexible recommendations and not legal rules. EEOC lacks formal rulemaking authority. Accordingly, the Guidelines may be recognized as interpretations of Title VII by the enforcement agencies, but not as substantive, mandatory regulations.

2. Clear and understandable guidelines that conform to the standards of conduct established by Title VII provide assistance to enforcement authorities and employers in determining appropriate methods of assessing the legality of conduct

The enforcement agencies have a legitimate interest under federal equal employment laws in protecting groups covered by the Guidelines from discrimination and ensuring that nondiscriminatory selection procedures are utilized. This interest is best protected when the enforcement agencies develop a consistent enforceable interpretation of the requirements of Title VII and other equal employment laws. Consistent interpretation serves the interest of the enforcement agencies as well as that of employers. It follows that guidelines should be simple and should not contain provisions that are inconsistent with, contrary to, or in excess of the requirements of Title VII. Important portions of the current Guidelines, as discussed below, do not conform with this principle.

Also, requirements of the Guidelines that are inconsistent with the accepted practices of the psychological profession are not appropriate. *See, e.g., United States v. South Carolina*, 445 F. Supp. 1094, 1112-13 (D.S.C. 1977), *aff'd mem. sub nom. National Education Association v. South Carolina*, 434 U.S. 1026 (1978). Enforcement agencies should recognize that the field of industrial psychology and validation methodologies are in the process of evolution and development. A detailed prescription for validation evidence is neither desirable nor possible.

3. Employment tests provide valuable information about prospective employees

It is widely recognized that employment tests provide valuable information about prospective employees (p. 16, *infra*). Currently there exist no feasible alternatives to job-related tests that are as informative, technically adequate and economically viable. Such tests serve both the employer's interest in selecting qualified and productive employees and the enforcement agencies' interest in ensuring that selection is based on the ability to perform the job and not on prohibited factors such as race, sex or national origin. The use of job-related tests should therefore be encouraged by developing a set of workable guidelines with which compliance is possible and by other appropriate means, including the allowance of increased transportability of evidence of validity from one employer to another and provision for a more flexible use of content-oriented selection procedures.

4. The Guidelines should not contain unworkable, impractical or arbitrary policies or rules

To demand in the Guidelines a higher level of test development and validation than is currently attainable is improper. It places virtually all employers in a posture of noncompliance and enables the enforcement agencies to use the Guidelines as a litigation vehicle against even those employers who have instituted "state-of-the-art" selection procedures. The federal agencies should acknowledge that the Guidelines can legitimately contain only those principles or recommendations that are generally accepted by the courts and by the psychological profession and that are capable of attainment given the current level of expertise of employers and members of the psychological profession.

Examples of unworkable or impractical policies contained in the Guidelines are discussed below. Among them are the requirement that the employer conduct a "search for alternatives" despite federal case law which places this burden on the plaintiff or the enforcement agencies and the requirement of "fairness" studies despite a substantial body of research which shows such studies to be unjustified. Other examples are provisions relating to the use of content validity, transportability of validity evidence and the failure to include a test of practical and statistical significance in the "four-fifths" rule.

5. The validity of selection procedures may be demonstrated by any method consistent with Title VII law rather than by adherence to a single standard, such as the Guidelines

No single set of inflexible, detailed rules can be applied to testing and employee selection in a dynamic employment environment. This fact is implicit in Title VII which neither recognizes nor endorses any *single* standard by which the job relatedness of a selection procedure is to be judged. Indeed, between 1966 and 1976, three of the four principal enforcement agencies adhered to different standards of job relatedness. Rather, as indicated above, courts have recognized that selection procedures need not conform in all respects with the Uniform Guidelines, but must conform only "to the essential purposes of Title VII." *Guardians*, 630 F.2d at 110. *See also United States v. State of New York*, 21 FEP Cases 1286, 1337 (N.D.N.Y. 1979) ("[T]he legal principle to be applied with regard to the job-relatedness of an employee selection procedure is one of generally accepted standards of the psychological profession.").

Consequently, alternative sources of accepted professional practices, *in addition to the Guidelines*, should be available to an employer to show the job relatedness of a selection procedure. Among these alternatives are:

a. Principles for the Validation and Use of Personnel Selection Procedures (Division 14 Principles)

The Division 14 *Principles* represent the official statement of the Division of Industrial-Organizational Psychology of the American Psychological Association (APA). Division 14 is the Division of the APA which is most concerned with employment testing. The *Principles* are addressed to the specific problems of decisionmaking in the area of employee selection.

b. Standards For Educational & Psychological Tests (APA Standards)

The *Standards* were prepared by a joint committee of the American Psychological Association (APA), the American Educational Research Association, and the National Council on Measurement in Education. Since they establish standards for tests that are essentially ideals, and as such address considerations that are virtually impossible to duplicate in the employment context, many of their provisions have limited practical application in employee selection. Nevertheless, they should be available to demonstrate test validity where appropriate.

c. Textbooks, journals or other research findings

Various textbooks, journals, and other research findings provide a valuable source of accepted practices of the psychological profession and should be available to an employer to demonstrate the job relatedness of a selection procedure.

d. Studies by industrial-organizational psychologists

Studies by industrial-organizational psychologists with special expertise in equal employment and employee selection problems should also be an available alternative. For example, an EEAC Ad Hoc Committee, consisting of industrial-organizational psychologists who are recognized experts in the employee selection area, has conducted a professional study of the Uniform Guidelines to determine their conformity with professional practice. As a result of its study, the committee has prepared a revised set of guidelines which conform to generally accepted professional practice. See Appendix B.

> e. *Section 713(b) opinion letter regarding the validity of selection procedures*

The enforcement agencies might consider establishing a nonmandatory procedure whereby employers, at their discretion, could seek an opinion as to the validity of their selection procedures in accordance with section 713(b) of Title VII. Any such procedure should be wholly voluntary and should contain sufficient safeguards to ensure that the confidentiality of the selection procedures would be maintained. It should also ensure that those employers who do choose to seek an opinion as to the validity of their selection procedures would not be subject to agency enforcement actions based on their submissions. At the same time, there should be no negative inference if an employer elects not to use the procedure.

> f. *Other sources representing generally accepted practices of the psychological profession*

There may be other sources of acceptable practices not mentioned above upon which employers should be able to rely. Also, the generally accepted practices of the psychological profession are constantly evolving. As new practices become acceptable, employers should be able to draw upon them to support the job relatedness of their selection procedures.

Where differences exist between the Guidelines and alternative sources of accepted professional practices, adherence to such sources by an employer should not be deemed by the agencies to be noncompliance with Title VII or other relevant laws. Because of the wide variety of expert opinions and practices found in this area of the law and the lack of certainty which prevails, in all cases the agencies should take into account the good faith attempts of an employer to comply with the Guidelines or acceptable alternative sources of professional practice.

6. Recordkeeping and costs of compliance should be reduced to the minimum essential to accomplish the objectives of the Guidelines

The recordkeeping requirements and other costs of complying with the Guidelines are now excessive. Many of these costs serve no legitimate equal employment purpose and could be reduced without harming legitimate agency interests related to enforcement of Title VII.

7. Federal agencies should continue to adhere to a "bottom-line" approach to enforcement actions

Employers with a satisfactory "bottom line" are not those toward whom the enforcement agencies should direct their limited resources.

PROBLEM AREAS IN THE CURRENT GUIDELINES

Employer concerns with the Uniform Guidelines are centered around a number of problem areas. Those which have proved most troublesome include the difficulty of compliance, lack of conformity with Title VII precedent, inconsistency with accepted practices of the psychological profession, burdensome recordkeeping requirements, excessive costs of validation, the standard for adverse impact, and agency and court reluctance to give weight to a favorable "bottom line."

1. Difficulty of Compliance

Perhaps foremost of these concerns is that even the largest employers, whose staffs of industrial psychologists can provide "state-of-the-art" assistance in developing and validating selection procedures, have found it impossible to comply fully with the Guidelines. Employer concern in this regard was recently reinforced by the report of the National Academy of Sciences entitled *Ability Testing: Uses, Consequences, and Controversies*, Washington, D.C., National Academy Press, 1982. The *Ability Testing* report is the result of over three years work by a distinguished, multidisciplinary group established under the auspices of the National Research Council and charged with the responsibility of conducting a broad examination of the role of testing in American society. The report concluded that "[i]t is disingenuous to impose test validation requirements that employers, even with the best will and a sizable monetary investment, cannot meet."

2. Lack of Conformity with Title VII Precedent

Another frequently voiced concern of employers is that, in a number of important aspects, the Guidelines do not conform to federal court precedent under Title VII. An important example is the requirement that the employer, as part of a validity study, conduct a costly investigation of alternative selection procedures and alternative methods of use of the procedures. In *Albemarle Paper Co. v. Moody*, 422 U.S. 405, 425 (1975), the Supreme Court stated that if an employer meets its burden of showing that its selection procedures are job related, the *complaining party* still may show that there are other selection procedures without a similar adverse effect which would serve the employer's interest. Such a showing, the Court said, would be evidence that the employer was using its tests as a "pretext" for discrimination. Thus, the Supreme Court in *Albemarle* placed the burden of showing suitable alternative procedures with a lesser adverse impact on the plaintiff or the enforcement agencies, not on the employer. This requirement was recently reiterated in *Connecticut v. Teal*, 102 S. Ct. 2525, 2531 (1982), where the Court stated that, when the employer has shown the relationship of the procedure to the job in question, to prevail the plaintiff must show that the employer was using the procedure as a pretext for discrimination.

The requirement of the Guidelines that the employer *must* conduct the search for alternatives is clearly inconsistent with *Albemarle* and *Teal* and should be revised to reflect Title VII case law. The employer may conduct such a search voluntarily but it is inappropriate under Title VII precedent to require the employer to do so. This conclusion is supported by the July 30, 1982, report of the GAO, which recommended that "it would be appropriate to reconsider the Guidelines' provision that users are responsible, as a matter of course, for searching for alternative selection procedures."

Another example of lack of conformity with Title VII is the emphasis in the Guidelines on increasing the pool of minority or female candidates by encouraging use of procedures (*i.e.*, use of cutoff scores or pass-fail procedures) that measure only minimum qualification levels. Federal case law under Title VII clearly establishes that an employer is only required to use selection procedures that are "job related" and is not required to use procedures that maximize the employment opportunities of minorities and women. *See Furnco Construction Co. v. Waters*, 438 U.S. 567, 577-78 (1978). *See also* the legislative history of Title VII at 118 Cong. Rec. 7213 (1964)("There is no requirement in Title VII that employers abandon bona fide qualification tests where, because of differences in background and education, members of some groups are able to perform better on these tests than members of other groups. An employer may set his qualifications as high as he likes, he may test to determine which applicants have these qualifications, and he may hire, assign, and promote on the basis of test performance."). While many employers have "affirmative action" obligations under E.O. 11246 and similar voluntary programs, it is inappropriate for the Guidelines to go beyond statutory law as interpreted by the courts and attempt to transform these obligations and programs into Title VII mandates.

3. Inconsistency with Generally Accepted Professional Practices

The continued adherence by the enforcement agencies to the Guidelines where differences exist between the Guidelines and the generally accepted practices of the psychological profession is also inconsistent with federal case law. *See, e.g., United States v. South Carolina*, 445 F. Supp. 1094, 1112-13 (D.S.C. 1977), *aff'd mem. sub nom. National Education Association v. South Carolina*, 434 U.S. 1026 (1978). An important example of this point is found in the extensive requirements of the Guidelines relating to "fairness" studies. These requirements are included despite the fact that a substantial body of research has indicated that test scores predict appropriate levels of job performance for both minority groups and the majority group. This research is supported by the *Ability Testing* report of the National Academy of Sciences referred to earlier. That study reported that in the instances where "test unfairness" has been discovered, the tests have more often predicted job performance of minorities to be better than it actually was. Furthermore, relative to the questions of whether test scores differ in validity for different groups, the National Academy of Sciences report stated that there was "little convincing evidence that well constructed and competently adminstered tests are more valid predictors for one population subgroup than for another: individuals with higher scores tend to perform better on the job, regardless of group identity."

Similarly, the requirements of the Guidelines relating to the use of content validity are in excess of generally accepted professional practices and unduly restrict the use of content-oriented validity strategies, which provide the only means which many employers feasibly can use to show the job relatedness of their selection procedures. *See Guardians*, 630 F.2d at 92, 93. The Guidelines cannot legitimately require more of an employer than is required by the generally accepted practices of the psychological profession. Thus, the requirements of the Guidelines which are inconsistent with these practices, such as those mandating "fairness" studies and discouraging content validation strategies, should be deleted.

The strict limitations which the Guidelines place on "transporting" evidence of validity from one user to another are still another example of requirements that are in excess of the accepted practices of the psychological profession and are unduly restrictive. See, e.g., *Friend v. Leidinger*, 588 F.2d 61, 65 (4th Cir. 1978)("To require local validation in every city, village and hamlet would be ludicrous."). In this regard, the *Ability Testing* study concluded that "[g]overnment agencies concerned with fair employment practices should accept the principle of cooperative validation research so that tests validated for a job category such as fire fighter in a number of localities can be accepted for use on the basis of the cumulated experience." By restricting the transporting of validity evidence, the Guidelines have actually operated to discourage the use of potentially valid selection procedures.

As indicated above, despite agency interpretations to the contrary, selection procedures need not conform in all respects with the Guidelines and professional practices, but must conform only "to the essential purposes of Title VII." *Guardians*, 630 F.2d at 110. The APA *Standards* and the Division 14 *Principles* more accurately state the proper objective. These standards and principles, which provide sources of accepted practices of the psychological profession, state that they are intended to be "statements of ideals or goals" and are "*not* written as law." As the "fairness" issue illustrates, the practices of the psychological profession regarding employment testing and selection are in a process of continual development and refinement and there is often a considerable divergence between accepted professional practice and the requirements of the Guidelines. Thus, the Guidelines should recognize that there are a number of alternative sources of accepted professional practice that will meet "the essential purposes of Title VII."

4. Burdensome Recordkeeping Requirements

Employers have found the recordkeeping requirements relating to the collection of adverse impact and validation data to be unnecessarily burdensome and costly. Frequently, they do not conform with the employer's established recordkeeping procedures and in many instances they do not serve any legitimate purpose under Title VII. The July 30, 1982, report of the GAO recommended an examination of problems associated with collecting and maintaining adverse impact data.

Examples of methods of reducing the currently burdensome recordkeeping requirements would be to provide employers with the option of collecting data on a job group rather than a job-by-job basis; to raise the threshold number of employees entitling an employer to use the simplified "small employer" recordkeeping provisions and to extend the "small employer" provisions to small establishments of any employer; to increase to a higher percentage the requirement that data be maintained for groups constituting two percent of the labor force in the relevant labor area; and to simplify and reduce current validity documentation requirements to a level consistent with the generally accepted practices of the psychological profession. The burdensome nature of the recordkeeping requirements of the Guidelines could be eased substantially by eliminating or altering these and other unnecessary requirements without jeopardizing the legitimate interest of the enforcement agencies in requiring the maintenance of such data.

5. Excessive Costs of Validation

Most employers have found the costs involved in attempting to comply with the Guidelines to be unnecessarily expensive. While employers in general recognize the benefits which they derive from the use of job-related selection procedures, nearly all employers believe that many of the costs associated with attempts to demonstrate validity under the Guidelines serve neither to increase equal employment opportunities nor productivity in their workforces. In addition to the cost savings which would accrue from simplified recordkeeping, the currently excessive costs of compliance with the Guidelines could be decreased substantially without detracting from equal employment opportunity by allowing increased transportability of validity evidence and by eliminating the requirements for differential prediction or fairness studies. These savings could be accomplished without an erosion of the principle of the Guidelines that tests which result in an adverse effect on an identifiable race, sex or ethnic group should be shown to be job related.

Most large and nearly all small employers do not possess the capability or staff to conduct their own validity studies. Consequently, the only way that such employers can establish the job relatedness or validity of their selection procedures is by transporting validity evidence produced elsewhere or by engaging in cooperative studies with other similarly situated employers. As set forth above, the Guidelines currently take an overly restrictive view of transporting validity evidence developed in another location and ignore the practical inability of many employers to conduct a study of their own. This situation could be corrected if the Guidelines recognized this practical problem and provided for increased transportability where the jobs are similar in terms of the work behaviors or knowledges, skills and abilities required for performance of the jobs.

The Guidelines should continue to encourage cooperative test development and validity research among similarly situated groups of employers. The resulting evidence developed in one setting could then be transported to other similar jobs. This expanded transportability is consistent with the recommendations of the *Ability Testing* report, as set forth above, that federal enforcement agencies should accept the principle of cooperative validation research so that tests validated for a job in one locality can be used in similar jobs in other settings. Transportability of validity evidence would enable more employers to use validated tests and would decrease the costs of doing so.

Also, as stated above, any requirements for conducting differential validity or "fairness" studies are inconsistent with the generally accepted practices of the psychological profession. No useful purpose is served by such studies and the cost savings which would result from their elimination from the Guidelines would be substantial.

The foregoing are examples of areas where excessive costs could be eliminated without detriment to the objectives of equal employment. These are not the only possibilities.

6. The Standard for Adverse Impact

Currently, the Guidelines provide that a selection rate for any race, sex or ethnic group which is less than four-fifths of the group with the highest rate will generally be regarded as evidence of discrimination. Many employers have found that this "four-fifths" rule for determining the adverse impact of selection procedures is often treated by the enforcement agencies as a rule of law rather than a "rule of thumb." Consequently, many employers have been faced with findings of adverse impact by the agencies where there is no underutilization of the group in question or where the differences in rates of selection are neither statistically nor practically significant.

If the Guidelines were to provide that a selection rate of less than four-fifths of the group with the highest rate does not automatically constitute evidence of adverse impact, but rather establishes a basis for the agency to seek additional information on the selection procedures at issue, the rule would be much less controversial. A selection rate of less than four-fifths might be considered evidence of adverse impact if it were significant in both practical and statistical terms, unless (1) the group's underutilization in the job or group of jobs compared to their availability in the relevant labor market is not statistically and practically significant; (2) the representation of the group among those selected is not substantially different from the group's representation in the relevant labor market; (3) the pool of applicants from the group in question is atypical of the normal pool from the relevant labor market; or (4) the differences are based on small numbers.

Thus, in the absence of underutilization of the group in question, there would be no reason for the agencies to scrutinize selection rates under the four-fifths rule. This approach to determining adverse impact would retain the four-fifths rule as an easily applied rule-of-thumb, yet would incorporate concepts of statistical significance and other factors that have been adopted by the courts under Title VII and which could affect the determination of adverse impact. *See, e.g., Hazelwood School District v. United States*, 433 U.S. 299 (1977). Such an application of the four-fifths rule would serve both the agencies' interest in having a rule that is practical and simple to apply and the employers' interest in a recognition that differences in rates of selection that are neither practically nor statistically significant do not constitute adverse impact.

7. The "Bottom Line"

Employers have long contended that the "bottom line" approach to enforcement actions serves the interests of employers and the enforcement agencies, as well as groups protected by Title VII. Currently, the Guidelines provide that the federal enforcement agencies, in the exercise of their prosecutorial discretion, ordinarily will not take enforcement action based upon a component of an employer's selection process where the overall result or "bottom line" of such process has no impact. It is clear after *Connecticut v. Teal*, 102 S. Ct. 2525 (1982), that a private claimant can establish a prima facie case under Title VII based upon the adverse impact of a pass-fail component of a multi-part selection process. However, *Teal* does not and should not control the agencies' discretion, as a matter of policy, to refrain from bringing enforcement actions where an employer's "bottom line" is satisfactory.

The protection from suit by the enforcement agencies currently available to employers who possess a satisfactory "bottom line" provides a major incentive for the employment of minorities and women in numbers approximating their representation in the relevant labor market. While the vulnerability to a lawsuit from private claimants lessens this incentive, it would be eroded further by the elimination of the protection from federal agency action and could result in the employment of fewer minorities and women. Employers may currently be willing, in appropriate instances, to incur the added risks of "reverse discrimination" suits in order to reach an acceptable "bottom line." They may not be willing to incur such risks if they still will face actions by the enforcement agencies.

8. Additional Concerns

In addition to the areas of concern set forth above, there are other serious problem areas in the Guidelines where changes should be made. For example, it would be more realistic if the protected groups covered by the Guidelines were narrowed by eliminating references to religious groups and by confining national origin group coverage to those set forth in section 4B. The section on method of use of selection procedures and selection for higher level jobs could be modified. Training success and other organizational criteria relating to job performance could be specifically identified as acceptable criterion measures. The sections relating to review of validity evidence for currency could be modified. Also, the section on disparate treatment could be amended and certain definitions in section 16 modified.

9. The National Academy of Sciences Report

As indicated above, the findings of the National Academy of Sciences *Ability Testing* study reinforce employer concerns about the current Guidelines. While recognizing the "tension" that sometimes exists between employers' legitimate interest in promoting workforce efficiency and the government's efforts to ensure equal employment opportunity, the report states that employment tests provide valuable information about prospective employees and that no alternatives presently exist to job-related tests that are as informative, as technically adequate and as economically and politically viable. The report recommends that the validity of the testing process should not be compromised in order to ensure the distribution of the workforce.

Characterizing the policies adopted by EEOC as "those that would be adopted if the desired effect were to force employers to a quota system to achieve a representative workforce," the report repeats employer concerns that this rigid interpretation of the Guidelines by the enforcement agencies and the courts has made it exceedingly difficult for test users to defend even "state-of-the-art" testing procedures. This has resulted in a situation where good tests are being abandoned or struck down along with the bad. The report cautions that while there is room for improving the quality of even the more useful tests, there is a significant danger that the abandonment of comparatively valid selection procedures because of pressure from the enforcement agencies will result in a lowering of the morale of the workforce and the productivity of the economy. Finally, the report concludes that as long as minority groups protected by Title VII continue to have a relatively high proportion of less educated and more disadvantaged members of our society, those facts are likely to be reflected in test scores so that even highly valid tests will have adverse impact.

CONCLUSION

As indicated at the beginning of this position statement, EEAC will continue to develop specific recommendations for implementing the principles outlined above. Other organizations and individuals are engaged in a similar effort. We hope the principles will be useful to all who are interested in nondiscriminatory selection procedures.

REVISION OF THE UNIFORM GUIDELINES ON EMPLOYEE SELECTION PROCEDURES—A PROPOSED ALTERNATIVE

by
Ad Hoc Committee on Employee Selection

As a result of two years of in-depth study, the Ad Hoc Committee proposes a section-by-section revision of the Uniform Guidelines on Employee Selection Procedures based on its professional and legal analysis that there is substantial conflict between the Uniform Guidelines and the requirements of Title VII of the 1964 Civil Rights Act and generally accepted practices of the psychological profession. The proposed revisions, among other things, would: (1) conform the Guidelines to Title VII precedent; (2) conform the Guidelines to the standards of the psychological profession; (3) permit transporting of validity evidence for comparable or similar jobs between locations; (4) eliminate the requirement to conduct differential prediction or fairness studies; and (5) reduce adverse impact recordkeeping and documentation of validity evidence requirements.

The Ad Hoc Committee on Employee Selection was formed in 1981 as a separate, specialized committee within the Equal Employment Advisory Council to address professional and legal issues relating to the Uniform Guidelines. It is composed of experienced EEO practitioners, lawyers, and industrial psychologists concerned with employee selection problems, all of whom are recognized experts on employee selection and the Uniform Guidelines.

REVISION OF THE UNIFORM GUIDELINES ON EMPLOYEE SELECTION PROCEDURES—A PROPOSED ALTERNATIVE

Introduction

Since the publication of the Uniform Guidelines on Employee Selection Procedures in 1978, equal employment practitioners, lawyers and industrial psychologists have expressed concern over the conflict between the Uniform Guidelines and the legal requirements of Title VII of the Civil Rights Act of 1964, as amended, and generally accepted practices of the psychological profession. In 1981, the Ad Hoc Committee on Employee Selection was formed as a separate, specialized committee within the Equal Employment Advisory Council (EEAC) to address legal and professional issues relating to the Uniform Guidelines. It is composed of experienced EEO practitioners, lawyers and industrial psychologists concerned with employee selection problems, all of whom are recognized experts on employee selection and the Uniform Guidelines.

Almost all of the Committee were members of the Ad Hoc Group on the Uniform Selection Guidelines which had been formed in 1974 to contribute a legal and professional perspective to the enforcement agencies' development of guidelines on selection procedures. Two of the Committee's members—Paul Sparks and Mary L. Tenopyr—were past presidents of the Division of Industrial-Organizational Psychology (Division 14) of the American Psychological Association (APA), the Division of the APA most concerned with employment testing. They, along with two other Committee members—Frank Erwin and Virginia Boehm—were directly involved in the development of the *Principles for the Validation and Use of Personnel Selection Procedures* (1980), which is the official statement of Division 14 concerning procedures for validation research and personnel selection. In addition, one member of the Committee—James Sharf—served as a staff psychologist to the Equal Employment Opportunity Commission during the development of the Uniform Guidelines.

Beginning in 1981, under the leadership of Mary Tenopyr, Paul Sparks, and Marilyn Quaintance, the Ad Hoc Committee began a professional study of the Uniform Guidelines to determine if alternative guidelines could be developed that would meet Title VII's legal requirements and generally accepted professional practice. The following revision of the Uniform Guidelines and the professional and legal analysis supporting an alternative approach to the current Guidelines are the result of two years of work by the Ad Hoc Committee. It is intended to be of assistance to the enforcement agencies as well as to all others interested in the development of sound employee selection procedures. The Ad Hoc Committee believes that the Revised Guidelines are consistent with the accepted practices of the psychological profession as well as with Title VII precedent.

The following persons served on the Ad Hoc Committee and contributed to the development of the revised employee selection guidelines: Mary L. Tenopyr, Chairperson (American Telephone & Telegraph Co.); Val H. Markos, Vice-Chair (United States Steel Corporation); V. Jon Bentz (Sears, Roebuck & Company); Virginia R. Boehm (Standard Oil of Ohio); Patricia J. Dyer (International Business Machines Corporation); Joyce Lawson (General Electric Company); John R. Murray, III (Prudential Insurance Company); Diane Prange (CNA Insurance); John M. Rauschenberger (Armco, Inc.); C. Paul Sparks (Exxon Company); H. Paul Stuber (Reynolds Metals Company); Jerry E. Toomer (Dow Chemical); John N. Turner (Ford Motor Company); Laurence Vickery (General Motors Corporation); Frank Erwin (Richardson, Bellows, Henry & Co.) (ex officio); James Sharf (Richardson, Bellows, Henry & Co.) (ex officio); and Marilyn Quaintance (International Personnel Management Association) (ex officio).

The professional and legal analysis of the revised employee selection guidelines was prepared by: Joyce Lawson (General Electric Company); Val H. Markos (United States Steel Corporation); and Mary L. Tenopyr (American Telephone & Telegraph Co.). Edward E. Potter and Thomas R. Bagby of the law firm of McGuiness & Williams, Washington, D.C., provided assistance on the legal aspects of the analysis. The analysis highlights the differences between the Revised Guidelines and the Uniform Guidelines and offers the professional and legal reasons for the revisions. It is designed to allow the reader to conduct a section-by-section comparison of the Revised Guidelines with the Uniform Guidelines. The professional and legal analysis that follows represents the professional opinion of the Ad Hoc Committee and is not an official position of the Equal Employment Advisory Council.

SECTION-BY-SECTION COMPARISON AND PROFESSIONAL AND LEGAL ANALYSIS

Table of Contents

		Page
Section 1.	Statement of Purpose[1]	24
Section 2.	Scope	27
Section 3.	Relationship Between Use of Selection Procedures and Job Relatedness	31
Section 4.	Information on Impact	36
Section 5.	General Recommendations for Validity Evidence	41
Section 6.	Use of Selection Procedures Which Have Not Been Validated	52
Section 7.	Use of Other Validity Evidence	54
Section 8.	Cooperative Validation Efforts	59
Section 9.	No Assumption of Validity	60
Section 10.	Employment Agencies and Employment Services	62
Section 11.	Disparate Treatment	63
Section 12.	Retesting of Applicants	65
Section 13.	Affirmative Action	66
Section 14.	Technical Recommendations for Validity Evidence	67
Section 15.	Documentation of Impact and Validity Evidence	89
Section 16.	Definitions	117
Section 17.	Policy Statement on Affirmative Action	125

---

[1]The captions for each section are those used by the Ad Hoc Committee in its proposed revision of the Uniform Guidelines.

Section 1. Statement of Purpose.

Uniform Guidelines
A. Need for uniformity—Issuing agencies. The Federal government's need for a uniform set of principles on the question of the use of tests and other selection procedures has long been recognized. The Equal Employment Opportunity Commission, the Civil Service Commission, the Department of Labor, and the Department of Justice jointly have adopted these uniform guidelines to meet that need, and to apply the same principles to the Federal Government as are applied to other employers.

Revised Guidelines
A. Need for uniformity—Issuing agencies. The Federal government's need for a uniform set of principles on the question of the use of tests and other selection procedures continues to be recognized. The Equal Employment Opportunity Commission, Office of Personnel Management, the Department of Labor, and the Department of Justice jointly have adopted these uniform guidelines to meet that need, and to apply the same principles to the Federal Government as are applied to other employers.

Professional and Legal Analysis

The only change here is to acknowledge the substitution of the Office of Personnel Management for the Civil Service Commission.

Uniform Guidelines
B. Purpose of guidelines. These guidelines incorporate a single set of principles which are designed to assist employers, labor organizations, employment agencies, and licensing and certification boards to comply with requirements of Federal law prohibiting employment practices which discriminate on grounds of race, color, religion, sex, and national origin. They are designed to provide a framework for determining the proper use of tests and other selection procedures. These guidelines do not require a user to conduct validity studies of selection procedures where no adverse impact results. However, all users are encouraged to use selection procedures which are valid, especially users operating under merit principles.

Revised Guidelines
B. Purpose of guidelines. These guidelines represent a set of recommendations which are intended to assist employers, labor organizations, and employment agencies in understanding the requirements of Federal law prohibiting employment practices which illegally discriminate on grounds of race, color, sex, and national origin as these classifications are defined in section 4B. They are designed to provide a framework for determining the proper use of tests and other selection procedures. These guidelines do not require a user to provide evidence of validity for selection procedures where no adverse impact

Section 1 (continued)

results. However, all users are encouraged to use selection procedures that are job related.

Professional and Legal Analysis

The first proposed change in this section is designed to ensure that the Guidelines are viewed by the agencies and the courts as "recommendations" and not as legally-binding "principles" which must be followed by employers. This is consistent with Title VII case law which increasingly has acknowledged that the Guidelines are recommendations and not legal rules. *See, e.g., Guardians Ass'n of New York City v. Civil Service,* 630 F.2d 79, 110 (2d Cir. 1980), *cert. denied,* 101 S. Ct. 3083 (1981)("The Guidelines remain useful as a source of guidance, but they need not be adhered to in every detail as if they were substantive regulations.").

The next revision relates to the elimination of religion from Guidelines' coverage and the limitation of national origin coverage to those national origin groups for whom recordkeeping requirements are imposed in section 4B (*i.e.,* American Indians, Asians and Hispanics). There are no recordkeeping requirements for maintaining information on religion, either under the Guidelines or for EEO-1 reporting purposes. Cases alleging religious discrimination have almost uniformly arisen in situations of disparate *treatment* and not disparate *impact.* Consequently, it is inappropriate to include religion as a basis for Guidelines' coverage. In addition, there currently exist extensive guidelines issued by EEOC relating to religious discrimination. *See* 29 C.F.R. Part 1605. The subject of religious discrimination, therefore, is more appropriately dealt with under EEOC's Religion Guidelines and not under the Selection Guidelines.

Currently, recordkeeping requirements relating to national origin are limited to those ethnic groups included in section 4B. This is intended to be consistent with the Equal Employment Opportunity Standard Form 100, Employer Information Report EEO-1 series. The revision is designed to ensure that only those national origin groups included in the recordkeeping requirements of section 4B (and not others, such as Polish, Norwegian, *etc.*) are covered by the Guidelines. EEOC's National Origin Guidelines, 29 C.F.R. Part 1606, adequately cover members of any other ethnic groups who believe that they have been discriminated against because of their national origin.

The previous reference to "licensing and certification boards" has been deleted. Such boards are not "employers" or "employment agencies" within the meaning of Title VII and should be excluded

Section 1 (continued)

from coverage under the Guidelines. *See, e.g., Tyler v. Vickery,* 517 F.2d 1089 (5th Cir. 1975), *cert. denied,* 426 U.S. 940 (1976); *Lavender-Cabellero v. Department of Consumer Affairs,* 458 F. Supp. 213 (S.D.N.Y. 1978).

Finally, the last sentence has been changed in recognition of the fact that means other than a showing of "validity" exist under federal law for demonstrating that a selection procedure is "job related." While a validation study is normally the means employed to demonstrate the job relatedness of a written test, many selection procedures may appropriately be justified by a showing of job relatedness other than by means of a validity study. *See, e.g., Furnco Construction Company v. Waters,* 438 U.S. 567, 577-78 (1978). *See also Hawkins v. Anheuser-Busch, Inc.,* 30 FEP cases 1171, 1175 (8th Cir. 1983) ("We cannot say, however, that validation studies are always required....").

Uniform Guidelines **C. Relation to prior guidelines.** These guidelines are based upon and supersede previously issued guidelines on employee selection procedures. These guidelines have been built upon court decisions, the previously issued guidelines of the agencies, and the practical experience of the agencies, as well as the standards of the psychological profession. These guidelines are intended to be consistent with existing law.

Revised Guidelines **C. Relation to prior guidelines.** These guidelines supersede previously issued guidelines on employee selection procedures.

Professional and Legal Analysis

This section provides that these Guidelines supersede previously issued guidelines because, as set forth herein, the previously issued Guidelines are inconsistent in a number of important areas with federal case law under Title VII and/or with the accepted practices of the psychological profession.

Uniform Guidelines **D. Implementation and interpretation.** [There is no current guideline on this subject.]

Revised Guidelines **D. Implementation and interpretation.** It is not expected that users will be able to implement completely every recommendation contained in these guidelines. The applicability of specific provisions of the guidelines depends on the particular circumstances of the user. Likewise, these guidelines are not intended to limit or prohibit professional development or innovation. Any interpretation of these guidelines should be made in light of any new and generally accepted professional research findings relevant to any issue in question.

Section 1 (continued)

Professional and Legal Analysis

This new section is designed to ensure that the Guidelines will be interpreted by the enforcement agencies and by the courts in a flexible manner. This flexibility is achieved by reiterating the fact that the Guidelines are recommendations and not legal rules, by emphasizing that the applicability of particular recommendations depends on the circumstances of the user, and by allowing for professional innovation. Thus, this section envisions a case-by-case determination of compliance with the Guidelines, taking into account the good faith efforts of the employer to comply with them.

This section also provides that the Guidelines will be interpreted in light of new and generally accepted professional research findings. Thus, the new section provides a means by which new developments of the psychological profession can be incorporated into the Guidelines without having to revise them each time new developments become generally acceptable.

Section 2. Scope.

Uniform Guidelines   **A. Application of guidelines.** These guidelines will be applied by the Equal Employment Opportunity Commission in the enforcement of Title VII of the Civil Rights Act of 1964, as amended by the Equal Employment Opportunity Act of 1972 (hereinafter "Title VII"); by the Department of Labor, and the contract compliance agencies until the transfer of authority contemplated by the President's Reorganization Plan No. 1 of 1978, in the administration and enforcement of Executive Order 11246, as amended by Executive Order 11375 (hereinafter "Executive Order 11246"); by the Civil Service Commission and other Federal agencies subject to section 717 of Title VII; by the Civil Service Commission in exercising its responsibilities toward State and local governments under section 208(b)(1) of the Intergovernmental-Personnel Act; by the Department of Justice in exercising its responsibilities under Federal law; by the Office of Revenue Sharing of the Department of the Treasury under the State and Local Fiscal Assistance Act of 1972, as amended; and by any other Federal agency which adopts them.

Revised Guidelines   **A. Application of guidelines.** These guidelines will be applied by the Equal Employment Opportunity Commission in the enforcement of Title VII of the Civil Rights Act of 1964, as amended by the Equal Employment Opportunity Act of 1972 (hereinafter "Title VII"); by the Department of Labor in the administration and enforcement of Executive Order 11246, as amended by Executive Order 11375 (hereinafter "Executive

Section 2 (continued)

Order 11246"); by the Office of Personnel Management and other Federal agencies subject to section 717 of Title VII; by the Office of Personnel Management in exercising its responsibilities toward State and local governments under section 208(b)(1) of the Intergovernmental-Personnel Act; by the Department of Justice in exercising its responsibilities under Federal law; by the Office of Revenue Sharing of the Department of the Treasury under the State and Local Fiscal Assistance Act of 1972, as amended; and by any other Federal agency which adopts them.

Professional and Legal Analysis

The only changes in this section are to eliminate the reference to "contract compliance agencies" and to acknowledge the renaming of the Civil Service Commission as the Office of Personnel Management.

Uniform Guidelines **B. Employment decisions.** These guidelines apply to tests and other selection procedures which are used as a basis for any employment decision. Employment decisions include but are not limited to hiring, promotion, demotion, membership (for example, in a labor organization), referral, retention, and licensing and certification, to the extent that licensing and certification may be covered by Federal equal employment opportunity law. Other selection decisions, such as selection for training or transfer, may also be considered employment decisions if they lead to any of the decisions listed above.

Revised Guidelines **B. Employment decisions.** These guidelines apply to selection procedures which are used as a basis for any employment decision. Employment decisions include but are not limited to hiring, promotion, demotion, membership (for example, in a labor organization), referral, and retention. Other selection decisions, such as selection for training or transfer, may also be considered employment decisions if they lead to any of the decisions listed above.

Professional and Legal Analysis

This section eliminates references to "licensing and certification." See discussion under section 1B.

Uniform Guidelines **C. Selection procedures.** These guidelines apply only to selection procedures which are used as a basis for making employment decisions. For example, the use of recruiting procedures designed to attract members of a particular race, sex, or ethnic group, which were previously denied employment opportunities or which are currently underutilized, may be necessary to bring an employer into compliance with Federal law, and is frequently an essential element of any effective

Section 2 (continued)

affirmative action program; but recruitment practices are not considered by these guidelines to be selection procedures. Similarly, these guidelines do not pertain to the question of the lawfulness of a seniority system within the meaning of section 703(h), Executive Order 11246 or other provisions of Federal law or regulation, except to the extent that such systems utilize selection procedures to determine qualifications or abilities to perform the job. Nothing in these guidelines is intended or should be interpreted as discouraging the use of a selection procedure for the purpose of determining qualifications or for the purpose of selection on the basis of relative qualifications, if the selection procedure had been validated in accord with these guidelines for each such purpose for which it is to be used.

Revised Guidelines C. **Selection procedures.** These guidelines apply only to selection procedures which are used as a basis for making employment decisions. Such procedures include the full range of assessment techniques from traditional paper and pencil tests, performance tests, training programs, and physical, educational and work experience requirements through informal or casual interviews and unscored application forms.

Recruitment, activities of college placement offices, and affirmative action practices are not considered by these guidelines to be selection procedures. Similarly, these guidelines do not pertain to the question of the lawfulness of a seniority system within the meaning of section 703(h), Executive Order 11246 or other provisions of Federal law or regulation, except to the extent that such systems utilize selection procedures to determine qualifications or abilities to perform the job. Nothing in these guidelines is intended or should be interpreted as discouraging the use of a job-related selection procedure for the purpose of determining employment qualifications or for the purpose of selection on the basis of relative qualifications.

Professional and Legal Analysis

The second sentence of the Revised Guidelines is new to this section. It is taken, in part, from the definition of "selection procedure," as set forth in section 16Q of the Uniform Guidelines.

The revised section expressly continues the exclusion of recruitment activities from coverage under the Guidelines and also excludes activities of college placement offices and affirmative action practices. Under the Uniform Guidelines, a college placement office could, in certain instances, be covered by the Guidelines. *See* Question and Answer (Q&A) 4, 44 Fed. Reg. 11997 (March 2, 1979). The revision makes it clear that college placement offices are not covered by the Guidelines.

The example relating to recruitment which is included in the Uniform Guidelines has been deleted, since it carries the implication that recruitment activities may be necessary because of the previous

Section 2 (continued)

denial of employment opportunities to members of a particular race, sex or ethnic group or "to bring an employer into compliance with federal law." Such practices, however, can be voluntarily undertaken by an employer or undertaken in order to fulfill affirmative action obligations under Executive Order 11246 under circumstances in which the employer has no prior history of discrimination.

Finally, the last sentence of the revision retains the Guidelines' acceptance of the use of procedures to determine qualifications or to select on the basis of relative qualifications, but the sentence makes clear that means other than formal validation are available under federal law to demonstrate that a selection procedure is "job related."

Uniform Guidelines
D. Limitations. These guidelines apply only to persons subject to Title VII, Executive Order 11246, or other equal employment opportunity requirements of Federal law. These guidelines do not apply to responsibilities under the Age Discrimination in Employment Act of 1967, as amended, not to discriminate on the basis of age, or under sections 501, 503, and 504 of the Rehabilitation Act of 1973, not to discriminate on the basis of handicap.

Revised Guidelines
D. Limitations. These guidelines apply only to Title VII, the nondiscrimination provisions of Executive Order 11246, or other equal employment opportunity requirements of Federal law. These guidelines do not apply to responsibilities under the Age Discrimination in Employment Act of 1967, as amended, not to discriminate on the basis of age, or under sections 501, 503, and 504 of the Rehabilitation Act of 1973, not to discriminate on the basis of handicap, or under section 402 of the Vietnam Era Veterans Readjustment Assistance Act, not to discriminate against Vietnam Era or disabled veterans.

Professional and Legal Analysis

The revised section clarifies that the Guidelines should apply only to the nondiscrimination provisions of Executive Order 11246 and not to the portions of the Executive Order relating to affirmative action responsibilities of federal contractors because many of the affirmative action obligations are in addition to the recommendations contained in the Guidelines. Because the Vietnam Era Veterans Readjustment Assistance Act is not covered by the Guidelines, this statute has been added to those statutes to which the Guidelines are not applicable.

Uniform Guidelines
E. Indian preference not affected. These guidelines do not restrict any obligation imposed or right granted by Federal law to users to extend a preference in employment to Indians

Section 2 (continued)

living on or near an Indian reservation in connection with employment opportunities on or near an Indian reservation.

Revised Guidelines   **E. Indian preference not affected.** These guidelines do not affect any obligation imposed or right granted by Federal law to users to extend a preference in employment to Indians living on or near an Indian reservation in connection with employment opportunities on or near an Indian reservation.

Professional and Legal Analysis

The only change is the substitution of the word "affect" for "restrict."

Section 3. Relationship Between Use of Selection Procedures and Job Relatedness.[2]

Uniform Guidelines   **A. Procedure having adverse impact constitutes discrimination unless justified.** The use of any selection procedure which has an adverse impact on the hiring, promotion, or other employment or membership opportunities of members of any race, sex, or ethnic group will be considered to be discriminatory and inconsistent with these guidelines, unless the procedure has been validated in accordance with these guidelines, or the provisions of section 6 below are satisfied.

Revised Guidelines   **A. Procedure having adverse impact.** The use of any selection procedure which results in an adverse impact as defined in section 4D in the hiring, promotion, or other employment or membership opportunities of members of any race, sex, or ethnic group will be considered to be inconsistent with the recommendations contained in these guidelines, unless the procedure can otherwise be shown to be job related.

Professional and Legal Analysis

The revisions to this section are designed to tie the concept of adverse impact to its definition as set forth in section 4D, including the requirement of statistical and practical significance and the other exceptions contained in section 4D. The revised section does not attempt to define discrimination as do the Uniform Guidelines. In conjunction with section 1B, this section limits considerations of

---

[2] The Uniform Guidelines caption for this section is "Discrimination defined: Relationship between use of selection procedures and discrimination."

Section 3 (continued)

adverse impact to those national origin groups for whom record-keeping requirements are contained in section 4B.

The revised section reemphasizes that the Guidelines are recommendations and not legal rules and that methods other than formal validation exist for showing a procedure to be job related. By removing the language requiring that selection procedures having adverse impact must be "validated in accordance with these guidelines," the Revised Guidelines take a more flexible approach to the requirements for showing the job relatedness of a selection procedure. In so doing, the revised section is brought into line with the accepted practices of the psychological profession and court precedent. See *Guardians,* 630 F.2d at 110 (Selection procedures need not conform in all respects with the Guidelines and the APA *Standards,* but must conform only "to the essential purposes of title VII."). See also the cautionary language in the Division 14 *Principles for the Validation and Use of Personnel Selection Procedures* (2d ed. 1980) (hereafter *Principles*) at page 2 and the *Standards for Educational and Psychological Testing* (1974) (hereafter *Standards*) of the American Psychological Association (APA) at page 8 that the "standards are statements of ideals or goals" and are "*not* written as law."

Finally, the revised section eliminates the reference to section 6 as an option to showing the job relatedness of a selection procedure which has adverse impact. A discussion of section 6 is contained below.

Uniform Guidelines **B. Consideration of suitable alternative selection procedures.** Where two or more selection procedures are available which serve the user's legitimate interest in efficient and trustworthy workmanship, and which are substantially equally valid for a given purpose, the user should use the procedure which has been demonstrated to have the lesser adverse impact. Accordingly, whenever a validity study is called for by these guidelines, the user should include, as a part of the validity study, an investigation of suitable alternative selection procedures and suitable alternative methods of using the selection procedure which have as little adverse impact as possible, to determine the appropriateness of using or validating them in accord with these guidelines. If a user has made a reasonable effort to become aware of such alternative procedures and validity has been demonstrated in accord with these guidelines, the use of the test or other selection procedure may continue until such time as it should reasonably be reviewed for currency. Whenever the user is shown an alternative selection procedure with evidence of less adverse impact and substantial evidence of validity for the same job in similar circumstances, the user should investigate it to determine the appropriateness of using or validating it in accord with these guidelines. This subsection is not intended to preclude the

Section 3 (continued)

combination of procedures into a significantly more valid procedure, if the use of such a combination has been shown to be in compliance with the guidelines.

Revised Guidelines **B. Consideration of suitable alternative selection procedures.** Whenever the user is shown a feasible alternative selection procedure with appropriately documented evidence of at least equal validity and substantially less adverse impact, the user should investigate it to determine the feasibility and appropriateness of using or validating it in accordance with the recommendations of these guidelines. This subsection is not intended to preclude the combination of procedures into a more valid procedure.

Professional and Legal Analysis

This section has been revised to conform to federal court precedent which places the burden of showing suitable alternative selection procedures on the plaintiff or the enforcement agencies. In *Albemarle Paper Co. v. Moody*, 422 U.S. 405, 425 (1975), the Supreme Court stated that if an employer meets its burden of showing that its selection procedures are job related, it remains open to the *complaining party* to show that there are other selection procedures without a similar racial effect which would serve the employer's interest. Such a showing, the Court said, would be evidence that the employer was using its selection procedures as a "pretext" for discrimination. Thus, the Supreme Court in *Albemarle* placed the burden of showing suitable alternative procedures with a lesser adverse impact on the plaintiff or the enforcement agencies. This requirement was recently reiterated in *Connecticut v. Teal*, 102 S. Ct. 2525 (1982), where the Court stated that when the employer has shown the relationship of the procedure to the job in question, the plaintiff may prevail if he shows that the employer was using the procedure as a pretext for discrimination. Thus, the requirement of the 1978 Guidelines that the employer must conduct the search for alternatives is clearly inconsistent with *Albemarle* and *Teal* and has been revised to reflect Title VII case law. The revision of this section is also in accord with the July 30, 1982, report of the General Accounting Office, entitled "Uniform Guidelines on Employee Selection Procedures Should Be Reviewed and Revised," which recommended that "it would be appropriate to reconsider the Guidelines' provision that users are responsible, as a matter of course, for searching for alternative selection procedures."

The requirement in the Uniform Guidelines that the employer conduct an investigation of suitable alternatives and "suitable alternative methods of using the selection procedure" is also incon-

Section 3 (continued)

sistent with federal case law which holds that an employer is not required to use selection procedures that maximize the employment opportunities of minorities and women. *See Furnco,* 438 U.S. at 577-78. In addition, the requirement regarding alternative uses of a selection procedure is inconsistent with the accepted practices of the psychological profession that, in usual circumstances, selection by rank order from a job-related selection procedure is preferred. See the discussion below in section 5G.

The revisions to this section also allow an employer to consider the feasibility (*i.e.*, cost effectiveness and practical utility) of using a suggested alternative selection procedure. The appropriateness of taking cost into account in determining which selection procedures to use has been recognized by the courts. *See United States v. South Carolina,* 445 F. Supp. 1094 (D. S.C. 1977), *aff'd mem. sub nom. National Education Association v. South Carolina,* 434 U.S. 1026 (1978); *Spurlock v. United Air Lines, Inc.,* 475 F.2d 216 (10th Cir. 1972).

In addition to the introduction of the concept of feasibility, the revised section also provides that suggested alternative selection procedures must have "appropriately documented evidence of at least equal validity" and "substantially less adverse impact." Generally accepted practices of the psychological profession encourage the use of selection procedures which are more valid or job related over those of lesser validity, because the more valid a procedure the more likely it is to select a more productive workforce that possesses a greater likelihood of success on the job. Consequently, unless an alternative selection procedure is shown to be equally as valid as the procedure used by the employer, the employer should have no obligation to investigate the feasibility and appropriateness of using it. Because an employer should not be required or encouraged to abandon a selection procedure of proven validity for one whose validity has not been demonstrated, an employer should be under no obligation to investigate a suggested alternative unless the validity of the alternative has been demonstrated in accordance with professionally accepted practices. The requirement that an alternative selection procedure must be shown to have a "substantially less adverse impact" is included to discourage the abandonment of a valid selection procedure in favor of an alternative whose lesser adverse impact is not statistically or practically significant.

Section 4. Information on Impact.

Uniform Guidelines

A. Records concerning impact. Each user should maintain and have available for inspection records or other information which will disclose the impact which its tests and other selection procedures have upon employment opportunities of persons by identifiable race, sex, or ethnic group as set forth in subparagraph B below in order to determine compliance with these guidelines. Where there are large numbers of applicants and procedures are administered frequently, such information may be retained on a sample basis, provided that the sample is appropriate in terms of the applicant population and adequate in size.

Revised Guidelines

A. Records concerning impact. Each user should maintain and have available for inspection records for each race, sex or ethnic group constituting five percent (5%) of the labor force in the relevant labor market. See section 15B. These records will disclose the degree of adverse impact which the user's selection procedures have upon employment opportunities of persons by identifiable race, sex, or ethnic group as set forth in subparagraph B below in order to determine consistency with the recommendations contained in these guidelines. These records should be maintained on the basis of the job or group of jobs for which the particular selection procedure was applied. Where there are large numbers of applicants and procedures are administered frequently, such information may be retained on a sample basis, provided that the sample is appropriate in terms of the applicant population and adequate in size.

Professional and Legal Analysis

The two major changes in this section are that records need only be maintained for groups constituting five percent of the labor force in the relevant labor market and that the employer is given the option of maintaining such records on either a job or a job group basis. The limitation of data collection to those groups constituting five percent of the relevant labor market is intended to reduce the costly and burdensome recordkeeping requirements under the 1978 Guidelines. Information on workforce makeup and hires for groups constituting less than five percent of the labor force would be available to the enforcement agencies through the EEO-1 reports which would continue to be filed with the government pursuant to the Equal Employment Opportunity Commission's recordkeeping requirements.

Section 4 (continued)

The Uniform Guidelines require in section 15A(2) that documentation of the adverse impact of a selection procedure should be maintained for each job. Compiling impact data in this manner is burdensome to employers and in many instances does not produce useful information for the enforcement agencies because often too few employment decisions are made for a particular job to be meaningful. The revised section would give employers the option of maintaining data on a job group basis where the various jobs utilize the same selection procedures.

Uniform Guidelines **B. Applicable race, sex, and ethnic groups for recordkeeping.** The records called for by this section are to be maintained by sex, and the following races and ethnic groups: Blacks (Negroes), American Indians (including Alaskan Natives), Asians (including Pacific Islanders), Hispanic (including persons of Mexican, Puerto Rican, Cuban, Central or South American, or other Spanish origin or culture regardless of race), whites (Caucasians) other than Hispanic, and totals. The race, sex, and ethnic classifications called for by this section are consistent with the Equal Employment Opportunity Standard Form 100, Employer Information Report EEO-1 series of reports. The user should adopt safeguards to insure that the records required by this paragraph are used for appropriate purposes such as determining adverse impact, or (where required) for developing and monitoring affirmative action programs, and that such records are not used improperly. See sections 4E and 17(4), below.

Revised Guidelines **B. Applicable race, sex, and ethnic groups for recordkeeping.** The records called for by this section are to be maintained by sex, and the following races and ethnic groups: Blacks (Negroes), American Indians (including Alaskan Natives), Asians (including Pacific Islanders), Hispanics (including persons of Mexican, Puerto Rican, Cuban, Central or South American, or other Spanish origin or culture regardless of race), whites (Caucasians) other than Hispanics. The race, sex, and ethnic classifications called for by this section are consistent with the Equal Employment Opportunity Standard Form 100, Employer Information Report EEO-1 series of reports. The user should adopt safeguards to insure that the records recommended by this paragraph are used only for appropriate purposes such as determining adverse impact, or (where required) for developing and monitoring affirmative action programs.

Professional and Legal Analysis

The minor revisions to this section include the elimination of the need to record "totals" for all groups combined, and the clarification that the recordkeeping provisions of the Guidelines are recommendations and not legally binding regulations.

Section 4 (continued)

Uniform Guidelines

C. Evaluation of selection rates. The "bottom line." If the information called for by sections 4A and B above shows that the total selection process for a job has an adverse impact, the individual components of the selection process should be evaluated for adverse impact. If this information shows that the total selection process does not have an adverse impact, the Federal enforcement agencies, in the exercise of their administrative and prosecutorial discretion, in usual circumstances, will not expect a user to evaluate the individual components for adverse impact, or to validate such individual components, and will not take enforcement action based upon adverse impact of any component of that process, including the separate parts of a multipart selection procedure or any separate procedure that is used as an alternative method of selection. However, in the following circumstances the Federal enforcement agencies will expect a user to evaluate the individual components for adverse impact and may, where appropriate, take enforcement action with respect to the individual components: (1) where the selection procedure is a significant factor in the continuation of patterns of assignments of incumbent employees caused by prior discriminatory employment practices, (2) where the weight of court decisions or administrative interpretations hold that a specific procedure (such as height or weight requirements or no-arrest records) is not job related in the same or similar circumstances. In unusual circumstances, other than those listed in (1) and (2) above, the Federal enforcement agencies may request a user to evaluate the individual components for adverse impact and may, where appropriate, take enforcement action with respect to the individual component.

Revised Guidelines

C. Evaluation of selection rates. If the information called for by sections 4A and B above shows that the total selection process for a job has an adverse impact, the individual components of the selection process should be evaluated for adverse impact. If this information shows that the total selection process does not have an adverse impact, the Federal enforcement agencies, in the exercise of their administrative and prosecutorial discretion, in usual circumstances, will not expect a user to evaluate the individual components for adverse impact, or to validate such individual components, and will not take enforcement action based upon adverse impact of any component of that process, including the separate parts of a multipart selection procedure, or any separate procedure that is used as an alternative method of selection. However, in the following circumstances the Federal enforcement agencies will expect a user to evaluate the individual components for adverse impact and may, where appropriate, take enforcement action with respect to the individual components: (1) where the selection procedure is a significant factor in the continuation of patterns of assignments of incumbent employees caused by prior discriminatory employment practices, (2) where the weight of court decisions or administrative interpretations hold that a specific procedure (such as height or weight requirements or no-arrest records) is not job related in the same or similar circumstances. In unusual circumstances, other than

Section 4 (continued)

those listed in (1) and (2) above, the Federal enforcement agencies may request a user to evaluate the individual components for adverse impact and may, where appropriate, take enforcement action with respect to the individual component.

Professional and Legal Analysis

The Supreme Court's decision in *Connecticut v. Teal*, 102 S. Ct. 2525 (1982), does not require the enforcement agencies to change their discretionary policy of refraining from bringing enforcement actions where the employer's "bottom line" is satisfactory. No change in this section is necessary, therefore.

Uniform Guidelines

D. Adverse Impact and the "four-fifths rule." A selection rate for any race, sex, or ethnic group which is less than four-fifths (4/5) (or eighty percent) of the rate for the group with the highest rate will generally be regarded by the Federal enforcement agencies as evidence of adverse impact, while a greater than four-fifths rate will generally not be regarded by Federal enforcement agencies as evidence of adverse impact. Smaller differences in selection rate may nevertheless constitute adverse impact, where they are significant in both statistical and practical terms or where a user's actions have discouraged applicants disproportionately on grounds of race, sex, or ethnic group. Greater differences in selection rate may not constitute adverse impact where the differences are based on small numbers and are not statistically significant, or where special recruiting or other programs cause the pool of minority or female candidates to be atypical of the normal pool of applicants from that group. Where the user's evidence concerning the impact of a selection procedure indicates adverse impact but is based upon numbers which are too small to be reliable, evidence concerning the impact of the procedure over a longer period of time and/or evidence concerning the impact which the selection procedure had when used in the same manner in similar circumstances elsewhere may be considered in determining adverse impact. Where the user has not maintained data on adverse impact as required by the documentation section of applicable guidelines, the Federal enforcement agencies may draw an inference of adverse impact of the selection process from the failure of the user to maintain such data, if the user has an underutilization of a group in the job category, as compared to the group's representation in the relevant labor market or, in the case of jobs filled from within, the applicable work force.

Revised Guidelines

D. Adverse Impact and the "four-fifths rule." A selection rate for any race, sex, or ethnic group which is less than four-fifths (4/5) (or eighty percent) of the rate for the group with the highest rate merely establishes a numerical basis for the enforcement agencies to seek further information. A less than four-fifths rate may be considered evidence of adverse impact if it is significant in both statistical and practical terms during

Section 4 (continued)

the relevant time period unless (1) the group's underutilization in the job or group of jobs when compared to their availability in the relevant labor market is not statistically and practically significant, (2) the representation of the group among those selected is not substantially different from the group's representation in the relevant labor market, (3) the pool applicants from the group in question is atypical of the normal pool from the relevant labor market, or (4) the differences are based on small numbers. In the absence of differences which are large enough to meet the four-fifths rate or a test of statistical significance, there is no reason to assume that the differences are reliable, or that they are based upon anything other than chance.

Professional and Legal Analysis

The first important change in this section provides that a selection rate for any race, sex, or ethnic group which is less than four-fifths of the rate for the group with the highest rate establishes a basis for the agencies to seek additional information regarding the selection procedures at issue. Under the Uniform Guidelines, a less than four-fifths selection rate is generally regarded as evidence of adverse impact. This change, which is consistent with Q&A 19, 44 Fed. Reg. 11999, was made in order to reflect the enforcement agencies' intent that determinations of adverse impact would not be made without investigating factors which mitigate against such a finding.

The second major change in this section is the inclusion of a standard of statistical and practical significance as part of the four-fifths rule calculation. This is consistent with established federal court decisions which have found adverse impact only where the differences in selection rates were "substantial." *See Griggs v. Duke Power Co.*, 401 U.S. 424 (1971); *cf. Hazelwood School District v. United States*, 433 U.S. 299 (1977). Where the adverse effect of an employer's selection procedures have been at issue, courts have nearly uniformly accepted a defense of a lack of statistical significance. *See, e.g., Williams v. Tallahassee Motors, Inc.*, 607 F.2d 689 (5th Cir. 1979); *Mayor of Philadelphia v. Educational Equality League*, 415 U.S. 605 (1974). Because this defense is clearly available to an employer in litigation with an enforcement agency, there is no persuasive reason why it should not be considered in the pre-enforcement stage.

In situations where a less than four-fifths rate of selection is present, the revised section lists four exceptions which would prevent a finding of adverse impact. The first exception is where the group's underutilization in the job or group of jobs when compared to its availability in the relevant labor market is not statistically or practically significant. This concept was the methodological basis

Section 4 (continued)

of the Supreme Court's decision in *Hazelwood*, 433 U.S. 299 (1977). In this instance, the inference of discrimination that might otherwise arise from a selection rate of less than four-fifths is dispelled by the fact that the group at issue is represented in the job in relative proportion to their representation in the qualified labor market. Thus, adverse impact in this instance might merely be an aberration in an otherwise good employment record.

The second exception arises where the representation among those selected is not substantially different from the group's representation in the relevant labor market. This could arise where an employer had engaged in affirmative recruitment efforts in order to increase the pool of applicants. Thus, despite the fact that the selection process has violated the eighty percent rule, there should be no determination of adverse impact because the employer has selected members of the group in question in proportion to their representation in the relevant labor market. The third and fourth exceptions involve instances where the pool of applicants is atypical of the normal pool from the relevant labor market, and where the differences are based on small numbers, respectively. These exceptions are included in the 1978 Guidelines. In sum, none of these exceptions provide circumstances which would justify enforcement action by the agencies.

Excluded from the revised section are the provisions found in the Uniform Guidelines relating to: the accumulation of impact data over a period of time where employment decisions have been too few to make impact determinations; the use of impact data from other sources which used the selection procedures in a similar manner; and the inference of impact which the agencies may draw where an employer has not maintained impact data and where an underutilization exists in the challenged job. The accumulation of data and the use of impact data from other sources were eliminated due to their unreliability and their inconsistency with accepted practices of the psychological profession. Also deleted is the "inference of adverse impact" provision because of the unfairness of drawing such an inference in the absence of a statutory or legal standard that adverse impact data must be maintained. In addition, such an inference fails to take into account legitimate reasons which might explain the apparent underutilization.

Uniform Guidelines **E. Consideration of user's equal employment opportunity posture.** In carrying out their obligations, the Federal enforcement agencies will consider the general posture of the user with respect to equal employment opportunity for the job

Section 4 (continued)

or group of jobs in question. Where a user has adopted an affirmative action program, the Federal enforcement agencies will consider the provisions of that program, including the goals and timetables, which the user has adopted and the progress which the user has made in carrying out that program and in meeting the goals and timetables. While such affirmative action programs may in design and execution be race, color, sex, or ethnic conscious, selection procedures under such programs should be based upon the ability or relative ability to do the work.

Revised Guidelines **E. Consideration of user's equal employment opportunity posture.** In carrying out their obligations, the Federal enforcement agencies will consider the general posture of the user with respect to equal employment opportunity for the job or group of jobs in question. Where a user has adopted an affirmative action program, the Federal enforcement agencies will consider the provisions of that program, including the goals and timetables. Selection procedures under such programs should be based upon the ability or relative ability to do the work.

Professional and Legal Analysis

This section retains the current language that the agencies will consider the general equal employment posture of the employer for the job or job group at issue, including any affirmative action program (AAP) which the employer may have adopted. The revised section deletes the portion of the Uniform Guidelines relating to consideration of progress in meeting goals and timetables under an AAP and that portion relating to the allowance of race, color, sex and ethnic-conscious affirmative action programs. These were deleted because they relate primarily to affirmative action obligations, whether voluntary or not, and not to equal employment obligations under Title VII.

Section 5. General Recommendations for Validity Evidence.[3]

Uniform Guidelines **A. Acceptable types of validity studies.** For the purposes of satisfying these guidelines, users may rely upon criterion-related validity studies, content validity studies or construct

---

[3]The Uniform Guidelines caption for this section is "General standards for validity studies."

Section 5 (continued)

validity studies, in accordance with the standards set forth in the technical standards of these guidelines, section 14 below. New strategies for showing the validity of selection procedures will be evaluated as they become accepted by the psychological profession.

Revised Guidelines

A. Acceptable types of validity evidence. For the purposes of satisfying the recommendations of these guidelines, users may rely upon criterion-related, both predictive and concurrent, and content or construct validity evidence, in accordance with accepted practices of the psychological profession. It is recognized that the lines of demarcation among these validity strategies are not absolute. Additional strategies for showing the validity of selection procedures may be adopted by users as they become generally accepted by the psychological profession.

Professional and Legal Analysis

This section has been revised to acknowledge expressly that both predictive and concurrent criterion-related validity strategies are appropriate. See Division 14 *Principles* at pages 6-7. The revised section also provides that the validation efforts of employers or users will be judged by the "accepted practices of the psychological profession" and not solely by the technical recommendations set forth in the Guidelines. This reliance on the generally-accepted practices of the psychological profession where the technical recommendations of the Guidelines depart from accepted professional practice is consistent with federal case law and with the more pragmatic approach of the psychological profession. See *U.S. v. South Carolina*, 445 F. Supp. at 1113 ("To the extent that the EEOC Guidelines conflict with well-grounded expert opinion and accepted professional standards, they need not be controlling."); *Guardians*, 630 F.2d at 91 ("Thus, the Guidelines should always be considered, but they should not be regarded as conclusive unless reason and statutory interpretation support their conclusions.").

A sentence has been added to the section to reflect the fact that the psychological profession recognizes that the "lines of demarcation" among the various validation strategies are not always clear. See Division 14 *Principles* at page 3. The distinction between content and construct validity strategies is perhaps the most difficult to determine. See *Guardians*, 630 F.2d at 92-93. The additional sentence allows for more flexibility in deciding which validation strategy is appropriate under the particular circumstances faced by an employer.

Finally, the revised section provides that employers may use additional validation strategies as they become generally accepted

Section 5 (continued)

by the psychological profession. The Uniform Guidelines state that new strategies will be "evaluated" as they become accepted by the psychological profession. As a practical matter, the enforcement agencies have limited technical competence to "evaluate" additional validation strategies. The revision, therefore, eliminates the role of the enforcement agencies in determining what the accepted practices of the psychological profession should be. Thus, as additional validation strategies become generally accepted in the psychological profession, these strategies may be used by employers without any need for enforcement agency "evaluation" or approval.

Uniform Guidelines

B. Criterion-related, content and construct validity. Evidence of the validity of a test or other selection procedure by a criterion-related validity study should consist of empirical data demonstrating that the selection procedure is predictive of or significantly correlated with important elements of job performance. See section 14B below. Evidence of the validity of a test or other selection procedure by a content validity study should consist of data showing that the content of the selection procedure is representative of important aspects of performance on the job for which the candidates are to be evaluated. See section 14C below. Evidence of the validity study should consist of data showing that the procedure measures the degree to which candidates have identifiable characteristics which have been determined to be important in successful performance in the job for which the candidates are to be evaluated. See section 14D below.

Revised Guidelines

B. Criterion-related, content and construct validity evidence. Evidence of the criterion-related validity of a selection procedure typically consists of a demonstration of a statistically significant relationship between the results of the selection procedure (predictor or predictors) and one or more relevant measures of job or training or organizational success (criterion or criteria). Evidence of content validity of a selection procedure consists of a demonstration that a selection procedure samples one or more relevant job or training domains. Evidence of construct validity of a selection procedure should show that the procedure measures the construct (essentially a theoretical concept) and that individual differences on the construct are related to individual differences on the job or training.

Professional and Legal Analysis

The definition of criterion-related validity has been revised to include measures of training or organizational success as appropriate criterion measures. The courts and the psychological profession recognize that measures of training or organizational success may serve as appropriate criterion measures. *See Washington v. Davis*, 426 U.S. 229, 250 (1976); Division 14 *Principles* at page 7.

Section 5 (continued)

The definition of content-oriented validation strategies has been revised to reflect the views of the psychological profession that a selection procedure which is sought to be justified by a content validation strategy should sample "one or more relevant job or training domains." See Division 14 *Principles* at page 12. The 1978 Guidelines require that a selection procedure should be "representative of important aspects of performance on the job." The revision is designed to provide for more flexibility in the use of content-oriented strategies by eliminating the current requirements under the Uniform Guidelines that the selection procedure must virtually replicate the job in order for content validity to be appropriate. The content sampling of training as well as job domains is in accord with case law and accepted practices of the psychological profession. *See U.S. v. South Carolina*, 445 F. Supp. at 1112-1113; Division 14 *Principles* at page 12. Similarly, the definition of construct validity has been revised so that differences in training, in addition to job performance, may be related to individual differences on the construct which a selection procedure measures.

Uniform Guidelines **C. Guidelines are consistent with accepted professional standards.** The provisions of these guidelines relating to validation of selection procedures are intended to be consistent with generally accepted professional standards for evaluating standardized tests and other selection procedures, such as those described in the Standards for Educational and Psychological Tests prepared by a joint committee of the American Psychological Association, the American Educational Research Association, and the National Council on Measurement in Education (American Psychological Association, Washington, D.C., 1974) (hereinafter "A.P.A. Standards") and standard textbooks and journals in the field of personnel selection.

Revised Guidelines **C. Guidelines are consistent with accepted professional practices.** The recommendations of these guidelines relating to validation of selection procedures are intended to be consistent with generally accepted professional practices for evaluating standardized tests and other selection procedures. Such practices may be set forth in a number of sources including, but not limited to, the *Standards for Educational and Psychological Tests* prepared by a joint committee of the American Psychological Association, the American Educational Research Association and the National Council on Measurement in Education (American Psychological Association, Washington, D.C., 1974), the *Principles for Validation and Use of Personnel Selection Procedures* prepared by the Division of Industrial-Organizational Psychology, American Psychological Association (2d ed. 1980), and standard textbooks and professional journals in the field of personnel selection.

Section 5 (continued)

Professional and Legal Analysis

The revision to this section confirms that the Guidelines are intended to be consistent with the generally accepted practices of the psychological profession. Such practices may be set forth in a number of sources, including but not limited to, the APA *Standards*, the Division 14 *Principles* and standard textbooks and journals of the profession. Reference to the Division 14 *Principles* was added as they are an important source of standards of those members of the psychological profession who work in the employment selection area.

The 1978 Guidelines, in Q&A 40, 44 Fed. Reg. 12002, state that where differences exist between the Guidelines and professional opinion, the Guidelines will be given precedence by the enforcement agencies. This is inconsistent with federal case law. *See U.S. v. South Carolina*, 445 F. Supp. at 1113 n. 20; *Guardians*, 630 F.2d at 91; see also Division 14 *Principles* at page 2; APA *Standards* at page 8. If the Q&A's are revised along with the Guidelines, they should specify that where differences exist between the Guidelines and accepted professional practices, adherence to professional practices should not be deemed by the agencies to be noncompliance with the Guidelines.

Uniform Guidelines **D. Need for documentation of validity.** For any selection procedure which is part of a selection process which has an adverse impact and which selection procedure has an adverse impact, each user should maintain and have available such documentation as is described in section 15 below.

Revised Guidelines **D. Need for documentation of validity.** For any selection procedure for which validity evidence is necessary in accord with these guidelines, each user should maintain and have available such documentation as is described in section 15 below.

Professional and Legal Analysis

The language in this section has been clarified.

Uniform Guidelines **E. Accuracy and standardization.** Validity studies should be carried out under conditions which assure insofar as possible the adequacy and accuracy of the research and the report. Selection procedures should be administered and scored under standardized conditions.

Revised Guidelines **E. Accuracy and standardization.** Selection procedures should be administered and scored under standardized conditions to the extent this is practically possible.

Section 5 (continued)

Professional and Legal Analysis

This section was revised to reflect the fact that absolute standardized administration and scoring of all types of selection procedures will not always be practically possible. The amendment will ensure that the Guidelines will be interpreted by the enforcement agencies in a flexible manner.

Uniform Guidelines	**F. Caution against selection on basis of knowledges, skills, or ability learned in brief orientation period.** In general, users should avoid making employment decisions on the basis of measures of knowledges, skills, or abilities which are normally learned in a brief orientation period, and which have an adverse impact.
Revised Guidelines	**F. Caution against selection on basis of a knowledge, skill, or ability learned in brief orientation period.** In general, users should avoid making employment decisions on the basis of measures of a knowledge, skill, or ability that the user expects a person to learn in a brief orientation period.

Professional and Legal Analysis

The generally accepted practice of the psychological profession is that users should not make employment decisions on the basis of a knowledge, skill, or ability that it expects a person to learn in a brief orientation period. Because this principle applies to selection procedures which do not have adverse impact as well as to ones that do, the last part of the sentence relating to adverse impact has been deleted.

Uniform Guidelines	**G. Method of use of selection procedures.** The evidence of both the validity and utility of a selection procedure should support the method the user chooses for operational use of the procedure, if that method of use has a greater adverse impact than another method of use. Evidence which may be sufficient to support the use of a selection procedure on a pass/fail (screening) basis may be insufficient to support the use of the same procedure on a ranking basis under these guidelines. Thus, if a user decides to use a selection procedure on a ranking basis, and that method of use has a greater adverse impact than use on an appropriate pass/fail basis (see section 5H below), the user should have sufficient evidence of validity and utility to support the use on a ranking basis. See sections 3B, 14B (5) and (6), and 14C (8) and (9).
	H. Cutoff scores. Where cutoff scores are used, they should normally be set so as to be reasonable and consistent with normal expectations of acceptable proficiency within the work force. Where applicants are ranked on the basis of properly validated selection procedures and those applicants scoring

Section 5 (continued)

below a higher cutoff score than appropriate in light of such expectations have little or no chance of being selected for employment, the higher cutoff score may be appropriate, but the degree of adverse impact should be considered.

Revised Guidelines
G. Method of use of selection procedures. Selection standards may be set as high or as low as the purposes of the user require, as long as they are based on job-related procedures. In usual circumstances, the relationship between a predictor and a criterion may be assumed to be linear. Consequently, selecting from the top scorers on down is the most effective procedure for maximizing the utility of the selection procedure providing there is an adequate amount of variance in the predictor.

Selection procedures supported by content or construct validity evidence that differentiate adequately among people usually can be assumed to have a linear relationship to job or training behavior. Consequently, ranking on the basis of scores on a job-related procedure is appropriate.

H. [Deleted.]

Professional and Legal Analysis

Sections 5G and H have been totally revised as a result of the inconsistency of the Uniform Guidelines with accepted practices of the psychological profession. The major points set forth in this revised section are that job-related selection standards may be set as high or as low as the purposes of the user require and that job-related selection procedures are assumed to have a linear relationship to job or training behaviors, so that ranking on the basis of a job-related selection procedure is appropriate. *See Griggs*, 401 U.S. at 434 n. 11; 110 Cong. Rec. 7213 (1964)(Memorandum of Senators Clark and Case).

The Uniform Guidelines provide that a user should have evidence of validity and utility to support the method of use of a selection procedure and that evidence sufficient to support the use of a selection procedure on a pass-fail basis may be insufficient to support the use of the procedure on a ranking basis. The Uniform Guidelines also require the user to have sufficient evidence of validity and utility to support the use of a procedure on a ranking basis, where use on a ranking basis results in a greater adverse impact than use on a pass-fail basis.

The current Guidelines apparently are designed to further affirmative action by encouraging the use of pass-fail procedures rather than rank ordering, especially where a content-oriented validation strategy is used. They make it difficult to justify the use of a content-

Section 5 (continued)

oriented selection procedure on a rank-order basis without some form of criterion-related or other empirical validity evidence. This position is contrary to established federal case law and to the generally accepted practices of the psychological profession and fails to consider the substantial loss of productivity resulting from the selection of persons with lower levels of performance on job-related selection procedures. In *Griggs*, 401 U.S. at 436, the Supreme Court endorsed the appropriateness of selection based on relative qualifications by stating that "Congress has not commanded that the less qualified be preferred over the better qualified simply because of minority origins." Similarly, in *Furnco*, 438 U.S. at 577-78, the court held that employers are not required to use selection procedures which maximize the employment opportunities of minorities.

The Division 14 *Principles* at page 18 discuss the issue of rank ordering based on a valid selection procedure as follows:

> Selection standards may be set as high or as low as the purposes of the organization require, if they are based on valid predictors. This implies that (a) the purposes of selection are clear and (b) they are acceptable in the social and legal context in which the employing organization functions. In usual circumstances, the relationship between a predictor and a criterion may be assumed to be linear. Consequently, selecting from the top scores on down is almost always the most beneficial procedure from the standpoint of an organization if there is an appropriate amount of variance in the predictor. Selection techniques developed by content-oriented procedures and discriminating adequately within the range of interest can be assumed to have a linear relationship to job behavior. Consequently, ranking on the basis of scores on these procedures is appropriate.

The *Principles* also recognize that "non-linear selection decision rules (*e.g.*, random selection from among those scoring above a cutoff) typically reduce the utility of valid selection procedures." The revisions to this section have been taken almost directly from this portion of the Division 14 *Principles* which reflects the accepted practices of the members of the profession most actively involved in the employee selection area.

Section 5H of the Uniform Guidelines, entitled "cutoff scores," has been deleted due to its inconsistency with federal case law and the accepted practices of the psychological profession. This section was deemed to be unnecessary based on the changes made to section 5G regarding methods of use of selection procedures.

Section 5 (continued)

By requiring that cutoff scores be set based on "normal expectations of acceptable proficiency within the workforce," the current Guidelines fail to take into consideration an employer's legitimate interest in attempting to effectuate improvements in its workforce. See *Griggs*, 401 U.S. at 436. It is also inconsistent with Division 14 *Principles* which state that job-related selection standards may be set as high or as low as the purposes of the organization require and that, where a critical score is set, there should be a reasonable rationale for the score. The Division 14 *Principles* expressly "[do] not recommend critical scores in preference to other interpretive methods."

Uniform Guidelines

I. Use of selection procedures for higher level jobs. If job progression structures are so established that employees will probably, within a reasonable period of time and in a majority of cases, progress to a higher level, it may be considered that the applicants are being evaluated for a job or jobs at the higher level. However, where job progression is not so nearly automatic, or the time span is such that higher level jobs or employees' potential may be expected to change in significant ways, it should be considered that applicants are being evaluated for a job at or near the entry level. A "reasonable period of time" will vary for different jobs and employment situations but will seldom be more than 5 years. Use of selection procedures to evaluate applicants for a higher level job would not be appropriate:

(1) If the majority of those remaining employed do not progress to the higher level job;
(2) If there is a reason to doubt that the higher level job will continue to require essentially similar skills during the progression period; or
(3) If the selection procedures measure knowledges, skills, or abilities required for advancement which would be expected to develop principally from the training or experience on the job.

Revised Guidelines

H. Use of selection procedures for higher level jobs. Use of a selection procedure to evaluate applicants or candidates for a higher level job or job group than that for which candidates are initially selected is appropriate, if (1) the majority of the individuals who remain employed and are available for advancement progress to the higher level within a reasonable period of time, or (2) the user maintains a promotion-from-within policy in which candidates in the lower level job or group are generally the pool from which persons are selected for those higher level jobs. These guidelines recognize that the considerations applicable to the promotion of clerical and hourly employees may vary substantially from those involving managerial and professional employees and therefore a flexible application of this section is necessary.

Section 5 (continued)

Professional and Legal Analysis

Section 5I of the Uniform Guidelines has been revised and redesignated section 5H. It has been amended to provide for a more flexible approach to the use of selection procedures for higher level jobs. The revised section provides that an employer can evaluate applicants for above entry level positions if the majority of persons who remain employed and are available for advancement progress to a higher level within a reasonable period of time. This is consistent with the Division 14 *Principles* at page 9. The five year time period contained in the 1978 Guidelines has been eliminated because it failed to take into account the instability of progression periods, especially in higher level or management jobs. The revised section also permits evaluation for a higher level job where the employer maintains a promotion-from-within policy in which candidates in lower level jobs are the pool from which higher level jobs are filled. The revised section specifically notes that flexibility is required in recognition of the different considerations applicable to the promotion of clerical or hourly employees as opposed to managerial and professional employees.

The portion of section 5I which provides that it is inappropriate to evaluate applicants for a higher level job "if the selection procedure measures knowledges, skills, or abilities required for advancement which would be expected to develop principally from the training or experience on the job" has been deleted. This was deleted because it failed to take into account the fact that persons already possessing the knowledges, skills, or abilities needed for advancement may be more productive earlier and may advance at a faster rate. The failure to take into account these already possessed knowledges, skills and abilities is to ignore experience as a major influencing factor in determining a person's capability to advance.

Uniform Guidelines   **J. Interim use of selection procedures.** Users may continue the use of a selection procedure which is not at the moment fully supported by the required evidence of validity, provided: (1) The user has available substantial evidence of validity, and (2) the user has in progress, when technically feasible, a study which is designed to produce the additional evidence required by these guidelines within a reasonable time. If such a study is not technically feasible, see section 6B. If the study does not demonstrate validity, this provision of these guidelines for interim use shall not constitute a defense in any action, nor shall it relieve the user of any obligations arising under Federal law.

Revised Guidelines   **I. Interim use of selection procedures.** Users may continue the use of a selection procedure which is not at the moment

Section 5 (continued)

fully supported by the evidence of validity recommended in these guidelines, provided that the additional evidence, as recommended by these guidelines, will be gathered and/or examined within a reasonable period of time.

Interim use of a selection procedure is to be differentiated from the transportability of a selection procedure having demonstrated validity. Transportability enables a user to use a selection procedure that has not been validated by the user for a particular job or group of jobs when the user's job or group of jobs and the job or group of jobs for which the validity evidence was examined or gathered include substantially the same major work behavior(s) or substantially the same major knowledge(s), skill(s), or abilility(ies) or other worker characteristic(s) as measured by the selection procedure in question. See section 7B. A user may transport such validity evidence without further requirement to provide additional validity evidence, provided that the work behavior(s), relevant knowledge(s), skill(s) or ability(ies), or other worker characteristic(s) involved can be shown to be comparable.

Professional and Legal Analysis

Section 5J of the Uniform Guidelines has been revised and redesignated section 5I. The revised section provides for the continued use of a selection procedure not fully supported by the evidence of validity recommended by the Guidelines "provided that the additional evidence, as recommended by these guidelines, will be gathered and/or examined within a reasonable period of time." The proviso in the current Guidelines requiring "substantial evidence of validity" has been eliminated due to its indefiniteness and because it was not deemed necessary in light of the fact that sufficient evidence of validity would be available within a reasonable period of time.

The revised section also draws the important distinction between interim use of a selection procedure which is not fully supported by evidence of validity, and the use of a selection procedure which has been shown to be validated in another setting and has been transported by an employer for use in a comparable setting. A user may transport validity evidence from another setting without providing additional evidence of validity, provided that the recommendations of section 7 regarding validity transportability are met.

Uniform Guidelines **K. Review of validity studies for currency.** Whenever validity has been shown in accord with these guidelines for the use of a particular selection procedure for a job or group of jobs, additional studies need not be performed until such time as the validity study is subject to review as provided in section 3B above. There are no absolutes in the area of determining the currency of a validity study. All circumstances concerning the study, including the validation strategy used, and changes

Section 5 (continued)

Revised Guidelines

in the relevant labor market and the job should be considered in the determination of when a validity study is outdated.

J. Review of validity evidence for currency. Whenever validity has been shown to be in accord with professional practices for the use of a particular selection procedure for a job or group of jobs, additional evidence need not be gathered or examined. There are no absolutes in the area of determining the currency of validity evidence and time in and of itself is not necessarily a factor. The primary factor to be considered is whether major changes in the job or group of jobs make the validity evidence no longer relevant.

Professional and Legal Analysis

Section 5K of the Uniform Guidelines has been revised and redesignated section 5J. The section was modified to emphasize that the major factor in reviewing the currency of validity evidence is whether "major changes in the job or group of jobs make the validity evidence no longer relevant." The revised section also emphasizes that the passage of time alone is not necessarily a factor in determining the currency of validity evidence.

References to the "validation strategy used, and changes in the relevant labor market" have been deleted because accepted practices of the psychological profession do not consider them to be relevant factors in reviewing the currency of validity evidence. Neither the validation strategy used nor changes in the labor market have been shown to affect the currency of validity evidence. The reference to a review of changes in the relevant labor market appears to be based on the theory of differential validity, which is unsupported by professional research findings and, therefore, is inappropriately required by the 1978 Guidelines.

Section 6. Use of selection procedures which have not been validated.

Uniform Guidelines

A. Use of alternate selection procedures to eliminate adverse impact. A user may choose to utilize alternative selection procedures in order to eliminate adverse impact or as part of an affirmative action program. See section 13 below. Such alternative procedures should eliminate the adverse impact in the total selection process, should be lawful and should be as job related as possible.

Revised Guidelines

A. [Deleted.]

52

Section 6 (continued)

Professional and Legal Analysis

Section 6A of the Uniform Guidelines has been deleted because it is redundant and reflects principles adequately set forth in sections 3B and 13. Moreover, in view of the Supreme Court's decision in *Connecticut v. Teal,* 102 S. Ct. 2525 (1982), elimination of adverse impact in the total selection process may be insufficient to comply with the requirements of Title VII.

Uniform Guidelines

B. Where validity studies cannot or need not be performed. There are circumstances in which a user cannot or need not utilize the validation techniques contemplated by these guidelines. In such circumstances, the user should utilize selection procedures which are as job related as possible and which will minimize or eliminate adverse impact, as set forth below.

(1) *Where informal or unscored procedures are used.* When an informal or unscored selection procedure which has an adverse impact is utilized, the user should eliminate the adverse impact, or modify the procedure to one which is a formal, scored or quantified measure or combination of measures and then validate the procedure in accord with these guidelines, or otherwise justify continued use of the procedure in accord with Federal law.

Revised Guidelines

There exist circumstances in which a user cannot or need not gather the validation evidence contemplated by these guidelines. In such circumstances, the user should utilize selection procedures which are as job related as possible.

A. **Where informal or unscored procedures are used.** When an informal or unscored selection procedure which has an adverse impact is utilized, the user may (a) eliminate the adverse impact, (b) modify the procedure, if feasible, to one which is a formal, scored or quantified measure or combination of measures and then validate the procedure in accord with accepted professional practices, (c) adopt a standardized procedure and validate it or support it in accordance with sections 5I and 7B, or (d) otherwise justify continued use of the procedure in accord with Federal law.

Professional and Legal Analysis

The proposed change introduces the standard of technical feasibility in modifying unscored procedures to formal, scored procedures. It also establishes that a standardized procedure may be validated by the transporting of validity evidence between locations for similar jobs. See section 7B. As such, the changes reflect the consensus of professionals and "state of the art" alternatives to modifying informal or unscored procedures.

Section 6 (continued)

Uniform Guidelines
(2) **Where formal and scored procedures are used.** When a formal and scored selection procedure is used which has an adverse impact, the validation techniques contemplated by these guidelines usually should be followed if technically feasible. Where the user cannot or need not follow the validation techniques anticipated by these guidelines, the user should either modify the procedure to eliminate adverse impact or otherwise justify continued use of the procedure in accord with Federal law.

Revised Guidelines
B. **Where formal and scored procedures are used.** When a formal and scored selection procedure is used which has an adverse impact, the validation strategies recommended by these guidelines usually should be followed if technically feasible. Where it is not necessary or feasible to gather the validation evidence anticipated by these guidelines, the user may (a) modify the use of the procedure to eliminate adverse impact, (b) support the procedure in accordance with section 7B, (c) adopt another standardized procedure and validate it or support it in accordance with section 7B, or (d) otherwise justify continued use of the procedure in accord with Federal law.

Professional and Legal Analysis

In certain circumstances, it may not be professionally necessary or technically feasible to gather validity evidence. The revision provides that one additional alternative not currently provided for in the Guidelines would be to support the procedure by transporting validity evidence. See section 7B.

Section 7. Use of other validity evidence.[4]

Uniform Guidelines
A. **Validity studies not conducted by the user.** Users may, under certain circumstances, support the use of selection procedures by validity studies conducted by other users or conducted by test publishers or distributors and described in test manuals. While publishers of selection procedures have a professional obligation to provide evidence of validity which meets generally accepted professional standards (see section 5C above), users are cautioned that they are responsible for compliance with these guidelines. Accordingly, users seeking to obtain selection procedures from publishers and distributors should be careful to determine that, in the event the user becomes subject to the validity requirements of these guidelines, the necessary information to support validity has been determined and will be made available to the user.

---

[4] The Uniform Guidelines caption for this section is "Use of other validity studies."

Section 7 (continued)

Revised Guidelines
A. Validity evidence not gathered by the user. Users may support the use of selection procedures with validity evidence gathered by other users or gathered by test publishers or distributors and described in test manuals provided that evidence meets accepted professional practice. Users obtaining selection procedures from other sources should be careful to determine, in advance of operational use of the procedure, that the information necessary to document validity is available and sufficient in terms of the recommendations of sections 5I, 7B and 15C(5) of these guidelines.

Professional and Legal Analysis

Revised section 7A states that users may support the use of selection procedures with validity evidence gathered by others in another setting provided that the evidence of validity meets accepted professional practice. The revised section also cautions that users obtaining selection procedures from other sources should determine prior to the use of a selection procedure that sufficient evidence of validity exists. The second sentence of the present guideline regarding the user's responsibility for compliance with the Guidelines has been deleted as unnecessary because the revised section provides that the evidence of validity gathered elsewhere should meet professional practices.

Uniform Guidelines
B. Use of criterion-related validity evidence from other sources. Criterion-related validity studies conducted by one test user, or described in test manuals and the professional literature, will be considered acceptable for use by another user when the following requirements are met:

(1) *Validity evidence.* Evidence from the available studies meeting the standards of section 14B below clearly demonstrates that the selection procedure is valid;

(2) *Job similarity.* The incumbents in the user's job and the incumbents in the job or group of jobs on which the validity study was conducted perform substantially the same major work behaviors, as shown by appropriate job analyses both on the job or group of jobs on which the validity study was performed and on the job for which the selection procedure is to be used; and

(3) *Fairness evidence.* The studies include a study of test fairness for each race, sex, and ethnic group which constitutes a significant factor in the borrowing user's relevant labor market for the job or jobs in question. If the studies under consideration satisfy (1) and (2) above but do not contain an investigation of test fairness, and it is not technically feasible for the borrowing user to conduct an internal study of test fairness, the borrowing user may utilize the study until studies conducted elsewhere meeting the requirements of these guide-

Section 7 (continued)

lines show test unfairness, or until such time as it becomes technically feasible to conduct an internal study of test fairness and the results of that study can be acted upon. Users obtaining selection procedures from publishers should consider, as one factor in the decision to purchase a particular selection procedure, the availability of evidence concerning test fairness.

Revised Guidelines

B. Use of validity evidence from other sources. Validity evidence gathered by one user or described in test manuals and the professional literature is appropriate for use by another user when the following conditions exist:

(1) *Validity evidence.* The validity evidence gathered in accordance with accepted professional practices and the recommendations of these guidelines demonstrates that the selection procedure is valid for the job or group of jobs in question; and

(2) *Job similarity.* The work performed in the user's job or group of jobs and in the job or group of jobs for which the validity evidence was examined or gathered includes substantially the same major work behavior(s), or involves substantially the same major knowledge(s), skill(s), ability(ies), or worker characteristic(s) as measured by the selection procedure in question.

Professional and Legal Analysis

Revised section 7B contains the recommendations for the transportability of evidence of validity gathered from sources other than the user. This revised section is extremely important because many large and nearly all small employers do not possess the capability, staff or number of employees required to conduct their own validity studies. Consequently, the only way that many employers can establish the job relatedness or validity of their selection procedures is by transporting evidence of validity produced elsewhere. The revisions of section 7B are designed to recognize this problem and to provide for increased transportability where jobs are similar in terms of work behaviors, or knowledges, skills and abilities required for performance of the jobs.

The transportability of validity evidence from one location or user to another has been recognized by the courts. In *Friend v. Leidinger*, 588 F.2d 61, 65 (4th Cir. 1978), the court upheld the validity of a test given for entry level firefighters in the Richmond, Virginia, Fire Bureau based on evidence of validity gathered in California. In so doing, the court stated:

> A part of the validation study was done in California and plaintiffs objected to a study not conducted in Richmond. However, plaintiffs have shown no difference in the duties of a fireman in the 55 areas of California, where the test was validated, from the duties of a Richmond fireman. *To*

Section 7 (continued)

require local validation in every city, village and hamlet would be ludicrous. (Emphasis added.)

See also *Pegues v. Mississippi State Employment Services*, 488 F. Supp. 239, 403 (N.D. Miss. 1980), *aff'd in relevant part*, No. 80-3212 (5th Cir. Mar. 11, 1983) ("Empirical research has demonstrated that validity is not perceptably changed by differences in location, differences in specific job duties or applicant populations. Valid tests do not become invalid when these circumstances change."); *Ability Testing: Uses, Consequences, and Controversies*, Part I (1982) at page 148 ("Government agencies concerned with fair employment practices should accept the principle of cooperative validation research so that tests validated for a job category such as fire fighter in a number of localities can be accepted for use on the basis of the cumulated experience.").

Revised section 7B sets forth two conditions for the use of validity evidence gathered by one user for use by another user. The first is that the validity evidence, gathered in accordance with accepted professional practices and the recommendations of the Guidelines, should demonstrate that the selection procedure is valid for the job or job group involved. The reference to gathering validity evidence in accordance with accepted professional practices was added to clarify that literal adherence to the requirements of the Uniform Guidelines may in many instances be in excess of the practices of the psychological profession. In addition, the 1978 Guidelines' requirement that evidence "clearly" demonstrate that the selection procedure is valid was deleted as unnecessary. The portion in the section 7B(1) of the Uniform Guidelines requiring validity evidence to "meet the standards of section 14B" is inconsistent with section 15A(3)(b), which deals with studies conducted before the issuance of the 1978 Guidelines and which satisfied the requirements of previous guidelines.

The second condition set forth in the revised section in connection with the transportability of validity evidence is that the job or job groups involved should include substantially the same major work behaviors or knowledges, skills and abilities. The Uniform Guidelines provide only that criterion-related validity evidence may be transported and that job similarity must be judged by whether the job or job groups contain the same major work behaviors. The revised section would allow the transportability of content or construct validity evidence in addition to criterion-related validity evidence. This recognizes the fact that two jobs may involve the same major knowledges, skills or abilities without necessarily involving

Section 7 (continued)

the same work behaviors. Consequently, there is no reason to limit transportability to instances of criterion-related validity or to similar job behaviors.

Examples of frequently cited content valid tests which would be readily transportable are tests of general typing ability, road tests for truck drivers and tests of arithmetic computation, among others. In instances where content valid tests are available, there is no reason why the Guidelines should not allow the transportability of such valid tests, nor is there reason to require an employer to conduct a criterion-related validity study in order to show the job relatedness of the selection procedure. For many employers, the failure of the agencies to allow the transportability of valid selection procedures will result in encouraging the continued use by the employer of selection procedures whose validity for the particular job is unknown.

The requirement of the Uniform Guidelines for "job analyses both on the job or group of jobs on which the validity study was performed and on the job for which the selection procedure is to be used" has been eliminated. Most test publisher's manuals do not contain job analysis information in sufficient detail to meet the current requirement. In addition, most employers do not possess the resources necessary for conducting a complete job analysis that would meet present requirements for selection purposes. Moreover, accepted professional practices for transporting evidence of validity do not require that the entire job be examined through a complete job analysis. Rather, it is sufficient under accepted professional practices that the two jobs possess substantially similar common element(s). Section 7B(2) has been modified accordingly.

Section 7B(3) has been deleted from the Revised Guidelines because studies conducted by the psychological profession have shown overwhelmingly that there is no further need for the requirement of test "fairness" studies. A discussion of the "fairness" issue is contained in the comments under revised section 14B(7).

Uniform Guidelines

C. Validity evidence from multiunit study. If validity evidence from a study covering more than one unit within an organization satisfies the requirements of section 14B below, evidence of validity specific to each unit will not be required unless there are variables which are likely to affect validity significantly.

D. Other significant variables. If there are variables in the other studies which are likely to affect validity significantly, the user may not rely upon such studies, but will be expected either to conduct an internal validity study or to comply with section 6 above.

Section 7 (continued)

Revised Guidelines **C. Validity evidence from multiunit study.** If validity evidence gathered from more than one unit within an organization satisfies section 7B, evidence of validity specific to each unit will not be required. See also section 8B.

D. [Deleted.]

Professional and Legal Analysis

This section has been revised to provide that if validity evidence gathered from more than one unit satisfies section 7B, evidence specific to each unit will not be required. Since revised section 7B references professional practices, it should be sufficient under revised section 7C for evidence to meet professional practices and not the requirements of section 14B of the Uniform Guidelines, which in many instances are in excess of accepted professional practices. The reference in section 7C to "variables which are likely to affect validity significantly" has been deleted because of its indefiniteness. If this is a reference to the issues of "differential prediction" or "fairness," an additional reason for deleting this portion is that such studies are not supported by a consensus of the psychological profession. Accordingly, section 7D has been deleted for the same reasons.

Section 8. Cooperative validation efforts.[5]

Uniform Guidelines **A. Encouragement of cooperative studies.** The agencies issuing these guidelines encourage employers, labor organizations, and employment agencies to cooperate in research, development, search for lawful alternatives, and validity studies in order to achieve procedures which are consistent with these guidelines.

Revised Guidelines **A. Encouragement of cooperative validation efforts.** The agencies issuing these guidelines encourage users to cooperate in gathering validation evidence.

Professional and Legal Analysis

The changes are editorial in nature. Cooperative or consortium studies are an effective and efficient means to develop reliable and valid selection procedures and should be encouraged under the Guidelines. Many users lack the financial resources to conduct va-

---

[5]The Uniform Guidelines caption for this section is "Cooperative studies."

Section 8 (continued)

lidity studies. Cooperative studies provide economies of scale and should provide more reliable results because of the larger samples involved.

Uniform Guidelines **B. Standards for use of cooperative studies.** If validity evidence from a cooperative study satisfies the requirements of section 14 below, evidence of validity specific to each user will not be required unless there are variables in the user's situation which are likely to affect validity significantly.

Revised Guidelines **B. Recommendations for use of cooperative validation efforts.** If validity evidence from a cooperative validation effort has been gathered in accordance with accepted professional practices and the recommendations of these guidelines, evidence of validity specific to each user will not be required.

Professional and Legal Analysis

The reference to other significant variables is unnecessary and has been deleted. If a cooperative validation study has been conducted in accordance with accepted professional practices, nothing more is required to establish its validity.

Section 9. No assumption of validity.

Uniform Guidelines **A. Unacceptable substitutes for evidence of validity.** Under no circumstances will the general reputation of a test or other selection procedures, its author or its publisher, or casual reports of it's [sic] validity be accepted in lieu of evidence of validity. Specifically ruled out are: assumptions of validity based on a procedure's name or descriptive labels; all forms of promotional literature; data bearing on the frequency of a procedure's usage; testimonial statements and credentials of sellers, users, or consultants; and other nonempirical or anecdotal accounts of selection practices or selection outcomes.

Revised Guidelines **A. Unacceptable substitutes for evidence of validity or relationship to job performance.** Under no circumstances will the general reputation of a test or other selection procedure, its author or its publisher, or casual reports of its validity be accepted in lieu of evidence of validity or its job relatedness. Specifically ruled out are: assumptions of validity based on a procedure's name or descriptive labels; promotional literature that does not include the information required for users to determine the quality and transportability of the procedures; data bearing on the frequency of a procedure's usage; testimonial statements and credentials of sellers, users, or consultants; and other nonempirical or anecdotal accounts of

Section 9 (continued)

selection practices or selection outcomes. Similarly, casual reports of test results in other settings, or court or agency findings regarding a procedure in other settings, should not be used as evidence of adverse impact or lack of validity with respect to the selection procedure.

Professional and Legal Analysis

The portion of section 9A relating to the use of promotional literature to establish the job relatedness of a selection procedure was modified to exclude only promotional literature "that does not include the information required for users to determine the quality and transportability of the procedures." This modification was made to ensure that "promotional literature," under appropriate circumstances, may be used in support of the transportability of selection procedures.

The last sentence in revised section 9A was added to ensure that casual reports of test results in other settings and court and agency findings would not be used as evidence of adverse impact or lack of validity. This requires the enforcement agencies to evaluate selection procedures based on the adverse impact and validity evidence available to the user and not on isolated prior reports or findings which may not be relevant to the user's situation.

Uniform Guidelines   **B. Encouragement of professional supervision.** Professional supervision of selection activities is encouraged but is not a substitute for documented evidence of validity. The enforcement agencies will take into account the fact that a thorough job analysis was conducted and that careful development and use of a selection procedure in accordance with professional standards enhance the probability that the selection procedure is valid for the job.

Revised Guidelines   **B. Encouragement of professional supervision.** Professional supervision of selection activities is encouraged but is not a substitute for documented evidence of validity.

Professional and Legal Analysis

The Revised Guidelines delete the last sentence in section 9B, which states that the agencies will take into account the thoroughness of the job analysis and the care in development and use of selection procedures. This was deleted because the thoroughness of a job analysis will in many instances have no relationship to the establishment of the job relatedness of a selection procedure. For example, while a job analysis is essential to content-oriented validity

Section 9 (continued)

strategies, it is often much less important in criterion-related studies. Consequently, the last sentence has been deleted.

Section 10. Employment agencies and employment services.

Uniform Guidelines **A. Where selection procedures are devised by agency.** An employment agency, including private employment agencies and State employment agencies, which agrees to a request by an employer or labor organization to devise and utilize a selection procedure should follow the standards in these guidelines for determining adverse impact. If adverse impact exists the agency should comply with these guidelines. An employment agency is not relieved of its obligation herein because the user did not request such validation or has requested the use of some lesser standard of validation than is provided in these guidelines. The use of an employment agency does not relieve an employer or labor organization or other user of its responsibilities under Federal law to provide equal employment opportunity or its obligations as a user under these guidelines.

Revised Guidelines **A. Where selection procedures are devised by agency.** An employment agency, including private employment agencies and State employment agencies, which agrees to a request by a user to devise and utilize a selection procedure should follow the recommendations in these guidelines. The use of an employment agency does not relieve a user of its responsibilities under Federal law.

Professional and Legal Analysis

The changes are editorial in nature. An employment agency which devises and administers a selection procedure should be held to the same standards of validity and job relatedness as other users of selection procedures. *See Pegues v. Mississippi State Employment Services*, 488 F. Supp. 239 (N.D. Miss. 1980), *aff'd in relevant part*, No. 80-3212 (5th Cir. Mar. 11, 1983). The use of an employment agency by an employer or labor organization does not relieve them of their responsibilities under federal law to monitor the results of the selection procedures to assure that they result in equal employment opportunity.

Uniform Guidelines **B. Where selection procedures are devised elsewhere.** Where an employment agency or service is requested to administer a selection procedure which has been devised elsewhere and to make referrals pursuant to the results, the employment agency or service should maintain and have available evidence of the impact of the selection and referral

Section 10 (continued)

procedures which it administers. If adverse impact results the agency or service should comply with these guidelines. If the agency or service seeks to comply with these guidelines by reliance upon validity studies or other data in the possession of the employer, it should obtain and have available such information.

Revised Guidelines
B. Where selection procedures are devised elsewhere. Where an employment agency or service is requested to administer a selection procedure which has been devised elsewhere and to make referrals pursuant to the results, the employment agency or service should follow the recommendations in these guidelines. The agency or service may rely on validity evidence or other data in the possession of the employer in accordance with section 7B.

Professional and Legal Analysis

Consistent with the revision of section 7B, the change in this section recognizes that employment agencies and services may transport validity evidence for similar jobs that have been developed in accordance with the Guidelines by another user.

Section 11. Disparate treatment.

Uniform Guidelines
The principles of disparate or unequal treatment must be distinguished from the concepts of validation. A selection procedure—even though validated against job performance in accordance with these guidelines—cannot be imposed upon members of a race, sex, or ethnic group where other employees, applicants, or members have not been subjected to that standard. Disparate treatment occurs where members of a race, sex, or ethnic group have been denied the same employment, promotion, membership, or other employment opportunities as have been available to other employees or applicants. Those employees or applicants who have been denied equal treatment, because of prior discriminatory practices or policies, must at least be afforded the same opportunities as had existed for other employees or applicants during the period of discrimination. Thus, the persons who were in the class of persons discriminated against during the period the user followed the discriminatory practices should be allowed the opportunity to qualify under less stringent selection procedures previously followed, unless the user demonstrates that the increased standards are required by business necessity. This section does not prohibit a user who has not previously followed merit standards from adopting merit standards which are in compliance with these guidelines; nor does it preclude a user who has previously used invalid or unvalidated selection procedures from developing and using procedures which are in accord with these guidelines.

Section 11 (continued)

Revised Guidelines The principles of disparate or unequal treatment must be distinguished from the concepts of validation. Disparate treatment occurs where identifiable members of a race, sex, or ethnic group have been intentionally denied the same selection, promotion, membership, or other employment opportunities as have been available to other employees or applicants during the relevant time period. Those specific employees or applicants who have been denied equal treatment must at least be afforded the same opportunities as had existed for other employees or applicants during the relevant time period. This section does not prohibit a user who had not previously followed merit standards from adopting merit standards which are consistent with these guidelines; nor does it preclude a user who has previously used invalid or unvalidated selection procedures from developing and/or using procedures which are in accord with these guidelines.

Professional and Legal Analysis

The revisions to this section are designed to ensure that only *identifiable* persons who were *intentionally* denied the same employment opportunities as others *during the relevant time period* are covered. The changes are in accord with federal case law dealing with claims of disparate treatment and limitations periods under Title VII. In *International Brotherhood of Teamsters v. United States*, 431 U.S. 324 (1977), the Supreme Court distinguished claims of disparate treatment from adverse impact claims, holding that proof of purposeful or intentional discrimination against identifiable persons was a prerequisite to a finding of liability on disparate treatment claims. Thus, only those persons who can be identified as having been intentionally denied the same employment opportunities as others are covered under this section, and not an unidentified class of persons who may or may not have been denied such opportunities. *Accord, Connecticut v. Teal*, 102 S. Ct. 2525 (1982). The revised section also covers only those identifiable persons who were denied the same opportunities during the relevant time period under Title VII. The Supreme Court held in *United Air Lines v. Evans*, 431 U.S. 553 (1977), that allegedly discriminatory acts which occurred prior to the period covered by a timely Title VII charge (*i.e.*, usually either 180 or 300 days, depending on whether the charge is filed in a deferral jurisdiction) are not unlawful and the later effects of such acts do not constitute a violation of Title VII. Thus, the concept of the "relevant time period" has been added to this section.

The second sentence in the Uniform Guidelines version prohibits the imposition of a selection procedure on one ethnic, race or sex group where other employees have not been subjected to the same

Section 11 (continued)

procedure. This sentence has been deleted from the revised section because it imposes unduly severe restrictions on an employer's ability to develop and implement job-related selection procedures. The current language could be read to prohibit the implementation of job-related selection procedures when incumbent employees were hired without having to complete successfully such procedures. The use of job-related selection procedures should not be so discouraged, as long as selection procedures are not adopted and implemented as a "pretext" for discrimination. Thus, elimination of this portion of the 1978 Guidelines would allow more latitude in adapting selection procedures to jobs that become more technical or require higher levels of skills.

Section 12. Retesting of applicants.

Uniform Guidelines   Users should provide a reasonable opportunity for retesting and reconsideration. Where examinations are administered periodically with public notice, such reasonable opportunity exists, unless persons who have previously been tested are precluded from retesting. The user may however take reasonable steps to preserve the security of its procedures.

Revised Guidelines   Users should provide a reasonable opportunity for retesting and reconsideration. Where examinations are administered periodically with public notice, such reasonable opportunity exists, unless persons who have previously been tested are precluded from retesting. The user may, however, take reasonable steps to preserve the security of its procedures. This will often mean limiting the time and frequency of retaking the test.

Professional and Legal Analysis

The proposed revision adds the requirement that users, in taking reasonable steps to preserve the security of their selection procedures, may limit the time and frequency of retaking a test. Division 14 *Principles* recognize that "[e]mployers should provide reasonable opportunities for reconsidering candidates *whenever alternative forms of* assessment exist and reconsideration is technically feasible." With regard to technical feasibility, the professional analysis for this section in *A Professional and Legal Analysis of the Uniform Guidelines on Employee Selection Procedures* (1981) [hereafter *Professional and Legal Analysis*] published by the American Society for Personnel Administration states at page 137:

Section 12 (continued)

It must be noted however, that in many employment situations alternate forms are not available and therefore retesting will not be technically feasible. Moreover, almost never are more than two alternate forms available to any employer. Retesting without alternate forms destroys the security of the test items and can result in a very inaccurate interpretation of a candidate's test score.

Unless it is recognized that retesting is frequently infeasible, this Section could be interpreted to require widespread retesting, which could in turn render tests invalid and therefore virtually useless.

Section 13. Affirmative action.

Uniform Guidelines

A. Affirmative action obligations. The use of selection procedures which have been validated pursuant to these guidelines does not relieve users of any obligations they may have to undertake affirmative action to assure equal employment opportunity. Nothing in these guidelines is intended to preclude the use of lawful selection procedures which assist in remedying the effects of prior discriminatory practices, or the achievement of affirmative action objectives.

B. Encouragement of voluntary affirmative action programs. These guidelines are also intended to encourage the adoption and implementation of voluntary affirmative action programs by users who have no obligation under Federal law to adopt them; but are not intended to impose any new obligations in that regard. The agencies issuing and endorsing these guidelines endorse for all private employers and reaffirm for all governmental employers the Equal Employment Opportunity Coordinating Council's "Policy Statement on Affirmative Action Programs for State and Local Government Agencies" (41 FR 38814, September 13, 1976). That policy statement is attached hereto as appendix, section 17.

Revised Guidelines

The use of selection procedures which have been validated pursuant to these guidelines does not relieve users of any obligations they may have to undertake affirmative action to assure equal employment opportunity.

Professional and Legal Analysis

The first sentence of section 13A of the Uniform Guidelines has been retained and the remainder of the section has been deleted because it was deemed to be inappropriate for inclusion in the Se-

Section 13 (continued)

lection Guidelines. The deleted portions would be more appropriately dealt with in guidelines having to do with affirmative action, such as EEOC's Guidelines on Affirmative Action, 29 C.F.R. Part 1608.

Section 14. Technical recommendations for validity evidence[6]

Introduction

The proposed revision of the technical requirements of the Guidelines is based on the 1976 Federal Executive Agency (FEA) Guidelines, 41 Fed. Reg. 51734 (November 23, 1976), because they conform more closely to accepted professional practices and are less burdensome and complicated than the Uniform Guidelines. They are couched as recommendations instead of requirements in recognition that "the science of testing is not as precise as physics or chemistry, nor its conclusions as provable." *Guardians*, 630 F.2d at 89. "The danger of too rigid an application of technical testing principles is that tests for all but the most mundane tasks would lack sufficient validity to permit their use. At least that is the role given the current state of the art of employment testing." *Id.* at 90. Consequently, the proposed technical standards should be viewed as recommendations recognizing that "it is not at all clear that *Griggs* requires observance of all the intricate details of the Guidelines." *Id.* at 91.

Uniform Guidelines	The following minimum standards, as applicable, should be met in conducting a validity study. Nothing in these guidelines is intended to preclude the development and use of other professionally acceptable techniques with respect to validation of selection procedures. Where it is not technically feasible for a user to conduct a validity study, the user has the obligation otherwise to comply with these guidelines. See sections 6 and 7 above.
Revised Guidelines	The following recommendations, as applicable, should be followed in gathering validity evidence. Nothing in these guide-

---

[6]The Uniform Guidelines caption for this section is "Technical standards for validity studies."

Section 14 (continued)

lines is intended to preclude the development and use of other professionally acceptable techniques with respect to the validation of selection procedures.

Professional and Legal Analysis

The changes are editorial. The revised prefatory language acknowledges that the guidelines permit the development and use of other professionally acceptable validation techniques, thereby providing implicit recognition that the field of industrial psychology is in the process of development and refinement.

Uniform Guidelines **A. Validity studies should be based on review of information about the job.** Any validity study should be based upon a review of information about the job for which the selection procedure is to be used. The review should include a job analysis except as provided in section 14B(3) below with respect to criterion-related validity. Any method of job analysis may be used if it provides the information required for the specific validation strategy used.

Revised Guidelines **A. Validity studies should be based on review of information about the job.** Any validity evidence should be based upon a review of information about the job for which the selection procedure is to be used. Any method of job review may be used if it provides the information appropriate to the specific validation strategy used.

Professional and Legal Analysis

The revision is editorial. As with the Uniform Guidelines and the 1976 FEA Guidelines, the proposal provides that any validity study should be based upon a review of information about the job for which the selection procedure is to be used. It also recognizes that a full job analysis is not required in all situations. The Division 14 *Principles* at page 4 expressly recognize these concepts:

> A systematic examination of the job and the context in which it is performed will provide an enhanced understanding of the selection problem. . . . A number of job analysis procedures exist, each differing in terms of the possible contribution to the objectives of the particular study or a portion of a study.

Uniform Guidelines **B. Technical standards for criterion-related validity studies. (1) *Technical feasibility.*** Users choosing to validate a selection procedure by a criterion-related validity strategy should determine whether it is technically feasible (as defined

Section 14 (continued)

in section 16) to conduct such a study in the particular employment context. The determination of the number of persons necessary to permit the conduct of a meaningful criterion-related study should be made by the user on the basis of all relevant information concerning the selection procedure, the potential sample and the employment situation. Where appropriate, jobs with substantially the same major work behaviors may be grouped together for validity studies, in order to obtain an adequate sample. These guidelines do not require a user to hire or promote persons for the purpose of making it possible to conduct a criterion-related study.

Revised Guidelines   **B. Criterion-related strategy.** (1) Users choosing a criterion-related validity strategy should determine whether it is technically feasible (as defined in section 16) to gather such evidence in the particular employment context. For example, the determination of the number of persons necessary to permit the conduct of a meaningful criterion-related study should be made by the user on the basis of all relevant information concerning the selection procedure, the potential sample and the employment situation. These guidelines do not require that a user hire or promote persons for the purpose of making it possible to conduct a criterion-related study.

Professional and Legal Analysis

Section 14B(1) of the Uniform Guidelines limits grouping of jobs to those situations in which the jobs have "substantially the same major work behaviors." As was pointed out in the *Professional and Legal Analysis* at page 143:

> This limitation implies that job grouping is only appropriate with jobs such as typist and keypunch operator where the skill requirements for performing the *entire* job are very similar. The profession, however, recognizes that a validity study may deal with only a segment of the overall requirements of several jobs. If a given segment or a given requirement of two jobs is similar, and the validation study is aimed at this segment, it would be professionally sound to combine the jobs in the study. This means that jobs might be combined differently in different validation studies (or in the same study).

For these reasons, the limitations on the grouping of jobs has been eliminated from the proposed revision. See also section 5B.

Uniform Guidelines   **(2) Analysis of the job.** There should be a review of job information to determine measures of work behavior(s) or performance that are relevant to the job or group of jobs in question. These measures or criteria are relevant to the extent that they represent critical or important job duties, work behaviors or

Section 14 (continued)

work outcomes as developed from the review of job information. The possibility of bias should be considered both in selection of the criterion measures and their application. In view of the possibility of bias in subjective evaluations, supervisory rating techniques and instructions to raters should be carefully developed. All criterion measures and the methods for gathering data need to be examined for freedom from factors which would unfairly alter scores of members of any group. The relevance of criteria and their freedom from bias are of particular concern when there are significant differences in measures of job performance for different groups.

Revised Guidelines (2) There should be a review of job or training information to determine measures of work or training behaviors, performance, or organizational outcomes that are relevant to the job in question. These measures or criteria are relevant to the extent that they represent one or more critical or important job duties, work behaviors or work outcomes as developed from the review of job information.

Professional and Legal Analysis

Section 14B(2) of the Uniform Guidelines erroneously assumes that bias can be identified, quantified and eliminated. Division 14's *Principles* at pages 7 to 8 point out the difficulties of objectifying bias:

> It is therefore apparent that the presence or absence of bias cannot be detected from a knowledge of criterion scores alone. If objective and subjective criteria disagree, bias in the more subjective measure may be suspected, although bias is not limited to subjective measures. There is no clear path to truth in these matters. A criterion difference between older and younger employees or day and night shifts may reflect bias in raters, equipment or conditions, or it may also reflect genuine differences in performance. What is required is the anticipation and reduction of the possibility of bias, alertness to this possibility, protection against it insofar as is feasible, and use of the best judgment possible in evaluating the data.

The *Professional and Legal Analysis* of the Guidelines at page 145 also provides a useful instruction in this regard:

> While the absence of bias cannot be assured, supervisory ratings should be focused or based on specific or important job duties, work behaviors, work requirements or work outcomes, and instructions to the raters should be detailed and carefully developed in order to maximize the objectivity of

Section 14 (continued)

the procedures and to sensitize them to factors that can contribute to rating error.

Consequently, although steps can be taken to minimize bias, it is virtually impossible to quantify and eliminate. See Revised Guidelines, Section 14B(3). Accordingly, the current requirement has been deleted as not being in conformance with accepted professional practices.

Uniform Guidelines — **(3) Criterion measures.** Proper safeguards should be taken to insure that scores on selection procedures do not enter into any judgments of employee adequacy that are to be used as criterion measures. Whatever criteria are used should represent important or critical work behavior(s) or work outcomes. Certain criteria may be used without a full job analysis if the user can show the importance of the criteria to the particular employment context. These criteria include but are not limited to production rate, error rate, tardiness, absenteeism, and length of service. A standardized rating of overall work performance may be used where a study of the job shows that it is an appropriate criterion. Where performance in training is used as a criterion, success in training should be properly measured and the relevance of the training should be shown either through a comparison of the content of the training program with the critical or important work behavior(s) of the job(s), or through a demonstration of the relationship between measures of performance in training and measures of job performance. Measures of relative success in training include but are not limited to instructor evaluations, performance samples, or tests. Criterion measures consisting of paper and pencil tests will be closely reviewed for job relevance.

Revised Guidelines — (3) Proper safeguards should be taken to insure that scores on selection procedures do not enter into any judgments of employee adequacy that are to be used as criterion measures. Criteria may consist of measures other than work proficiency including but not limited to length of service, regularity of attendance, work samples, training time or success in job training. Where performance in training is used as a criterion, the relevance of the training should be shown either through a comparison of the content of the training program with one or more critical or important work behavior(s) of the job(s), or through a demonstration of the relationship between measures of training and job success. Measures of relative success in training may include but are not limited to instructor evaluations, performance samples, or tests.

Whatever criteria are used should represent one or more important or critical work behaviors or work outcomes. Certain job behaviors including but not limited to production rate, error rate, job level achieved, progression rate, evaluation of potential, absenteeism and turnover, may be used as criteria without a full job review. A rating of overall work performance may be utilized where it is based on carefully defined job relevant characteristics. Although it is virtually impossible to

Section 14 (continued)

identify and quantify bias in subjective evaluation ratings, instructions to raters should be carefully developed so as to minimize that possibility. It should be recognized that group average differences in subjective evaluation ratings are not necessarily indicative of bias.

Professional and Legal Analysis

The changes in this section are largely editorial in nature except for the deletion of the last sentence in section 14B(3). As a legal requirement, the statement that "measures consisting of paper and pencil tests will be closely reviewed for job relevance" appears to be contrary to *Washington v. Davis*, 426 U.S. 229, 249-50 (1976), in which the Court accepted the relevance of a paper and pencil test to training, not to the job. The sentence suggests that paper and pencil tests are suspect as criterion measures. As pointed out at page 145 in the *Professional and Legal Analysis* of the Guidelines:

> This is an especially vexing problem to companies that engage in a large amount of apprenticeship or similarly expensive and lengthy training. Often, paper and pencil tests are the only efficient means of assessing trainee performance.

> An additional point is that trainees in industrial training programs are typically paid during training. "Trainee" or apprenticeship job titles are common. Therefore, performance in training is in effect performance on the job and should not be singled out for special treatment by the Guidelines.

For these reasons, the last sentence has been deleted, there being no professional basis for highlighting paper and pencil tests for special scrutiny.

Uniform Guidelines

(4) Representativeness of the sample. Whether the study is predictive or concurrent, the sample subjects should insofar as feasible be representative of the candidates normally available in the relevant labor market for the job or group of jobs in question, and should insofar as feasible include the races, sexes, and ethnic groups normally available in the relevant job market. In determining the representativeness of the sample in a concurrent validity study, the user should take into account the extent to which the specific knowledges or skills which are the primary focus of the test are those which employees learn on the job.

Where samples are combined or compared, attention should be given to see that such samples are comparable in terms of

Section 14 (continued)

the actual job they perform, the length of time on the job where time on the job is likely to affect performance, and other relevant factors likely to affect validity differences; or that these factors are included in the design of the study and their effects identified.

Revised Guidelines
(4) The sample should be appropriate for the purposes of the researcher's investigation. Race, sex, and ethnic variables should not be assumed to influence the obtained validity in the absence of explicit evidence that they do. Where samples are combined or compared, attention should be given to see that such samples are at least comparable in terms of the most relevant job or training behaviors or associated knowledges, skills and abilities.

Professional and Legal Analysis

The requirement in section 14B(4) that the sample of subjects in a study should be representative of the "relevant labor market," including its racial, sexual and ethnic composition, is an outgrowth of the requirement in section 14B(8) to conduct differential validity or test fairness studies. As discussed below, there is little professional support for fairness studies. The importance of having a representative sample is well established in the profession but the assumption that race and ethnic considerations are instrumental in determining the representativeness of the sample is incorrect. In the opinion of many professionals, questions of sample representativeness are most appropriately addressed in terms of score distributions. The Uniform Guidelines, moreover, do not define the "relevant labor market," and the term is usually in dispute in Title VII litigation. *See, e.g., Hazelwood,* 433 U.S. 299 (1977). In sum, the concept of relevant labor market has little professional basis and is likely to result in wide disagreement between users and the enforcement agencies as to what constitutes a representative sample. Therefore, the reference to relevant labor market has been deleted.

The Uniform Guidelines provide that "where samples are combined or compared, attention should be given to see that such samples are comparable in terms of the actual job they perform." It is professionally sound, however, to compare segments of jobs, even though the jobs may appear dissimilar. The Guidelines have therefore been revised to include comparison of the "most relevant job or training behaviors or associated knowledges, skills, and abilities."

Uniform Guidelines
(5) **Statistical relationships.** The degree of relationship between selection procedure scores and criterion measures should be examined and computed, using professionally acceptable statistical procedures. Generally, a selection procedure is con-

Section 14 (continued)

sidered related to the criterion, for the purposes of these guidelines, when the relationship between performance on the procedure and performance on the criterion measure is statistically significant at the 0.05 level of significance, which means that it is sufficiently high as to have a probability of no more than one (1) in twenty (20) to have occurred by chance. Absence of a statistically significant relationship between a selection procedure and job performance should not necessarily discourage other investigations of the validity of that selection procedure.

Revised Guidelines (5) The degree of relationship between selection procedure scores and criterion measures should be examined and computed, using professionally acceptable statistical procedures. Generally, a selection procedure is considered related to the criterion, for purposes of these guidelines, when the relationship between the procedure and at least one relevant criterion is statistically significant, *i.e.*, is sufficiently high as to have a probability of no more than one (1) in twenty (20) to have occurred by chance. Absence of a statistically significant relationship between a selection procedure and a criterion should not necessarily discourage other investigations of the validity of the selection procedures or inclusion of that procedure in a combination which is statistically significant. There are no minimum correlation coefficients applicable in an employment situation.

Professional and Legal Analysis

The changes are editorial in nature. The reference to the .05 level of significance has been deleted because in circumstances in which a small number are to be selected from among a large number of applicants, procedures with validities which do not reach the .05 level could be professionally acceptable. In this regard, Division 14 *Principles* state at page 10 that:

Traditionally, a validity coefficient or similar statistic which has a probability of less than one in twenty of having occurred by chance may be considered as establishing significant validity. There may be exceptions to this rule; professional standards have never insisted on a specific level of significance. However, departures from this convention should be based on reasons which can be stated in advance (such as power functions, utility, economic necessity, etc.).

Uniform Guidelines (6) **Operational use of selection procedures.** Users should evaluate each selection procedure to assure that it is appropriate for operational use, including establishment of cutoff scores or rank ordering. Generally, if other factors remain the same, the greater the magnitude of the relationship (e.g., cor-

Section 14 (continued)

relation coefficient) between performance on a selection procedure and one or more criteria of performance on the job, and the greater the importance and number of aspects of job performance covered by the criteria, the more likely it is that the procedure will be appropriate for use. Reliance upon a selection procedure which is significantly related to a criterion measure, but which is based upon a study involving a large number of subjects and has a low correlation coefficient will be subject to close review if it has a large adverse impact. Sole reliance upon a single selection instrument which is related to only one of many job duties or aspects of job performance will also be subject to close review. The appropriateness of a selection procedure is best evaluated in each particular situation and there are no minimum correlation coefficients applicable to all employment situations. In determining whether a selection procedure is appropriate for operational use the following considerations should also be taken into account: The degree of adverse impact of the procedure, the availability of other selection procedures of greater or substantially equal validity.

Revised Guidelines   (6) **[Deleted.]**

Professional and Legal Analysis

This subsection has been deleted as being inconsistent with accepted professional practices regarding the critical elements of utility determinations. In this regard, Division 14's *Principles* at page 18 provide that:

The utility of a selection procedure should be considered in considering whether to apply it operationally. In reaching the decision, consideration should be given to relative costs and benefits to both the organization and its employees. It is not recommended that procedures of marginal usefulness be applied, but a procedure with at least some demonstrated utility is ordinarily preferable to one of unknown validity or usefulness. Under usual circumstances, utility has a direct relationship to the coefficient of correlation...and, as mentioned previously, some methods of doing cost-benefit analysis on this basis have been developed....

The consideration of the degree of adverse impact is not a legal requirement in assessing the appropriateness of a selection procedure if the selection procedure is job related. *See Griggs v. Duke Power Co.*, 401 U.S. 424 (1971). Indeed, the Supreme Court in *Furnco*, 438 U.S. at 577-78, expressly held that employers are not required to adopt a "best" hiring procedure that would permit them "to at least consider...the most minority employees" or that maximizes the hiring of minority employees. Similarly, "the availability of other

Section 14 (continued)

selection procedures of greater or substantially equal validity" is not relevant. It only serves as evidence of pretext of discrimination if the user knew or should have known about such alternatives. *See Albemarle Paper Co.*, 422 U.S. at 425.

Uniform Guidelines	**(7) Overstatement of validity findings.** Users should avoid reliance upon techniques which tend to overestimate validity findings as a result of capitalization on chance unless an appropriate safeguard is taken. Reliance upon a few selection procedures or criteria of successful job performance when many selection procedures or criteria of performance have been studied, or the use of optimal statistical weights for selection procedures computed in one sample, are techniques which tend to inflate validity estimates as a result of chance. Use of a large sample is one safeguard: cross-validation is another.
Revised Guidelines	(6) Users should avoid reliance upon techniques that tend to overestimate validity findings as a result of capitalization on chance unless an appropriate safeguard is taken. Use of a large sample is one safeguard; cross-validation is another. Standard statistical corrections for range restriction and unreliability are not considered to be techniques that overestimate validity findings.

Professional and Legal Analysis

The second sentence of the current guideline has been deleted due to its inconsistency with the accepted practices of the psychological profession. The deleted portion fails to consider that, even where statistically significant evidence of validity is found for only one of several criteria, the evidence of validity of that criterion may well justify continued use of the procedure. The final sentence has been added to acknowledge that certain generally accepted statistical corrections do not overestimate validity findings. With regard to the overestimation of the validity issue, Division 14 *Principles* provide at page 11 that:

> *Researchers Should Guard Against Overestimates of Validity Resulting from Capitalization on Chance.* Especially when initial sample size is small, estimates of the validity of a composite battery developed on the basis of a regression equation should be adjusted using the appropriate *shrinkage formula* or be cross-validated on a new sample. It should be noted that the assignment of either rational or unit weights to predictors does not result in shrinkage in the usual sense. Where a smaller number of predictors is selected for use based on sample validity coefficients from a larger number included in the study, most shrinkage formulas are inap-

Section 14 (continued)

propriate and the alternative is cross-validation unless sample sizes are large.

Uniform Guidelines

(8) *Fairness*. This section generally calls for studies of unfairness where technically feasible. The concept of fairness or unfairness of selection procedures is a developing concept. In addition, fairness studies generally require substantial numbers of employees in the job or group of jobs being studied. For these reasons, the Federal enforcement agencies recognize that the obligation to conduct studies of fairness imposed by the guidelines generally will be upon users or groups of users with a large number of persons in a job class, or test developers; and that small users utilizing their own selection procedures will generally not be obligated to conduct such studies because it will be technically infeasible for them to do so.

(a) *Unfairness defined*. When members of one race, sex, or ethnic group characteristically obtain lower scores on a selection procedure than members of another group, and the differences in scores are not reflected in differences in a measure of job performance, use of the selection procedure may unfairly deny opportunities to members of the group that obtains the lower scores.

(b) *Investigation of fairness*. Where a selection procedure results in an adverse impact on a race, sex, or ethnic group identified in accordance with the classifications set forth in section 4 above and that group is a significant factor in the relevant labor market, the user generally should investigate the possible existence of unfairness for that group if it is technically feasible to do so. The greater the severity of the adverse impact on a group, the greater the need to investigate the possible existence of unfairness. Where the weight of evidence from other studies shows that the selection procedure predicts fairly for the group in question and for the same or similar jobs, such evidence may be relied on in connection with the selection procedure at issue.

(c) *General considerations in fairness investigations*. Users conducting a study of fairness should review the A.P.A. Standards regarding investigation of possible bias in testing. An investigation of fairness of a selection procedure depends on both evidence of validity and the manner in which the selection procedure is to be used in a particular employment context. Fairness of a selection procedure cannot necessarily be specified in advance without investigating these factors. Investigation of fairness of a selection procedure in samples where the range of scores on selection procedures or criterion measures is severely restricted for any subgroup samples (as compared to other subgroup samples) may produce misleading evidence of unfairness. That factor should accordingly be taken into account in conducting such studies and before reliance is placed on the results.

(d) *When unfairness is shown*. If unfairness is demonstrated through a showing that members of a particular group perform

Section 14 (continued)

better or poorer on the job than their scores on the selection procedure would indicate through comparison with how members of other groups perform, the user may either revise or replace the selection instrument in accordance with these guidelines, or may continue to use the selection instrument operationally with appropriate revisions in its use to assure compatibility between the probability of successful job performance and the probability of being selected.

(e) *Technical feasibility of fairness studies.* In addition to the general conditions needed for technical feasibility for the conduct of a criterion-related study (see section 16, below) an investigation of fairness requires the following:

(i) An adequate sample of persons in each group available for the study to achieve findings of statistical significance. Guidelines do not require a user to hire or promote persons on the basis of group classifications for the purpose of making it possible to conduct a study of fairness; but the user has the obligation otherwise to comply with these guidelines.
(ii) The samples for each group should be comparable in terms of the actual job they perform, length of time on the job where time on the job is likely to affect performance, and other relevant factors likely to affect validity differences; or such factors should be included in the design of the study and their effects identified.

(f) *Continued use of selection procedures when fairness studies not feasible.* If a study of fairness should otherwise be performed, but is not technically feasible, a selection procedure may be used which has otherwise met the validity standards of these guidelines, unless the technical infeasibility resulted from discriminatory employment practices which are demonstrated by facts other than past failure to conform with requirements for validation of selection procedures. However, when it becomes technically feasible for the user to perform a study of fairness and such a study is otherwise called for, the user should conduct the study of fairness.

Revised Guidelines **(7) Fairness or differential prediction of the selection procedure.** Differential prediction, unfairness or bias, as typically defined, have not been sufficiently demonstrated for race, sex, and ethnic groups to warrant a guideline recommendation to gather evidence related to these issues. Such evidence is therefore not required by these guidelines.

Professional and Legal Analysis

Fairness studies should not be required under the Guidelines. There is presently insufficient research evidence to support the present standard to collect such evidence. After reviewing the available evidence on differential prediction and fairness, the recent National Academy of Sciences study on *Ability Testing* concluded at page 146 (Part I) that: "We find little convincing evidence that well-constructed and competently administered tests are more valid predic-

Section 14 (continued)

tors for one population subgroup than for another: individuals with higher scores tend to perform better on the job regardless of group identity." Moreover, Part II of the *Ability Testing* study at page 382 concluded that "where differences are found, a single equation based on the majority group or the combined minority and majority groups usually tends to overpredict the actual criterion performance of minority group employees." It is therefore inappropriate for the Guidelines to require that fairness studies be routinely conducted as part of a criterion-related validity study. Such studies increase substantially the costs of establishing the job relatedness of a selection procedure without furthering the goals of equal employment opportunity.

Uniform Guidelines

C. Technical standards for content validity studies.
(1) *Appropriateness of content validity studies.* Users choosing to validate a selection procedure by a content validity strategy should determine whether it is appropriate to conduct such a study in the particular employment context. A selection procedure can be supported by a content validity strategy to the extent that it is a representative sample of the content of the job. Selection procedures which purport to measure knowledges, skills, or abilities may in certain circumstances be justified by content validity, although they may not be representative samples, if the knowledge, skill, or ability measured by the selection procedure can be operationally defined as provided in section 14C(4) below, and if that knowledge, skill, or ability is a necessary prerequisite to successful job performance.

A selection procedure based upon inferences about mental processes cannot be supported solely or primarily on the basis of content validity. Thus, a content strategy is not appropriate for demonstrating the validity of selection procedures which purport to measure traits or constructs, such as intelligence, aptitude, personality, commonsense, judgment, leadership, and spatial ability. Content validity is also not an appropriate strategy when the selection procedure involves knowledges, skills, or abilities which an employee will be expected to learn on the job.

Revised Guidelines

C. Content-oriented strategy. (1) There should be a definition of a content domain(s) with respect to the job(s) in question. Content domains may be defined through job review of the work or training behaviors or activities, or by the pooled judgments of persons having knowledge of the job. Content domains include one or more critical or important work or training behaviors, work products, work activities, job duties, or the knowledges, skills or abilities or work characteristics shown to be necessary for performance of the duties, behaviors, activities or the production of work. Where a content domain has been defined as a knowledge, skill or ability, that knowledge, skill or ability should be operationally defined. A selec-

Section 14 (continued)

tion procedure based on inferences about abstract psychological processes cannot be supported by content validity alone, unless the process can be operationally defined. Content validity by itself is not an appropriate validation strategy for intelligence, personality or interest tests. Content validity is also not an appropriate validation strategy when the selection procedure involves knowledges, skills or abilities which an employee will be expected to learn in a brief orientation period on the job.

(2) A selection procedure which is an appropriate sample of a content domain of the job or training as defined in accordance with subsection (1) above is a content valid procedure for that domain. Where the domain or domains measured are critical to the job, or constitute a substantial proportion of the job, the selection procedure will be considered to be content valid for the job. The reliability of selection procedures justified on the basis of content validity should be a matter of concern to the user. Whenever it is feasible to do so, appropriate statistical estimates should be made of the reliability of the selection procedures.

(3) A demonstration of the relationship between the content of the selection procedure and the content domain is critical to content validity. Content validity may be shown if the knowledges, skills or abilities or worker characteristics demonstrated in and measured by the selection procedure substantially correspond to the knowledges, skills, abilities or worker characteristics shown to be necessary for job or training success. The closer the content of the selection procedure is to actual work samples, behaviors, or activities, the stronger is the basis for showing content validity. The need for careful documentation of the relationship between the content domain of the selection procedure and that of the job increases as the content of the selection procedure less resembles that of the content domain.

Professional and Legal Analysis

Section 14C(1) has been rewritten and is incorporated in subsections C(1), C(2) and C(3) of the Revised Guidelines because it contains a number of principles that are not professionally supportable. For example, it is not necessary under accepted professional practice that a selection procedure be a representative sample of the content of the *entire* job to support a content validity strategy. Division 14's *Principles* provide that a procedure may be a sample of a given domain if that domain is an important part of the job, *i.e.*, is a representative sample of the content of one or more critical work behaviors of the job. The domain "does not have to cover the entire universe of topics covered in a training course or of duties in a particular job." *Principles* at page 12. See also discussion of section 14C(4) below.

Section 14 (continued)

It is misleading to say that "content validity is not an appropriate strategy when the selection procedure involves knowledges, skills, or abilities (KSA's) which an employee will be expected to learn on the job." This statement does not give appropriate recognition to the time it takes to learn the job or the knowledge or experience that is brought to the job. As stated in the *Principles* at page 14:

> The point here is that selection does not occur independently of training and this fact must be taken into account. The principle stated here does not preclude relegating different levels of the same ability to selection and training. For example, the fact that an employee is taught to read and interpret company technical manuals does not mean that the job applicant should not be evaluated for basic reading skills.

Section 14C(1) of the Uniform Guidelines states that content validation cannot be used to support tests or other procedures purporting to measure traits or constructs. As noted in the *Professional and Legal Analysis* of the Guidelines at page 159, this is inconsistent with professional practice:

> Not all "constructs" are broad abstract traits. Many constructs, particularly those in the ability area, can be defined quite narrowly and may lend themselves to measurement by procedures developed through content validation . . . . Thus, where a construct is operationally defined in terms of work behaviors and the selection procedure is an objective measure of these behaviors, the construct may be seen as a convenient label for an aggregate of work behaviors and may properly be validated by a content strategy.

See also *Guardians*, 630 F.2d at 93 ("If the job in question involves primarily abilities that are somewhat abstract, content validation should not be rejected simply because these abilities could be categorized as constructs.").

Uniform Guidelines (2) *Job analysis for content validity.* There should be a job analysis which includes an analysis of the important work behavior(s) required for successful performance and their relative importance and, if the behavior results in work product(s), an analysis of the work product(s). Any job analysis should focus on the work behavior(s) and the tasks associated with them. If work behavior(s) are not observable, the job analysis should identify and analyze those aspects of the be-

Section 14 (continued)

havior(s) that can be observed and the observed work products. The work behavior(s) selected for measurement should be critical work behavior(s) and/or important work behavior(s) constituting most of the job.

Revised Guidelines (2) [Deleted and revised as part of section 14C(1), C(2) and C(3) above.]

Professional and Legal Analysis

The Uniform Guidelines express a preference for a task-based job analysis but the Division 14 *Principles* permit a more limited analysis. Specifically, the *Principles* state at page 13 that:

A content domain should ordinarily be defined in terms of tasks, activities or responsibilities or *specific abilities, knowledge, or job skills found to be prerequisite to effective behavior in the domain.* (Emphasis added.)

Accordingly, because the Uniform Guidelines are inconsistent with professional practice, this section has been rewritten as part of section 14C(1)-C(3) above.

Uniform Guidelines (3) **Development of selection procedures.** A selection procedure designed to measure the work behavior may be developed specifically from the job and job analysis in question, or may have been previously developed by the user, or by other users or by a test publisher.

Revised Guidelines (3) [Deleted.]

Professional and Legal Analysis

Because of the emphasis of the Uniform Guidelines on work sample tests, retention of this subsection effectively precludes pencil and paper tests and limits training and experience requirements. Accordingly, this subsection has been deleted.

Uniform Guidelines (4) **Standards for demonstrating content validity.** To demonstrate the content validity of a selection procedure, a user should show that the behavior(s) demonstrated in the selection procedure are a representative sample of the behavior(s) of the job in question or that the selection procedure provides a representative sample of the work product of the job. In the case of a selection procedure measuring a knowledge, skill, or ability, the knowledge, skill, or ability being measured should be operationally defined. In the case of a selection procedure measuring a knowledge, the knowledge being measured should be operationally defined as that body of learned information which is used in and is a necessary prerequisite for observable

Section 14 (continued)

aspects of work behavior of the job. In the case of skills or abilities, the skill or ability being measured should be operationally defined in terms of observable aspects of work behavior of the job. For any selection procedure measuring a knowledge, skill, or ability the user should show that (a) the selection procedure measures and is a representative sample of that knowledge, skill, or ability; and (b) that knowledge, skill, or ability is used in and is a necessary prerequisite to performance of critical or important work behavior(s). In addition, to be content valid, a selection procedure measuring a skill or ability should either closely approximate an observable work behavior, or its product should closely approximate an observable work product. If a test purports to sample a work behavior or to provide a sample of a work product, the manner and setting of the selection procedure and its level and complexity should closely approximate the work situation. The closer the content and the context of the selection procedure are to work samples or work behaviors, the stronger is the basis for showing content validity. As the content of the selection procedure less resembles a work behavior, or the setting and manner of the administration of the selection procedure less resemble the work situation, or the result less resembles a work product, the less likely the selection procedure is to be content valid, and the greater the need for other evidence of validity.

Revised Guidelines   (4) [Deleted and revised as part of section 14C(1) above.]

Professional and Legal Analysis

The emphasis of the Uniform Guidelines on content validity being a demonstration that the content of the selection procedure is representative of important aspects of performance on the job is inconsistent with accepted professional definitions of content validity, which go beyond the work sample approach of the Guidelines and include identification of critical knowledges, skills and abilities as well. The Division 14 *Principles* provide at page 12 that:

Appropriate development of a selection procedure on the basis of *content* requires developing the procedure to be an appropriate sample of a specified content domain. If a selection procedure is to be used for employment decisions, the relevant content domain is *performance* (or the knowledge, skill, or ability necessary for performance) on the job, in relevant job training, or on specified aspects of either. . . .

* * * * * * *

The more a selection procedure has point-in-time fidelity to exact job operations, the less likely it is to have enough

Section 14 (continued)

generality to remain appropriate in view of job changes. Also, the more a selection procedure is a specific sample of a domain involved in one job, the less likely it is to apply to other similar jobs. Specificity and generality form the ends of a continuum, and no one except the researcher can determine how general a selection procedure should be. The important thing is that the researcher be aware in advance of conditions which may affect the generality decision; and that the generality decision must have a clear rationale based on the specific selection situation at hand, organizational needs, anticipated changes in technology, equipment, and work assignments, and human and economic considerations. This principle also applies in the development of content-oriented criteria for use in a predictive or concurrent criterion-related study. The degree to which the results of the study can be generalized will depend partly on the generality of the criteria and their applicability over time and jobs.

The thrust of the Uniform Guidelines, however, is to require exact fidelity of a content validated selection procedure to the content of the job. This would result in a continual need to change selection procedures, particularly when work requirements are variable and subject to change. Therefore, this subsection has been deleted and incorporated into section 14C(1) to conform it with professional practice.

Uniform Guidelines   (5) **Reliability.** The reliability of selection procedures justified on the basis of content validity should be a matter of concern to the user. Whenever it is feasible, appropriate statistical estimates should be made of the reliability of the selection procedure.

Revised Guidelines   (5) [Deleted and incorporated as part of section 14C(2) above.]

Professional and Legal Analysis

This subsection has been incorporated without change in section 14C(2) of the proposed revision.

Uniform Guidelines   (6) **Prior training or experience.** A requirement for or evaluation of specific prior training or experience based on content validity, including a specification of level or amount of training or experience, should be justified on the basis of the relationship between the content of the training or experience and the

Section 14 (continued)

content of the job for which the training or experience is to be required or evaluated. The critical consideration is the resemblance between the specific behaviors, products, knowledges, skills, or abilities in the experience or training and the specific behaviors, products, knowledges, skills, or abilities required on the job, whether or not there is close resemblance between the experience or training as a whole and the job as a whole.

Revised Guidelines (4) A requirement for specific prior training or for work experience based on content validity, including a specification of level or amount of training or experience, should be justified on the basis of the relationship between the content of the training or experience and the content domain of the job for which the training or experience is to be required. The critical consideration is the resemblance between the specific behaviors, products, knowledges, skills, or abilities in the experience or training and the specific behaviors, products, knowledges, skills, or abilities required on the job, whether or not there is close resemblance between the experience or training as a whole and the job as a whole.

Professional and Legal Analysis

The proposed revision is virtually identical to the existing provision. No substantive change is intended.

Uniform Guidelines (7) **Content validity of training success.** Where a measure of success in a training program is used as a selection procedure and the content of a training program is justified on the basis of content validity, the use should be justified on the relationship between the content of the training program and the content of the job.

Revised Guidelines (7) [Deleted.]

Professional and Legal Analysis

This subsection has been deleted because it requires an absolute duplication of training and job duties. Rather, users should show the relationship of training content to one or more domains of job content.

Uniform Guidelines (8) **Operational use.** A selection procedure which is supported on the basis of content validity may be used for a job if it represents a critical work behavior (i.e., a behavior which is necessary for performance of the job) or work behaviors which constitute most of the important parts of the job.

Revised Guidelines (8) [Deleted.]

Section 14 (continued)

Professional and Legal Analysis

See legal and professional analysis with respect to section 14C(1).

Uniform Guidelines (9) **Ranking based on content validity studies.** If a user can show, by a job analysis or otherwise, that a higher score on a content valid selection procedure is likely to result in better job performance, the results may be used to rank persons who score above minimum levels. Where a selection procedure supported solely or primarily by content validity is used to rank job candidates, the selection procedure should measure those aspects of performance which differentiate among levels of job performance.

Revised Guidelines (5) Under usual circumstances, a content-oriented selection procedure with adequate differentiation can be assumed to have a linear relationship to job or training or organizational behaviors and the results may be used to rank people.

Professional and Legal Analysis

The Division 14 *Principles* expressly recognize the professional practice of ranking pursuant to content valid selection procedures and section 14C(9) of the Uniform Guidelines has been amended accordingly. The *Principles* at page 15 provide in this regard that:

> Interpretation of content-oriented selection procedures may reflect the measurement properties of the given procedure. If a selection instrument yields reliable results, and provides adequate discrimination in the score ranges involved, persons may be ranked upon the basis of its results. However, if an instrument is constructed more in the manner of a training mastery test, in which the examinee is expected to get all or nearly all of the items correct, a critical score may be in order. A critical score is also in order in situations such as those in which the greater speed at which a typist can type cannot be reflected in production because of equipment or process limitations. In this case, the selection procedure should be designed with the limiting conditions considered.

The effect of the current Guidelines, however, is to require a criterion-related study if a content valid test is to be useful. See discussion under section 5G above.

Uniform Guidelines D. **Technical standards for construct validity studies.** (1) **Appropriateness of construct validity studies.** Construct validity is a more complex strategy than either crite-

Section 14 (continued)

rion-related or content validity. Construct validation is a relatively new and developing procedure in the employment field, and there is at present a lack of substantial literature extending the concept to employment practices. The user should be aware that the effort to obtain sufficient empirical support for construct validity is both an extensive and arduous effort involving a series of research studies, which include criterion related validity studies and which may include content validity studies. Users choosing to justify use of a selection procedure by this strategy should therefore take particular care to assure that the validity study meets the standards set forth below.

(2) Job analysis for construct validity studies. There should be a job analysis. This job analysis should show the work behavior(s) required for successful performance of the job, or the groups of jobs being studied, the critical or important work behavior(s) in the job or group of jobs being studied, and an identification of the construct(s) believed to underlie successful performance of these critical or important work behaviors in the job or jobs in question. Each construct should be named and defined, so as to distinguish it from other constructs. If a group of jobs is being studied the jobs should have in common one or more critical or important work behaviors at a comparable level of complexity.

(3) Relationship to the job. A selection procedure should then be identified or developed which measures the construct identified in accord with subparagraph (2) above. The user should show by empirical evidence that the selection procedure is validly related to the construct and that the construct is validly related to the performance of critical or important work behavior(s). The relationship between the construct as measured by the selection procedure and the related work behavior(s) should be supported by empirical evidence from one or more criterion-related studies involving the job or jobs in question which satisfy the provisions of section 14B above.

(4) Use of construct validity study without new criterion-related evidence. (a) *Standards for use.* Until such time as professional literature provides more guidance on the use of construct validity in employment situations, the Federal agencies will accept a claim of construct validity without a criterion-related study which satisfies section 14B above only when the selection procedure has been used elsewhere in a situation in which a criterion-related study has been conducted and the use of a criterion-related validity study in this context meets the standards for transportability of criterion-related validity studies as set forth above in section 7. However, if a study pertains to a number of jobs having common critical or important work behaviors at a comparable level of complexity, and the evidence satisfies subparagraphs 14B (2) and (3) above for those jobs with criterion-related validity evidence for those jobs, the selection procedure may be used for all the jobs to which the study pertains. If construct validity is to be generalized to other jobs or groups of jobs not in the group studied, the Federal enforcement agencies will expect at a minimum

Section 14 (continued)

additional empirical research evidence meeting the standards of subparagraphs section 14B (2) and (3) above for the additional jobs or groups of jobs.

(b) *Determination of common work behaviors.* In determining whether two or more jobs have one or more work behavior(s) in common, the user should compare the observed work behavior(s) in each of the jobs and should compare the observed work product(s) in each of the jobs. If neither the observed work behavior(s) in each of the jobs nor the observed work product(s) in each of the jobs are the same, the Federal enforcement agencies will presume that the work behavior(s) in each job are different. If the work behaviors are not observable, then evidence of similarity of work products and any other relevant research evidence will be considered in determining whether the work behavior(s) in the two jobs are the same.

Revised Guidelines

D. Construct Validity. Construct validity is a more complex strategy than either criterion-related or content validity. Accordingly, users choosing to validate a selection procedure by use of this strategy should be careful to follow professionally accepted practices.

(1) There should be a review of information about the job. This job review should result in a determination that the construct of interest is relevant to successful performance of one or more important or critical parts of a job.

(2) A selection procedure should be selected or developed which measures the construct(s) identified in accord with subparagraph (1) above.

(3) A selection procedure may be used operationally if the recommendations of subparagraphs (1) and (2) are met and there is sufficient empirical research evidence showing that the procedure is validly related to one or more critical job duties.

(4) Where a selection procedure satisfies the recommendations of subsections (1), (2) and (3) above, it may be used operationally for other jobs which are shown by an appropriate job review to include the same construct(s) as an essential element in job performance.

Professional and Legal Analysis

Although the Uniform Guidelines at section 5A give equal standing to content, criterion, and construct validity strategies, section 14D effectively negates the construct strategy as an alternative. Construct validity is professionally recognized as being a more complex strategy and this section has been redrafted accordingly.

Section 15. Documentation of impact and validity evidence.

Uniform Guidelines **A. Required information.** Users of selection procedures other than those users complying with section 15A(1) below should maintain and have available for each job information on adverse impact of the selection process for that job and, where it is determined a selection process has an adverse impact, evidence of validity as set forth below.

Revised Guidelines **A. Required information.** Users of selection procedures other than those users complying with section 15A(1) below should maintain and have available for each job or job group information on the impact of the selection process for that job or job group and, where necessary, validity evidence.

Professional and Legal Analysis

This section has been revised to allow for the collection of adverse impact data on a job *or* a "job group" basis. The "job group" option was added to reflect the fact that many jobs have common skill or ability components and selection for them may be by a common selection procedure. In many instances, collection of data on a job only basis will not provide sufficient numbers of persons for a meaningful impact analysis to be undertaken. In addition, the allowance of data collection on a job group basis is consistent with many employers' recordkeeping practices and in many instances will facilitate the gathering of data required for a validity study because such studies are often based on job groups rather than a single job.

Uniform Guidelines **(1) Simplified recordkeeping for users with less than 100 employees.** In order to minimize recordkeeping burdens on employers who employ one hundred (100) or fewer employees, and other users not required to file EEO-1, et seq., reports, such users may satisfy the requirements of this section 15 if they maintain and have available records showing, for each year:

(a) The number of persons hired, promoted, and terminated for each job, by sex, and where appropriate by race and national origin;
(b) The number of applicants for hire and promotion by sex and where appropriate by race and national origin; and
(c) The selection procedures utilized (either standardized or not standardized).

These records should be maintained for each race or national origin group (see section 4 above) constituting more than two

Section 15 (continued)

percent (2%) of the labor force in the relevant labor area. However, it is not necessary to maintain records by race and/or national origin (see § 4 above) if one race or national origin group in the relevant labor area constitutes more than ninety-eight percent (98%) of the labor force in the area. If the user has reason to believe that a selection procedure has an adverse impact, the user should maintain any available evidence of validity for that procedure (see sections 7A and 8).

Revised Guidelines **(1) Simplified recordkeeping for users with 250 or fewer employees.** In order to minimize recordkeeping burdens on employers with establishments who employ two hundred fifty (250) or fewer employees, and other users not required to file EEO-1, *et seq.*, reports, such users may satisfy the requirements of this section if they maintain and have available records showing, for each year:

(a) The number of persons hired, promoted, and terminated for each job or job group, by race, sex and national origin;
(b) The number of applicants for hire and promotion by race, sex and national origin; and
(c) The selection procedures utilized (either standardized or not standardized).

These records should be maintained for each race or national origin group (see section 4 above) constituting more than five percent (5%) of the labor force in the relevant labor market. However, it is not necessary to maintain records by race and/or national origin (see section 4 above) if one race or national origin group in the relevant labor market constitutes more than ninety-five percent (95%) of the labor force in the relevant labor market. It is advisable to maintain evidence of job relatedness.

Professional and Legal Analysis

The revisions to this section extend small employer recordkeeping requirements to employers with 250 or fewer employees and to larger employers with establishments of 250 or fewer employees. The revisions are intended to lessen the recordkeeping burdens on small employers and small establishments and are consistent with proposals to reduce the recordkeeping requirements of federal contractors. The extension of small employer recordkeeping requirements to small establishments is designed to reflect the fact that, for many employers, decisions regarding selection are often made by individual establishments, which have no greater recordkeeping ability than small employers, and not from a central personnel office. *See, e.g., Stastny v. Southern Bell Tel. & Tel.*, 628 F.2d 267, 279 (4th Cir. 1980)("[T]here were in effect as many labor pools as there were separate and essentially autonomous facilities.").

The "job group" option, as discussed in section 14A, above, has been included in subsection (1)(a) as well. In addition, the section

Section 15 (continued)

has been amended in accordance with section 4A to provide that records be kept only for groups constituting more than 5% of the labor force in the relevant labor market. The "relevant labor market" language has been added to this section because the use of raw labor force data without consideration of the source of the qualified pool of applicants may not, in many instances, appropriately define the relevant labor market. The final sentence has been modified to advise users to maintain evidence of job relatedness, which might in appropriate cases consist of evidence other than formal validity studies.

Uniform Guidelines

(2) Information on impact. (a) *Collection of information on impact.* Users of selection procedures other than those complying with section 15A(1) above should maintain and have available for each job records or other information showing whether the total selection process for that job has an adverse impact on any of the groups for which records are called for by sections [sic] 4B above. Adverse impact determinations should be made at least annually for each such group which constitutes at least 2 percent of the labor force in the relevant labor area or 2 percent of the applicable workforce. Where a total selection process for a job has an adverse impact, the user should maintain and have available records or other information showing which components have an adverse impact. Where the total selection process for a job does not have an adverse impact, information need not be maintained for individual components except in circumstances set forth in subsection 15A(2)(b) below. If the determination of adverse impact is made using a procedure other than the "four-fifths rule," as defined in the first sentence of section 4D above, a justification, consistent with section 4D above, for the procedure used to determine adverse impact should be available.

(b) *When adverse impact has been eliminated in the total selection process.* Whenever the total selection process for a particular job has had an adverse impact, as defined in section 4 above, in any year, but no longer has an adverse impact, the user should maintain and have available the information on individual components of the selection process required in the preceding paragraph for the period in which there was adverse impact. In addition, the user should continue to collect such information for at least two (2) years after the adverse impact has been eliminated.

(c) *When data insufficient to determine impact.* Where there has been an insufficient number of selections to determine whether there is an adverse impact of the total selection process for a particular job, the user should continue to collect, maintain and have available the information on individual components of the selection process required in section 15(A)(2)(a) above until the information is sufficient to determine that the overall selection process does not have an adverse impact as defined in section 4 above, or until the job has changed substantially.

Section 15 (continued)

Revised Guidelines

B. Information on impact. Users of selection procedures who have more than 250 employees should maintain and have available for each job or group of jobs to which the selection procedure was applied records or other information showing the impact of the total selection process for that job or group of jobs for which records are called for by section 4B above. Adverse impact determinations should be made annually for each such group which constitutes at least 5 percent of the labor force in the relevant labor market. Where a total selection process for a job or job group has an adverse impact, the user should maintain and have available records or other information showing which components have an adverse impact. Where the total selection process for a job or job group does not have an adverse impact, information need not be maintained for individual components.

Professional and Legal Analysis

Section 15A(2)(a) has been changed to reflect the previously discussed increase in small employer coverage to 250 employees, the use of job groups, the increase to 5% for covered groups, and the concept of the relevant labor market. The portion of the Uniform Guidelines requiring impact determinations for groups constituting a designated percentage of "the applicable workforce" has been deleted as unnecessary because the revised language would cover any instances where impact determinations should be made.

The final sentence of section 15A(2)(a) has been deleted in the Revised Guidelines. This sentence is no longer necessary in view of the revisions in section 4C relating to the incorporation of tests of practical and statistical significance and the four listed exceptions.

Section 15A(2)(b) has been deleted as well as the reference to it in section 15A(2)(a) in the Revised Guidelines. It requires the maintenance of impact data on components for the period during which an adverse impact occurred, even after the impact in the overall process has been eliminated. In addition, the current section provides that the user should continue to collect such data for two years after the impact has been eliminated. The requirements of section15A(2)(b) create a costly and burdensome obligation on employers which serves no legitimate interest of the enforcement agencies. For these reasons, it has been deleted.

Section 15A(2)(c) covers situations where an insufficient number of selections have been made to determine the impact of the selection procedures and requires the maintenance of information on individual components until such time as a sufficient number of decisions have been made to calculate adverse impact. This section was deleted in the Revised Guidelines because fluctuations in prac-

Section 15 (continued)

tices may make data accumulated over a long period of time misleading, and because the effect of the provision on employers making few selection decisions is to require the continuous maintenance of data on all components of a selection process. As a practical matter, employers who make too few selection decisions in a year to conduct an adequate adverse impact analysis are not employers on whom the enforcement agencies should be focusing their resources.

Uniform Guidelines (3) **Documentation of validity evidence.** (a) *Types of evidence.* Where a total selection process has an adverse impact (see section 4 above) the user should maintain and have available for each component of that process which has an adverse impact, one or more of the following types of documentation:

(i) Documentation evidence showing criterion-related validity of the selection procedure (see section 15B, below).
(ii) Documentation evidence showing content validity of the selection procedure (see section 15C, below).
(iii) Documentation evidence showing construct validity of the selection procedure (see section 15D, below).
(iv) Documentation evidence from other studies showing validity of the selection procedure in the user's facility (see section 15E, below).
(v) Documentation evidence showing why a validity study cannot or need not be performed and why continued use of the procedure is consistent with Federal law.

(b) *Form of report.* This evidence should be compiled in a reasonably complete and organized manner to permit direct evaluation of the validity of the selection procedure. Previously written employer or consultant reports of validity, or reports describing validity studies completed before the issuance of these guidelines are acceptable if they are complete in regard to the documentation requirements contained in this section, or if they satisfied requirements of guidelines which were in effect when the validity study was completed. If they are not complete, the required additional documentation should be appended. If necessary information is not available the report of the validity study may still be used as documentation, but its adequacy will be evaluated in terms of compliance with the requirements of these guidelines.

(c) *Completeness.* In the event that evidence of validity is reviewed by an enforcement agency, the validation reports completed after the effective date of these guidelines are expected to contain the information set forth below. Evidence denoted by use of the word "(Essential)" is considered critical. If information denoted essential is not included, the report will be considered incomplete unless the user affirmatively demonstrates either its unavailability due to circumstances beyond the user's control or special circumstances of the user's study which make the information irrelevant. Evidence not so denoted is desirable but its absence will not be a basis for considering a report incomplete. The user should maintain and

Section 15 (continued)

have available the information called for under the heading "Source Data" in sections 15B(11) and 15D(11). While it is a necessary part of the study, it need not be submitted with the report. All statistical results should be organized and presented in tabular or graphic form to the extent feasible.

Revised Guidelines C. **Documentation of validity evidence.** (1) For selection procedures having an adverse impact, the user should maintain and have available one of the following types of documentation evidence:

(a) Documentation evidence showing criterion-related validity of the selection procedure.
(b) Documentation evidence showing content validity of the selection procedure.
(c) Documentation evidence showing construct validity of the selection procedure.
(d) Documentation evidence from other studies showing validity of the selection procedure.
(e) Documentation evidence showing why validation is not feasible or not appropriate and why continued use of the procedure is consistent with Federal law.

This evidence should be compiled in a reasonably complete and organized manner to permit direct evaluation of the validity evidence. Previously written employer or consultant reports of validity are acceptable if they are reasonably complete in regard to the following documentation recommendations, or if they are reasonably complete in terms of guidelines which were in effect when the study was completed. If necessary information is not available, the validity report may still be used as documentation, but its adequacy will be evaluated in terms of the recommendations contained in these guidelines.

Professional and Legal Analysis

Revised section 15C(1) sets out the types of evidence of validity or job relatedness that are discussed throughout the remainder of the documentation section. As with the revised technical recommendations in section 14, the FEA Guidelines instead of the Uniform Guidelines are used as the basis for the revisions. The changes in this section are largely editorial with the major ones being the introduction of feasibility for a validity study in section 15C(1)(e) and the inclusion of a "reasonableness" factor with regard to the completeness of reports of validity.

Section 15A(3)(c) of the current Guidelines has been deleted because it is in excess of the accepted practices of the psychological profession regarding the completeness of validity evidence. The designation of those things deemed by the agencies to be "essential" as mandatory requirements is beyond the accepted practices of the psychological profession. Thus, the Revised Guidelines have deleted

Section 15 (continued)

any reference to "essential" items. The large number of items deemed by the Uniform Guidelines to be "essential" makes it nearly impossible for an employer to comply fully with the Guidelines.

Uniform Guidelines	**B. Criterion-related validity studies.** Reports of criterion-related validity for a selection procedure should include the following information:
	(1) *User(s), location(s), and date(s) of study.* Dates and location(s) of the job analysis or review of job information, the date(s) and location(s) of the administration of the selection procedures and collection of criterion data, and the time between collection of data on selection procedures and criterion measures should be provided (Essential). If the study was conducted at several locations, the address of each location, including city and State, should be shown.
Revised Guidelines	**(2)** *Criterion-related validity.* Reports of criterion-related validity of selection procedures should contain the following information:
	(a) *Time Period(s) of Study.* The time period of administration of selection procedures and collection of criterion data and, where appropriate, the time between collection of data on selection procedures and criterion measures should be shown.

Professional and Legal Analysis

Section 15B of the Uniform Guidelines has been redesignated as section 15C(2). Information regarding dates and locations of the job analysis or review have been deleted as unnecessary because a knowledge of job requirements may be derived from numerous sources over a long period of time. Likewise, the requirement for the locations where the study was conducted has been deleted because many criterion studies will involve numerous locations, a listing of which will not add to the adequacy of the study.

Uniform Guidelines	**(2)** *Problem and setting.* An explicit definition of the purpose(s) of the study and the circumstances in which the study was conducted should be provided. A description of existing selection procedures and cutoff scores, if any, should be provided.
Revised Guidelines	(b) *Purpose and setting.* An explicit definition of the purpose(s) and the circumstances in which the validity evidence was gathered should be provided.

Professional and Legal Analysis

The second sentence has been deleted as being unnecessary.

Section 15 (continued)

Uniform Guidelines

(3) **Job analysis or review of job information.** A description of the procedure used to analyze the job or group of jobs, or to review the job information should be provided (Essential). Where a review of job information results in criteria which may be used without a full job analysis (see section 14B(3)), the basis for the selection of these criteria should be reported (Essential). Where a job analysis is required a complete description of the work behavior(s) or work outcome(s) and measures of their criticality or importance should be provided (Essential). The report should describe the basis on which the behavior(s) or outcome(s) were determined to be critical or important, such as the proportion of time spent on the respective behaviors, their level of difficulty, their frequency of performance, the consequences of error, or other appropriate factors (Essential). Where two or more jobs are grouped for a validity study, the information called for in this subsection should be provided for each of the jobs, and the justification for the grouping (see section 14B(1)) should be provided (Essential).

Revised Guidelines

(c) *Review of job information.* Where a review of job information results in criteria which are measures other than work proficiency, the basis for the selection of these criteria should be reported. Where a job review is conducted, the report should include either:

(i) the important duties performed on the job and the basis on which such duties were determined to be important; or
(ii) the knowledges, skills, abilities and/or other worker characteristics and bases on which they were determined to be important. Published descriptions from industry sources or the Dictionary of Occupational Titles, Fourth Edition, United States Government Printing Office (1977) are satisfactory if they reasonably describe the job. If appropriate, a brief supplement to the published description should be provided.
(iii) if two or more jobs are grouped for a validity study, a justification for this grouping should be provided.

Professional and Legal Analysis

This section has been extensively revised to reflect professional opinion that numerous methods of job analysis are acceptable. Thus, the revised section provides that either a work-oriented (duty or task-based) or worker-oriented (identification of knowledge, skills, abilities or other worker characteristics (KSAO's)) is sufficient. The current language in section 15B(3) implying that only a work-behavior-oriented job analysis is sufficient has been deleted as inconsistent with accepted professional practices and other aspects of the Guidelines. The revised section recognizes that there may be differences in the level of thoroughness for a criterion-related review of job information than for a content-oriented analysis.

Section 15 (continued)

Uniform Guidelines (4) **Job titles and codes.** It is desirable to provide the user's job title(s) for the job(s) in question and the corresponding job title(s) and code(s) from U.S. Employment Service's Dictionary of Occupational Titles.

Revised Guidelines (d) *Job titles and codes.* It is desirable to provide the user's job title(s) for the job(s) in question and the corresponding job title(s) and code(s) from U.S. Employment Service's Dictionary of Occupational Titles.

Professional and Legal Analysis

No change.

Uniform Guidelines (5) **Criterion measures.** The bases for the selection of the criterion measures should be provided, together with references to the evidence considered in making the selection of criterion measures (essential). A full description of all criteria on which data were collected and means by which they were observed, recorded, evaluated, and quantified, should be provided (essential). If rating techniques are used as criterion measures, the appraisal form(s) and instructions to the rater(s) should be included as part of the validation evidence, or should be explicitly described and available (essential). All steps taken to insure that criterion measures are free from factors which would unfairly alter the scores of members of any group should be described (essential).

Revised Guidelines (e) *Criteria.* A full description of all criteria on which data were collected, including a rationale for selection of the final criteria and means by which they were gathered and quantified should be provided. If rating techniques are used as criterion measures, a copy of the appraisal form(s) and instructions to the rater(s) should be included as part of the validation evidence.

Professional and Legal Analysis

The changes are largely editorial with the exception of the deletion of the last sentence which has to do with steps taken to ensure that criterion measures are free from bias. This sentence was deleted because accepted professional practices deem attempts to maximize rating standardization, reliability and validity to be sufficient to eliminate potential biases in ratings.

Uniform Guidelines (6) **Sample description.** A description of how the research sample was identified and selected should be included (essential). The race, sex, and ethnic composition of the sample, including those groups set forth in section 4A above, should be described (essential). This description should include the

Section 15 (continued)

Revised Guidelines — size of each subgroup (essential). A description of how the research sample compares with the relevant labor market or work force, the method by which the relevant labor market or work force was defined, and a discussion of the likely effects on validity of differences between the sample and the relevant labor market or work force, are also desirable. Descriptions of educational levels, length of service, and age are also desirable.

(f) *Sample.* A description of how the research sample was selected should be included.

Professional and Legal Analysis

Only the first sentence of the present Guidelines has been retained. The remainder of the section has been deleted because it relates to the continued agency adherence to the professionally rejected concept of differential validity. See discussion of section 14B(8) at page 78, *supra.*

Uniform Guidelines — **(7) Description of selection procedures.** Any measure, combination of measures, or procedure studied should be completely and explicitly described or attached (essential). If commercially available selection procedures are studied, they should be described by title, form, and publisher (essential). Reports of reliability estimates and how they were established are desirable.

Revised Guidelines — (g) *Selection procedure.* The measure, combination of measures, or procedures studied should be described or attached. If commercially available selection procedures are used, they should be described by title, form and publisher. A rationale for choosing the selection procedures investigated should be included.

Professional and Legal Analysis

In addition to editorial changes, the last sentence requiring reports of reliability estimates in the current Guidelines has been deleted and replaced with a recommendation that the rationale for choosing the selection procedures should be included.

Uniform Guidelines — **(8) Techniques and results.** Methods used in analyzing data should be described (essential). Measures of central tendency (e.g., means) and measures of dispersion (e.g., standard deviations and ranges) for all selection procedures and all criteria should be reported for each race, sex, and ethnic group which constitutes a significant factor in the relevant labor market (essential). The magnitude and direction of all relationships between selection procedures and criterion measures investigated should be reported for each relevant race, sex, and ethnic group and for the total group (essential). Where groups

Section 15 (continued)

are too small to obtain reliable evidence of the magnitude of the relationship, need not be reported separately. Statements regarding the statistical significance of results should be made (essential). Any statistical adjustments, such as for less then perfect reliability or for restriction of score range in the selection procedure or criterion should be described and explained; and uncorrected correlation coefficients should also be shown (essential). Where the statistical technique categorizes continuous data, such as biserial correlation and the phi coefficient, the categories and the bases on which they were determined should be described and explained (essential). Studies of tests fairness should be included where called for by the requirements of section 14B(8) (essential). These studies should include the rationale by which a selection procedure was determined to be fair to the group(s) in question. Where test fairness or unfairness has been demonstrated on the basis of other studies, a bibliography of the relevant studies should be included (essential). If the bibliography includes unpublished studies, copies of these studies, or adequate abstracts or summaries, should be attached (essential). Where revisions have been made in a selection procedure to assure compatability between successful job performance and the probability of being selected, the studies underlying such revisions should be included (essential). All statistical results should be organized and presented by relevant race, sex, and ethnic group (essential).

Revised Guidelines

(h) *Techniques and results.* Methods used in analyzing data should be described. Measures of central tendency (*e.g.,* means) and measures of dispersion (*e.g.,* standard deviations and ranges) for all selection procedures and all criteria should be reported. Where appropriate, statistical results should be organized and presented in tabular or graphical form. Selection procedure-criterion relationships should be reported. Statements regarding the statistical significance or confidence intervals surrounding results should be made.

Any statistical adjustments, such as for less than perfect predictor reliability or for restriction of score range in the selection procedure or criterion, or both, should be described; and unadjusted correlation coefficients should also be shown. Where the statistical technique used categorizes continuous data, such as biserial correlation, the bases for such categories should be described.

Professional and Legal Analysis

The revised section eliminates the requirements for reporting data on means, standard deviations and correlation coefficients by race, sex and ethnic groups, and also eliminates all references to "fairness studies."

Uniform Guidelines

(9) **Alternative procedures investigated.** The selection procedures investigated and available evidence of their impact

Section 15 (continued)

should be identified (essential). The scope, method, and findings of the investigation, and the conclusions reached in light of the findings, should be fully described (essential).

Revised Guidelines (9) **[Deleted.]**

Professional and Legal Analysis

Section 15B(9) of the Uniform Guidelines has been deleted because the burden of the search for alternatives has been placed on the plaintiff or the enforcement agencies by the relevant court decisions. See discussion at section 3B above.

Uniform Guidelines (10) **Uses and applications.** The methods considered for use of the selection procedure (e.g., as a screening device with a cutoff score, for grouping or ranking, or combined with other procedures in a battery) and available evidence of their impact should be described (essential). This description should include the rationale for choosing the method for operational use, and the evidence of the validity and utility of the procedure as it is to be used (essential). The purpose for which the procedure is to be used (e.g., hiring, transfer, promotion) should be described (essential). If weights are assigned to different parts of the selection procedure, these weights and the validity of the weighted composite should be reported (essential). If the selection procedure is used with a cutoff score, the user should describe the way in which normal expectations of proficiency within the work force were determined and the way in which the cutoff score was determined (essential).

Revised Guidelines (i) *Uses and applications.* A description of the way in which each selection procedure is used (*e.g.*, as a screening device with a cutoff score or combined with other procedures in a battery) and application of the procedure (*e.g.*, selection, transfer, promotion) should be provided. If weights are assigned to different parts of the selection procedure, these weights and the validity of the weighted composite should be reported.

(j) *Cutoff scores.* Where cutoff scores are to be used, both the cutoff scores and the way in which they were determined should be described.

Professional and Legal Analysis

The revised section eliminates the requirement for documentation of adverse impact based on the method of use of the procedure and also eliminates the need for including a rationale for the method of use and the utility of the procedure. See discussion at sections 3B and 5G, above.

Section 15 (continued)

With respect to cutoff scores, the revised section is consistent with the Division 14 *Principles* at page 19 which state that "[t]he only justification which can be demanded is that critical scores are determined on the basis of a reasonable rationale." The revision eliminates the reference to "normal expectations of proficiency within the workforce" because this fails to take into account an employer's legitimate interest in upgrading the quality of the workforce. The language is also inconsistent with decisions of the federal courts that employers are free to select based on the relative qualifications of applicants. *See Griggs*, 401 U.S. at 436.

Uniform Guidelines	(11) **Source data.** Each user should maintain records showing all pertinent information about individual sample members and raters where they are used, in studies involving the validation of selection procedures. These records should be made available upon request of a compliance agency. In the case of individual sample members these data should include scores on the selection procedure(s), scores on criterion measures, age, sex, race, or ethnic group status, and experience on the specific job on which the validation study was conducted, and may also include such things as education, training, and prior job experience, but should not include names and social security numbers. Records should be maintained which show the ratings given to each sample member by each rater.
Revised Guidelines	(k) *Source data.* Each user should maintain records showing all pertinent information about individual sample members in studies involving the validation of selection procedures. These records (exclusive of names and social security number) may be requested by an enforcement agency when it has identifiable questions concerning the adequacy of the report of validity evidence. These data should include selection procedure scores and criterion scores.

Professional and Legal Analysis

The requirements for maintaining information on raters and race, sex, ethnic and other data have been deleted from the revised section. The rater information was deleted because of its difficulty of attainment and due to the fact that rater confidences may be violated. In addition, there is no clear use related to legitimate agency concerns which could be made of such rater data. The maintenance of data relating to race, sex, ethnic and other factors was deleted as irrelevant because those factors have not been shown to influence validity evidence. Finally, the revised section provides that records regarding sample members may be requested by an enforcement agency only when it has "identifiable questions concerning the adequacy of the report of validity evidence."

Section 15 (continued)

Uniform Guidelines **(12) Contact person.** The name, mailing address, and telephone number of the person who may be contacted for further information about the validity study should be provided (essential).

Revised Guidelines (l) *Contact person.* It is desirable for the user to set forth the name, mailing address, and telephone number of the individual who may be contacted for further information about the validity evidence.

Professional and Legal Analysis

The changes are editorial.

Uniform Guidelines **(13) Accuracy and completeness.** The report should describe the steps taken to assure the accuracy and completeness of the collection, analysis, and report of data and results.

Revised Guidelines (13) [Deleted.]

Professional and Legal Analysis

Current section 15B(13) was deleted as unnecessary because accepted professional practices provide sufficient guidance for determining the accuracy and completeness of the studies.

Uniform Guidelines **C. Content validity studies.** Reports of content validity for a selection procedure should include the following information:

(1) User(s), location(s) and date(s) of study. Dates and location(s) of the job analysis should be shown (essential).

(2) Problem and setting. An explicit definition of the purpose(s) of the study and the circumstances in which the study was conducted should be provided. A description of existing selection procedures and cutoff scores, if any, should be provided.

Revised Guidelines **(3) Content Validity.** Reports of content validity of selection procedures should contain the following information:

Professional and Legal Analysis

Sections 15C(1) and (2) involving user, location, dates, and problem and setting have been deleted as not required by professional practice.

Uniform Guidelines **(3) Job analysis—Content of the job.** A description of the method used to analyze the job should be provided (essential).

Section 15 (continued)

The work behavior(s), the associated tasks, and, if the behavior results in a work product, the work products should be completely described (essential). Measures of criticality and/or importance of the work behavior(s) and the method of determining these measures should be provided (essential). Where the job analysis also identified the knowledges, skills, and abilities used in work behavior(s), an operational definition for each knowledge in terms of a body of learned information and for each skill and ability in terms of observable behaviors and outcomes, and the relationship between each knowledge, skill, or ability and each work behavior, as well as the method used to determine this relationship, should be provided (essential). The work situation should be described, including the setting in which work behavior(s) are performed, and where appropriate, the manner in which knowledges, skills, or abilities are used, and the complexity and difficulty of the knowledge, skill, or ability as used in the work behavior(s).

Revised Guidelines (a) *Definition of content domain.* A full description should be provided for the basis on which a content domain is defined. A complete and comprehensive definition of the content domain should also be provided.

Professional and Legal Analysis

The revision is designed to provide a more flexible approach to defining the content domain than is currently provided for under the Uniform Guidelines. The revised section acknowledges that no single method of job analysis is preferred and leaves the choice of what method will be utilized to the professional judgment of the psychologist or other person seeking to define the content domain. The Division 14 *Principles* at page 13 provide that "[a] content domain should ordinarily be defined in terms of tasks, activities or responsibilities or specific abilities, knowledge, or job skills found to be prerequisite to effective behavior in the domain." Thus, the rigid definition of job analysis in the 1978 Guidelines, which strongly favors the use of a behavior-oriented or task-based job analysis, is inconsistent with accepted professional practices.

Uniform Guidelines **Job title and code.** [There is no current Guideline provision on this subject.]

Revised Guidelines (b) *Job title and code.* It is desirable to provide the user's job title(s) and the corresponding job title(s) and code(s) from the United States Employment Service Dictionary of Occupational Titles.

Professional and Legal Analysis

This section is taken from section 13(c)(2) of the 1976 FEA Guidelines.

Section 15 (continued)

Uniform Guidelines

(4) Selection procedure and its content. Selection procedures, including those constructed by or for the user, specific training requirements, composites of selection procedures, and any other procedure supported by content validity, should be completely and explicitly described or attached (essential). If commercially available selection procedures are used, they should be described by title, form, and publisher (essential). The behaviors measured or sampled by the selection procedure should be explicitly described (essential). Where the selection procedure purports to measure a knowledge, skill, or ability, evidence that the selection procedure measures and is a representative sample of the knowledge, skill, or ability should be provided (essential).

Revised Guidelines

(c) *Selection procedures.* Selection procedures including those constructed by or for the user, specific training, education and experience requirements, composites of selection procedures, and any other procedure for which content validity is asserted should be completely and explicitly described or attached. If commercially available selection procedures are used, they should be described by title, form, and publisher. Evidence that the selection procedure measures the content domain should be provided.

Professional and Legal Analysis

Education and experience requirements have been added to the current section as requirements for which content validity may be asserted. Separate references in the Uniform Guidelines to the measurement or sampling of work behaviors or knowledges, skills and abilities has been replaced by the last sentence in the revised section which provides that evidence that the selection procedure measures the content domain should be provided. This is consistent with the change in revised section 15C(3)(a) of the definition of content domain and represents a move away from a rigid insistence of the enforcement agencies on the "representativeness" of the knowledge, skill or ability being sampled.

Uniform Guidelines

(5) Relationship between the selection procedure and the job. The evidence demonstrating that the selection procedure is a representative work sample, a representative sample of the work behavior(s), or a representative sample of a knowledge, skill, or ability as used as a part of a work behavior and necessary for that behavior should be provided (essential). The user should identify the work behavior(s) which each item or part of the selection procedure is intended to sample or measure (essential). Where the selection procedure purports to sample a work behavior or to provide a sample of a work product, a comparison should be provided of the manner, setting, and the level of complexity of the selection procedure with those

Section 15 (continued)

of the work situation (essential). If any steps were taken to reduce adverse impact on a race, sex, or ethnic group in the content of the procedure or in its administration, these steps should be described. Establishment of time limits, if any, and how these limits are related to the speed with which duties must be performed on the job, should be explained. Measures of central tendency (e.g., means) and measures of dispersion (e.g., standard deviations) and estimates of reliability should be reported for all selection procedures if available. Such reports should be made for relevant race, sex, and ethnic subgroups, at least on a statistically reliable sample basis.

Revised Guidelines (d) *Techniques and results.* The method by which the correspondence between the content of the selection procedure and the job content domain(s) was determined should be described. The adequacy of the sample coverage of the content domain should be described as precisely as possible. Measures of central tendency (*e.g.*, means) and measures of dispersion (*e.g.*, standard deviations) should be reported for all selection procedures as appropriate and feasible.

Professional and Legal Analysis

Section 15C(5) of the Uniform Guidelines has been almost wholly revised. The heading "Techniques and results" is taken from the FEA Guidelines, as is most of the text. The revisions are designed to bring the section into conformity with the more flexible practices of the psychological profession and to provide a workable basis for using a content-oriented validity strategy. In particular, the section reflects the change in definition of content domain set forth in revised section 14C(1). It is designed to eliminate the overly rigid requirements of the 1978 Guidelines relating to the identification of the relationship of work behaviors to each item in the selection procedure as well as the measurement of job complexity.

Uniform Guidelines **(6) Alternative procedures investigated.** The alternative selection procedures investigated and available evidence of their impact should be identified (essential). The scope, method, and findings of the investigation, and the conclusions reached in light of the findings, should be fully described (essential).

Revised Guidelines **(6) [Deleted.]**

Professional and Legal Analysis

Section 15C(6) has been eliminated because this burden properly rests with the plaintiff or the enforcement agencies. See discussion at section 3B, above.

Section 15 (continued)

Uniform Guidelines

(7) Uses and applications. The methods considered for use of the selection procedure (e.g., as a screening device with a cutoff score, for grouping or ranking, or combined with other procedures in a battery) and available evidence of their impact should be described (essential). This description should include the rationale for choosing the method for operational use, and the evidence of the validity and utility of the procedure as it is to be used (essential). The purpose for which the procedure is to be used (e.g., hiring, transfer, promotion) should be described (essential). If the selection procedure is used with a cutoff score, the user should describe the way in which normal expectations of proficiency within the work force were determined and the way in which the cutoff score was determined (essential). In addition, if the selection procedure is to be used for ranking, the user should specify the evidence showing that a higher score on the selection procedure is likely to result in better job performance.

Revised Guidelines

(e) *Uses and applications.* A description of the way in which each selection procedure is used (*e.g.*, as a screening device with a cutoff score or combined with other procedures in a battery) and the application of the procedure (*e.g.*, selection, transfer, promotion) should be provided. A rationale for the use of the procedure should be provided.

Professional and Legal Analysis

The first sentence in this revised section is taken from the 1976 FEA Guidelines. The current section contains two concepts which vastly undermine the practical usefulness of content validity. The first is the requirement for showing the "utility of the procedure as it is to be used." The satisfaction of the present requirement would entail considerable additional research, including in most instances a criterion-related study, and is professionally unnecessary because the utility of most uses of content-oriented selection procedures are evident.

The second concept which undermines the use of content-oriented selection procedures is the requirement that, when ranking is to be used, the user should specify the evidence showing that a higher score on the selection procedure will result in better job performance. The requirement in effect mandates criterion-related validity evidence and eliminates the practical usefulness of content strategies and undermines the Guidelines' earlier recognition of the equality of criterion, content and construct validity strategies. As set forth in revised section 5G above, the Division 14 *Principles* recognize that:

> Selection techniques developed by content-oriented procedures and discriminating adequately within the range of

Section 15 (continued)

interest can be assumed to have a linear relationship to job behavior. Consequently, ranking on the basis of scores on these procedures is appropriate.

Thus, the requirement with respect to ranking is wholly inconsistent with the accepted practices of the psychological profession and has been eliminated. The language relating to "normal expectations of proficiency within the work force" has also been eliminated. See discussion under revised section 15C(2)(i) at pages 100–101.

Uniform Guidelines	**(8) Contact person.** The name, mailing address, and telephone number of the person who may be contacted for further information about the validity study should be provided (essential).
Revised Guidelines	(f) *Contact person.* It is desirable for the employer to set forth the name, mailing address and telephone number of the individual who may be contacted for further information about the validation evidence.

Professional and Legal Analysis

The changes are editorial.

Uniform Guidelines	**(9) Accuracy and completeness.** The report should describe the steps taken to assure the accuracy and completeness of the collection, analysis, and report of data and results.
Revised Guidelines	(9) [Deleted.]

Professional and Legal Analysis

Section 15C(9) has been eliminated as being unnecessary.

Uniform Guidelines	**D. Construct validity studies.** Reports of construct validity for a selection procedure should include the following information:
	(1) Users(s), location(s), and date(s) of study. Date(s) and location(s) of the job analysis and the gathering of other evidence called for by these guidelines should be provided (essential).
	(2) Problem and setting. An explicit definition of the purpose(s) of the study and the circumstances in which the study was conducted should be provided. A description of existing selection procedures and cutoff scores, if any, should be provided.
Revised Guidelines	(4) *Construct validity.* Reports of construct validity of selection procedures should contain the following information:

Section 15 (continued)

Professional and Legal Analysis

Section 15D(1) of the Uniform Guidelines has been eliminated because this information is often unavailable for studies conducted by other users and examined by the current user as part of the development of a construct-oriented selection procedure. Section 15D(2) has also been deleted as in excess of the accepted practices of the psychological profession.

Uniform Guidelines	(3) **Construct definition.** A clear definition of the construct(s) which are believed to underlie successful performance of the critical or important work behavior(s) should be provided (essential). This definition should include the levels of construct performance relevant to the job(s) for which the selection procedure is to be used (essential). There should be a summary of the position of the construct in the psychological literature, or in the absence of such a position, a description of the way in which the definition and measurement of the construct was developed and the psychological theory underlying it (essential). Any quantitative data which identify or define the job constructs, such as factor analyses, should be provided (essential).
Revised Guidelines	(a) *Construct definition.* A clear definition of the construct should be provided, explained in terms of empirically observable behavior.

Professional and Legal Analysis

The revised section is taken from the 1976 FEA Guidelines. Eliminated is reference to "levels of construct performance" because this information is usually not included in construct definitions. Consequently, it is often impossible to relate "levels of construct performance" to the job for which the selection procedure is used.

Uniform Guidelines	(4) **Job Analysis.** A description of the method used to analyze the job should be provided (essential). A complete description of the work behavior(s) and, to the extent appropriate, work outcomes and measures of their criticality and/or importance should be provided (essential). The report should also describe the basis on which the behavior(s) or outcomes were determined to be important, such as their level of difficulty, their frequency of performance, the consequences of error or other appropriate factors (essential). Where jobs are grouped or compared for the purposes of generalizing validity evidence, the work behavior(s) and work product(s) for each of the jobs should be described, and conclusions concerning the similarity of the jobs in terms of observable work behaviors or work products should be made (essential).
Revised Guidelines	(b) *Job review.* The job review should show how the constructs are related to important job or training behaviors.

Section 15 (continued)

Professional and Legal Analysis

This section has been revised in recognition of the more flexible approach to job review which the psychological profession has found to be acceptable. The current emphasis on observable work behaviors is particularly inappropriate where a construct-oriented strategy is used because constructs involve largely unobservable traits and characteristics. Adherence to observable work behaviors is in excess of accepted professional practices and the section has been revised accordingly. The revised section also allows a showing of the construct's relationship to training behavior.

Uniform Guidelines (5) **Job titles and codes.** It is desirable to provide the selection procedure user's job title(s) for the job(s) in question and the corresponding job title(s) and code(s) from the United States Employment Service's dictionary of occupational titles [sic].

Revised Guidelines (c) *Job titles and codes.* It is desirable to provide the selection procedure user's job title(s) for the job(s) in question and the corresponding job title(s) and code(s) from the United States Employment Service's Dictionary of Occupational Titles.

Professional and Legal Analysis

The changes are editorial.

Uniform Guidelines (6) **Selection procedure.** The selection procedure used as a measure of the construct should be completely and explicitly described or attached (essential). If commercially available selection procedures are used, they should be identified by title, form and publisher (essential). The research evidence of the relationship between the selection procedure and the construct, such as factor structure, should be included (essential). Measures of central tendency, variability and reliability of the selection procedure should be provided (essential). Whenever feasible, these measures should be provided separately for each relevant race, sex and ethnic group.

Revised Guidelines (d) *Selection procedure.* The selection procedure used as a measure of the construct should be completely and explicitly described or attached. If commercially available selection procedures are used, they should be identified by title, form and publisher. The evidence demonstrating that the selection procedure is in fact a proper measure of the construct should be included.

Professional and Legal Analysis

The first two sentences are unchanged. The third sentence is taken from the 1976 FEA Guidelines. The current requirement for

Section 15 (continued)

providing measures of central tendency, variability and reliability by race, sex and ethnic group have been eliminated because this requirement is apparently based on professionally discredited theory of differential prediction. See discussion under section 14B(8) at page 78.

Uniform Guidelines
(7) Relationship to job performance. The criterion-related study(ies) and other empirical evidence of the relationship between the construct measured by the selection procedure and the related work behavior(s) for the job or jobs in question should be provided (essential). Documentation of the criterion-related study(ies) should satisfy the provisions of section 15B above or section 15E(1) below, except for studies conducted prior to the effective date of these guidelines (essential). Where a study pertains to a group of jobs, and, on the basis of the study, validity is asserted for a job in the group, the observed work behaviors and the observed work products for each of the jobs should be described (essential). Any other evidence used in determining whether the work behavior(s) in each of the jobs is the same should be fully described (essential).

Revised Guidelines
(e) *Anchoring.* The empirical evidence showing that performance on the selection procedure is related to performance of critical job or training behaviors should be included and that individual differences on the construct are related to individual differences on the job or training should be included.

Professional and Legal Analysis

The revised section is taken largely from the 1976 FEA Guidelines and replaces section 15D(7). It eliminates the requirement that all studies used must meet the requirements of the Guidelines. Because it is often necessary to use studies completed before the issuance of the Guidelines, the present standard virtually eliminates efforts to use construct validity.

Uniform Guidelines
(8) Alternative procedures investigated. The alternative selection procedures investigated and available evidence of their impact should be identified (essential). The scope, method, and findings of the investigation, and the conclusions reached in light of the findings should be fully described (essential).

Revised Guidelines
(8) [Deleted.]

Professional and Legal Analysis

Section 15D(8) has been deleted because this burden properly rests with the plaintiff or the enforcement agencies. See discussion at section 3B, above.

Section 15 (continued)

Uniform Guidelines
(9) *Uses and applications.* The methods considered for use of the selection procedure (e.g., as a screening device with a cutoff score, for grouping or ranking, or combined with other procedures in a battery) and available evidence of their impact should be described (essential). This description should include the rationale for choosing the method for operational use, and the evidence of the validity and utility of the procedure as it is to be used (essential). The purpose for which the procedure is to be used (e.g., hiring, transfer, promotion) should be described (essential). If weights are assigned to different parts of the selection procedure, these weights and the validity of the weighted composite should be reported (essential). If the selection procedure is used with a cutoff score, the user should describe the way in which normal expectations of proficiency within the work force were determined and the way in which the cutoff score was determined (essential).

Revised Guidelines
(f) *Uses and applications.* A description of the way in which each selection procedure is used (*e.g.*, as a screening device with a cutoff score or combined with other procedures in a battery) and application of the procedure (*e.g.*, selection, transfer, promotion) should be provided. If weights are assigned to different parts of the selection procedure, these weights (and the validity of the weighted composite) should be reported.

Professional and Legal Analysis

The revisions to this section are taken from the FEA Guidelines. References to evidence for the utility of the method of use chosen and to "normal expectations of proficiency within the workforce" were eliminated. See discussion in revised section 15C(3)(e), above.

Uniform Guidelines
Cutoff scores.
[There is no current Guideline provision on this subject.]

Revised Guidelines
(g) *Cutoff scores.* Where cutoff scores are to be used, both the cutoff scores and the way in which they were determined should be described.

Professional and Legal Analysis

This section was taken from the 1976 FEA Guidelines.

Uniform Guidelines
(10) *Accuracy and completeness.* The report should describe the steps taken to assure the accuracy and completeness of the collection, analysis, and report of data and results.

Revised Guidelines
(10) [Deleted.]

Section 15 (continued)

Professional and Legal Analysis

Section 15D(10) has been deleted as being unnecessary.

Uniform Guidelines
(11) *Source data.* Each user should maintain records showing all pertinent information relating to its study of construct validity.

Revised Guidelines
(h) *Source data.* Each user should maintain records showing all pertinent information about individual sample members in studies involving the validation of selection procedures. These records (exclusive of names and social security number) may be requested by an enforcement agency when it has identifiable questions concerning the adequacy of the report of validity evidence. These data should include selection procedure scores and criterion scores.

Professional and Legal Analysis

This revised section was taken in part from the FEA Guidelines. See discussion of revised section 15C(2)(k) at page 100.

Uniform Guidelines
(12) *Contact person.* The name, mailing address, and telephone number of the individual who may be contacted for further information about the validity study should be provided (essential).

Revised Guidelines
(i) *Contact person.* It is desirable for the user to set forth the name, mailing address and telephone number of the individual who may be contacted for further information about the validity evidence.

Professional and Legal Analysis

The changes are editorial.

Uniform Guidelines
E. **Evidence of validity from other studies.** When validity of a selection procedure is supported by studies not done by the user, the evidence from the original study or studies should be compiled in a manner similar to that required in the appropriate section of this section 15 above. In addition, the following evidence should be supplied:

Revised Guidelines
(5) *Evidence of validity from other studies.* When validity of a selection procedure is supported by studies not conducted by the user, the evidence from the original study or studies should be compiled in a manner similar to that required above. See section 7A. In addition, the following evidence should be supplied:

Section 15 (continued)

Professional and Legal Analysis

The changes are largely editorial and include a reference to section 7A regarding the transportability of evidence of validity.

Uniform Guidelines   (1) **Evidence from criterion-related validity studies.**—a. *Job information.* A description of the important job behavior(s) of the user's job and the basis on which the behaviors were determined to be important should be provided (essential). A full description of the basis for determining that these important work behaviors are the same as those of the job in the original study (or studies) should be provided (essential).

Revised Guidelines   (a) *Evidence from criterion-related validity studies.* (i) *Job information.* A description of the important behaviors or the knowledge(s), skill(s), ability(ies), or worker characteristic(s) of the user's job and the basis on which they were determined to be important should be provided. A full description of the basis for determining that these important job or training behaviors or knowledge(s), skill(s), ability(ies) or worker characteristic(s) are sufficiently similar to those of the job in the original study (or studies) to warrant use of the selection procedure in the new situation should be provided. For purposes of this section, a comparison based on job description in the Dictionary of Occupational Titles, Fourth Edition, 1977, will be satisfactory.

Professional and Legal Analysis

The revisions to this section are designed to achieve consistency with the revisions to section 7 on transportability of validity evidence. The revised section recognizes that job information may be based on KSAO's as well as on job behaviors. The revised section also acknowledges that training as well as job behaviors may be compared in order to determine whether the selection procedure may be used in a new situation.

The Uniform Guidelines' overly rigid requirement that work behaviors must be shown to be the "same" as those in the original study has been changed to provide that the job or training behaviors or KSAO's should be shown to be "sufficiently similar" to warrant the use of the procedure in the new setting. The present requirement of showing that the work behaviors in the compared jobs are identical makes it virtually impossible to make use of the transportability provisions. The section provides that a comparison based on job descriptions contained in the Dictionary of Occupational Titles is sufficient. This ensures that the job or training behaviors or KSAO's are sufficiently similar to warrant transportability of the procedures without imposing unduly restrictive requirements on the potential

Section 15 (continued)

user. Workable standards for transporting evidence of validity are extremely important because this is the only means available to most employers to demonstrate the validity of their selection procedures.

Uniform Guidelines   b. *Relevance of criteria.* A full description of the basis on which the criteria used in the original studies are determined to be relevant for the user should be provided (essential).

Revised Guidelines   (ii) *Relevance of criteria.* A full description of the basis on which the criteria used in the original studies are determined to be relevant for the user should be provided.

Professional and Legal Analysis

No change except for deletion of "(essential)."

     c. *Other variables.* The similarity of important applicant pool or sample characteristics reported in the original studies to those of the user should be described (essential). A description of the comparison between the race, sex and ethnic composition of the user's relevant labor market and the sample in the original validity studies should be provided (essential).

     (c) [Deleted.]

Professional and Legal Analysis

Current section 15E(1)(c) has been deleted. See discussion of section 7C above.

Uniform Guidelines   d. *Use of the selection procedure.* A full description should be provided showing that the use to be made of the selection procedure is consistent with the findings of the original validity studies (essential).

Revised Guidelines   (iii) *Use of the selection procedure.* A full description should be provided showing that the use to be made of the selection procedure is consistent with the original validity evidence.

Professional and Legal Analysis

The changes are editorial.

Uniform Guidelines   (e) *Bibliography.* A bibliography of reports of validity of the selection procedure for the job or jobs in question should be provided (essential). Where any of the studies included an investigation of test fairness, the results of this investigation should be provided (essential). Copies of reports published in

Section 15 (continued)

journals that are not commonly available should be described in detail or attached (essential). Where a user is relying upon unpublished studies, a reasonable effort should be made to obtain these studies. If these unpublished studies are the sole source of validity evidence they should be described in detail or attached (essential). If these studies are not available, the name and address of the source, an adequate abstract or summary of the validity study and data, and a contact person in the source organization should be provided (essential).

Revised Guidelines (iv) *Bibliography.* A bibliography of reports of validity of the selection procedure for the job or jobs in question should be provided. Where a user is relying upon unpublished studies, a reasonable effort should be made to obtain these studies. If these unpublished studies are the sole source of validity evidence they should be described in detail or attached. If these studies are not available, the name and address of the source, an abstract or summary of the validity study and data, and a contact person in the source organization should be provided.

Professional and Legal Analysis

References to fairness studies have been eliminated. See discussion of section 14B(8) at page 78, *supra.* The reference to reports published in journals not commonly available has been deleted.

Uniform Guidelines (2) **Evidence from content validity studies.** See section 14C(3) and section 15C above.

Revised Guidelines (b) *Evidence from content validity studies—Similarity of content domains.* A full description should be provided of the similarity between the content domain in the user's job and the content domain measured by a selection procedure developed and shown to be content valid by another user.

Professional and Legal Analysis

This revised section is taken largely from the 1976 FEA Guidelines, with the substitution of "content" for "performance" domain. This is in accordance with the approach to content validity taken by the Division 14 *Principles* and by the revisions to section 15C(3)(a).

Uniform Guidelines (3) **Evidence from construct validity studies.** See sections 14D(2) and 15D above.

Revised Guidelines (c) *Evidence from construct validity studies—Uniformity of construct.* A description should be provided of the basis for determining that the construct identified as underlying successful job or training behavior by the user's job review is the same as the construct measured by the selection procedure.

Section 15 (continued)

Professional and Legal Analysis

The revision is taken largely from the FEA Guidelines and recognizes that "training" as well as job behaviors may be used.

Uniform Guidelines

F. Evidence of validity from cooperative studies. Where a selection procedure has been validated through a cooperative study, evidence that the study satisfies the requirements of sections 7, 8 and 15E should be provided (essential).

G. Selection for higher level job. If a selection procedure is used to evaluate candidates for jobs at a higher level than those for which they will initially be employed, the validity evidence should satisfy the documentation provisions of this section 15 for the higher level job or jobs, and in addition, the user should provide: (1) a description of the job progression structure, formal or informal; (2) the data showing how many employees progress to the higher level job and the length of time needed to make this progression; and (3) an identification of any anticipated changes in the higher level job. In addition, if the test measures a knowledge, skill or ability, the user should provide evidence that the knowledge, skill or ability is required for the higher level job and the basis for the conclusion that the knowledge, skill or ability is not expected to develop from the training or experience on the job.

H. Interim use of selection procedures. If a selection procedure is being used on an interim basis because the procedure is not fully supported by the required evidence of validity, the user should maintain and have available (1) substantial evidence of validity for the procedure, and (2) a report showing the date on which the study to gather the additional evidence commenced, the estimated completion date of the study, and a description of the data to be collected (essential).

Revised Guidelines

F. [Deleted.]

G. [Deleted.]

H. [Deleted.]

Professional and Legal Analysis

Sections 15F, 15G and 15H have been deleted as being unnecessary. With regard to sections 15G and H, see discussion at sections 5H and I above.

Section 16. Definitions.

Introduction

Several definitions which are included in the Uniform Guidelines have been deleted from the Revised Guidelines: ability, compliance with these guidelines, content validity, construct validity, criterion-related validity, enforcement action, job analysis, job description, knowledge, observable, should, skill, unfairness of selection procedure, validated in accord with these guidelines or properly validated, and work behavior. These definitions were deleted either because they were inconsistent with legal precedent or accepted professional practices or because of changes which were made in the Revised Guidelines which made the definition inaccurate or unnecessary.

Uniform Guidelines	The following definitions shall apply throughout these guidelines:
Revised Guidelines	The following definitions shall apply throughout these guidelines:

Professional and Legal Analysis

No change.

Uniform Guidelines	**A. Ability.** A present competence to perform an observable behavior or a behavior which results in an observable product.
Revised Guidelines	A. [Deleted.]

Professional and Legal Analysis

See introduction to this section.

Uniform Guidelines	**B. Adverse impact.** A substantially different rate of selection in hiring, promotion, or other employment decision which works to the disadvantage of members of a race, sex, or ethnic group. See section 4 of these guidelines.

Section 16 (continued)

Revised Guidelines   **A. Adverse impact.** See section 4D of these guidelines.

Professional and Legal Analysis

The definition set forth in revised section 4D is adopted by reference.

Uniform Guidelines   **C. Compliance with these guidelines.** Use of a selection procedure is in compliance with these guidelines if such use has been validated in accord with these guidelines (as defined below), or if such use does not result in adverse impact on any race, sex, or ethnic group (see section 4, above), or, in unusual circumstances, if use of the procedure is otherwise justified in accord with Federal law. See section 6B, above.

Revised Guidelines   **C. [Deleted.]**

Professional and Legal Analysis

See introduction to this section.

Uniform Guidelines   **Content domain.** [There is no definition on this subject in the current Guidelines.]

Revised Guidelines   **B. Content domain.** A body of knowledge and/or a set of tasks or other behaviors defined so that given facts or behaviors, as appropriate, may be classified as included or excluded.

Professional and Legal Analysis

This definition has been added to achieve consistency with the Division 14 *Principles* and to move away from the present rigid adherence to observable work behaviors in the Uniform Guidelines.

Uniform Guidelines   **D. Content validity.** Demonstrated by data showing that the content of a selection procedure is representative of important aspects of performance on the job. See section 5B and section 14C.

Revised Guidelines   **D. [Deleted.]**

Professional and Legal Analysis

See introduction to this section.

Section 16 (continued)

> **E. Construct validity.** Demonstrated by data showing that the selection procedure measures the degree to which candidates have identifiable characteristics which have been determined to be important for successful job performance. See section 5B and section 14D.
>
> **E. [Deleted.]**

Professional and Legal Analysis

See introduction to this section.

> **F. Criterion-related validity.** Demonstrated by empirical data showing that the selection procedure is predictive of or significantly correlated with important elements of work behavior. See sections 5B and 14B.
>
> **F. [Deleted.]**

Professional and Legal Analysis

See introduction to this section.

Uniform Guidelines   **G. Employer.** Any employer subject to the provisions of the Civil Rights Act of 1964, as amended, including State or local governments and any Federal agency subject to the provisions of section 717 of the Civil Rights Act of 1964, as amended, and any Federal contractor or subcontractor or federally assisted construction contractor or subcontractor covered by Executive Order 11246, as amended.

Revised Guidelines   **C. Employer.** Any employer subject to the provisions of the Civil Rights Act of 1964, as amended, including State or local governments and any Federal agency subject to the provisions of section 717 of the Civil Rights Act of 1964, as amended, and any Federal contractor or subcontractor or federally assisted construction contractor or subcontractor covered by Executive Order 11246, as amended.

Professional and Legal Analysis

No change.

Uniform Guidelines   **H. Employment agency.** Any employment agency subject to the provisions of the Civil Rights Act of 1964, as amended.

Revised Guidelines   **D. Employment agency.** Any employment agency subject to the provisions of the Civil Rights Act of 1964, as amended.

Section 16 (continued)

Professional and Legal Analysis

No change.

Uniform Guidelines	**I. Enforcement action.** For the purposes of section 4 a proceeding by a Federal enforcement agency such as a lawsuit or an administrative proceeding leading to debarment from or withholding, suspension, or termination of Federal Government contracts or the suspension or withholding of Federal Government funds; but not a finding of reasonable cause or a conciliation process or the issuance of right to sue letters under title VII or under Executive Order 11246 where such finding, conciliation, or issuance of notice of right to sue is based upon an individual complaint.
Revised Guidelines	**I. [Deleted.]**

Professional and Legal Analysis

See introduction to this section.

Uniform Guidelines	**J. Enforcement agency.** Any agency of the executive branch of the Federal Government which adopts these guidelines for purposes of the enforcement of the equal employment opportunity laws or which has responsibility for securing compliance with them.
Revised Guidelines	**E. Enforcement agency.** Any agency of the executive branch of the Federal Government which adopts these guidelines for purposes of the enforcement of the equal employment opportunity laws or which has responsibility for securing compliance with them.

Professional and Legal Analysis

No change.

Uniform Guidelines	**K. Job analysis.** A detailed statement of work behaviors and other information relevant to the job.
Revised Guidelines	**K. [Deleted.]**

Professional and Legal Analysis

See introduction to this section.

Uniform Guidelines	**L. Job description.** A general statement of job duties and responsibilities.

Section 16 (continued)

Revised Guidelines L. [Deleted.]

Professional and Legal Analysis

See introduction to this section.

Uniform Guidelines M. **Knowledge.** A body of information applied directly to the performance of a function.

Revised Guidelines M. [Deleted.]

Professional and Legal Analysis

See introduction to this section.

Uniform Guidelines N. **Labor organization.** Any labor organization subject to the provisions of the Civil Rights Act of 1964, as amended, and any committee subject thereto controlling apprenticeship or other training.

Revised Guidelines F. **Labor organization.** Any labor organization subject to the provisions of the Civil Rights Act of 1964, as amended, and any committee subject thereto controlling apprenticeship or other training.

Professional and Legal Analysis

No change.

Uniform Guidelines O. **Observable.** Able to be seen, heard, or otherwise perceived by a person other than the person performing the action.

Revised Guidelines O. [Deleted.]

Professional and Legal Analysis

See introduction to this section.

Uniform Guidelines P. **Race, sex, or ethnic group.** Any group of persons identifiable on the grounds of race, color, religion, sex, or national origin.

Revised Guidelines G. **Race, sex, or ethnic group.** Any group of persons identifiable on the grounds of race, color, sex, or national origin as specified in section 4B.

Section 16 (continued)

Professional and Legal Analysis

This definition was revised to limit coverage to those groups specified in section 4B.

Uniform Guidelines   Q. **Selection procedure.** Any measure, combination of measures, or procedure used as a basis for any employment decision. Selection procedures include the full range of assessment techniques from traditional paper and pencil tests, performance tests, training programs, or probationary periods and physical, educational, and work experience requirements through informal or casual interviews and unscored application forms.

Revised Guidelines   H. **Selection procedure.** Any measure, combination of measures, or procedure, other than a bona fide seniority system, used as a basis for any employment decision. Selection procedures include the full range of assessment techniques from traditional paper and pencil tests, performance tests, training programs, or probationary periods and physical, educational, and work experience requirements through informal or casual interviews and unscored application forms.

Professional and Legal Analysis

In accordance with *Teamsters*, this definition expressly excludes actions pursuant to a "bona fide seniority system" from the definition of selection procedure.

Uniform Guidelines   R. **Selection rate.** The proportion of applicants or candidates who are hired, promoted, or otherwise selected.

Revised Guidelines   I. **Selection rate.** The proportion of applicants or candidates who are hired, promoted, or otherwise selected.

Professional and Legal Analysis

No change.

Uniform Guidelines   S. **Should.** The term "should" as used in these guidelines is intended to connote action which is necessary to achieve compliance with the guidelines, while recognizing that there are circumstances where alternative courses of action are open to users.

Revised Guidelines   S. [Deleted.]

Professional and Legal Analysis

See introduction to this section.

Section 16 (continued)

Uniform Guidelines **T. Skill.** A present, observable competence to perform a learned psychomoter act.

Revised Guidelines **T. [Deleted.]**

Professional and Legal Analysis

See introduction to this section.

Uniform Guidelines **U. Technical feasibility.** The existence of conditions permitting the conduct of meaningful criterion-related validity studies. These conditions include: (1) An adequate sample of persons available for the study to achieve findings of statistical significance; (2) having or being able to obtain a sufficient range of scores on the selection procedure and job performance measures to produce validity results which can be expected to be representative of the results if the ranges normally expected were utilized; and (3) having or being able to devise unbiased, reliable and relevant measures of job performance or other criteria of employee adequacy. See section 14B(2). With respect to investigation of possible unfairness, the same considerations are applicable to each group for which the study is made. See section 14B(8).

Revised Guidelines **J. Technical feasibility.** The existence of conditions permitting the conduct of meaningful criterion-related validity studies. These conditions include: (1) an adequate and appropriate sample of persons available for the study to achieve findings of statistical significance; (2) having or being able to obtain a sufficient range of scores on the selection procedure and job performance measures to produce validity results which can be expected to be representative of the results if the ranges normally expected were utilized; and (3) having or being able to devise unbiased, reliable and relevant measures of job or training peformance or other criteria of employee adequacy.

Professional and Legal Analysis

The changes in this definition include the addition of the concept of the appropriateness of the sample and the addition of training performance as a measure of employee adequacy. References to fairness studies have been deleted.

Uniform Guidelines **V. Unfairness of selection procedure.** A condition in which members of one race, sex, or ethnic group characteristically obtain lower scores on a selection procedure than members of another group, and the differences are not reflected in differences in measures of job performance. See section 14B(7).

Revised Guidelines **V. [Deleted.]**

Section 16 (continued)

Professional and Legal Analysis

See introduction to this section and discussion at section 14B(7).

Uniform Guidelines   W. User. Any employer, labor organization, employment agency, or licensing or certification board, to the extent it may be covered by Federal equal employment opportunity law, which uses a selection procedure as a basis for any employment decision. Whenever an employer, labor organization, or employment agency is required by law to restrict recruitment for any occupation to those applicants who have met licensing or certification requirements, the licensing or certifying authority to the extent it may be covered by Federal equal employment opportunity law will be considered the user with respect to those licensing or certification requirements. Whenever a State employment agency or service does no more than administer or monitor a procedure as permitted by Department of Labor regulations, and does so without making referrals or taking any other action on the basis of the results, the State employment agency will not be deemed to be a user.

Revised Guidelines   K. User. Any employer, labor organization or employment agency, to the extent it may be covered by Federal equal employment opportunity law, which uses a selection procedure as a basis for any employment decision. Whenever a State employment agency or service does no more than administer or monitor a procedure as permitted by Department of Labor regulations, and does so without making referrals or taking any other action on the basis of the results, the State employment agency will not be deemed to be a user.

Professional and Legal Analysis

References to licensing and certification boards have been deleted consistent with the revision of section 1B.

Uniform Guidelines   X. Validated in accord with these guidelines or properly validated. A demonstration that one or more validity study or studies meeting the standards of these guidelines has been conducted, including investigation and, where appropriate, use of suitable alternative selection procedures as contemplated by section 3B, and has produced evidence of validity sufficient to warrant use of the procedure for the intended purpose under the standards of these guidelines.

Revised Guidelines   X. [Deleted.]

Professional and Legal Analysis

See introduction to this section.

Section 16 (continued)

Uniform Guidelines	**Y. Work behavior.** An activity performed to achieve the objectives of the job. Work behaviors involve observable (physical) components and unobservable (mental) components. A work behavior consists of the performance of one or more tasks. Knowledges, skills, and abilities are not behaviors, although they may be applied in work behaviors.
Revised Guidelines	**Y. [Deleted.]**

Professional and Legal Analysis

See introduction to this section.

Section 17. Policy statement on affirmative action.

Professional and Legal Analysis

Revision or comment on this section is beyond the scope of Ad Hoc Committee's study. Section 17 of the Uniform Guidelines may be found in Appendix C of this monograph.

CONCLUSION

The Ad Hoc Committee believes that the foregoing proposed revision of the Uniform Guidelines is a professionally and legally sound alternative to the present Guidelines which should be adopted by the federal enforcement agencies and the courts.

DETERMINING THE VALIDITY OF TESTS THROUGH THE EEOC OPINION LETTER PROCESS

by
Bruce A. Nelson

The author's thesis is that because of the uncertainty surrounding whether any particular test is valid under Title VII of the 1964 Civil Rights Act and the interest of the Equal Employment Opportunity Commission (EEOC) in promoting the use of job-related selection procedures and criteria, the EEOC should make use of its opinion letter process as a means of ascertaining in advance whether a test is valid. The opinion letter process has not been used in the employee selection area because the EEOC has no established means of handling requests regarding the validity of written tests and has not developed the expertise necessary to render an opinion, the author states. Moreover, test users have feared that materials submitted to the EEOC might be disclosed, resulting in competitive and legal harm. The author suggests a number of alternative approaches which could overcome these problems and recommends that the EEOC institute a pilot program to assess the appropriateness of a permanent opinion letter procedure to assess the validity of selection procedures.

Bruce A. Nelson, educated at the University of Michigan (B.B.A.; J.D.), has practiced employment law in San Francisco since 1968, and is a partner in the law firm of Morrison & Foerster, which has offices in San Francisco, Los Angeles, Denver, Washington, D.C., and London. He is the author of many books and articles, including *Wage Discrimination and the "Comparable Worth" Theory in Perspective*, Winter 1980 edition of the University of Michigan Journal of Law Reform, and *Burdens of Proof Under Employment Discrimination Legislation*, published in the 1980 Journal of College and University Law. Mr. Nelson is a frequent lecturer in employment matters and has represented many major corporations in Title VII class action litigation and OFCCP compliance reviews. He is a member of the American Bar Association, Litigation and Labor Sections; the ABA Committee on Equal Employment Opportunity Law; the Advisory Board of the California Business Law Institute; and the Board of Development of the University of Michigan Graduate School of Business Administration.

DETERMINING THE VALIDITY OF TESTS THROUGH THE EEOC OPINION LETTER PROCESS

As the lead equal employment enforcement agency in the federal government, the Equal Employment Opportunity Commission (EEOC) should encourage the use of job-related selection devices that maximize productivity in the workplace while at the same time preventing unlawful discrimination.[1] The use of job-related written tests provides perhaps the best means of furthering both objectives: a job-related test maximizes productivity and can eliminate subjectivity in selection. However, the policies adopted by EEOC in the past often have operated to discourage the use of even highly useful and validated written tests.

EEOC's attempts to ensure that written tests are not used in a discriminatory manner have resulted in the imposition of such stringent test validation requirements that many employers have abandoned even "state-of-the-art" testing in favor of less valid or subjective procedures, either because they could not afford to conduct a costly validity study or because of fears that they could not meet EEOC's stringent requirements for validation. Employers have found that even valid selection procedures are likely to result in adverse impact against one or more protected groups, thus resulting in strict agency scrutiny of the procedure. As a result of the high costs and uncertainty surrounding attempts to demonstrate the validity of their selection procedures, many employers adopted a "bottom line" approach to employee selection, under which they made conscious efforts to ensure that the overall selection process did not result in adverse impact.[2] However, as a result of the decision of the Supreme Court in *Connecticut v. Teal*, employers may no longer rely on a nondiscriminatory "bottom line" as a defense to an action based upon the adverse impact of a pass-fail component of the selection process.[3]

---

[1] By Executive Order 12067 (1978), EEOC was granted lead authority to develop a uniform approach to the equal employment efforts of the federal government.
[2] The Uniform Guidelines on Employee Selection Procedures, adopted by the Departments of Justice and Labor, EEOC and the Office of Personnel Management, provide in section 4C that the federal enforcement agencies, in the exercise of their prosecutorial discretion and in usual circumstances, will not require validation of individual components of a process where the overall selection process does not have an adverse impact. 29 C.F.R. § 1607.4C.
[3] 102 S. Ct. 2525 (1982). In *Teal*, the State of Connecticut used a multicomponent promotion process that required persons to pass a written test in order to be considered further for promotion. The written test had an adverse impact on blacks, but the "bottom line" of persons actually promoted resulted in blacks being promoted at a

Thus, employers are faced on the one hand with the stringent validation requirements of the Uniform Guidelines, which most employers are simply unable to meet, and on the other hand with the effective elimination, by the decision in *Teal*, of the protection formerly thought to be available to employers who could demonstrate a nondiscriminatory "bottom line." Consequently, employers have been left with virtually no means of ensuring that even state-of-the-art validated selection procedures will not subject them to possible liability.

One available means which might provide a degree of certainty to the employee selection area is the "opinion letter" process of the EEOC. Any employer or test developer currently is free to ask for an opinion letter from EEOC regarding the validity of any test for a particular job or group of jobs. For several reasons, employers and the EEOC heretofore have not made extensive use of the opinion letter process in the employee selection area.

The first of these reasons is that the EEOC has no established means for handling opinion letter requests regarding the validity of written tests and has not developed the practically-oriented expertise necessary to render an opinion. The second reason why the opinion letter process has not been used in the employee selection area is the fear of test users that materials submitted to the agency might be disclosed to the public, resulting in competitive and legal harm to the submitter. Given the uncertainty to employers surrounding the use of selection procedures and the interest of the EEOC in promoting the use of job-related selection devices, the opinion letter process has significant potential to be of benefit to the enforcement agencies, test users and developers, and ultimately to persons protected by Title VII.

EEOC OPINION LETTER PROCESS

Section 713(b)[4] of Title VII of the Civil Rights Act of 1964, as amended, provides a defense for actions of an employer taken pursuant to written interpretations or opinions of the EEOC:

> (b) In any action or proceeding based on any alleged unlawful employment practice, no person shall be subject to

---

substantially higher rate than whites. The Supreme Court held that a "bottom line" result favorable to blacks as a group did not preclude individual blacks who failed the written test from establishing a prima facie case based on the adverse impact of the single component of the process.
[4] 42 U.S.C. § 2000e-12(b).

any liability or punishment for or on account of (1) the commission by such person of an unlawful employment practice if he pleads and proves that the act or omission complained of was in good faith, in conformity with, and in reliance on any written interpretation or opinion of the Commission. . . . Such a defense, if established, shall be a bar to the action or proceeding, notwithstanding that (A) after such act or omission, such interpretation or opinion is modified or rescinded or is determined by judicial authority to be invalid or of no legal effect. . . .

EEOC has issued regulations which set forth its policy for issuing interpretations or opinions.[5] Section 1601.31 of these regulations provides that any person may request a written opinion or interpretation, the issuance of which will be discretionary. Section 1601.32 sets forth what should be included in a request for an interpretation or opinion letter. Among the items which should be included are "[a] statement of all known relevant facts" and "[a] statement of reasons why the interpretation or opinion should be issued." Section 1601.33 defines what constitutes a "written interpretation or opinion of the Commission" within the meaning of section 713(b) of Title VII. This section provides that "[a] letter entitled 'opinion letter' and signed by the General Counsel on behalf of the Commission" and "[m]atter published and specifically designated as such in the Federal Register" may be relied upon as a written interpretation or opinion.

At present, EEOC has no established means for handling such opinion letter requests in a manner which would provide a professionally and legally adequate assessment of validity evidence that is submitted to the agency. In addition, the Uniform Guidelines, as they have been interpreted by EEOC in the past, do not provide an appropriate measure of validity that test users and developers are likely to be able to fulfill. Thus, in order for the opinion letter process to function to its fullest advantage, a revision of the current Guidelines should be undertaken in order to eliminate those requirements that are in excess of the accepted practices of the psychological profession and Title VII case law. However, even if an immediate revision of the Guidelines is not undertaken, the opinion letter process may still provide a meaningful and useful procedure if EEOC undertakes a number of specific actions which are necessary to implement effectively the opinion letter process.

---

[5] 29 C.F.R. §§ 1601.31-1601.33.

DEVELOPMENT OF AGENCY EXPERTISE

The first step which EEOC must undertake in order to ensure the success of the opinion letter process is to develop the practically-oriented expertise necessary to determine the adequacy of validity data offered in support of a request for an opinion letter. Currently, the EEOC employs only one industrial psychologist. It is doubtful that any single agency employee would possess sufficiently broad practical experience in test development and validation to be used as the sole determiner of the validity of tests submitted pursuant to an opinion letter request. However, this broad expertise could be attained by enlisting a panel of industrial psychologists to evaluate technical validation data. Any psychologists used by the agency should have extensive field experience in test validation. The validation data could be submitted directly to such a panel and reviewed by them at a non-agency location. Following a review of the technical evidence of validity, the psychologists would be in a position to render an opinion as to whether the validity evidence was consistent with the accepted practices of the psychological profession.[6] The opinion of the psychologists could then be submitted to the agency for approval.

As mentioned above, implicit in such a process is the need to revise the current Uniform Guidelines in order to eliminate or revise those portions that are in excess of the legal requirements of Title VII and the accepted practices of the psychological profession, and to establish a realistic, up-to-date standard for job relatedness which can be used by the psychologists reviewing validity documentation. If the Guidelines are not revised, it is essential that the psychologists chosen for such a panel be persons who are familiar with and able to apply the accepted practices of the psychological profession in order to determine the validity of the test in question.

CONFIDENTIALITY OF ACCOMPANYING DOCUMENTATION

The second step which the EEOC must undertake in order to increase the likelihood of success of the opinion letter process is to ensure that test users or developers who are considering seeking an

---

[6]Alternative sources of accepted professional practices, in addition to the Guidelines, which could be used to demonstrate the job relatedness of a selection procedure include the *Principles for the Validation and Use of Personnel Selection Procedures* (Division 14 *Principles*); *Standards for Educational & Psychological Tests* (APA *Standards*); and textbooks, journals, research findings or studies by industrial-organizational psychologists, among others.

opinion letter are not discouraged by the fear that a failure to secure an opinion letter from the agency will be used against them or that the validity documentation data offered in support of their selection device will be released to their competitive or legal disadvantage. Such fears can be alleviated by providing that requests for an opinion letter should be made anonymously and that the agency will establish appropriate safeguards to ensure that agency records do not contain the identity of the requesting entity. Such regulations also should establish clearly that the failure to obtain an opinion letter will not be considered probative of the validity of the selection device in any way. Only by installing such safeguards will the agency be able to convince test users or developers to take advantage of the opinion letter process.

The Uniform Guidelines currently contain provisions relating to the documentation of validity evidence. The documentation requirements are extensive and have been applied by EEOC in determining whether a given selection procedure has been shown to be job related or valid. Section 15B of the Guidelines relates to the documentation requirements for demonstrating criterion validity and is illustrative of the documentation of validity currently required under the Guidelines. Among the requirements set forth in section 15B are the following:

1. A description of the procedure used to analyze the job or group of jobs, or to review the job information;
2. A description of the proportion of time spent on various job behaviors, their level of difficulty and the consequences of error in the conduct of these behaviors;
3. Job titles and codes from the U.S. Employment Services Dictionary of Occupational Titles;
4. A full description of criterion measures used;
5. The race, sex and ethnic composition of the research sample, and a description of how the research sample compares to the relevant labor market;
6. Descriptions of educational levels, length of service and age of sample;
7. An explicit description or attachment of any measure or procedure studied;
8. An identification of the selection procedures investigated and evidence of their adverse impact;
9. Methods considered for use of the selection procedure and the rationale for choosing the method to be used;
10. Source data including scores on the procedures, scores

on criterion measures, age, sex, race, or ethnic group status, and experience on the job studied.

Thus, the documentation required by the current Guidelines provides a wealth of valuable information regarding the business operations of a test user. Disclosure of information not otherwise public to business competitors could cause substantial harm to the competitive position of the user whose materials were disclosed. The documentation required by the Guidelines would also enable a competitor to institute selection procedures virtually identical to those used by the submitting test user. As a result, the competitive advantage which the test user may have gained by developing and validating its own selection procedures would be lost if the procedures and validity documentation were disclosed to its competitors. Furthermore, the disclosure of the contents of the test itself would eliminate any usefulness which the device may have had because the test questions and answers would be compromised by their release.

The disclosure of such information may, as a practical matter, undermine one of the essential purposes of Title VII. As set forth above, one of the ways in which Title VII seeks to prevent unlawful discrimination is by ensuring that selection decisions are based on factors related to the ability to perform the job and not on such prohibited factors as race, sex or ethnic status. Thus, the purposes of Title VII are served to the extent that the opinion letter process can encourage and expand the use of job-related or valid tests by offering immunity from an action based on the use of such a test. If test users believe that the documentation submitted to EEOC in conjunction with an opinion letter request may be disclosed to the public, many users will not be willing to risk such disclosure by seeking an opinion letter. Thus, in order to institute a workable opinion letter process, the agency must be able to offer reasonable assurances that materials submitted will not be disclosed pursuant to the Freedom of Information Act (FOIA) or otherwise.

The Freedom of Information Act

The FOIA[7] requires government agencies to disclose information contained in agency records upon request unless that information falls within nine exemptions enumerated in section 552(b) of the FOIA. The nondisclosure of information pursuant to these exemptions is discretionary, not mandatory.[8] The exemptions which

---

[7] 5 U.S.C. §§ 552 *et seq.*, as amended.
[8] *Chrysler Corp. v. Brown*, 441 U.S. 281 (1979).

most often are applied to documents submitted by employers to EEOC and which are most pertinent in this area state:

(b) This section does not apply to matters that are—

* * * * * *

(3) specifically exempted from disclosure by statute (other than Section 552b of this title), provided that such statute (A) requires that the matters be withheld from the public in such a manner as to leave no discretion on the issue, or (B) establishes particular criteria for withholding or refers to particular types of matter to be withheld;

(4) trade secrets and commercial or financial information obtained from a person and privileged or confidential;

Unlike the other FOIA exemptions, Exemption 3 does not specify documents that may be withheld. Instead, it exempts from disclosure documents that are already exempted by other statutes. Thus, interpretation of this exemption involves reconciling the FOIA with numerous nondisclosure statutes, such as the Trade Secrets Act,[9] which antedate it.

Of all the exemptions to the FOIA, Exemption 4 is most clearly addressed to the prevention of disclosure of confidential business information. It provides that trade secrets and commercial and financial information which are "privileged or confidential" need not be made available to the public. However, as indicated above, the mere fact that records fall within Exemption 4 does not preclude the agency from releasing the information—it only has discretion not to do so.

In applying Exemption 4, most courts since 1974 have generally

---

[9]The Trade Secrets Act, 18 U.S.C. § 1905, provides:

Whoever, being an officer or employee of the United States or of any department or agency thereof, publishes, divulges, discloses, or makes known in any manner or to any extent *not authorized by law* any information coming to him in the course of his employment or official duties or by reason of any examination or investigation made by, or return, report or record made to or filed with, such department or agency or officer or employee thereof, which information concerns or relates to trade secrets, *processes, operations, style of work, or apparatus, or to the identity, confidential statistical data, amount or source of any income, profits, losses, or expenditures of any person, firm, partnership, corporation, or association*; or permits any income return or copy thereof to be seen or examined by any person except as provided by law; shall be fined not more than $1,000 or imprisoned not more than one year, or both; and shall be removed from office or employment. (Emphasis added.)

followed the standard established in *National Parks and Conservation Ass'n v. Morton*.[10] That is, commercial or financial information is "confidential" within the meaning of Exemption 4 only if it is shown that disclosure would cause *substantial competitive injury* to the party from whom the information was obtained or if disclosure would impair the government's ability to obtain such information in the future. With respect to the "substantial competitive injury" test, analysis of the legislative history reveals that, although avoidance of competitive injury was one of the reasons for enacting Exemption 4, Congress apparently did not intend that the existence or extent of competitive injury would be the determining standard for the applicability of Exemption 4.[11] Moreover, in *National Parks and Conservation Ass'n v. Kleppe* ("National Parks II"),[12] the Court of Appeals for the District of Columbia Circuit explained that, where it can be shown that submitters actually face competition, the likelihood of substantial competitive harm to their competitive positions is "virtually axiomatic."

In *Chrysler Corp. v. Brown*, the Supreme Court recognized that "under the FOIA third parties have been able to obtain Government files containing information submitted by corporations and individuals who thought that the information would be held in confidence."[13] However, the Court in *Chrysler* held that the FOIA exemptions are *not* mandatory bars to disclosure, but merely permit an agency to withhold certain information.[14] Consequently, it concluded that because "Congress did not limit an agency's discretion to disclose information when it enacted the FOIA [,] [i]t necessarily follows that the Act does not afford Chrysler any right to enjoin agency disclosures."[15]

The Court also held that the Trade Secrets Act does not afford a private right of action to enjoin disclosure in violation of the statute. But since section 10(e) of the Administrative Procedure Act (APA) requires agency action to be "in accordance with law,"[16] the

---

[10] 498 F.2d 765, 770 (D.C. Cir. 1974).
[11] Both the House and Senate reports concerning Exemption 4 stated that the exemption was intended to protect traditional privacy interests by excluding from disclosure information that was submitted to the government in confidence or that was not customarily disclosed to the public by the submitter. *See* H.R. Rep. No. 89-1497, 89th Cong., 1st Sess. 6 (1965); S. Rep. No. 89-813, 89th Cong., 1st Sess. 9 (1965).
[12] 547 F.2d 673, 684 (D.C. Cir. 1976).
[13] 441 U.S. at 285.
[14] *Id.* at 293.
[15] *Id.* at 294.
[16] The pertinent provisions of section 10(e) of the APA, 5 U.S.C. § 706, provide that a reviewing court shall:

Court concluded that a reviewing court can prevent any disclosure that would violate section 1905 of the Trade Secrets Act.[17] Thus, companies may prevent disclosure by the government of confidential corporate information only by seeking review of the agency's decisions to disclose under the procedures of the APA. The Court in *Chrysler* did not decide, however, whether the agency's decision would be subject to *de novo* review by a federal district court, or would be subject merely to a review of the administrative record of the agency.

The Court also left unanswered "[t]he relative ambits of Exemption 4 [of the FOIA] and § 1905... or whether § 1905 is an exempting statute within the terms of... Exemption 3...."[18] Consequently, even after *Chrysler*, the scope of Exemptions 3 and 4 has not been clearly defined. As a result, a determination of whether documentation submitted in conjunction with a request for an opinion letter might be subject to disclosure under the FOIA will depend largely on conjecture as to how a court faced with such an FOIA request would rule.

Suggestions for Safeguarding Confidential Information

Despite safeguards which might be undertaken by EEOC and employers to ensure that confidential business information will not be disclosed, any documents submitted to the agency and made a part of agency records are *potentially* subject to disclosure. Even where the agency has determined that the documents fall within an exemption of the FOIA and agrees not to disclose the information, there remains the danger that a person seeking the information can convince a court to order the release of the documents. Thus, there is a real danger that tests or other selection procedures submitted to EEOC as part of a request for an opinion letter *may* be subject to disclosure in whole or in part in a lawsuit brought by a requestor.[19]

---

(2) hold unlawful and set aside agency action, findings, and conclusions found to be—
(A) arbitrary, capricious, an abuse of discretion, or otherwise not in accordance with law;
* * * * * *
(F) unwarranted by the facts to the extent that the facts are subject to trial *de novo* by the reviewing court.

[17] 441 U.S. at 317-18; 441 U.S. at 319 (Marshall, J., concurring).
[18] 441 U.S. at 319 n. 49.
[19] Another danger is that information could be released by one federal agency to another and that the second agency would not protect the confidentiality of the information. 44 U.S.C. § 3508 offers some protection in this regard by providing that "all the provisions of law including penalties which relate to the unlawful disclosure of information" apply to the second agency as well. However, EEOC should establish

Set forth below are five ways in which the agency and test users can attempt to ensure that documents submitted in conjunction with an opinion letter request will not be disclosed to the public.

1. Ensure that Documents Do Not Become "Agency Records"

The safest way to ensure that materials accompanying an opinion letter request are not subject to disclosure is to make certain that such materials do not become part of "agency records," since only "agency records" are subject to release under the FOIA. The Records Disposal Act,[20] provides that "agency records" consist of documents "made or received by an agency." Thus, in *Forsham v. Harris*,[21] the Supreme Court held that data generated by a private organization which received federal grants but which data was not at any time obtained by the agency, were not "agency records" subject to disclosure under the FOIA.

The likelihood that the documents to be reviewed will become agency records depends largely on the opinion letter mechanism which EEOC establishes for reviewing tests and other selection procedures. If the agency were to establish a panel of non-agency industrial-organizational psychologists, the documents could be delivered directly to them at a non-agency location for their review.[22] Following their review, they could be returned to the employer and no copies should be retained by the panel or the agency. When the review is completed, any notes taken by the panel should remain with the employer or should be kept at a non-agency location.

Whether the documents would be considered to be agency records would depend on an interpretation of whether they have been "received" or "obtained" by the agency within the meaning of *Forsham*. *Forsham* expressly declined to decide "what agency conduct

---

safeguards in its regulations to ensure that confidential information is not disclosed by another agency.
[20]44 U.S.C. § 3301.
[21]445 U.S. 169 (1980).
[22]If EEOC personnel were used to determine the validity of a certain test, the agency personnel could conduct a review of the validity evidence at the place of business of the test user. Under these circumstances, the documents reviewed by the agency would remain in the custody and control of the user and should not be considered to be "agency records" subject to disclosure under the FOIA. In such instances, the agency personnel should review the documents without making copies. Although this procedure may be viewed as somewhat impractical for the agency, it does have the advantage of providing agency personnel with easier access to relevant records. However, despite the fact that these documents never become part of agency files, there is no assurance that a requestor might not be able to secure their release in a sympathetic court.

is necessary to support a finding that it has 'obtained' documents."[23] Thus, there is at least a possibility that a FOIA request filed during the time that the panel is in possession of the documents might be upheld by the courts.[24] In the absence of a request while the panel is in possession of the documents and after the documents are returned to the test user or developer, they should not be subject to disclosure.[25] Consequently, the procedure which would appear to give the greatest assurance that the tests or other selection procedures reviewed would not be subject to disclosure would be for a non-agency panel to review them outside of the agency, either at the place of business of the test user or at some other non-agency location.

If the agency determines that the above procedures are not feasible or desirable, there are a number of other safeguards set forth below which the agency and test users can take to help prevent disclosure of confidential information that is submitted to the agency in conjunction with an opinion letter request. The maximum protection can be afforded by combining a number of these safeguards. However, even with these safeguards there is no absolute assurance that a requestor of information will not be able to secure disclosure of some or all of a user's selection procedures and other documentation submitted to the agency.

2. Regulations Providing for Nondisclosure

The first safeguard that could be adopted by the agency to ensure that confidential information relating to selection procedures and validity studies submitted as part of the opinion letter process would not be disclosed would be the promulgation of regulations by the agency setting forth a policy of nondisclosure of such materials. These regulations could be published as part of the agency regulations pertaining to opinion letters,[26] the availability of records under the FOIA,[27] or as part of any revision of the Uniform Guidelines[28] which might occur. As the basis for these regulations, the agency

---

[23]445 U.S. at 186 n. 17.
[24]Many individuals and organizations have instituted the practice of standing or continuing FOIA requests for certain types of information. Permitting such a practice jeopardizes the viability of any opinion letter procedure.
[25]*Kissinger v. Report. Com. for Freedom of the Press*, 445 U.S. 136, 150 (1980)("Congress did not mean that an agency improperly withholds a document which has been removed from the possession of the agency prior to the filing of the FOIA request.").
[26]29 C.F.R. §§ 1601.31-1601.33.
[27]29 C.F.R. § 1610.1.
[28]29 C.F.R. Part 1607.

could set forth the fact that the information submitted in conjunction with an opinion letter request is submitted voluntarily; that the information is protected from disclosure under Exemptions 3 and/or 4 of the FOIA; that the agency believes a central purpose of Title VII of encouraging the use of job-related and valid selection procedures is furthered by the free use of the opinion letter process without fear that the documents submitted will be disclosed; that the disclosure of such information pertaining to the selection process of the test user would compromise that process and make it unusable; and that the interests of the agency, the test user and the public are served by a policy of nondisclosure of such information. The regulations should state that EEOC believes the information to be exempt from disclosure under the FOIA and that the agency will not exercise its discretion to release any or all of the information.[29] Other agencies have adopted similar regulations.[30]

3. Presubmission Reviews and Advance Determinations

An alternative procedure which EEOC could adopt involves a presubmission review or advance determination of confidentiality of voluntarily submitted data or information. This procedure has been used by Food and Drug Administration (FDA) as well as by Environmental Protection Agency (EPA).[31] Thus, EEOC could adopt a procedure which would provide an opportunity for a test user to secure an advance determination as to whether or not the agency will afford confidential treatment to the information submitted.[32] However, there is a possibility that documents submitted for an advance confidentiality determination may be the subject of an FOIA request while the confidentiality request is pending. In addition, of course, the ultimate determination of the confidentiality of requested materials will in many instances be made by the courts.

---

[29] In the event that the agency were to ignore its regulations and order release of all or a portion of any documents pertaining to selection procedures of the test user and submitted in conjunction with an opinion letter request, the test user would have a cause of action under section 10(e) of the APA, 5 U.S.C. § 706, to prevent such disclosure.

[30] See 21 C.F.R. § 20.111(d) (Food and Drug Administration); 40 C.F.R. § 2.207 (Environmental Protection Agency).

[31] See 21 C.F.R. § 20.44(a) (FDA); and 40 C.F.R. § 2.206(a) (EPA).

[32] In the event that EEOC adopts either the "advance determination" or "class" nondisclosure process, the agency should also commit itself to defend in court against any request for disclosure and to consult with the test user regarding such defense.

4. Test User Request for Confidentiality

The test user requesting an opinion letter may gain further protection by expressly claiming in the letter requesting an opinion letter the confidentiality of the documents submitted.[33] The letter should also state that the user retains the ownership of the documents and that the documents must be returned to the user after a determination on the opinion letter request is made by the agency. In addition, the letter should set forth who is to be contacted in the event that an issue arises as to the confidentiality of the submitted documents. Finally, the documents themselves should be marked "Confidential" and should also identify who is to be notified in the event the confidentiality of the documents is questioned. This procedure may be useful with a direct opinion letter request or in conjunction with any presubmission review which the agency might adopt.

5. Notice to Test User

In the event that the agency receives a request for disclosure of any of the materials submitted in conjunction with an opinion letter request, the test user should be notified immediately of such a request. Where the agency has made a "class" determination by regulation that the materials are not subject to release, or where an advance determination of confidentiality has been obtained, the agency should inform the requestor that the documents will not be disclosed.[34] If the agency has not made a "class" determination or has not made an advance determination of confidentiality, the test user should be notified when a request for any documents submitted in conjunction with its opinion letter request is made and should be allowed the opportunity to demonstrate, prior to a determination of whether the documents may be released, that the materials should remain confidential. Advance notice should also be provided the test user if the agency decides that the information should be disclosed.[35]

---

[33]This is consistent with the procedure proposed by the Office of Federal Contract Compliance Programs (OFCCP) of the Department of Labor in § 60-2.5(c) of its proposed regulations governing the affirmative action obligations of federal contractors. 45 Fed. Reg. 42968, 42993 (August 25, 1981).
[34]If the agency in either of these instances determines that release of the documents is appropriate, the test user could seek a review of such decision under the APA, 5 U.S.C. § 706.
[35]These notice requirements are consistent with the procedure proposed by OFCCP. Under the proposed OFCCP regulations governing the affirmative action obligations of federal contractors, notification to the contractor is required when the agency

PROPOSAL FOR A PILOT PROGRAM

Because neither EEOC nor test users or developers have had significant experience with opinion letters in this area, and because there are a number of substantial problems which must be solved in order to implement a meaningful opinion letter process, an experimental pilot program may provide a means of determining whether the opinion letter process can be used effectively in this area. Under such a pilot program, EEOC could use one or two outside industrial psychologists as experts to evaluate a limited number of validity studies (perhaps four or five). These studies probably should come from test users rather than test developers because test developers might gain advantage over their competitors from a favorable opinion letter ruling. These four or five studies should comprise a variety of validation methodologies, as well as a variety of jobs or job groups. The agency and participating test users should attempt to incorporate safeguards, such as those outlined above, to ensure that information accompanying an opinion letter is not disclosed to the competitive and legal disadvantage of the submitter. Finally, the pilot program should be of a limited duration (perhaps one year initially), with a thorough review of the process at the conclusion of the pilot program. Such a review would enable the agency and test users and developers to determine what changes, if any, should be made in the process and to establish a permanent process if that is deemed to be warranted.

CONCLUSION

While there are substantial problems surrounding the use of opinion letters in the employee selection area, the development and use of such a process offers a number of potential advantages to the agency, test users and developers, and persons protected by Title VII. The opinion letter process encourages the use of job-related, objective selection devices, which should operate to ensure that selection devices are based on the ability to perform the job and not on prohibited factors such as race, sex or ethnic status. The process also may accomplish a substantial reduction in the legal risk to test

---

receives a request under the FOIA for disclosure of information obtained from contractors. Section 60-2.5(c), 45 Fed. Reg. at 42993. The contractor is given an opportunity to submit a statement of reasons why the information should be withheld. *Id.* In the event that OFCCP determines that the information is disclosable under the FOIA, the regulations provide for notice of the agency's intent to disclose the information at least ten days prior to disclosure.

users associated with the use of selection procedures, while encouraging voluntary compliance with Title VII by test users and developers. The process also should reduce substantially the current high costs to test users of developing and validating selection procedures. Such costs could be reduced by enabling other test users to transport tests and evidence of validity, deemed by an opinion letter to be sufficient, for use in jobs or job groups possessing similar job duties or knowledges, skills and abilities. Finally, the opinion letter process will encourage an increase in productivity by basing selection decisions on tests which are tied more closely to the abilities and skills required for performance of the job. Thus, the use of the opinion letter process in the employee selection area is an idea worth pursuing because it offers the potential for substantial benefits and because the problems associated with implementing such a process probably can be kept within tolerable limits.

THE IMPACT OF PROFESSIONAL STANDARDS ON EMPLOYEE TESTING AND EQUAL EMPLOYMENT

by

Val H. Markos and John M. Rauschenberger

The authors contend that the proposed Joint Technical Standards for Educational and Psychological Testing, if adopted by the sponsoring professional organizations as proposed in their February 1983 draft, will have a profound effect on employment testing and equal employment opportunity. The authors express concern about: (1) the numerous technical standards that only the largest test developers and corporations with substantial resources can possibly meet and which fail to recognize the realities of test validation in the dynamic work environment; (2) the obstacles the proposed Standards establish to using job-related selection procedures and the adverse implications this has for national productivity; (3) the negative context in which tests are portrayed and the implications this has on the protection of individual rights; and (4) the lack of references supporting the Standards, their overall lack of clarity and their inconsistency with research evidence, professional practice, and the Uniform Guidelines on Employee Selection Procedures. Finally, the authors question the document's intent that the proposed Standards be enforced by the federal enforcement agencies and the courts rather than serving as a technical guide as has been the case with all prior professional standards.

Val H. Markos has been Staff Supervisor for Testing and Counseling, U.S. Steel Corporation since 1979. In that capacity he is responsible for all development, validation, and implementation of employee selection criteria within U.S. Steel, and he advises the Corporate Director of Employment on all testing and selection matters. Prior to joining U.S. Steel, Dr. Markos was Test Validation Supervisor for the City of Miami, Florida. Dr. Markos is a member of several professional associations including the American Psychological Association and the Association for the Advancement of Science. He has authored a number of articles on employment testing and psychological measurement. Dr. Markos received his B.A. in psychology from Weber State College and his M.S. and Ph.D. in industrial psychology from the University of Georgia.

John M. Rauschenberger is the Supervisor of Corporate Personnel Research for Armco, Inc. He holds Masters and Doctoral degrees in Industrial and Organizational Psychology from Michigan State University and is a member of the American Psychological Association (APA), the Society for Industrial and Organizational Psychology, Inc. (Division 14 of the APA) and the Academy of Management. In addition to having co-authored research articles on such topics as test validation, utility and fairness, he was also a contributor to *A Professional and Legal Analysis of the Uniform Guidelines on Employee Selection Procedures* (1981) published by the American Society for Personnel Administration.

THE IMPACT OF PROFESSIONAL STANDARDS ON EMPLOYEE TESTING AND EQUAL EMPLOYMENT

Introduction

The widespread use of objective and standardized tests in the United States to select employees in the private sector began in the early 1900's. Testing for employee selection as one aspect of psychology is still a science in the process of evolution. Psychology itself is a relatively young science and psychological measurement, the measuring of cognitive skills and abilities, personality, temperament, *etc.*, is a still growing and developing body of knowledge. Increasingly, employment tests have been developed and validated in accordance with practices generally accepted by the psychological profession and based on this evolving body of knowledge. Acceptance of these practices recognizes the fact that employment test development and validation research is conducted in a dynamic work environment. Because of this environment, applied researchers experience problems very different from those experienced by the scientist in a controlled laboratory setting. As V. Jon Bentz, head of the Psychological Research and Services Division of Sears, Roebuck & Co. has stated:

> Validity research takes place in an incredibly complicated milieu, where such scientific necessities as control and standardization are extremely difficult to achieve. The attention that needs to be given to criterion and test development, the analysis and interpretation of data, are all arduous in the extreme, calling for very high-level quantitative skills and powers of abstraction.[1]

Notwithstanding these difficulties, a prestigious, multidisciplinary committee studying ability testing under the aegis of the National Academy of Sciences found "no evidence of alternatives to testing that are equally informative, equally adequate technically, and also economically and politically viable" in the employment setting.[2]

---

[1]Statement of V. Jon Bentz at the hearings of the Committee on Ability Testing, National Research Council, Washington, D.C. (November 17-18, 1978) reported in *Ability Testing: Consequences and Controversies* (Part I), National Academy Press (1982) at pp. 139-140 [hereafter *Ability Testing*].
[2]*Ability Testing* (Part I) at 144.

In addition to empirical research knowledge and professional recommendations, employment testing is scrutinized under the 1978 Uniform Guidelines on Employee Selection Procedures. Section 5C of the Uniform Guidelines states that:

> The provisions of these guidelines relating to validation of selection procedures are intended to be consistent with generally accepted professional standards for evaluating standardized tests such as the Standards for Educational and Psychological Tests prepared by a joint committee of the American Psychological Association, the American Educational Research Association and the National Council on Measurement in Education (American Psychological Association, Washington, D.C., 1974) (hereinafter "A.P.A. Standards") and standard textbooks and journals in the field of personnel selection.[3]

The *Ability Testing* study observed with respect to the reference to the *Standards for Educational and Psychological Tests* (hereafter 1974 *Standards*) in the Guidelines that:

> While the *Standards* reflect the best professional expertise, they are rarefied for the everyday world of employment testing. By incorporating them in the Guidelines, EEOC [Equal Employment Opportunity Commission] transformed what had been a state-of-art professional judgment, which the individual psychologist was expected to adopt in the light of particular circumstances, into ground rules for an employer's compliance with the [1964] Civil Rights Act.[4]

Fundamentally then, the 1974 *Standards* and the Uniform Guidelines were written for wholly different purposes and any inconsistencies associated with a researcher's ability to comply simultaneously with the provisions contained in both documents can be traced back to this fact.

Significantly, when the Uniform Guidelines have been shown to vary from professional standards, a number of courts have held that professional standards and practices take precedence over the Uniform Guidelines.[5] Furthermore, when validity evidence has been

---

[3] 29 C.F.R. 1607.5C.
[4] *Ability Testing* (Part I) at 105.
[5] *See, e.g., United States v. South Carolina,* 445 F. Supp. 1094, 1113 n. 20 (D.S.C. 1977), *aff'd mem. sub nom. National Education Association v. South Carolina,* 434 U.S. 1026 (1978); *Guardians Ass'n of New York v. Civil Service,* 630 F.2d 79, 91 (2d Cir. 1980), *cert. denied,* 101 S. Ct. 3083 (1981).

required under specific provisions of the Guidelines, testing programs with significant adverse impact have not passed court scrutiny. In fact, whole testing programs have been struck down with the decisions being influenced by such professionally unsupportable reasons as the inadequacy of a generally accepted approach to job analysis,[6] failure to conduct a differential validity study,[7] use of unvalidated cutoff scores,[8] failure to validate ranked scores,[9] use of concurrent rather than predictive criterion-related validity design,[10] and use of job-related training performance as a criterion.[11] This has been true despite the substantial resources which may have been devoted to a validity study.[12] This may help explain why almost one-half of the respondents to an Equal Employment Advisory Council survey on the Uniform Guidelines stated that their companies had discontinued the use of some or all tests because of the complexity and cost of the Uniform Guidelines.[13] It also may help explain why another 15 percent of the respondents specifically ceased using tests because of court decisions.[14]

Revision of the 1974 *Standards*

Because psychological measurement is evolving, the standards established by professional organizations as a guide to test users and developers are revised from time to time. The American Psychological Association (APA), the American Educational Research Association (AERA) and the National Council for Measurement in Education (NCME) have been the most active in promulgating standards for testing. The first standards were established in 1954 with the publication of the *Technical Recommendations for Psychological Tests and Diagnostic Techniques* by the APA. The 1954 *Technical Recommendations* focused primarily on the standards for reporting information about tests. In 1955, the AERA and the NCME prepared *Technical Recommendations for Achievement Tests*. In 1966,

---

[6]*See, e.g., United States v. State of New York*, 21 FEP Cases 1286 (N.D.N.Y. 1979).
[7]*See, e.g., United States v. Georgia Power Co.*, 474 F.2d 906 (5th Cir. 1973).
[8]*See, e.g., Boston Chapter, NAACP v. Beecher*, 504 F.2d 1017 (1st Cir. 1974), *cert. denied*, 421 U.S. 910 (1975).
[9]*See, e.g., Allen v. City of Mobile*, 464 F. Supp. 433 (S.D. Ala. 1978).
[10]*See, e.g., United States v. Georgia Power Co.*, 474 F.2d 906 (5th Cir. 1973).
[11]*See, e.g., Ensley Branch, NAACP v. Seibels*, 616 F.2d 812 (5th Cir. 1980), *cert. denied*, 449 U.S. 1061 (1980).
[12]*See, e.g., United States v. State of New York*, 21 FEP Cases 1286 (N.D.N.Y. 1979). (In monetary terms, over one million dollars spent in the test development and validation effort).
[13]See Appendix A of this Monograph.
[14]*Id.*

both sets of standards were combined and revised as the *Standards for Educational and Psychological Tests and Manuals*. The 1966 revision concerned test producer obligations and was referenced in the 1970 Employee Selection Guidelines of the Equal Employment Opportunity Commission (EEOC) as one possible source of minimum standards for validation.[15] The *Standards* were subsequently revised in 1974 to encompass competency in testing practice as the *Standards for Educational and Psychological Tests* and, as mentioned previously, these were incorporated by reference in the 1978 Uniform Guidelines.[16]

The 1974 *Standards* currently are undergoing revision. For the past year a Standards Review Committee appointed by the three sponsoring organizations has been working to produce what will become new *Joint Technical Standards for Educational and Psychological Testing*. The work product of the Committee has been subject to the review and comment of approximately 100 psychologists. After consideration of their comments, the revised draft *Joint Technical Standards* were distributed to the public in February 1983. After review of the public comments, another draft will be distributed to the public in August 1983 with public hearings to be held in September 1983. The resulting draft *Joint Technical Standards* will then be subject to comment by all committees and divisions of the APA before their submission for final approval to the Council of Representatives of the APA in August 1984.

The draft *Joint Technical Standards* made public in February 1983 is the current draft of the Standards Review Committee. The initial draft caused a substantial negative response from a number of psychologists who reviewed it and found it overly restrictive and sometimes inconsistent with testing literature.[17] Due to the efforts of many psychologists serving as advisors to the Standards Review Committee, as well as a motion of the membership of the Society of Industrial and Organizational Psychology (Division 14 of the APA),[18]

---

[15] 29 C.F.R. 1607.5(a) (1970).
[16] They were earlier referenced in the 1976 Federal Executive Agency Guidelines published by the Departments of Labor and Justice and the U.S. Civil Service Commission.
[17] The *Joint Technical Standards* will apply not only to tests, but also to interviews, personal history data and almost anything a psychologist may use in evaluating people.
[18] Division 14, Division of Industrial and Organizational Psychology, is the division of the APA most concerned with employment testing. In 1975, Division 14 issued its *Principles for the Validation and Use of Personnel Selection Procedures* as a statement of good practice in the use of standardized tests and other employee selection procedures. The 1975 *Principles* were intended to be consistent with the 1974 APA

the ratification process, originally scheduled to be completed in September1983, has been slowed and substantial criticism has been aired.

As mentioned, the process now will be extended through August 1984. There is an indication in the publicly released draft that the Standards Review Committee has made modifications to respond to a number of the criticisms. Although there have been modifications, there are still a number of issues that are or should be of concern to the psychologists, test users and developers who will have to refer to the *Joint Technical Standards* as a professional guide. The following discussion outlines several aspects of these issues.

Standards. In 1980, the *Principles* were revised. As stated in the Statement of Purpose of the 1980 *Principles*:

> Its purpose is to specify principles of good practice in the choice, development, and evaluation of personnel selection procedures. (Page 1.)

> The *Principles* are not meant to be at variance with the *Standards for Educational and Psychological Tests* (APA, 1974). However, the *Standards* were written for measurement problems in general while the *Principles* are addressed to the specific problems of decision making in the areas of employee selection, placement, promotion, etc. (Page 2.)

Like the *Standards*, the *Principles* stated here present ideals toward which the members of this Division and other researchers and practitioners are expected to strive. Circumstances in any individual study or application will affect the importance of any given principle. Researchers and practitioners should, however, consider very carefully any factors suggesting that a general principle is inapplicable or that its implementation is not feasible. It is most appropriate to bear in mind the following statement from the *Standards*, cited in full in the 1975 *Principles* and now repeated here:

> A final caveat is necessary in view of the prominence of testing issues in litigation. This document is prepared as a technical guide for those within the sponsoring professions; it is *not* written as law. What is intended is a set of standards to be used, in part, for self-evaluation by test developers and test users. An evaluation of their competence does not rest on the literal satisfaction of every relevant provision of this document. The individual standards are statements of ideals or goals, some having priority over others. Instead, an evaluation of competence depends on the degree to which the intent of this document has been satisfied by the test developer or user (APA, 1974, p. 8).

The *Principles* are intended to represent the consensus of professional knowledge and thought as it exists today, albeit not a *consensus omnium* since this is probably unattainable. Also, it is to be noted that personnel selection research and development is still an evolving field and techniques and decision-making models are subject to change. This document contains references for further reading and for support of the principles enunciated. It is expected that both researchers and practitioners will maintain an appropriate level of awareness of developments in the field. (Page 2.)

Protection of Individual Rights

The language of the proposed *Joint Technical Standards* appropriately implies that improper test use can have a negative and damaging effect on individuals. A further appropriate implication to be drawn from the draft is that an unethical or misinformed test developer or user is in a position to violate, unwittingly or otherwise, the rights of individuals by the use of tests. It is disturbing to many practitioners, however, that the document makes only short, passing reference to the benefits which accrue not only to individuals but to our society as a whole from the *proper* use of testing.

The consequences of this imbalance could be serious. Because it has been the case with the current 1974 *Standards*, it is reasonable to expect the *Joint Technical Standards* will often be relied upon in litigation regarding psychological testing, by governmental agencies in their investigation of discrimination complaints, by arbitrators in labor-management disputes over testing and selection issues, and by others in those arenas where testing has been and will continue to be under review. Because the language of the draft focuses primarily on a negative, one-sided view of the possible ramifications of psychological testing, an independent reviewer (*e.g.*, a judge or arbitrator) will be very likely to interpret the consensus of professional opinion as suggesting that psychological testing practices should be summarily considered "guilty until proven innocent."

This negative and unbalanced picture will do little to help further a well-rounded understanding of the individual and societal ramifications associated with psychological testing. Undoubtedly, it will be used by independent audiences as evidence to justify a restricted use of psychological tests in educational and industrial arenas. This would, of course, be ironic given the conclusion of the *Ability Testing* study of the superiority of tests over other alternatives.[19]

With or without tests, decisions concerning the selection of individuals for schools or jobs will continue to be made. If test use is restricted, the resulting impact will be more decisions made on the basis of subjective, judgmental inferences of unknown validity. Many of these inferences may be far less appropriate than those made in light of the results of validated tests. The appropriateness of inferences made from a properly validated test can be determined by validation evidence and the consequences associated with making them can be both rationally and empirically demonstrated. There

---

[19]See p. 147, *supra*.

is no evidence to suggest that subjective, judgmental inferences of unknown validity will better protect individuals or their rights in the decisionmaking process. Rather, it would seem that they would offer less protection. As noted earlier, while the protection of individuals and their rights is an appropriate concern in the 1974 *Standards* revision process, an unbalanced presentation of the potential consequences associated with psychological testing is not an effective way to deliver that protection, and may, in the final analysis, only serve to reduce it.

Burdensome Nature of Requirements

In their entirety, the proposed *Joint Technical Standards* establish provisions representing an even greater burden than now exists on test developers and users. A general criticism aired by many psychologists concerns the overall length and massive nature of the *Joint Technical Standards*. There are 266 individual Standards presented in the document. The document, including the preface, introduction and incomplete glossary, covers 198 single spaced pages.

Part of the reason for the length of the document is the fact that the *Joint Technical Standards* are organized into three parts with Part I (6 chapters) covering Test Instrumentation, Part II (11 chapters) covering Test Use and Part III (2 chapters) discussing specific issues. Part II discusses separately each of a number of differing settings in which tests may be used. Thus, Standards for the use of tests in personnel selection are separate from those for use of tests in a clinical setting. At first glance it would appear that for practitioners involved in personnel testing, eight chapters would apply or be pertinent to their work.[20] This alone would involve 165 individual Standards and over 100 pages. However, after reading the introduction to Chapter 7, one finds that the Committee identifies Standards in Chapters 10 (Clinical Testing), 11 (Counseling and Guidance) and 17 (Educational Testing of Linguistic Minorities) as being relevant as well. When one notes the statement in the Introduction that none of the chapters can stand alone, it becomes evident that the number of Standards with which practitioners have to be concerned is actually 266.

The Standards Review Committee has expressed the opinion that the number of Standards is not extreme because not every

---

[20]This would include all of Part I, as well as Chapter 7 on Personnel Selection and Chapter 16 on Testing of the Handicapped.

Standard will apply to every situation. In reality, however, it is simply too easy to interpret a situation as necessitating the application of an inappropriate Standard. This is especially likely when the reviewer is one who is unfamiliar with test validation research, such as a judge or arbitrator.

In comparison with the 1974 *Standards*, there is a 20 percent overall increase in the number of Standards, from 220 to 266. Furthermore, considering those Standards identified as essential in the 1974 *Standards* and those labeled "A"[21] in the *Joint Technical Standards*, the increase is about 47 percent or from 151 to 222. One must keep in mind that progress in this respect is not indicated by increasing the number of technical requirements, but in decreasing the number consistent with research findings.

A major cause of the increase in the number of Standards is the requirement throughout the draft *Joint Technical Standards* for explanations, rationale, and information concerning the appropriateness of procedures and approaches. It is clear that the document is asking for very specific information to provide for outside review and evaluation of techniques and procedures. In this respect the *Joint Technical Standards* will be seen less and less as a helpful guide to test development and use, and will be viewed more and more as requirements having to be met because of possible repercussions.

To increase the present burden means that even those with substantial resources (staff, as well as money) will find it difficult to comply with such rigorous Standards. But as was observed in the *Ability Testing* report: "It is disingenuous to impose test validation requirements that employers, even with the best will and a sizable monetary investment, cannot meet."[22] Thus, one consequence of the *Joint Technical Standards*, as proposed, could be the creation of a competitive advantage for large companies over their smaller competitors. Perhaps more significant, however, is the potential impact on the individual practitioner: the clinician in private practice, the school psychologist, and any other practitioner who does not have the benefit of the substantial financial and technical support in his

---

[21] The draft *Joint Technical Standards* refers to Standards as primary "A" and secondary "B" with the "A" category being Standards which all tests should meet. This represents an even stronger requirement than the essential rating in the 1974 *Standards*. The 218 "A" Standards identified included 22 "A/B" standards. The "A/B" designation is defined in the document as a necessary requirement for all but low-volume, unpublished tests.

[22] *Ability Testing*, Part I at 107.

or her individual applied research settings that would be necessary to comply with the proposed *Joint Technical Standards.*

Perhaps most significant is the potential impact on the nation as a whole. If, as one might expect, the burdensome nature of these provisions were to cause a reduction in the use of psychological tests in educational, industrial, or other arenas, then in addition to the potential consequences on individual rights discussed previously, one should also consider the impact of such an outcome on national productivity.

Notwithstanding the current recessionary economy, there has been a growing concern in America about our continued decline in productivity in comparison to other nations. Researchers have been able to document the cost-benefits of testing in terms of the productivity increases obtainable from a workforce selected with the aid of validated psychological measures. While it is obvious that the use of validated personnel selection methods alone will not reverse a national decline in productivity, it can make a quantifiable contribution to the effort.[23] It would be unfortunate and disappointing to many practicing industrial psychologists if the psychological profession unwittingly were to establish a roadblock to the contribution that could be made to help overcome this national concern.

Finally, the preface of the document contains a statement identifying government enforcement agencies and courts as potential enforcers of the *Joint Technical Standards.* The concern over this point is more clearly understood with recognition of the fact that the proviso in the 1974 *Standards* that they were prepared as a technical guide, not written as law, has been modified.[24] The 1974 *Standards* identified the purpose of self-evaluation and technical guidance as an important objective. While including a statement explaining that they are not written as law, the *Joint Technical Standards* identify a major role they will play in providing the courts with a basis for evaluating the proper use of tests. Apparently, it is not the intent of the Standards Review Committee to write statements of ideals and goals as was the stated purpose of the 1974 *Standards.* In fact, the preface of the current draft clearly identifies that an objective of the Committee is to provide government agen-

---

[23]*See* J. E. Hunter and F. L. Schmidt, "Fitting People into Jobs: The Impact of Personnel Selection on National Productivity," in *Human Performance and Productivity* (E. A. Fleishman, ed.) (1981) (Estimated annual productivity increase of $43 to $75 billion resulting from all U.S. employers adopting ability based selection standards).
[24]See note 18, *supra.*

cies, the courts and others with the ability to address social, legal and political concerns from a sound technical base. In this respect, the *Joint Technical Standards* are not written as much to provide assistance to the informed practitioner as they are to provide a tool for a third party without testing expertise to evaluate and review the practices of the professional.

One has to question the wisdom of any professional organization inviting outside interpretation and enforcement of its own standards. Many practitioners are concerned that when the *Joint Technical Standards* are utilized by the courts and enforcement agencies, the probability of someone being able to identify an aspect of a test that is "not up to Standard" will be almost assured with this large number of rules, even when the user otherwise adheres to most other Standards, uses the test in an appropriate context, and draws appropriate inferences from test scores.

References or Documentation of Standards

As implied in the introduction to this paper, it is the essence of good scientific practice that professional standards be written to reflect the evolving body of empirical knowledge in that science. It is, therefore, ironic that the draft *Joint Technical Standards* contain no specific references or documentation. This document is in contrast to Division 14's *Principles*, which at least contain some references enabling the reader to evaluate the empirical research evidence supporting the existence of the *Principles*, especially for those issues those issues which represent departures from previous thinking or practices. This lack of citation to authority is important because there are several proposed requirements for which there appear to be either little or no empirical support and which, if adopted, could have profound implications for equal employment litigation and compliance.

As mentioned, given the intent that the *Joint Technical Standards* be interpreted and enforced by nonprofessional audiences, it is only fair that they be established on and supported by specific references to sound technical research. It must be noted in this regard that the Standards Review Committee was *not* charged with the task of *creating* new standards of professional practice. Rather, it was asked to write statements which reflect the consensus of professional opinion as to what empirical research knowledge suggests those professional practices ought to be. To understand the difference in these two approaches, we merely note that citation of references is possible for the latter but not for the former.

Technical Standards

Much of the criticism of the original draft of the *Joint Technical Standards* was centered on specific technical Standards. While it is apparent that many of these Standards have been subject to further modification, it is difficult to evaluate whether the modifications resolve the issues. There are two contributing factors. First, at the end of the draft, a glossary is provided with over 150 terms to be defined but with no definitions attached. Because numerous technical Standards can be altered by the definition of an individual term, the glossary becomes an extremely important part of the document. Obviously, a major concern of practitioners will be the possibility of there being modifications to the *Joint Technical Standards* only to have apparent progress removed through a controversial definition of terms. In fact, until all the concerned parties have had the opportunity to review a completed glossary, none of the 266 Standards, the comments accompanying them, or the commentary associated with the chapters can be accepted without concern.

The second contributing factor is the confusion introduced by the actual organization of the draft. As discussed above, because of the numerous chapters covering various aspects of test use and the long commentary prefacing each chapter, the same principle or technical issue may be introduced several times throughout the document. This in and of itself makes the *Joint Technical Standards* not only difficult to understand, but difficult to use. Additionally, each discussion of a principle or issue may not be completely consistent with other discussions of the same topic.

An example of this inconsistency can be seen with respect to the issue of differential prediction. Standard 2.21 requires a differential prediction study for those groups for which previous research has established a probability of differential prediction. The comment associated with the Standard mentions the fact that it does not appear that differential prediction by race is often found in employment testing and that there is little evidence of the existence or nonexistence of gender differences. The commentary in the introduction of Chapter 2 states that the evidence suggests no differential prediction for blacks versus whites and that evidence of other minority comparisons is limited. Then in Chapter 8, Standard 8.7 requires, where feasible, the study of differential prediction for selected groups. It does not designate which selected groups. The comment associated with that Standard, moreover, speaks of the difficulty of conducting this research due to small samples and suggests cooperative studies.

An employer may want to read these Standards and comments as not requiring differential prediction studies for a given minority group (*e.g.*, Hispanics). However, it is unclear just what the requirement is and, if it appears unclear to testing practitioners, one must ask how a judge or enforcement agency representative will interpret the issue. Thus, the organization of the draft itself makes it difficult for users to understand just what is required by the *Joint Technical Standards*.

A similar example surrounds the notion introduced in Standard 2.1 that all three approaches to validation—content, construct, and criterion-related strategies—are necessary to demonstrate a test's validity. Historically, these three components have represented different aspects of validity and different strategies in test validation. Validation has always meant the providing of evidence through one approach or another that appropriate inferences are made from test results. Both the Uniform Guidelines and Division 14 *Principles* recognize that the valid use of a test can be established based on any of these strategies alone. The modification of Standard 2.1 introduces the requirement that an appropriate mix of these three approaches be justified by presentation of the rationale for that mix.

The introductory comments to Chapter 2 state that the strongest statements of validity would include evidence of all three components though all "are not always necessary" for the valid use of a test. Chapter 7 (Personnel Selection) identifies criterion-related validity as often representing the principle validity concept with an alternative approach being a combination of content and construct validity, if criterion-related is not feasible. Chapter 8 on Educational Admissions Testing identifies all three components as being vital. Chapter 9 cites the "content component, supplemented by construct analysis and, where feasible, by generalizations based on criterion-related evidence" as primary to licensing and certification test validation. Further references to the three approaches are found in other chapters. The result of the numerous references to this issue is that the practitioner is left questioning what is acceptable short of providing evidence of all three components.

The providing of validity evidence for all three components represents an unnecessary research burden not required by professional practice. However, the justifiable fear is that with the document's numerous references to the three components of validity, it would be easy to interpret the *Joint Technical Standards* as requiring all three approaches to validity for most tests.

There are other examples of proposed technical standards which depart from past practices and research findings. One example is the preference demonstrated in the *Joint Technical Standards* for a predictive rather than concurrent design of criterion-related validity studies. This distinctive preference for predictive validity contradicts the Division 14 *Principles* which establish no such preference. Moreover, the Standard ignores published research literature that has discussed this point. [25]

CONCLUSION

The result of the effort to revise the *Standards for Educational and Psychological Tests* is still to be seen. It is apparent, however, that we are witnessing a change from a guide for professionals to a tool for enforcement agencies and the courts to evaluate professional practices. Without further modification, the *Joint Technical Standards* would create a heavier burden for practitioners and test users to bear. Because of this, the *Joint Technical Standards* could influence further the trend of less sharing of data and research findings and less publishing of applied personnel selection research, even though they are explicit in their encouragement and support of such professional activities. One cannot help but wonder as to how useful these *Joint Technical Standards* will prove to be, in the final analysis, in helping this relatively young science to achieve progress.

It would be unfair to assume that the final version of the revised *Joint Technical Standards* will contain all of the problems mentioned in this paper. Nonetheless, it would be safe to say that unless the course is changed, the boat will continue to drift in this direction. It is also safe to assume that there will be little change in its course unless more practitioners and other affected parties come forward to put their oars in the water.

---

[25]*See, e.g.*, G. V. Barrett, J.S. Phillips, & R. A. Alexander, *Concurrent and Predictive Validity Designs: A Critical Reanalysis*, 66 J. of App. Psy. 1 (1981); K. Pearlman, F. L. Schmidt, and J. E. Hunter, *Validity Generalization Results for Tests Used to Predict Job Proficiency and Training Success in Clerical Occupations*, 65 J. of App. Psy. 373 (1980); S. E. Bemis, *Occupational Validity of the General Aptitude Battery*, 52 J. of App. Psy. 240 (1968).

THE IMPACT OF *CONNECTICUT V. TEAL* ON EMPLOYEE SELECTION, EEO COMPLIANCE AND LITIGATION

by
Edward E. Potter and Thomas R. Bagby

The authors contend that the Supreme Court's decision in State of Connecticut v. Teal (1982) has significant implications for Title VII litigation and compliance, affirmative action, personnel testing and employee selection procedures. The authors discuss the factual circumstances of Teal, the lower court decisions, and the Supreme Court's majority and dissenting opinions. The burdens of proof in Title VII litigation are described and the authors suggest alternative approaches to such litigation depending on whether the selection procedure involves pass-fail components and/or subjective or objective criteria, and whether there is adverse impact when the actual selection decisions are made. The effect of Teal on affirmative action practices and judicial remedies, the use of affirmative action as a defense, and the employment of protected classes are analyzed. Whether Teal will result in revision of the Uniform Guidelines on Employee Selection Procedures with respect to the "bottom line" standard, the search for alternatives provision, and the "80 percent" rule also are examined. The authors also suggest a number of practical selection procedure alternatives after Teal depending on the employer's circumstances and priorities. Finally, recent legal developments are analyzed.

Edward E. Potter is a partner in the law firm of McGuiness & Williams specializing in labor, equal employment opportunity, and international labor law. In this capacity, he has represented management in equal employment matters of various types including factfinding and court proceedings under Title VII of the 1964 Civil Rights Act, the Age Discrimination Act and other equal employment statutes; and compliance reviews and administrative proceedings under Executive Order 11246. For the past two years, Mr. Potter has served as legal counsel to the Ad Hoc Committee on Employee Selection. In addition, he has taught EEO seminars on the use of statistics in EEO litigation, availability, and employee selection procedures to several hundred management officials and lawyers. Mr. Potter received a B.A. in economics from Michigan State University, an M.S. in collective bargaining and labor economics from Cornell University, and a J.D. from American University. He is a member of the District of Columbia Bar, the Labor and Employment Law Section of the American Bar Association, and the Federal Bar Association.

Thomas R. Bagby has been associated with the law firm of McGuiness & Williams since 1981. He served as law clerk to the Honorable June L. Green, United States District Judge for the District of Columbia from 1975 to 1977. From 1977 to 1981 Mr. Bagby was a trial attorney in the Civil Rights Division of the Department of Justice. In that capacity he represented the United States in a number of major Title VII pattern and practice cases against state and local governments involving testing and test validation under the Uniform Guidelines on Employee Selection Procedures. In addition, he was responsible for the investigation, negotiation, entry and enforcement of numerous consent decrees against state and local governments and was also involved in investigations, negotiations and enforcement actions under Executive Order 11246. Mr. Bagby received his undergraduate and law degrees from the University of Virginia and is a member of the Virginia and District of Columbia Bars.

THE IMPACT OF *CONNECTICUT v. TEAL* ON EMPLOYEE SELECTION, EEO COMPLIANCE AND LITIGATION

Introduction

Personnel administrators, supervisors and others make employment decisions on a daily basis based on objective and subjective assessments of the relative qualifications of applicants and candidates for available positions in the workforce. Because of the incentives inherent in hiring and promoting the most productive individuals, employers usually act in their economic self interest and select those who they believe to be the best qualified individuals available. Tests are one tool used in personnel selection whose use is premised on the reality that people differ in their ability to perform a job. Tests have been shown to be a source of valuable information about prospective employees and often provide the only information related to ability and skills that an employer has in making selection decisions.[1] No alternative to tests is currently available that is equally informative, and as technically and economically viable, with respect to assessing the capabilities of individuals.[2] On the other hand, even highly valid or job-related tests are likely to have varying degrees of disparate impact against minorities.[3]

Title VII of the Civil Rights Act of 1964, as amended, was enacted by Congress to protect the right of individuals to be free from employment practices that discriminate against them on the basis of their race, color, religion, sex or national origin. In implementing Title VII's nondiscrimination mandate, the courts have recognized that individuals may seek to vindicate their rights by alleging that they have been subjected to disparate treatment, *i.e.*, intentional discrimination, or that they have been victims of a facially neutral practice, such as a test, which has a disparate impact on their protected group.

---

[1] National Academy of Sciences, *Ability Testing: Uses, Consequences and Controversies* (Part I), (1982) [hereafter *Ability Testing*] at 143-144.
[2] *Id.* at 144.
[3] R. Linn, "Ability Testing: Individual Differences, Prediction, and Differential Prediction" in *Ability Testing* (Part II) at 365-366; R. I. Samuda, *Psychological Testing of American Minorities* (1975) at 1; R.L. Flaugher, *The Many Definitions of Test Bias*, 33 American Psychology 672-73 (July 1978); and D. J. Weiss and M. L. Davison, *Review of Test Theory Methods* (1981) at 27.

In *Griggs v. Duke Power Co.*[4] and *Albemarle v. Moody*,[5] the Supreme Court established the standards for determining when the use of an employment test or other facially neutral selection procedure or criterion violates TitleVII. In *Griggs*, the Court concluded that "Congress directed the thrust of the Act to the *consequences* of employment practices, not simply the motivation."[6] "If an employment practice which operates to exclude [a protected class] cannot be shown to be related to performance, the practice is prohibited."[7] In *Albemarle*, the Court stated that the employer's burden of proving the job relatedness of a particular job requirement arises "only after the complaining party or class has made out a prima facie case of discrimination, *i.e.*, has shown that the tests in question *select* applicants for hire or promotion in a racial pattern significantly different from the pool of applicants."[8] If an employer meets its burden of proving the job relatedness of its tests, the burden of proof shifts to "the complaining party to show that other tests or selection devices, without a similarly undesirable racial effect, would also serve the employer's legitimate interest in 'efficient and trustworthy workmanship.' "[9]

Both *Griggs* and *Albemarle* involved factual circumstances in which the overall selection results of a multicomponent selection process had adverse impact against minorities.[10] However, in *Connecticut v. Teal*,[11] decided June 21, 1982, the Court in a 5 to 4 decision found that the plaintiffs had established a prima facie case of discrimination in a selection process whose overall results favored minorities.

In *Teal*, the State of Connecticut had established a multicomponent promotion process that required individuals entering the process to pass a written test in order to be considered further for promotion. The results of the written test had a disparate impact on blacks. But after other selection criteria were applied to the remaining candidates, blacks actually were promoted at a higher rate than whites. In its decision the Court held that a "bottom line" result favorable to blacks as a group did not preclude individual black employees, who failed the written test and were thereby pre-

---

[4] 401 U.S. 424 (1971).
[5] 422 U.S. 405 (1975).
[6] 401 U.S. at 432.
[7] *Id.* at 431.
[8] 422 U.S. at 425 (emphasis added).
[9] *Id.*
[10] *See also Dothard v. Rawlinson*, 433 U.S. 321 (1977).
[11] 102 S. Ct. 2525 (1982).

cluded from further consideration, from establishing a prima facie case based on the disparate impact of the single component of the selection process. The Court further held that the favorable "bottom line" did not provide the employer with a defense to such a prima facie case.

Prior to *Teal*, many employers thought that a clean bottom line, *i.e.*, no adverse impact at the point of the selection decision, provided a defense to Title VII suits premised on a disparate impact theory (but not a disparate treatment theory).[12] This view was based on a number of considerations. First, the Court on a number of occasions had stressed that Title VII encourages voluntary compliance and previously had encouraged employers to take "effective steps" to improve the employment opportunities of protected class members.[13] Second, the Equal Employment Opportunity Commission (EEOC), the primary agency charged with enforcement of Title VII, also had encouraged such voluntary action in its Affirmative Action Guidelines.[14] Under those Guidelines, if self analysis reveals that an employer's employment practices have or tend to have adverse effect, the employer may take reasonable action designed to correct the problem.[15] Third, the four principal enforcement agencies under Title VII—the EEOC, the Department of Justice, the Office of Federal Contract Compliance Programs (OFCCP) of the Department of Labor, and the U.S. Civil Service Commission (now the Office of Personnel Management)—in the Uniform Guidelines on Employee Selection Procedures encouraged voluntary action to eliminate the overall adverse impact of a selection process and, as a matter of administrative and prosecutorial discretion, adhered to a bottom line

---

[12] It was well-established before the Court's decision in *Teal* that the overall selection process' lack of discriminatory impact would not defeat a claim of intentional discrimination, although it would be relevant to such a claim. See *McDonnell Douglas Corp. v. Green*, 411 U.S. 792, 804-05 (1973); *International Brotherhood of Teamsters v. United States*, 431 U.S. 324, 340 n. 20 (1977); *Furnco Construction Corp v. Waters*, 438 U.S. 567, 580 (1978); *New York City Transit Authority v. Beazer*, 440 U.S. 568, 584 n.25 (1979).

[13] *See, e.g., United Steelworkers of America v. Weber*, 443 U.S. 193, 204 (1979); *Alexander v. Gardner-Denver Co.*, 415 U.S. 36, 44 (1974).

[14] 29 C.F.R. Part 1608.

[15] 29 C.F.R. § 1608.4. In addition, both private and public employers are subject to various mandatory affirmative action requirements. Federal contractors at some 325,000 establishments are subject to the affirmative action obligations of Executive Order 11246, 30 Fed. Reg. 12319 (1965), *as amended by* 32 Fed. Reg. 14302 (1967) and 43 Fed. Reg. 46501 (1978). Likewise many public employers, like the State of Connecticut, are subject to various state affirmative action statutes. *See, e.g.*, Conn. Stat. § 46a-68. Unlike under Title VII, the statistical imbalances that trigger these affirmative action requirements need not be connected to any showing of past or present discrimination.

standard for purposes of enforcement.[16] Finally, most of the lower courts that had considered the question had concluded that there was no violation of Title VII based on a disparate impact theory if there was no adverse impact at the bottom line.[17] Thus, employers, like the State of Connecticut, reasonably concluded that corrective action to eliminate adverse impact at the bottom line was sufficient to avoid discrimination suits based on the results of a facially neutral component of a selection process, absent evidence of intentional discrimination.

The *Teal* decision, therefore, has significant implications for Title VII litigation and compliance, affirmative action, personnel testing and employee selection procedures. The purpose of this paper is to examine these implications in depth. The paper discusses the facts and the Supreme Court's majority and dissenting opinions in *Teal* and analyzes the effect of the decision on EEO compliance, affirmative action and the burdens of proof under Title VII. The paper also suggests alternative selection procedure strategies employers may consider after *Teal*.

CONNECTICUT V. TEAL

Facts and Lower Court Decisions

The State of Connecticut utilized a multicomponent, merit selection process to assess the qualifications of candidates for promotion to supervisor positions in the Department of Income Maintenance. Candidates for these positions were required to complete successfully a multicomponent selection process. Candidates were first required to take a professionally-developed written test. Those employees receiving a passing score were then evaluated on the basis of past work performance, supervisors' recommendations, and seniority, in conjunction with their test scores. At the third stage of the process, the State made its selections from among the remaining qualified candidates.

In December 1978, the test was administered to 329 candidates. Because a cutoff score of 70 would have limited substantially the

---

[16] 29 C.F.R. Part 1607.
[17] *See, e.g., EEOC v. Greyhound Lines*, 635 F.2d 188 (3d Cir. 1980); *EEOC v. Navajo Refining Co.*, 593 F.2d 988 (10th Cir. 1979); *Friend v. Leidinger*, 588 F.2d 61 (4th Cir. 1978); *Rule v. Ironworkers Local 396*, 568 F.2d 558 (8th Cir. 1977); *Smith v. Troyan*, 520 F.2d 492 (6th Cir. 1975), cert. denied, 426 U.S. 934 (1976); *Brown v. New Haven Civil Service Board*, 474 F. Supp. 1256 (D. Conn. 1979); *Williams v. City of San Francisco*, 483 F. Supp. 335 (N.D. Calif. 1979); *Stewart v. Hannon*, 469 F. Supp. 1142 (N.D. Ill. 1979); *Lee v. City of Richmond*, 456 F. Supp. 756 (E.D. Va. 1978).

number of qualified blacks proceeding to the next step of the selection process, the State lowered the cutoff score to 65. Although the lower cutoff score permitted more blacks to participate in the remainder of the selection process, the percentage of blacks who passed was 54.2 percent, compared to 79.5 percent of the white candidates. Thus, the black pass rate was approximately 68% of the white pass rate, sufficient to establish "adverse impact" under the "4/5ths" or "80%" rule of the Uniform Guidelines.[18] However, when the actual promotions were made, after application of the other components of the selection process, there was no adverse impact against blacks. In fact, blacks were substantially favored by the State's selection process—23 percent of the blacks who initially entered the selection process were promoted, compared to 13.5 percent of the initial white candidates. Thus, the promotion rate of blacks was nearly 170 percent of the promotion rate of whites.

A suit under Title VII and other statutes was brought by four black candidates who scored lower than 65 on the examination and hence were eliminated from further consideration. Each had been promoted provisionally to supervisory positions prior to taking the test and had served in such positions for periods of up to two years. The suit alleged that the written test component of the selection process was unlawful because it had an adverse impact on blacks. Adopting the bottom line approach of the Uniform Guidelines, the district court [19] held that the favorable "bottom line" promotion rate of blacks precluded the plaintiffs from establishing a prima facie case of disparate impact and accordingly, that the State was not required to demonstrate the job relatedness of the written examination. Although the trial court received evidence regarding the validity of the examination, it did not rule on that issue.

The Second Circuit reversed, [20] holding that where a component of a selection process has a disparate impact on minorities and constitutes a barrier beyond which those failing that component cannot proceed, a prima facie case of discrimination is established even though the process taken as a whole does not result in disparate impact. To do otherwise, it stated, "would be adopting the position that regardless of the language of the statute Congress intended

---

[18] The "4/5ths" rule provides that "a selection rate for any race, sex, or ethnic group which is less than four-fifths (4/5) (or eighty percent) of the rate for the group with the highest rate will generally be regarded by the federal enforcement services as evidence of adverse impact...." 29 C.F.R. § 1607.40.
[19] The district court opinion is unofficially reported at 27 FEP Cases 1330 (D. Conn. 1980).
[20] *Teal v. Connecticut*, 645 F.2d 133 (2d Cir. 1981).

Title VII to protect faceless groups rather than individuals."[21] However, in instances where written test scores were but one part of an overall, cumulatively-scored process—*i.e.*, each candidate is permitted to participate in all steps of the selection process—the appellate court concluded that "the overall results of the process should be deemed a fair barometer of the fairness of the process."[22] From this opinion, the State of Connecticut petitioned the Supreme Court for certiorari.

The Majority Opinion

Justice Brennan, in his opinion joined by Justices White, Marshall, Blackmun and Stevens, held that the promotional examination, which operated as a barrier to plaintiffs' promotion and which had a discriminatory impact on black employees, falls within the language of section 703(a)(2) [23] of Title VII, which makes it an unlawful employment practice for an employer "to limit, segregate, or classify his employees or applicants for employment in any way which would deprive or tend to deprive any individual of employment opportunities . . . because of such individual's race, color, religion, sex, or national origin." In so doing, the majority continually emphasized that the statute speaks not in terms of actual jobs or promotions for racial *groups*, but in terms of limitations and classifications that may deprive *individuals* of employment *opportunities*.

The majority opinion reiterated that *Griggs v. Duke Power Co.*[24] and its progeny have established a three-part analysis for claims of disparate impact.[25] First, a plaintiff must show that a facially neutral employment practice has a significant discriminatory impact. Second, if that showing is made, the employer must demonstrate that the practice has "a manifest relationship to the employment in question." Third, the plaintiff may still prevail if he shows that the employer used the practice as a mere pretext for discrimination.

The majority stated that claims of adverse impact, as defined by the Court in *Griggs*, reflect the language of section 703(a)(2) and the intent of Congress to provide for equality of employment opportunities and to remove non-job-related barriers which have operated in the past to the disadvantage of minorities. Thus, the majority stated that:

---

[21] *Id.* at 138.
[22] *Id.* at 139.
[23] 42 U.S.C. § 2000e-2(a)(2).
[24] 401 U.S. 424 (1971).
[25] 102 S. Ct. at 2531.

When an employer uses a nonjob-related barrier in order to deny a minority or woman applicant employment or promotion, and that barrier has a significant adverse effect on minorities or women, then the applicant has been deprived of an employment *opportunity* "because of . . . race, color, religion, sex, or national origin."[26]

The majority stressed that in disparate impact cases the Court has consistently focused on requirements that create a discriminatory bar to individual *opportunities* and had never required the focus to be on the overall number of minorities or females actually hired or promoted. In this regard, the majority criticized the argument that disparate impact should be measured only at the bottom line of the selection process, stating that this "ignores the fact that Title VII guarantees these individual respondents the *opportunity* to compete equally with white workers on the basis of job-related criteria."[27] Thus, the Court concluded that the employees' rights under section 703(a)(2) were violated, unless the State could show that "the examination given was not an artificial, arbitrary, or unnecessary barrier, because it measured skills related to effective performance in the role of Welfare Eligibility Supervisor."[28]

The majority also rejected the suggestion of the United States,[29] as amicus curiae, that section 703(h)[30] of Title VII provided a defense to the State. Section 703(h) provides that it is not unlawful "to give and to act upon the results of any professionally developed ability test provided that such test, its administration or action upon the results is not designed, intended or used to discriminate." The Government had argued that the written test was not "used to discriminate" because it did not disproportionately deprive blacks of promotions. The majority, however, citing its conclusion in *Griggs* that section 703(h) protected only those tests which were job related, stated that:

> A nonjob-related test that has a disparate impact, and is used to "limit" or "classify" employees, is "used to discriminate" within the meaning of Title VII, whether or not it was "designed or intended" to have this effect and despite

---

[26] *Id.* at 2532.
[27] *Id.* at 2533.
[28] *Id.*
[29] The amicus brief filed by the United States was submitted by the Department of Justice. The Equal Employment Opportunity Commission (EEOC) expressly declined to join the brief.
[30] 42 U.S.C. § 2000e-2(h).

an employer's efforts to compensate for its discriminatory effect.[31]

The majority declined to impose an additional burden on plaintiffs for establishing a prima facie case or to recognize an affirmative defense in instances where the employer, despite the disparate impact of a component of a selection process, has a nondiscriminatory bottom line. To do so, the majority wrote, would be to redefine the protections guaranteed by Title VII.

The majority stated that the focus of Title VII is the protection of the individual employee rather than protection of the protected group as a whole. The majority drew no distinction in this regard between the protection of such individual rights under either a disparate treatment or disparate impact theory of discrimination. Instead, relying on a line of disparate treatment cases, the majority averred that every *individual* employee is protected against both discriminatory treatment and facially neutral practices which have a discriminatory impact.[32] Indeed, the majority indicated that the need for protection of the individual may be even greater when facially neutral procedures are used because "[r]equirements and tests that have a discriminatory impact are merely some of the more subtle, but also the more pervasive of the 'practices and devices which have fostered racially stratified job environments to the disadvantage of minority citizens.' " [33]

The suggestion that a nondiscriminatory bottom line may be a defense against an individual employee's claim is to confuse unlawful discrimination with discriminatory intent, the majority asserted. It declined to defer to the bottom line approach adopted by the federal enforcement agencies in the Uniform Guidelines, finding that the Guidelines expressly do not address the underlying question of law.[34] The Court, however, reaffirmed that a nondiscriminatory bottom line and an employer's good faith efforts to achieve a balanced workforce, might assist an employer in rebutting the inference in a disparate treatment case that a particular employment action was *intentionally* discriminatory. But under Title VII, the Court stated, "[a] racially balanced work force cannot immunize an employer from

---

[31] 102 S. Ct. at 2534.
[32] *Id.* at 2535. *See Los Angeles Department of Water & Power v. Manhart*, 435 U.S. 702, 708 (1978); *Furnco Construction Corp. v. Waters*, 438 U.S. 567, 580 (1978); *International Brotherhood of Teamsters v. United States*, 431 U.S. 324, 340 n.20 (1977); *Phillips v. Martin-Marietta Corp.*, 400 U.S. 542 (1971)(*per curiam*).
[33] 102 S. Ct at 2535 *quoting McDonnell Douglas Corp. v. Green*, 411 U.S. at 800.
[34] *Id.* at 2534 n.12.

liability for specific acts of discrimination,"[35] including the adverse results of facially neutral practices. Nor under the majority's opinion does affirmative action or favorable treatment of other members of a plaintiff's protected class insulate an employer from liability based on a disparate impact theory. Equating disparate treatment and disparate impact, the majority stated:

> Title VII does not permit the victim of a facially discriminatory policy to be told that he has not been wronged because other persons of his or her race or sex were hired. That answer is no more satisfactory when it is given to victims of a policy that is facially neutral but practically discriminatory.[36]

The Dissenting Opinion

Justice Powell, in a dissenting opinion joined by Chief Justice Burger and Justices Rehnquist and O'Connor, maintained that the majority decision blurs the distinction between disparate impact and disparate treatment cases. The dissent argued that in each disparate impact case which the Court has decided, it had looked not to whether an individual had been unlawfully classified, but rather to whether there had been an impact on the group to which the employee belongs. "Thus, while disparate-*treatment* cases focus on the way in which an individual has been treated, disparate-*impact* cases are concerned with the protected group."[37]

The dissent highlighted the fact that the Court's previous consideration of disparate impact cases had consistently focused on whether the *total selection process* had an adverse impact on a protected group.[38] Disagreeing with the reasoning of the majority, the dissent argues that:

> The Court, disregarding the distinction drawn by our cases, repeatedly asserts that Title VII was designed to protect individual, not group, rights. It emphasizes that some individual blacks were eliminated by the disparate impact of the preliminary test. But this argument confuses the *aim* of Title VII with the legal theories through which its aims

---

[35] *Id.* quoting *Furnco Construction Corp. v. Waters*, 438 U.S. at 579.
[36] *Id.*
[37] *Id.* at 2536.
[38] *Id.* & n.2. The dissent cited *Dothard v. Rawlinson*, 433 U.S. 321, 329 (1977); *Albemarle Paper Co. v. Moody*, 422 U.S. 405, 409-11 (1975); and *Griggs v. Duke Power Co.*, 401 U.S. at 431 for this principle.

were intended to be vindicated. It is true that the aim of Title VII is to protect individuals, not groups. But in advancing this commendable objective, Title VII jurisprudence has recognized two distinct methods of proof. In one set of cases—those involving direct proof of discriminatory intent—the plaintiff seeks to establish direct, intentional discrimination against him. In that type case, the individual is at the forefront throughout the entire presentation of evidence. In disparate impact cases, by contrast, the plaintiff seeks to carry his burden of proof by way of *inference*—by showing that an employer's selection process results in the rejection of a disproportionate number of members of a protected group to which he belongs. From such a showing a fair inference then may be drawn that the rejected applicant, as a member of that disproportionately excluded group, was himself a victim of that process's " 'built-in head winds.' " But this method of proof—which actually *defines* disparate impact theory under Title VII—invites the plaintiff to prove discrimination by reference to the group rather than to the allegedly affected individual. There can be no violation of Title VII on the basis of disparate impact in the absence of disparate impact on a *group*.[39]

The dissent asserted that regardless of whether a plaintiff's prima facie case focuses on the results of the overall selection process or on a single pass-fail component with a discriminatory impact, the employer's evidence showing that its overall selection process contained no discriminatory impact dispels any inference of discrimination which may have arisen from the plaintiff's evidence. The dissent would hold that under such circumstances the plaintiff has failed to show by a preponderance of the evidence that the selection process had adverse impact.[40]

---

[39] *Id.* at 2537 (citation and footnotes omitted). The dissent later in its opinion further explained:

> Our cases, cited above, have made clear that discriminatory-impact claims cannot be based on how an individual is treated in isolation from the treatment of other members of the group. Such claims necessarily are based on whether the group fares less well than other groups under a policy, practice, or test. Indeed, if only one minority member has taken a test, a disparate-impact claim cannot be made, regardless of whether the test is an initial step in the selection process or one of several factors considered by the employer in making an employment decision.

Id. at 2539 (footnote omitted).
[40] *Id.* & n.3.

The dissent would reaffirm earlier holdings of the Court that "Title VII does not require that employers adopt merit hiring or the procedures most likely to permit the greatest number of minority members to be considered for or to qualify for jobs and promotions."[41] It stated that "[e]mployers need not develop tests that accurately reflect the skills of every individual candidate" recognizing that "there are few if any tests that do so."[42] The majority, it averred, seemed unaware of this practical reality.

Finally, the dissent contends that the majority decision may force employers to eliminate tests entirely or to rely on expensive, job-related testing which may not be upheld if challenged. The dissent leaves open the possibility of integrating test scores into one overall cumulative score, which it states would not result in a finding of discrimination under the majority opinion unless the overall result had an adverse impact. However, the dissent notes that "if employers integrate test results into a single-step decision, they will be free to select *only* the number of minority candidates proportional to their representation in the workforce."[43] The dissent points out that the decision ironically may result in employers selecting fewer minority members than they might have if the bottom line defense had been accepted. Moreover, in the minority's view, the practical effect of the Court's decision may be quota hiring by state and local employers. This arbitrary method of employment is unfair to all applicants regardless of race, sex, or national origin, it argued, and "is not likely to produce a competent workforce."[44]

TITLE VII LITIGATION STANDARDS AFTER *TEAL*

Prior to the Supreme Court's decision in *Teal*, most employers and many officials in the federal enforcement agencies, as well as many other proponents of affirmative action in employment, believed that the bottom line approach adhered to by the agencies and by most courts provided a strong incentive to the employment of greater numbers of minorities and women. Under most circumstances, an employer, by maintaining a nondiscriminatory bottom line in its selection process, could ensure that the individual components of its selection process, including written tests, would not be evaluated separately. Thus, an employer with a nondiscriminatory bot-

---

[41] *Id.* at 2539 *citing Texas Dept. of Community Affairs v. Burdine*, 450 U.S. 248, 258-59 (1981); *Furnco*, 438 U.S. at 578.
[42] *Id.*
[43] *Id.* at 2540 n.8.
[44] *Id.* at 2540.

tom line was given more latitude in the procedures or standards that it used to select individuals for hire, promotion or other employment opportunities.

A nondiscriminatory bottom line also meant that an employer did not have to demonstrate the job relatedness or validity of various components of its selection process or the process as a whole. Many employers also found that the maintenance of a nondiscriminatory bottom line was helpful in meeting their affirmative action obligations under Executive Order 11246 and other affirmative action statutes, regulations or orders. Finally, a nondiscriminatory bottom line provided insulation to an employer from lawsuits alleging the adverse effect of a component of the process or the process as a whole.

Thus, persons who were eliminated by a component of a selection process could prevail only if they could demonstrate that the employer had engaged in discriminatory *treatment* by intentionally discriminating against them. On the other hand, the advantages that protected groups derived from a satisfactory bottom line were substantial. Many employers took steps to ensure that their bottom lines were without impact on those groups, with the resultant employment of increasing numbers of minorities and females. The decision in *Teal* has required those employers who have relied on a bottom line approach to reevaluate their entire selection process and to determine what, if any, changes should be made in light of *Teal*.

The principal legal effect of *Teal* on employers is that a facially neutral component of a selection process, *i.e.*, one that is not on its face discriminatory, that acts as a barrier to some employment opportunity and also has an adverse effect may be challenged by an individual screened out by the component even if the overall result of the selection process has no adverse impact, or, indeed, even if it favors minority employees. Thus, the first step that employers should take after *Teal* is to evaluate any pass-fail components of their selection process to determine whether the components are facially neutral procedures which may be subjected to a disparate impact analysis such as was undertaken on the written test results in *Teal*.[45]

---

[45] A cautious employer may also want to conduct such an analysis of components of its selection process which do not serve as a pass-fail hurdle but are part of a cumulatively-scored process. Even though the dissent in *Teal* stated that employers could integrate components or factors into an overall selection decision without fear of a finding of discrimination on the basis of the adverse effect of the component or factor unless the total selection process resulted in disparate impact, the Court's decision does not address this issue directly. But as has been cogently observed:

> Even in a cumulatively scored application process, a score on any single component might be so low as to preclude the accumulation of a total score meeting a minimum hiring requirement, . . . or a total score at

This initial evaluation to determine whether any facially neutral components may be susceptible to an adverse impact analysis is particularly important because of the different methods and burdens of proof involved in disparate impact and disparate treatment cases.

Burdens of Proof

The adverse or disparate impact method of proof under Title VII is used to attack employment selection criteria that are facially neutral or "fair in form," yet fall more harshly on a protected class of employees.[46] In order to establish a claim of disparate impact, a plaintiff must show that a facially neutral employment practice produces a significant adverse impact on a protected group of employees. The employer's intent to discriminate against a class of employees is not at issue.[47] Once the plaintiff has demonstrated the adverse impact of the selection procedure or criteria, the employer then has the burden of proving that the selection procedure is justified by a legitimate business reason or "business necessity."[48] As discussed below, this burden is substantially more difficult to satisfy than the employer's rebuttal burden in a disparate treatment case. If the employer establishes the job relatedness of the selection procedure, the burden of persuasion then shifts to the plaintiff to show that selection procedures with less adverse impact were available that would meet the employer's legitimate interest in efficiency and quality.

In contrast, the disparate treatment method of proof places a heavier burden of proof on the plaintiff because the burden of persuasion remains at all times with the plaintiff. In a disparate treatment analysis, a plaintiff must demonstrate a discriminatory motive or intent on the part of the employer. Once the plaintiff establishes a prima facie case of intentional discrimination by a preponderance of the evidence, the burden that shifts to the defendant is merely to produce evidence that the plaintiff was rejected for legitimate, nondiscriminatory reasons.[49] The evidence offered by the defendant need

---

least equal to that of the lowest scoring applicant who was hired. The fact that test scores are cumulated in an application process would not itself prevent scrutiny of a component, if that type of investigation were legally required.

Brown v. New Haven Civil Service Bd., 474 F. Supp. 1256, 1262 (D. Conn. 1979).
[46] *See, e.g., International Brotherhood of Teamsters v. United States*, 431 U.S. 324, 335 n.15 (1977).
[47] *Griggs*, 401 U.S. at 432.
[48] *Id.* at 431.
[49] *Texas Department of Community Affairs v. Burdine*, 450 U.S. 248 (1981).

not be sufficient to persuade the court of the legitimacy of the reasons, but the articulated reason must be clear and reasonably specific and admitted into evidence.[50]

In *Pouncy v. Prudential Insurance Company*,[51] the Fifth Circuit emphasized the importance of the distinction between disparate impact and disparate treatment cases. The plaintiff in *Pouncy* alleged that Prudential's performance appraisal and promotion system involved the use of subjective criteria, which had resulted in discrimination against the plaintiff specifically and disparate impact against blacks as a group. The plaintiff also alleged that Prudential's salary system resulted in class discrimination against minorities. The Fifth Circuit determined that "like the parties, the trial judge incorrectly employed a disparate impact analysis in deciding classwide claims which were properly viewed only as allegations of disparate treatment."[52] The court found that the plaintiff had not shown that an identifiable, facially neutral employment practice used by Prudential had an adverse effect on blacks. It held that none of the employment practices identified by the plaintiff—the failure to post job openings, the use of a level system, and the evaluation of employees with subjective criteria—constituted facially neutral employment practices to which the disparate impact theory could be applied. Consequently, the court evaluated plaintiff's claims under the more stringent disparate treatment standard and found for the defendant. Although it recognized that statistical evidence may be adequate to establish a prima facie case of disparate treatment, the court cautioned that the statistical evidence must be extremely strong to support the inference of intentional discrimination.[53] At least four other circuits have adopted the *Pouncy* reasoning concerning the distinction between claims of disparate impact and disparate treatment.[54]

The Fifth Circuit in *Pouncy* gave several examples of selection criteria which may be subjected to an adverse impact analysis. Mentioned by the court were aptitude and intelligence tests,[55] educa-

---

[50] *See* 450 U.S. at 254-58.
[51] 668 F.2d 795 (5th Cir. 1982).
[52] *Id.* at 797 n.1.
[53] *Id.* at 802. *See also Gay v. Waiters' Union*, 29 FEP Cases 1027, 1042 (9th Cir. August 24, 1982)("Although statistical data may, in a proper case, be sufficient alone to raise a prima facie case, the statistics must be considerably more stark than those involved here.").
[54] *Harris v. Ford Motor Co.*, 651 F.2d 609 (8th Cir. 1981); *Pope v. City of Hickory, N.C.*, 679 F.2d 20 (4th Cir. 1982); *Mortensen v. Callaway*, 672 F.2d 822 (10th Cir. 1982); *O'Brien v. Sky Chefs, Inc.*, 670 F.2d 864 (9th Cir. 1982).
[55] *See Griggs v. Duke Power Co.*, 401 U.S. 424 (1971).

tional requirements,[56] minimum height and weight requirements,[57] an employer's refusal to employ persons who use methadone,[58] credit ratings and arrest records. It should be emphasized that the absence of an identifiable facially neutral selection criterion will not prevent a plaintiff from alleging and seeking to prove under a disparate treatment theory that the employer has engaged in intentional discrimination. However, as noted above, the burden of proof on a plaintiff in disparate treatment cases is substantially greater than in disparate impact cases, and the Supreme Court in *Teal* acknowledged that a nondiscriminatory bottom line may be probative in rebutting the inference that particular actions were motivated by a discriminatory intent.[59] The reader is cautioned that the *Pouncy* reasoning regarding the difference between disparate impact and disparate treatment claims has not been adopted in all circuits, although it has been accepted in the circuits that have expressly considered the distinction.[60] Even in those circuits that have adopted a *Pouncy*-type analysis, defendants can expect claimants to attempt to portray selection practices as "facially neutral" devices susceptible to a disparate impact analysis. Thus, employers should remain prepared to rebut both disparate impact and treatment approaches while arguing that a *Pouncy* analysis mandates that all but true facially neutral practices be examined under a disparate treatment theory.

Business Necessity and Other Defenses

Consequently, as a first step, employers after *Teal* should evaluate the individual components of their selection process to determine whether they are susceptible to a disparate impact analysis. If an identifiable facially neutral selection criterion has a disparate effect and serves as a pass-fail hurdle, the employer should then determine whether the observed differences in rates of selection are

---

[56] *Id.*
[57] *See Dothard v. Rawlinson*, 433 U.S. 321 (1977).
[58] *See New York City Transit Authority v. Beazer*, 440 U.S. 568 (1979).
[59] 102 S. Ct. at 2535. In *Pouncy*, 668 F.2d at 804, the Fifth Circuit noted the steady increase in the percentage of black employees in all levels of Prudential's workforce and concluded that such evidence was inconsistent with any policy of discrimination during the time period relevant to the suit.
[60] *But cf. Rowe v. Cleveland Pneumatic Co.*, 29 FEP Cases 1682, 1685-86 (6th Cir. Oct. 20, 1982)(The subjective evaluations of foremen in considering rehires were analyzed under both disparate treatment and disparate impact theories because the appellate court noted that many TitleVII cases involving subjective evaluations have been analyzed under the disparate impact doctrine).

practically and statistically significant.[61] If a statistically significant impact does exist, the employer must demonstrate the job relatedness or business necessity of the practice in question.[62] In many instances, this will involve demonstrating validity of a written test instrument in accordance with the complex validation requirements of the Uniform Guidelines.[63]

After *Teal*, the employer remains free to show that the challenged component of the selection process which has adverse impact is valid (*i.e.*, job related) or otherwise justified by federal law. In *Teal*, the district court heard extensive testimony on the validity of the written test at issue, but expressly declined to rule on the validity issue, relying instead on the employer's nondiscriminatory bottom

---

[61] *See, e.g., Hazelwood School District v. United States*, 433 U.S. 299 (1977). A violation of the four-fifths or eighty percent rule under the Uniform Guidelines alone should be viewed as merely establishing a numerical basis for drawing an initial inference of adverse impact and for requiring additional information and not as conclusive evidence of adverse impact. Question and Answer 19, 43 Fed. Reg. 11996 (March 2, 1979), clarifying the Uniform Guidelines. The reader is cautioned, however, that if the four-fifths rule violation is all the evidence that a court has before it, it may find the violation probative of disparate impact. *See Rich v. Martin Marietta Corp.*, 467 F. Supp. 587, 612 (D. Colo. 1979). *See also, Hazelwood*, 433 U.S. at 307-08 ("Where gross [percentage] statistical disparities can be shown, they alone in a proper case constitute prima facie proof of a pattern or practice of discrimination.").

[62] The courts have adopted two inconsistent standards of business necessity. The first business necessity standard requires a showing that the practice is absolutely necessary or essential to the operation of the business. *See, e.g., Kirby v. Colony Furn. Co.*, 613 F.2d 696 (8th Cir. 1980); *Parson v. Kaiser Aluminum & Chemical Corp.*, 575 F.2d 1374, 1389 (5th Cir. 1978), *cert. denied*, 441 U.S. 968 (1979); *United States v. Bethlehem Steel Corp.*, 446 F.2d 652, 662 (2d Cir. 1971). The second standard equates business necessity with job relatedness and does not require the employment practice to be indispensable to job performance. *See, e.g., Contreras v. City of Los Angeles*, 656 F.2d 1267 (9th Cir. 1981), *cert. denied*, 102 S. Ct. 1719 (1982); *Chrisner v. Complete Auto Transit, Inc.*, 645 F.2d 1251 (6th Cir. 1981); *Spurlock v. United Airlines*, 475 F.2d 216 (10th Cir. 1972).

After *Teal*, the second standard would appear to be the proper standard, for the Court stated:

> Therefore, respondents' rights under § 703(a)(2) have been violated, unless petitioners can demonstrate that the examination given was not an artificial, arbitrary, or unnecessary barrier, because it measured *skills related to effective performance* in the role of Welfare Eligibility Supervisor.

102 S. Ct. at 2533 (emphasis added). *See also Griggs*, 401 U.S. at 431 ("If an employment practice which operates to exclude Negroes cannot be shown to be *related to job performance*, the practice is prohibited.")(emphasis added); *cf. Albemarle*, 422 U.S. at 431 (The "standard for job relatedness" is "that discriminatory tests are impermissible unless shown by professionally acceptable methods to be 'predictive of or significantly correlated with important elements of work behavior which comprise or are relevant to the job or jobs for which candidates are being evaluated.' ").

[63] 29 C.F.R. § 1607.14.

line as a defense. The Second Circuit, after finding that a nondiscriminatory bottom line was no defense to the claim of adverse impact of the written test component, remanded the case so that the district court could "evaluate the job-relatedness of the written examination in accordance with the EEOC Guidelines."[64] Accordingly, the State of Connecticut on remand still can prevail if it can demonstrate that the test is valid or job related.

Because plaintiffs may now establish a prima facie case based on the results of a facially neutral, pass-fail component even if the overall selection results show no adverse impact, establishing a prima facie case of disparate impact is now easier than before *Teal*.[65] The Supreme Court's decision in *Teal*, therefore, places increased emphasis on the validation of selection procedures, such as written tests, which have adverse impact.[66] The recent report of the National Academy of Sciences on *Ability Testing*[67] highlights the dilemma that this presents for employers. The *Ability Testing* report was the result of over three years work by a distinguished multidisciplinary group established under the auspices of the National Research Council and charged with the responsibility of conducting a broad examination of the role of testing in American society. The report concluded that as long as minority groups protected by Title VII continue to have a relatively high proportion of less educated and

---

[64] *Teal v. Connecticut*, 645 F.2d at 140.
[65] See bottom line cases cited in note 17, *supra*.
[66] Richard T. Sampson and Kathleen Pontone of the law firm of Semmes, Bowen & Semmes, in a paper prepared for a workshop for members of the Division of Industrial and Organizational Psychology of the American Psychological Association in August 1982 have commented:

> [T]houghtful practitioners have been advising their clients to validate any testing used for some time now . . . . To many attorneys specializing in the defense of Title VII litigation, the *Teal* decision was not a surprise. The Court has long held to the fundamental premise enunciated in *Griggs* and its progeny that where a selection process has an adverse impact, it must be demonstrated to be job related in order to be lawful. If an easily identifiable component of a selection process similarly had adverse impact, then that component must be demonstrated to be job related and to be a valid predictor of subsequent performance on the job. Many defense lawyers have been amazed that professional personnel practitioners have objected to this principle. It seems a matter of irresistible logic that if a selection process cannot be demonstrated to be job related, that it has little, if any, business utility. An employer has no reason to administer a test unless it does in fact have some business utility. It naturally then follows that an employer should be called upon to demonstrate the job relatedness of a selection component where its use has been called into question on the basis of its adverse impact on a particular group.

[67] See note 1, *supra*.

more disadvantaged members of society, these facts are likely to be reflected in test scores so that even highly valid tests will have adverse impact.[68] This finding is consistent with the experience of many employers who have found that standardized tests generally have resulted in adverse impact on one or more groups protected by Title VII.

In an effort to avoid the costly, time-consuming and uncertain process of test validation, many employers before *Teal* relied on a nondiscriminatory bottom line to support their selection procedures and to insulate them from lawsuits based on the impact of written tests. Because few tests with adverse impact had been shown to meet the stringent standards set forth in the Uniform Guidelines,[69] even those employers attempting to validate tests saw the bottom line option as the most certain defense. Because *Teal* has removed this defense from liability except possibly with respect to cumulatively-scored selection processes, the standards which govern whether a selection procedure has been shown to be valid or job related have become even more critical.

The burden which the courts and the enforcement agencies, through the Uniform Guidelines, have placed on employers for demonstrating the validity or job relatedness of selection procedures with adverse effect has been an extremely heavy one. Even the largest employers, whose staffs of industrial psychologists can provide "state-of-the-art" assistance in developing and validating selection procedures, have found it nearly impossible to comply fully with the requirements of the Guidelines. Prior to *Teal*, the *Ability Testing* report had noted that the rigid interpretation of the Guidelines by the enforcement agencies and the courts made it exceedingly difficult for test users to defend even such "state-of-the-art" testing procedures, and that good tests were being abandoned or struck down along with the bad.[70] The report cautioned that there was a significant danger that the abandonment of comparatively valid selection procedures because of pressures from the enforcement agencies would

---

[68] *Ability Testing*, Part I at 146. See also note 3, *supra*.
[69] *See, e.g., United States v. State of New York*, 21 FEP Cases 1286 (N.D. N.Y. 1979).
[70] *Ability Testing*, Part I at 146-47. In April 1976, David L. Rose, Chief of the Employment Section, Civil Rights Division, Department of Justice stated in a memorandum to the Deputy Attorney General:

> Under the present [1970] EEOC *Guidelines*, few employers are able to show the validity of any of their selection procedures, and the risk of their being held unlawful is high. Since not only tests, but all other procedures must be validated, the thrust of the present guidelines is to place almost all test users in a posture of noncompliance, to give great discretion to enforcement personnel to determine who would be prose-

result in a lowering of the morale of the workforce and the productivity of the economy.[71] Because most written tests will have adverse impact, after *Teal* there is a possibility that employers may be held liable each time they administer a written test on a screen-out basis, regardless of whether they have maintained a nondiscriminatory bottom line.

It is unclear after *Teal* if a different standard of job relatedness will be applied when an employer has a nondiscriminatory bottom line.[72] *Teal* states that the rights of the plaintiffs, who were screened out by the written test, have been violated "unless petitioners [the State] can demonstrate that the examination given was not an artificial, arbitrary, or unnecessary barrier, because it measured skills related to effective performance in the role of Welfare Eligibility Supervisor."[73] Some EEO practitioners have suggested that this burden may be less demanding than the standard imposed by some courts and administrative agencies. However, the "artificial, arbitrary and unnecessary" and "related to effective performance" language is taken from the Supreme Court's earlier opinion in *Griggs*.[74] Thus, this language may not signal any departure from the earlier standard established in *Griggs*. However, the language may send a message to those lower courts that have been applying the business necessity standard too stringently.[75]

Another possibility as a result of *Teal* is that the courts could adopt a sliding scale of job relatedness with respect to facially neutral, knockout components when there is no adverse impact at the bottom line. That is, the degree of job relatedness necessary to serve as a defense to a pass-fail component may be less if the bottom line

---

cuted, and to set aside objective selection procedures in favor of numerical hiring.
The 1970 EEOC Guidelines on Employee Selection Procedures, 35 Fed. Reg. 12333, referred to in the memorandum, were subsequently supplanted by the 1978 Uniform Guidelines. Former EEOC staff psychologist James C. Sharf, has commented, however, that: "While the *Uniform Guidelines* offer at least a choice between validation strategies that the 1970 EEOC *Guidelines* did not, the documentation requirements now add considerably to the likelihood that a full compliance review will find an employer to be in noncompliance. . . ." James C. Sharf, "Personnel Testing and the Law" in *Personnel Management* (K. Rowland & J. Ferris, eds.) (1982) at 178.
[71] *Ability Testing*, Part I at 147. One recent study estimates that an annual productivity increase between $43 billion and $75.7 billion could be achieved if all U.S. employers adopted ability-based selection standards. J.E.Hunter & F.L.Schmidt, "Fitting People to Jobs: The Impact of Personnel Selection on National Productivity" in *Human Performance and Productivity* (E.A.Fleishman, ed.) (1981).
[72] See note 62, *supra*.
[73] 102 S. Ct. at 2533.
[74] 401 U.S. at 431.
[75] See note 62, *supra*.

is nondiscriminatory.[76] Such an approach is supported by language in earlier Supreme Court precedent. In *Albemarle*, the Court stated that "[t]he question of job relatedness must be viewed in the context of the plant's operation and the history of the testing program."[77] There, the test perpetuated overt discrimination and the Court held that rigorous adherence to the requirements of the EEOC's 1970 Selection Guidelines was required. On the other hand, where as in *Teal* there is not a demonstrated history of past or present overt discrimination and the bottom line favors the plaintiff's class the probative value of the plaintiff's prima facie case is less. Accordingly, the degree of job relatedness required under Title VII to rebut the plaintiff's prima facie case should be less than under a *Albemarle* fact pattern. How much less would depend on the facts and circumstances of each case.[78]

Lower courts have recognized, moreover, that there are degrees of job relatedness[79] and that compliance with Title VII does not require that selection procedures conform in all respects with the Uniform Guidelines and professional practices, but only with "the essential purposes of Title VII."[80] Furthermore, as a technical matter

---

[76] Alternatively, Professor Alfred W. Blumrosen, former consultant to the EEOC, has suggested that a "rational relationship" standard should be applied in the absence of "overall adverse impact." Under Blumrosen's paradigm:

> The loose sense in which many tests can be considered to be "job related" on rational grounds involves an overall judgment that employees who can pass a particular hurdle are likely to be better qualified than those who cannot, but it does not require either detailed statistical evidence, or immediately obvious intuitive evidence, to back it up, which the EEOC Guidelines require. Nevertheless, there is a "tissue of rationality" in the connection between the test and the job. This tissue of rationality does *not* justify denying employment opportunities to minorities and women, where the entire selection process has an adverse impact. In that situation rigorous analyses and findings to demonstrate "job relatedness" are necessary to justify the effect on minorities or women. This was the case in both *Griggs* and in *Albemarle*.
>
> But where the "bottom line" is satisfied, the justification for a selection procedure need not be so detailed. More general considerations of job relatedness, which would not meet the standards of the Guidelines, may satisfy the requirement of *Teal*.

Daily Lab. Rep. D-5 (August 27, 1982) (footnotes omitted).
[77] 422 U.S. at 427.
[78] This is not inconsistent with the conclusion of the Supreme Court that statistics used to establish a prima facie case of discrimination may have differing degrees of probative value depending on their statistical significance and the level of qualifications of the job. See *Hazelwood*, 433 U.S. at 308 nn. 13 & 14; *Teamsters*, 431 U.S. at 339 n.20.
[79] See *Vulcan Society v. Civil Service Commission*, 490 F.2d 387, 396 (2d Cir. 1973); *Baker v. City of Detroit*, 483 F. Supp. 930, 974 (E.D. Mich. 1979).
[80] *Guardians Ass'n of New York City v. Civil Service*, 630 F.2d 79, 110 (2d Cir. 1980), cert. denied, 101 S. Ct. 3083 (1981).

of test validation, there are degrees of job relatedness. One method of demonstrating the "validity" of a test is by demonstrating a statistically significant correlation between test scores, for example, and job success. Such correlations exist on a continuum from −1 to +1, with +1 evidencing a perfect correlation of test scores with job success. Different selection procedures or criteria may have different statistically significant correlations for job success. All may be job related but to different degrees. In sum, case law and the practical realities of validation of selection procedures justify courts applying a sliding scale of job relatedness, especially when there is no adverse impact at the actual point of the selection decision(s).

The increased emphasis which *Teal* has placed on the validation of all facially neutral selection procedures that constitute screen-outs and that have disparate impact has made it imperative that the enforcement agencies and the courts devise workable validation standards that are capable of attainment given the current level of expertise of employers and members of the psychological profession who develop and validate tests. To do otherwise creates substantial incentives for employers to use less objective or subjective selection standards unrelated to productivity and which may offer greater opportunities for discrimination. As the *Ability Testing* report noted, "[i]t is disingenuous to impose test validation requirements that employers, even with the best will and a sizable monetary investment, cannot meet."[81] To demand a higher level of test development and validation than is currently attainable serves no purpose other than to place virtually all employers in a posture of noncompliance.

Determination of the Plaintiff's Entitlement to Relief

In many employment discrimination class actions, the courts bifurcate the issue of the defendant's liability: Stage I determines the employer's liability and Stage II determines individual entitlement to backpay and other relief. In *Teamsters*, the Supreme Court discussed the standards of proof for individual relief after the plaintiff has proven the employer's liability in Stage I. Once the plaintiff shows that he or she unsuccessfully applied for a position, "the burden then rests on the employer to demonstrate that the individual applicant was denied employment for lawful reasons."[82] This essentially involves a recreation by the court of the conditions and relationships that would have occurred had there been no unlawful

---

[81] *Ability Testing*, Part I at 107.
[82] 431 U.S. at 362.

discrimination.[83] "[T]he court [is] required to balance the equities of each minority employee's situation in allocating the limited number of vacancies that were discriminatorily refused to class members."[84] In usual circumstances, the burden on the plaintiff in the Stage II trial is to show that he or she applied for and was qualified for the position. The employer's rebuttal burden is to justify its decision not to hire or promote the plaintiff(s).

Teal can be distinguished from prior Supreme Court disparate impact cases where the allegation was that the plaintiff was unlawfully denied the *position* in question[85] and cases in which the plaintiff participates in the entire selection process. The *opportunity* that is denied in bottom line cases such as *Teal*, involving the adverse impact of components of a selection process, is the opportunity to compete in the remainder of the selection process with the candidates who successfully completed the written test component, rather than selection for the job itself. Thus, after *Teal* it apparently remains open to the state to demonstrate that even if the plaintiffs had been allowed to compete in the remainder of the selection process, they would not have been selected because the white candidates chosen were better qualified for the positions. This could involve a comparison by the parties and the district court of the relative qualifications of the candidates in order to determine whether any or all of the plaintiffs actually would have received promotions had they been allowed to compete in the remainder of the selection process after the written examination. This comparison could include the factors of past work performance, supervisors' recommendations and seniority that constituted the remaining components of the selection process, as well as such other factors as the parties and the district court may deem appropriate. Only if it is determined by this comparison that any or all of the plaintiffs would have been promoted had they not been screened out by the written test would the plaintiffs be entitled to selection for the position sought, together with such other equitable relief as the court may deem appropriate.[86] On

---

[83] *Id.* at 371-72.
[84] *Id.* at 372.
[85] *See, e.g., Griggs*, 401 U.S. at 431; *Albemarle*, 422 U.S. at 409-11; *Dothard*, 433 U.S. at 329.
[86] Professor Blumrosen has suggested alternatively that the sequence of proof might involve the following:

> (1) All qualifications of the whites who were promoted must be disclosed by the employer.
> (2) The plaintiffs should then indicate which of the white employees, in their view, would not have been promoted under non-discriminatory selection procedures. The parties will then be at issue over whether

remand in *Teal*, this comparison would not appear to be a difficult one because it would involve only the four plaintiffs and the thirty-five white candidates who received promotions. In other cases involving larger numbers of claimants and employment decisions, this task may be substantially more difficult to complete.

EFFECT OF *TEAL* ON AFFIRMATIVE ACTION

One irony of *Teal* is that, based on the facts presented, it would appear that both blacks and whites could establish claims under Title VII based on the results of the same selection process.[87] As set forth above, blacks could establish a prima facie case based on the disparate impact of the written test. It would appear that white candidates also could have maintained a claim because, despite their passing the written test at a substantially higher rate than blacks, the actual promotion rate of blacks was nearly 170 percent of the actual promotion rate of whites. Thus, it would appear that whites would be able to establish a prima facie claim of disparate treatment with regard to the remainder of the selection process which was considered in making the actual promotions.[88]

---

these white employees would have been preferred over the blacks under non-discriminatory selection procedures.
(3) The burden of going forward with the evidence in support of the actions taken should be on the employer. Where the ultimate burden of persuasion lies on the question is not clear, but it may not matter. If the court is convinced one way or the other, the burden of persuasion is irrelevant. Only when the evidence is in equipoise need the court resort to the burden of persuasion. In that event, the burden of demonstrating that the individual blacks were not the "victims" of discrimination already found may lie with the employer.

Daily Lab. Rep. D-5 (August 27, 1982)(footnote omitted).
[87] The court's holding in *Teal* increases the likelihood that adverse impact can be established at some point of the selection process by one or more protected classes. For example, if blacks, whites, Hispanics, men and women apply for a job with five identifiable, objective pass-fail hurdles (*e.g.*, written test, experience, seniority, medical examination, and height-weight requirement) there are twenty-five possible circumstances in which adverse impact could occur albeit by sheer chance alone. This is the problem, widely acknowledged in statistical texts, of multiple comparisons. That is, if there are many opportunities for a "rare event" to occur, *i.e.*, adverse impact in some component of a selection process, and courts search for adverse impact in a sufficiently large universe, we should not be surprised if courts find that one component of a selection process has adverse impact even when the overall process has no such impact. *See, e.g.*, Miller, *Simultaneous Statistical Inference* (1977); Maxwell, *Analyzing Qualitative Data* (1977); and Feinberg, *The Analysis of Cross-Classified Categorical Data* (1977).
[88] Based on a *Pouncy* analysis, the State of Connecticut could have argued that a disparate impact analysis is inappropriate as to the adverse effect of the selection

Affirmative Action as a Defense

Athough the issue of reverse discrimination is not discussed by the Court in *Teal*, in instances where white plaintiffs in factual circumstances similar to *Teal* allege disparate impact or treatment, a private sector employer's affirmative action could serve in an appropriate case as a defense to such an action. In enacting Title VII, Congress sought to improve the employment opportunities of minorities and women by assuring that selection decisions were made in a nondiscriminatory manner. "Accordingly, it was clear to Congress that 'the crux of the problem [was] to open employment opportunities for Negroes in occupations which have been traditionally closed to them,' [110] Cong. Rec. 6548 (1964) (remarks of Sen. Humphrey), and it was to this problem that Title VII's prohibition against racial discrimination in employment was primarily addressed."[89] While affirmative action is not required by Title VII, once undertaken, it becomes relevant to an assessment of the selection process.

It is well-established that Title VII does not require an employer to establish the "best" hiring or promotion procedure that would permit it "to at least consider . . . the most minority candidates."[90] But in *Weber* and other cases the Court has stressed that the "primary" objective of Title VII is the removal of barriers to minorities "that have operated in the past to *favor* an identifiable group of *white* employees over other employees."[91] It is also clear that voluntary compliance is the "preferred means" of eliminating employment discrimination,[92] and that employers are encouraged to "self-examine and to self-evaluate their employment practices."[93]

In keeping with Title VII's policy of self-examination, the federal enforcement agencies have adopted policies that encourage voluntary compliance and affirmative action. For example, in the 1978 Uniform Guidelines, the enforcement agencies concluded that affirmative action to eliminate the adverse impact of a selection procedure is permissible under Title VII. Section 6 of the Uniform Guidelines

---

criteria of past work performance and supervisors' recommendations on white candidates because they are not facially neutral. Instead, a disparate treatment theory should be applied. *See* pp. 176-177, *supra*. Of course, if facially neutral criteria are involved, the white candidates could proceed under either a disparate impact or a disparate treatment theory of discrimination.

[89] *United Steelworkers v. Weber*, 443 U.S. 193, 203 (1979).
[90] *Furnco*, 438 U.S. at 578.
[91] *Griggs*, 401 U.S. 429-30 (emphasis added); *Albemarle*, 422 U.S. at 417; and *Weber*, 443 U.S. at 204.
[92] *Alexander v. Gardner-Denver Co.*, 415 U.S. 36, 44 (1974).
[93] *Teamsters*, 431 U.S. at 364; and *Weber*, 443 U.S. at 204.

provides that where a selection procedure has adverse impact, the employer may (1) modify a formal, scored procedure such as a test to eliminate the adverse impact or (2) eliminate the adverse impact from unscored procedures, or (3) choose alternative selection procedures as part of an affirmative action program to eliminate the adverse impact.[94] Thus, the four federal enforcement agencies have encouraged employers to take affirmative action with respect to selection procedures having an adverse impact against minorities and women.

The EEOC's Affirmative Action Guidelines,[95] also encourage voluntary action. Section 1608.4 of the Guidelines provides that if self analysis shows that the employer's employment practices have or tend to have adverse effect, the employer may take reasonable action designed to correct the problem. Significantly, it is not necessary under the Guidelines that the self analysis establish a violation of Title VII.[96]

Thus, private employers faced with the circumstances presented in *Teal*, who analyze their workforce or applicant flow statistics and determine that there may be potential Title VII liability, may conclude that affirmative action is warranted so that their workforces more closely mirror the racial, ethnic or sexual composition of the qualified labor force in the relevant labor market. Even if it is not certain that an employer has discriminated, a self analysis of the surrounding circumstances may lead it to conclude that corrective action should be undertaken voluntarily. Relevant considerations

---

[94] 29 C.F.R. § 1607.6.
[95] 29 C.F.R. Part 1608.
[96] Reliance on the Affirmative Action Guidelines as the basis for taking affirmative action also invokes the "save harmless" provision, section 713(b) of TitleVII, 42 U.S.C. § 2000e-12(b). Under this section, employers who act in "good faith, in conformity with, and in reliance on any written interpretation or opinion of the EEOC" cannot be found in violation of TitleVII, even if the EEOC interpretation is later rejected by the courts. The Affirmative Action Guidelines expressly provide for section 713(b) protection for actions taken pursuant to the Guidelines. *See* 29 C.F.R. § 1608.2.

In addition to the voluntary equal employment mandate of Title VII, both public and private sector employers are also subject to various mandatory affirmative action requirements. Federal contractors at some 325,000 establishments are subject to the affirmative action obligations of Executive Order 11246, 30 Fed. Reg. 12319 (1965), *as amended by* 32 Fed. Reg. 14302 (1967) and 43 Fed. Reg. 46501 (1978). Unlike Title VII, the statistical imbalances that trigger these affirmative action requirements need not be connected to any showing of past or present discrimination. *See Hearings on S.2115, Before the Subcommittee on Labor of the Senate Committee on Labor and Public Welfare, 92d Cong. 1st Sess.* 77, 88 (1971); Nash, "Affirmative Action Under Executive Order 11246," 46 N.Y.U. L. Rev. 225, 229-230 (1971). Likewise public employers are subject to various state affirmative action statutes. *See, e.g.*, Conn. Stat. § 46a-68.

could include a desire to remedy the effects of past discrimination, the possibility of time consuming and costly processing of discrimination complaints, the uncertainty of the outcome of litigation, and a desire to avoid wasteful and expensive litigation. As the *Weber* decision indicates, the public policy of encouraging voluntary compliance could hardly be achieved if such actions were permitted only when discrimination could be established to a certainty.

In sum, affirmative action may properly serve as a defense to a private employer against putative white plaintiffs if the affirmative action is reasonable under the circumstances. That is, first, the affirmative action is "a temporary measure: it is not intended to maintain racial balance, but simply to eliminate manifest racial imbalance,"[97] and second, the affirmative action does not involve a quota or a specified number of selections from a particular racial, ethnic or sexual class.[98]

Two additional points should be kept in mind with regard to the selection process in *Teal* and with regard to affirmative action as a defense for public employers in general. First, the State of Connecticut expressly denied in its brief and oral argument before the Court that it took affirmative action in the portions of the selection process after the written test to overcome the impact on blacks which the written test produced.[99] Consequently, none of the courts discussed whether the job category in question exhibited a "demonstrable racial imbalance" which might have justified affirmative steps to increase the number of blacks in the position. In the absence of acknowledged affirmative action efforts and evidence of a job category with a demonstrable racial imbalance sufficient to justify such affirmative action, it would appear that an employer in the position in which the State of Connecticut was in *Teal* would be

---

[97] *Weber*, 443 U.S. at 208.
[98] *See Regents of the University of California v. Bakke*, 438 U.S. 265 (1978).
[99] This position was apparently taken because it viewed the Connecticut Human Rights and Opportunities Law, Title 46a-51, *et seq.*, Chapter 814c, Human Rights and Opportunities, Connecticut General Statutes, as an equal employment opportunity statute and not an affirmative action statute. The State apparently believed that to acknowledge that affirmative steps had been taken in the process after the written test to ensure the promotion of additional blacks would be to acknowledge that it had acted in excess of the state statute, as well as possibly in violation of the equal protection standards of the Fourteenth Amendment of the United States Constitution. The Supreme Court, however, noted that the Second Circuit had expressly found that the State used an affirmative action program to offset the effect of the written component of the selection process in order to ensure that a significant number of minority supervisors from the eligibility list resulting from the written examination were selected. The Court found it unnecessary to resolve this question. 102 S. Ct. at 2530 n.5.

subject to an action by whites who passed the test and failed to be promoted. Without an acknowledgment of affirmative action efforts designed to overcome a demonstrable racial imbalance in the job category, *Weber* would offer no defense to the employer.

The second point concerns the applicability of *Weber* to public sector employers. Because the affirmative action plan at issue in *Weber* did not involve state action, the case did not present an alleged violation of the Equal Protection Clause of the Fourteenth Amendment.[100] Because public employers are subject to the strictures of the Fourteenth Amendment, it is unclear to what extent, if any, public employers will be afforded protections similar to those afforded a private employer by *Weber*.[101]

Judicial Remedies

Another unaddressed and unanswered question raised by *Teal* is the extent to which the majority's emphasis on "individual" as opposed to "group" rights will affect the judicial relief which might be ordered in future employment discrimination cases. On numerous occasions courts have imposed "goals and timetables" or "quota" hiring or promotion relief after a finding of unlawful discrimination.[102] Many such cases have arisen in the public sector and often involved challenges to written tests which had an adverse effect on minorities. [103] "Goals and timetables" or "quotas" in such cases generally have involved relief over a specified number of years to a group which had been adversely affected by an employer's practices,

---

[100] *Weber*, 443 U.S. at 200.
[101] When Congress amended TitleVII in 1972 extending its nondiscriminatory requirements to state and local jurisdictions, "Congress expressly indicated the intent that the same TitleVII principles be applied to governmental and private employers alike." *Dothard v. Rawlinson*, 433 U.S. at 331 n. 14. See H.R. Rep. No. 92-238, 92d Cong., 1st Sess. 17 (1971); S. Rep. No. 92-415, 92d Cong., 1st Sess. 10 (1971). See also *Washington v. Davis*, 426 U.S. 229 (1976).

Several courts have concluded that a voluntary affirmative action plan implemented by a state employer will not violate TitleVII if it is valid under *Weber*. See *LaRivere v. EEOC*, 28 FEP Cases 1481, 1484 (9th Cir. 1982); *Detroit Police Officers Ass'n v. Young*, 608 F.2d 671, 688-90 (6th Cir. 1979), cert. denied, 101 S. Ct. 3079 (1981); *United States v. City of Miami*, 664 F.2d 435, 461 (5th Cir. 1981) (en banc).

[102] *See, e.g., United States v. City of Chicago*, 549 F.2d 415, 436-37 (7th Cir.), cert. denied sub nom. *Adams v. City of Chicago*, 434 U.S. 875 (1977); *Boston Chapter, NAACP, Inc. v. Beecher*, 504 F.2d 1017, 1026 (1st Cir. 1974), cert. denied sub nom. *Commissioners & Director of Civil Serv. v. Boston Chapter, NAACP, Inc.*, 421 U.S. 910 (1975); *Vulcan Society v. Civil Service Commission*, 490 F.2d 387, 398 (2d Cir. 1973).

[103] *See, e.g., Ass'n Against Discrimination v. City of Bridgeport*, 594 F.2d 306, 310 (2d Cir. 1979).

without regard to whether the individuals benefiting from such relief were the actual victims of such discrimination. Thus, some or all of the persons selected pursuant to such "goals" or "quotas" may not have applied for the position before the court's decision imposing "goal" or "quota" relief and, consequently, such persons may *not* have been actual victims of the employer's unlawful practices. It would appear, however, that the majority emphasis in *Teal* on "individual" as opposed to "group" rights under Title VII may be inconsistent with the award of "goal" or "quota" relief on such a group basis. In such instances, the "individual" rights emphasis in *Teal* may mandate that relief would only be available to identifiable victims of an employer's practices and not to that individual's race, sex or ethnic group as a whole. This is the position which the Department of Justice has taken on relief in Title VII cases.[104] However, *Teal* did not address the issue of relief and it is unclear whether the Court's reasoning on "individual" rights will carry over into the area of relief for proven violations.

Employment of Protected Classes and Maintaining the Bottom Line

While *Teal* was obviously intended by the Supreme Court majority to be a decision favorable to minority employment opportunities, it is open to serious question how the decision in the long run will affect the employment opportunities of minorities and females. Because a nondiscriminatory bottom line will no longer shield employers from liability for the adverse effect of a component of their selection processes, many employers may no longer view a nondiscriminatory bottom line to be as crucial to them as it was before *Teal*.

Many employers, especially those concerned with increasing productivity, may choose to place emphasis on validating the components of the selection process rather than on maintaining a nondiscriminatory bottom line. The use of valid selection procedures does not mean that such procedures will be without impact against groups protected under Title VII. In fact, as discussed previously, the *Ability Testing* study found that as long as minorities continue

---

[104] *See* "Administration Will Not Seek Job Quotas, Justice Official Tells House Subcommittee," Daily Lab. Rep. A-8 (September 23, 1981). *See also* briefs of the Department of Justice filed in the Supreme Court in *Beecher v. Boston Chapter NAACP*, Nos. 82-185, 82-246, 82-259 (S. Ct.), *reprinted* in Daily Lab. Rep. D-1 (December 17, 1982); and filed in the Fifth Circuit in *Williams v. City of New Orleans*, No. 82-3435 (5th Cir.) *reprinted* in Daily Lab. Rep. E-1 (January 10, 1983).

to have a relatively high proportion of less educated and more disadvantaged members of our society, those facts are likely to be reflected in test scores so that even highly valid tests will have adverse impact.[105] If an employer can demonstrate that a component of the selection process which has adverse effect is job related or valid, that showing will shield the employer from liability, not only based on the adverse effect of the component, but also in most instances from a suit based on an unsatisfactory bottom line. If the employer can show that an unsatisfactory bottom line is the result of the impact of a validated component of the process, then no cause of action would lie based on a discriminatory bottom line. Thus, perhaps the ultimate irony of *Teal* is that the substantial costs which employers may incur in order to conduct and defend validity studies to support selection components, might not, under the facts in *Teal*, result in the employment of any additional minorities or females, and may in fact result in the employment of fewer minorities and females. Given the limited funds available to all employers, it is quite possible that funds which might otherwise have gone to training, recruitment or other efforts to employ additional minorities and females, or to upgrade their job-related skills, will be shifted to test validation efforts.

Although *Teal* has reduced substantially the incentive of employers to maintain a nondiscriminatory bottom line, there do remain certain benefits which may be derived from a satisfactory bottom line. For employers covered by Executive Order 11246, for example, the efforts to maintain a satisfactory bottom line may be consistent, in many instances, with an employer's affirmative action obligations under the Order. Moreover, even the majority opinion noted that a nondiscriminatory bottom line may be probative in disparate treatment cases to demonstrate that a particular employment action was not motivated by discriminatory intent. As a practical matter, a nondiscriminatory bottom line may influence courts to accept more readily evidence of the job relatedness or validation of a selection component which has adverse effect.[106] Finally, and perhaps most importantly, a nondiscriminatory bottom line will be of substantial benefit if the enforcement agencies decide to continue their previously expressed intention to bring enforcement actions, in most instances, only against employers with a discriminatory bottom line, as discussed in the next section.

---

[105] *Ability Testing*, Part I at 146.
[106] *Compare Friend v. Leidinger*, 588 F.2d 61 (4th Cir. 1978) *with United States v. State of New York*, 21 FEP Cases 1286 (N.D.N.Y. 1979).

It is unclear at this point whether these remaining incentives for maintaining a nondiscriminatory bottom line will be sufficient to overcome the significant erosion of the protection from liability which *Teal* produced. A resolution of these competing concerns will determine over time whether *Teal* will have the favorable effect on the employment opportunities of minorities and females which the Court majority envisioned, or whether it will actually result in the employment of fewer minorities and females, as the dissent warned and as many observers fear.

REVISION OF THE UNIFORM GUIDELINES
The Bottom Line

Although *Teal* touched on a number of issues relating to the Uniform Guidelines, it is unclear whether the decision will result in substantial revisions of the Guidelines. With regard to the bottom line issue, the Guidelines currently provide that, in usual circumstances, the agencies will not take enforcement action against an employer based on the adverse impact of a component of a selection process where the overall process does not have adverse impact.[107] As recognized by the Court, the bottom line approach by the agencies, as set forth in the Guidelines, is based on the "exercise of their administrative and prosecutorial discretion" and is not a rule of law.[108] The *Teal* majority noted however, that the present Guidelines permit individual employees to file their own suits challenging selection components even when the overall process reveals no adverse impact against minorities and the federal agencies exercise their discretion not to prosecute.[109]

While it is clear after *Teal* that a private claimant (or the enforcement agencies) may establish a prima facie case under Title VII based upon the adverse effect of a pass-fail component of a multipart selection process, *Teal* does not control the agencies' discretion, as a matter of policy, to refrain from bringing enforcement actions where an employer's bottom line is nondiscriminatory.[110]

---

[107] 29 C.F.R. § 1607.4C.
[108] 102 S. Ct. at 2534 n.12.
[109] In this regard over 95 percent of all equal employment lawsuits are filed by individuals. Less than 5 percent are filed by the enforcement agencies.
[110] *See* OFCCP Order No. 660f12 (Jan. 4, 1983) at page 3, wherein the agency primarily charged with enforcement of Executive Order 11246 states:

> In the view of OFCCP, the *Teal* decision does not undercut or conflict with the Uniform Guidelines. . . . [R]egardless of the validity of the "bottom line" standard, the Government has elected that, in the usual case, it will not prosecute adverse impact in one element of a selection

Indeed, the bottom line approach to enforcement actions serves the interests of employers, the enforcement agencies and ultimately groups protected by Title VII. As mentioned above, the protection from suit by the enforcement agencies currently available to employers who possess a nondiscriminatory bottom line provides a major incentive for the employment of minorities and women in numbers approximating their representation in the relevant labor market. While the vulnerability to a lawsuit from private claimants lessens this incentive, it would be further eroded by the elimination of the protection from federal agency action and could result over a period of time in the employment of fewer minorities and women. Employers may currently be willing, in appropriate instances, to incur the added risks of "reverse discrimination" suits in order to reach an acceptable bottom line. They may not be willing to incur such risks if they still will face actions by the enforcement agencies.

The Search for Alternatives

Currently, the Uniform Guidelines place the burden of conducting an investigation of suitable alternative selection procedures on the employer.[111] This requirement has been established in contradiction of the Supreme Court's decision in *Albemarle Paper Co. v. Moody*,[112] which states that the burden placed by Title VII on employers is to show that a challenged selection device is job related or valid and not also to demonstrate that there are no available alternative selection devices with a lesser adverse effect. *Teal*, citing the Court's prior discussion of the issue in *Albemarle*, reinforces the position that the burden of conducting such a search rests with the plaintiff and the enforcement agencies and not with the employer.[113] While many employers and test users routinely conduct a search for available and acceptable alternative selection procedures *before* they decide which procedure to use to select persons, most employers have found that such a search *after* they have demonstrated the job relatedness of the challenged selection device is a costly process which rarely, if ever, produces any satisfactory alternatives.

---

process so long as the "bottom line" is acceptable. Nothing in *Teal* suggests that the Government does not have discretion to use its limited resources in this manner.

[111] 29 C.F.R. § 1607.3B.
[112] In *Albemarle*, the Court stated that if an employer meets its burden of showing that its selection procedure is job related, the complaining party may still show that there are other selection procedures without a similar adverse effect that would serve the employer's interest. Such a showing, the Court said, would be evidence that the employer was using its tests as a "pretext" for discrimination. 422 U.S. at 425.
[113] 102 S. Ct. at 2531.

A recent report of the General Accounting Office (GAO) [114] has suggested that the "search for alternatives" provision of the Guidelines should be reviewed to determine whether it should be revised. The GAO report recommended that "[i]n view of the perceived inconsistency between the procedures called for in the Guidelines and those enunciated by the Supreme Court in *Albemarle*, we believe it would be appropriate to reconsider the Guidelines' provision that users are responsible, as a matter of course, for searching for alternative selection procedures."[115]

The Eighty Percent Rule

Another issue of concern under the Guidelines was alluded to by the Court in *Teal* without discussion. The Guidelines provide that a selection rate that "is less than [80 percent] of the rate for the group with the highest rate will generally be regarded... as evidence of adverse impact."[116] Thus, the "four-fifths" or "eighty percent" rule has been used as a rule of thumb by the enforcement agencies for determining whether a selection procedure has adverse impact. Defendants have contended that a violation of the eighty percent rule should not constitute evidence of adverse impact where the differences are not practically and statistically significant. As recognized by the dissent in *Teal*, sample size often plays an important role in determining whether perceived differences are statistically significant or whether they may have occurred by chance.[117]

In discussing the passing rates of various groups of candidates on the written test in *Teal*, the majority stated that "[p]etitioners do not contest the District Court's implicit finding that the examination itself resulted in disparate impact under the 'eighty percent rule' of the Uniform Guidelines on Employee Selection Procedures adopted by the Equal Employment Opportunity Commission."[118] It should be noted that the State did not contest the finding that the examination resulted in disparate impact under the eighty percent rule and in fact the differences in passing rates were statistically significant.[119] Thus, the Court in *Teal* did not have occasion to ad-

---

[114] General Accounting Office, "Uniform Guidelines on Employee Selection Procedures Should be Reviewed and Revised," (July 30, 1982).
[115] *Id.* at 8.
[116] 29 C.F.R. § 1607.4D.
[117] 102 S. Ct. at 2539 n.7.
[118] *Id.* at 2529 n.4.
[119] The black mean score (64.90) on the examination differed from the white mean (71.63) by approximately 2.70 standard deviations, which is statistically significant at the .05 level, a generally accepted level of statistical significance. *See Hazelwood School District v. United States*, 433 U.S. at 308 n.14. Likewise, the passing ratio for

dress the use of the eighty percent rule in instances where the differences may not be statistically significant. Presumably, in such instances the Court would rely on tests of statistical significance and not on the eighty percent rule for determining whether adverse impact exists.[120]

SELECTION ALTERNATIVES AFTER *TEAL*

A number of alternatives remain open to employers after *Teal* for structuring their selection processes. Which of these a given employer chooses to adopt will depend largely on the organizational needs of the company. The *Ability Testing* study concluded that "[e]mployment selection is caught up in a destructive tension between employers' interest in promoting work force efficiency and the governmental effort to ensure equal employment opportunity."[121] Thus, while productivity and equal employment opportunity are not mutually exclusive, many employers will decide what alternative course to take after *Teal* based on whether they view themselves as productivity or equal employment oriented. Other employers may choose to take a middle course and attempt to accommodate both these concerns. Which alternatives an employer chooses will be determined largely by a number of factors including: the quality of the validity evidence for existing selection procedures or criteria; the resources available to conduct validity studies; the degree of adverse impact in components of existing procedures; the projected costs of compliance and litigation; the number of applicants or candidates and the number of openings available; whether the selections are for blue or white collar positions; preference for multiple hurdle versus cumulatively-scored selection processes; and whether there are adequate resources to make it feasible and acceptable for the company to use a cumulatively-scored process. Other factors which will be important in determining what procedures will be used are existing Title VII case law, the standards of compliance

---

blacks (54.17%) differed from the passing ratio for whites (79.53%) by approximately 3.76 standard deviations, also statistically significant. The district court on its decision set forth a chart at 27 FEP Cases 1331 with sufficient information to perform these two calculations using a "test concerning two means" and a "test of two proportions," respectively.
[120] *See* note 61, *supra*; *see also Hazelwood*, 433 U.S. at 308 n.14; *Teamsters*, 431 U.S. at 339 n. 20 (1977)("consideration of small sample size may, of course, detract from the value of such evidence"); 29 C.F.R. § 1607.4D ("Greater differences in selection rate may not constitute adverse impact where the differences are based on small numbers and are not statistically significant . . . .").
[121] *Ability Testing,* Part I at 147.

under federal selection guidelines, actual enforcement policies and practices of the federal agencies, generally accepted practices of the psychological profession, and revisions to the *Principles for Validation and Use of Personnel Selection Procedures*[122] and the *Standards for Educational and Psychological Tests.*[123]

Multiple Hurdle Selection Processes

A typical circumstance for many employers will involve a multicomponent selection process with one or more components having adverse impact. Because of inadequate resources and a desire to consider a smaller number of qualified candidates at each component of the process, many employers will have a strong preference for multiple or successive hurdle selection processes that preclude further participation of a candidate who does not meet a specified requirement or cutoff score. There are at least six alternatives that an employer using a multiple hurdle selection process could consider in such circumstances after *Teal.*

First, one or more of the pass-fail components of the process may involve a facially neutral procedure or criterion for which there is evidence of validity or job relatedness. For example, an employer may have a test with adverse impact as a knockout component of a selection process, but also possess evidence that the test is a valid measure of success on the job or in a training program or accurately samples the knowledges, skills or abilities required for the job. In such an instance, the employer could consider beginning the selection process with the written test because this is the component of the process for which the greatest evidence of validity exists. Thus, the employer could use the selection component(s) which has the greatest evidence of job relatedness or validity to absorb the brunt of the adverse impact of the process.

As a second alternative, Dr. Mary L. Tenopyr, Division Manager for Research and Testing, American Telephone & Telegraph Company, has suggested that employers may consider selectively combining selection procedures or criteria with a validated test early in

---

[122] Prepared by the Division of Industrial and Organizational Psychology (Division 14) of the American Psychological Association (2d ed. 1980). Division 14 is the division of the American Psychological Association most concerned with employment testing.
[123] Prepared by a joint committee of the American Psychological Association, American Educational Research Association and National Council on Measurement in Education. The 1974 *Standards* are presently undergoing revision and revised standards are expected in August 1984.

the selection process to serve cumulatively as a pass-fail component. Dr. Tenopyr states that they can be combined statistically in many instances in such a way as to remove adverse impact. Whether the employer chooses to use either method will depend on the nature and quality of the evidence of job relatedness which it possesses, the amount of adverse impact resulting from the validated procedure, an estimation of the likelihood of prevailing on the validity issue if the test or other device is challenged, and its preference for validated selection procedures.

As discussed previously, section 6B of the Uniform Guidelines provides that where a selection procedure has adverse impact, the employer may eliminate the adverse impact in lieu of validating the selection procedure.[124] Thus, the Uniform Guidelines encourage a third method for restructuring selection procedures. That is, at the completion of each step of the selection process, the employer could evaluate the component for adverse impact, and adjust the participation rates of those proceeding to the next component to eliminate any impact. The principal advantage of this approach is that a prima facie case of disparate impact could not be established by protected groups based on the adverse impact of a particular component. However, the elimination of impact in components may subject the employer to a suit by whites or other groups who are disfavored by the adjustments in participation rates.[125] In addition, depending on the level of impact of a component it may also permit further participation of candidates who may have little likelihood of being selected.

Professor Blumrosen has suggested a fourth alternative that may avoid this last difficulty. He states that "[w]here the employer has taken 'bottom line' affirmative action in selecting those minorities who passed [a] . . . test, the employer should review the qualifications of minorities who failed the test, to determine if there is any job-related reason to further consider them as compared to whites who passed the test."[126] In his opinion, "*Teal* may require no more than a 'second look' at the credentials of blacks who failed the test. Applicants who 'look good' should be processed further, others need not be."[127] Although Professor Blumrosen states that this "second

---

[124] 29 C.F.R. § 1607.6B.
[125] Elimination of the adverse impact of each component could still result in impact at the "bottom line." For example, if blacks fared 80% as well as whites at each stage of a 5-step selection procedure, based on the initial number of candidates entering the process, blacks would be selected at a rate 33% that of whites ($.8^5 = .328$) at the bottom line. *See, e.g., Vulcan Society v. Civil Service Commission*, 360 F. Supp. 1265, 1272 (S.D. N.Y.), *aff'd*, 490 F.2d 387 (2d Cir. 1973).
[126] Daily Lab. Rep. D-4 (August 27, 1982).
[127] *Id.*

look" would not be a burdensome effort, it could become quite cumbersome depending on the number of candidates, the kind of selection criteria involved and the nature of the job.

A fifth alternative for employers is to place subjective procedures and criteria, such as oral interviews, evaluation of biographical information, and evaluation of past work performance, at the beginning of the process in order to eliminate those persons who do not possess the minimum qualifications for the job or position in question and who are unlikely to be successful performers on the job. By eliminating those persons who do not possess the essential minimum qualifications for the job or position, the adverse effect of a written test given in a later stage of the process may be lessened. Employers should be aware that any objective or facially neutral minimum qualification, such as education used as part of such subjective stages of the selection process should be job related if it screens out candidates.[128] However, anyone challenging the effect of subjective procedures should be required to proceed on the more stringent disparate treatment theory of liability.[129]

A sixth alternative is to eliminate facially neutral components such as written tests altogether and use subjective devices such as oral interviews or performance ratings as a basis for screening out applicants. While such procedures lack the objective appeal of written tests, they may serve in appropriate instances the interests of a given employer.[130] Persons screened out by any of such subjective components or by the overall process should be required to proceed on a disparate treatment theory of liability.

The six alternatives outlined for use of pass-fail components after *Teal* are not intended to be exhaustive. Employers may find combinations of these alternatives or other methods more adaptable to their particular selection needs.

Cumulatively-Scored Selection Processes

The dissent in *Teal* suggested an alternative means by which employers may be able to avert liability based on the adverse effect of a component of a selection process:

---

[128] See notes 55-58, *supra*.
[129] See pp. 176-177, *supra*.
[130] Particularly for lower level jobs, the courts have permitted the use of subjective procedures if they are fair in form and contain adequate safeguards such as criteria related to job performance, written instructions, review by higher level management officials, and an opportunity to discuss the evaluation and add written comments.

Another possibility is that employers may integrate consideration of test results into one overall hiring decision based on that "factor" and additional factors. Such a process would not, even under the Court's reasoning, result in a finding of discrimination on the basis of disparate impact unless the actual hiring decisions had a disparate impact on the minority group. But if employers integrate test results into a single-step decision, they will be free to select *only* the number of minority candidates proportional to their representation in the workforce.[131]

Thus, it apparently remains open to employers to consider the test not as a pass-fail barrier based upon reaching a specified cutoff score, but rather as a part of a cumulatively-scored process under which the results of all selection components are consolidated.[132] Under such a cumulatively-scored process, it would appear that in most instances an employee could challenge only the overall result of the process absent evidence of intentional discrimination.[133] However, it should be noted that despite the intimations from the dissent that such a process would be acceptable under the majority opinion, *Teal* does not definitively decide this issue, nor does it decide whether a plaintiff may base a discrimination suit on a particular item or subcomponent of a selection procedure.[134]

Two other issues that are related to a cumulatively-scored pro-

---

See, e.g., *Pouncy v. Prudential Insurance Co.*, 23 FEP Cases 1349, 1364-65 (S.D. Tex. 1980), aff'd, 668 F.2d 795 (5th Cir. 1982). See also Bartholet, *Application of Title VII to Jobs in High Places*, 95 Harv. L. Rev. 945, 976 (1982)("On the upper level, courts have applied a far more lenient standard.").
[131] 102 S. Ct. at 2540.
[132] In a memorandum to clients, dated July 22, 1982, the law firm of Paul, Hastings, Janofsky & Walker has recommended that "the most prudent course is to eliminate 'knockouts' and open up the remaining steps of the selection process to all applicants, so as to avoid having any identifiable intermediate step at which adverse impact could be measured."
[133] But see note 45, *supra* and discussion below.
[134] Vice Chairman of the EEOC Cathie Shattuck has stated that *Teal* can be read narrowly in this regard even with respect to multiple hurdle processes. In remarks before the Annual Convention of the Federal Bar Association in Washington, D.C., (September 9, 1982) she stated:

> *Teal* can be read narrowly. The Court's repeated emphasis on "opportunity" indicates that the Court is not saying that *any* element which works a disparate impact on a protected group regardless of its effect on the overall selection process, will be found discriminatory. Moreover, if an element has a disparate impact, then it also must operate as a "built-in headwind" to equal employment opportunity, that is, the element must meet the standards set forth in *Griggs* . . . before the Court

cess were also left unanswered by *Teal*. The first involves instances where members of a protected group score sufficiently low on a component of the process (*i.e.*, a written test) that they are effectively, though not actually, precluded from consideration for employment opportunities.[135] *Teal* did not address this issue and it is unclear how far the logic of *Teal* would go if such a situation were to be challenged.

The second uncertainty surrounding a cumulatively-scored process arises out of the language of the dissent, quoted above, that "if employers integrate test results into a single-step decision, they will be free to select *only* the number of minority candidates proportional to their representation in the workforce."[136] This statement by the dissent is subject to at least two interpretations. First, the statement could be read to imply that an employer could select minorities only up to their representation in the available labor market without incurring possible liability from a reverse discrimination suit. Second, the language may have been intended to indicate that an employer using a cumulatively-scored process could hire fewer minorities than the State of Connecticut actually hired without incurring liability from those not hired. Although it is unclear which of these two interpretations was intended by the dissent, it would appear from the context in which the statement was made that the latter would be the correct interpretation.

In sum, although a cumulatively-scored procedure may afford a bottom line defense, employers who hire or promote large numbers of employees may find that a process that considers all applicants at each component stage is not economically feasible. In such situations, employers may want to consider selecting by use of pass-fail components using an alternative suggested above or by such other alternatives as it may find acceptable. Before making a decision, employers may also want to conduct an analysis of the costs and benefits of validating components of a pass-fail selection process versus the costs of maintaining a cumulatively-scored process. Any such analysis, where possible, should attempt to factor in the po-

---

will find discrimination and the employer have to show that it is job related.

See also discussion in The Supreme Court, 1981 Term, 96 Harv. L. Rev. 62, 284 (1982) ("[A] court would scrutinize subtests only when a plaintiff alleged that an intermediate test served as a crucial hurdle for employment or promotion had a desparate impact on a minority group.").

[135] See note 45, *supra*.
[136] 102 S. Ct. at 2540 n.8.

tential liability which the employer may incur under each of the selection processes considered.

Public Sector Considerations

The decision in *Teal* is particularly troublesome for public sector employers which often operate under merit system statutes or regulations that in many instances require the use of written tests and also may require the selection of candidates based upon rank order test results or from a limited number of persons who scored highest on the test. Because many public employers receive large numbers of applications, it may not be economically feasible, even for those able by law to do so, to abandon the use of pass-fail or cutoff scores. Thus, public employers after *Teal* will be forced to attempt to demonstrate the job relatedness or validation of their challenged selection components, even though few courts have found tests used in the public sector to be lawful.[137] The end result of *Teal* may be that such public employers no longer may be willing to risk "reverse discrimination" lawsuits which may result from affirmative efforts in later stages of the process to eliminate the disparate effects of a written test. As the dissent in *Teal* pointed out, the decision may have the unintended effect in the public sector of actually resulting in fewer minorities being selected.

RECENT LEGAL DEVELOPMENTS

A recent divided panel decision of the First Circuit in *Costa v. Markey*[138] illustrates the wide-ranging and potentially unpredictable impact that *Teal* may have as the courts, enforcement agencies and employers sort out the meaning of the Court's decision. *Costa* arose out of the rejection of a female applicant for a position on the New Bedford, Massachusetts, Police Department. The New Bedford Police Department made appointments for police officers from a list of eligible applicants certified to it from the state civil service personnel division. In 1974, following the retirement of a female police officer and based on the department's need to replace the retired officer with another female, New Bedford sought and received approval to engage in sex-specific hiring by hiring a female from a list

---
[137] *See, e.g., Guardians Ass'n of New York City v. Civil Service*, 630 F.2d 79 (2d Cir. 1980), *cert. denied*, 101 S. Ct. 3083 (1981); *United States v. State of New York*, 21 FEP Cases 1286 (N.D.N.Y. 1979).
[138] The opinion is unofficially reported at 30 FEP Cases 593 (1st Cir. December 3, 1982).

containing only the names of female applicants. The plaintiff, who had successfully passed a written and physical agility test, appeared first on the list supplied in order to fill the position at issue. However, the plaintiff was rejected at the interview stage because she failed to meet the five feet six-inch minimum height requirement then in effect. Two women who placed third and fourth on the eligibility list satisfied the minimum height requirement and were appointed.

Plaintiff brought suit under TitleVII under a disparate impact theory. Plaintiff produced evidence that eighty percent of the male population is at least five feet six-inches tall, while less than twenty percent of the female population reaches that height. The district court held that the application of the minimum height requirement violated TitleVII. In its initial decision, the First Circuit panel concluded that because the minimum height requirement in this instance was applied to an eligibility list consisting of women only, there could be no disparate impact and hence no prima facie case of disparate impact discrimination.[139] The first panel decision expressly declined to follow the Second Circuit's decision in *Teal*. Following the Supreme Court's decision in *Teal*, the First Circuit reconsidered the case and held (2 to 1) for the plaintiff.

In reversing its initial decision, the First Circuit stated that:

> *Teal* teaches that the proper place to evaluate the strength of a TitleVII plaintiff's prima facie case of disparate impact discrimination is the *point at which the employer's neutral criterion has a discriminatory effect*. The Court's focus must be on the first step in the employment process that produces an adverse impact on a group protected by Title VII, not the end result of the employment process as a whole.[140]

It is clear in this instance that the minimum height requirement was applied at a stage when *only women* were under consideration. However, the First Circuit concluded that "*Teal* requires us, however, to look behind the result [that does not reveal disproportionate adverse impact on the relevant minority labor pool] and evaluate the disparate impact of the height requirement itself, not the end result of its application in this particular case."[141] The court acknowledged the "sticking point" in the instant case that "in this instance of the city's application of its height requirement women

---

[139] The initial decision is reported at 677 F.2d 158 (1st Cir. 1982).
[140] 30 FEP Cases at 595 (emphasis added).
[141] *Id.* at 595-96.

were excluded only relative to other women."[142] The appellate court concluded, however, in holding for the plaintiff that:

> Were we to focus in this case on the city's hiring of only women we would be focusing on the "bottom line." It is undisputed that New Bedford's five feet six-inch height requirement resulted in far more women than men being classified as ineligible for appointment as police officers. The city routinely applied the height requirement to both male and female applicants. In this case the city applied the requirement to women only and hired only women. But this is no defense to a prima facie case of disparate impact discrimination. It seeks to justify the disparate effect of the rule in general by pointing to the end results of one particular application of the rule. This is the "bottom line" approach which is proscribed by *Teal*. In light of *Teal*, we hold that when, as here, an employer uniformly applies a rule to male and female applicants and applies it in one round of hiring decisions to a pool of only female applicants, the rule must be job-related if in its regular application it has a disparate effect on women.[143]

The dissent in *Costa* interprets the majority opinion to mean "that although women have not been discriminated against, the use of a criterion of choice—height—which in *other* circumstances *can* be a means of discriminating aginst women, is sufficient to make out a prima facie case here."[144] Unlike the majority, however, the dissent does not view the case as being controlled by *Teal*. The dissent distinguishes the case from *Teal* as follows:

> In *Costa* there was no discrimination to begin with; in *Teal* the initial discrimination was compensated for at the end. That timing is a crucial distinction between the two cases because, as we pointed out in *Costa I*, the initial decision in this case to hire only women meant that the pass-fail barrier never had any disparate effect on women. There was, therefore, no question of remedying the discriminatory effect of an element in a process with a nondiscriminatory bottom line. There was never any discriminatory effect.[145]

---

[142] *Id.* at 596.
[143] *Id.*
[144] *Id.* at 598.
[145] *Id.* at 599 (footnote omitted).

The dissent further maintained that no Title VII violation could have occurred in the instant case "when it is impossible that she was disadvantaged in relation to any man."[146] Finally, the dissent acknowledged that in another context, where males and females were in competition, the disparate impact on women resulting from a five feet six-inch minimum height requirement would establish a prima facie case of disparate impact and would require the employer to demonstrate that the height requirement was job related. However, the dissent concluded that "[w]hen only women were competing for a job as a police officer, a height requirement may be unfair but it is not a violation of Title VII."[147]

The decision in *Costa* raises a number of significant questions regarding the manner in which lower courts may interpret *Teal*. First, the case emphasizes the importance of isolating the component of a selection process which is challenged in order to determine whether the application of that component under the circumstances in which it was applied resulted in a disparate effect. The First Circuit majority cautioned that its "focus must be on the first step in the employment process that produces an adverse impact on a group protected by TitleVII, not the end result of the employment process as a whole."[148] It is clear from the facts in *Costa*, however, that the "first step" in the process where the height requirement was applied was at the interview stage when only women were under consideration. Thus, it would appear that the minimum height requirement *in this instance* operated to favor only taller women over shorter women, and not men over women as the court concluded. It is clear that in most instances where men and women are being evaluated, minimum height requirements such as the five feet six-inch requirement herein, would enable a woman screened out by the requirement to establish a prima facie case of disparate impact against women. In addition, had the minimum height requirement been applied to men and women in the instant case prior to the establishment of the eligibility list, *Teal* might well enable a woman who was screened out to establish a prima facie case based on the fact that she was denied the "opportunity" to proceed further in the selection process because of her sex. Thus, under *Teal*, the point in the selection process at which a facially neutral selection criteria is actually applied may determine whether or not a prima facie case can be established.

A second problem raised by *Costa* involves the extent to which the decision could be relied upon in other factual circumstances.

---
[146] *Id.*
[147] *Id.* at 600.
[148] *Id.* at 595.

Suppose, for example, that an employer administered a written test of cognitive abilities to a group of all black applicants and certain of the applicants were then eliminated from further consideration because of their failure to achieve the pass-fail score established for the test. From the group who passed the test, certain blacks were then chosen to fill the positions at issue. Because such tests, when applied to blacks and whites, have resulted in disparate impact against blacks, the logic of *Costa* would apparently dictate that a black person screened out by such a test could establish a prima facie case even though he was competing only against other blacks and despite the fact that blacks were chosen for the positions in question. Such a result, however, was not contemplated by *Teal* because the actual application of the test in the above example was to blacks only and could not have resulted, as so applied, in a disparate impact against blacks.[149]

---

[149] The Ninth Circuit in *Gerdom v. Continental Airlines*, 692 F.2d 602 (9th Cir. 1982), *pet. for cert. pending*, No.82-1388(U.S. Sup. Ct.) declined to reach the question of the applicability of a disparate impact analysis to employment conditions imposed exclusively on a job classification restricted to members of one sex. An earlier appellate court decision in the same case, decided prior to *Teal*, expressly held that a disparate impact theory was inappropriate in such circumstances and that the plaintiffs could only proceed on the basis of a disparate treatment theory. 648 F.2d 1223, 1226-27 (9th Cir. 1981).

The case involved a challenge to a policy requiring employees classified as "flight hostesses," a position held only by women, to comply with maximum weight requirements. No similar weight requirements were enforced for job classifications which included men. In deciding that the policy constituted unlawful disparate treatment against women, a six-judge majority in the second decision declined to reach the question of whether a disparate impact analysis could be used under those circumstances. 692 F.2d at 605. However, the five dissenting judges would have held that a disparate impact theory could not be advanced where all flight hostesses during the time in question were female. The dissent, in maintaining that *Teal* was not to the contrary, stated that:

> *Teal* is inapposite because it involved two different racial groups of employees subject to a facially neutral requirement that had a disparate impact on only one of the groups. The two groups present in the facts before this court are not distinguishable under the terms of TitleVII. The weight requirement discriminated against one group of women who could not meet Continental's weight requirement and favored a different group of women who could meet the standard. Gerdom did not allege that the weight requirement selected or rejected applicants or affected working conditions in a male-to-female ratio significantly different from that of the pool of flight hostesses or flight hostess applicants. No comparison can be made between male and female flight attendants because there were no male flight attendants during the period in question. Therefore, the disparate impact theory is not appropriate for analysis of these facts.

Id. at 612 (footnote omitted); *see also Stroud v. Delta Airlines, Inc.*, 544 F.2d 892 (5th Cir. 1977), *cert. denied*, 434 U.S. 844 (1977).

The decision in *Costa* may have resulted from the fact that the application of the height requirement to both men and women would have resulted in a disparate impact on women. Thus, the appellate court may have been influenced by the fact that only because of the unique factual circumstances of the city hiring from an all female list did the height requirement not operate to disproportionately screen out women. The First Circuit may not have been willing to allow the plaintiff to remain without a remedy for the use by the city of a selection criterion which in nearly all other applications would have resulted in a disparate impact against women. The court also may have viewed the failure of the city to offer evidence of the job relatedness of the height requirement and the subsequent abandonment of the requirement by the city as a tacit acknowledgment that the height requirement was not required for performance of the job.

The chances of fact patterns similar to *Costa* arising with any degree of frequency would appear to be remote because in most instances employers will be evaluating both men and women and/or blacks and whites as part of the same process. However, because the decision is one of the first appellate court decisions applying *Teal*, it will have to be addressed and possibly distinguished by other lower courts which are faced with situations which require an interpretation of *Teal*.

CONCLUSION

The decision of the Supreme Court in *Teal* will have a substantial effect on employee selection, Title VII compliance and litigation and affirmative action. Many employers may find it desirable after *Teal* to reevaluate and to consider alternatives, such as those suggested above, to their selection procedures to ensure that they are consistent with *Teal* and to ensure that such procedures are operating to select productive employees in a manner which minimizes the employer's potential for liability under Title VII. As the *Costa* decision illustrates, however, there will undoubtedly be a transition period during which employers, the federal enforcement agencies, the courts and members of groups protected by Title VII will engage in an evaluation of where employee selection stands after *Teal*. However, it may be several years before a final judgment can be rendered as to whether *Teal* was a pro-affirmative action decision, as the majority envisioned, or whether it will result over a period of time in the employment of fewer minorities and females, as the dissent warned.

Appendix A

SUMMARY OF EEAC SURVEY CONCERNING THE UNIFORM GUIDELINES ON EMPLOYEE SELECTION PROCEDURES

Forty-nine member companies representing a broad cross-section of industries responded to EEAC's questionnaire concerning their experience with the Uniform Guidelines on Employee Selection Procedures. A summary of the responses to each question is set forth below.

1. Does your company use tests for—white collar positions? —blue collar positions?—both?

Most companies—33 or 67% of all respondents—use tests for both blue and white collar positions. Three companies use tests for blue collar jobs only and nine companies reported that they use tests exclusively for white collar positions, of which four used them for clerical positions only. Four companies stated they did not use tests at all.

2. How does your company develop tests?—in house psychologist?—outside consultant?—other?

Only 2 companies develop tests exclusively by staff industrial psychologists. Otherwise companies use more than one source to develop tests. Twenty (20) companies use an in-house industrial psychologist to develop at least some of their tests, 16 use outside consultants, 33 purchase the test from a test developer, and 14 use other methods. Thus, of the possible sources of tests, 24 percent (20 of 83) are developed internally by companies.

3. If your company has ceased to use tests, why was the use of tests discontinued? What role, if any, did the complexity and cost of the Guidelines play in the decision to discontinue use of tests?

Forty (40) companies (82%) stated they have ceased the use of some or all tests. Fifty-eight (58) percent (23 of 40) discontinued their use because of the complexity and cost of the Guidelines. The remainder were discontinued for a variety of reasons including court decisions, insufficient validity, and sample sizes too small to conduct a validity study.

Typical of the explanations provided for their decisions are the following:

> Haven't discontinued testing, but the scope has been drastically reduced. The complexity and cost of the Guidelines were the primary considerations.

> The use of aptitude tests requiring criterion type validation was discontinued due to stringent guideline requirements and potential liabilities inherent in the system.

> Testing for some jobs was discontinued in the early 1970's after careful review of the degree to which internal research evidence supporting the use of the tests would meet the requirements of the Guidelines. The complexity and cost of the Guidelines play a major part in *every* decision whether to allocate resources to develop and validate tests for any job group in the company.

> We severely limit use of tests to content valid, knowledge or skill achievement tests. We were more influenced by *Griggs* and *Moody* than by the Guidelines.

> A drastic reduction in the use of tests was due to consent decrees and court cases. The role played by the Guidelines was in establishing a standard used by the court and in the consent decrees for determining the acceptability (or lack thereof) of a test.

4. If your company subsequently resumed testing, were substantial start-up costs involved? Explain.

Fourteen (14) companies responded that they subsequently resumed testing. Most of these responses (79% or 11 of 14) indicated that substantial start-up costs were involved. The costs to validate the new test ranged from $15,000 to $500,000. These costs were attributed to the cost of validating the test, expanding in-house capabilities, and the use of outside consultants.

5. Would your company be more inclined to use tests if the Guidelines permitted companies to use tests developed at other locations for similar jobs?

Eighty-three (83) percent (38 of 46) of the companies responding to the question indicated that they would be more likely to use tests

if the Guidelines permitted test transportability between locations for similar jobs.

6. What sections of the Guidelines have presented the most difficult problems of compliance? Explain.

Over four-fifths (83% or 36 of 44) of the companies answering the question stated that the validation requirements of the Guidelines presented the most difficult problem of compliance. One-third (1/3) of these (12 of 36) specifically highlighted the requirement to conduct fairness studies. The search for alternatives requirements was identified as a compliance problem in 23 percent (10 of 44) of the questionnaires, the definition of adverse impact and the bottom line in 14 percent (6 of 44), and the recordkeeping and documentation requirements in 11 percent (5 of 44).

7. What costs, in addition to those required by professional practice, has your company incurred in order to comply with the Guidelines? Explain.

The following costs, in addition to those required by professional practice, were identified by the responding companies: fairness studies, search for alternatives, recordkeeping and documentation requirements, and loss of productivity. Representative of some of the responses are the following:

> We have incurred and will incur over the next five years approximately $1,000,000 in incremental costs to conduct validity studies that we can be reasonably certain will withstand government scrutiny. These costs are associated primarily with: (1) placement on the job of a number of individuals who do not meet minimum ability (test) requirements in order to assure a sufficient range of scores to conduct a predictive validity study; and (2) development of "state of the art" job performance measures for validation criteria that are beyond reproach.

> The worst of the extra costs come from the fairness requirements. Accumulating samples to do fairness studies increase data collection costs by about a factor of 10 (*i.e.*, such studies are 10 times more expensive than otherwise required). When added to the level of detail required by the various guidelines, the cost of Guidelines' requirements amounts to about 90% of the study. Only 10% [of the costs] are really required for good professional practice.

Loss of productivity in selections where merit has lost out to quotas. Probably in the millions—only a utility analysis could estimate.

One company allocated the cost of compliance with the Guidelines as follows:

Development of procedures, instructions, computer techniques and misc. support	$150,000
Training of Field Personnel at Corporate Headquarters	25,000
Corporate Computer Support	15,000
Total	$192,000

8. What are the costs to your company of the recordkeeping requirements of the Guidelines? (Please document if possible.)

Most companies found it difficult to estimate the cost of the recordkeeping requirements under the Guidelines, but generally believed they were substantial. Where they were estimated, they ranged from $7,500 per year to $750,000 depending on the size of the company. One response identified the following annual recordkeeping costs:

Collecting and reporting data to Corporate Headquarters (105 locations, annually)	$100,000
Corporate computer processing of data	15,000
Locations' self-analysis and records retention	10,500
Total	$125,500

9. How have the Guidelines affected productivity? Your company's ability to meet corporate EEO and affirmative action goals?

Generally, the Guidelines were viewed by companies as having a negative effect on productivity because testing has been discouraged. See also responses to question 7. Representative of the responses are the following:

Productivity has been affected by moving from "more valid" (tests) to "less valid" (interviews) selection devices.

Profoundly negative—we have hired numbers and paid dearly.

Hard to determine effect on productivity beyond not hiring the best qualified applicant for the position.

The Guidelines have definitely lowered productivity during the time the study is being conducted. Productivity is also lower than necessary for jobs for which no test is used (a valid test would screen out many more poor performers) because the costs and complexities of the required research make supporting studies not feasible.

The Guidelines have greatly affected productivity by simply establishing a climate of strong hesitancy to utilize even valid testing in job selection and placement.

With respect to the impact of the Guidelines on EEO and affirmative action, most respondents concluded that the Guidelines have not diminished their ability to meet EEO and affirmative action goals. One respondent stated:

The Guidelines have had little effect on our ability to meet EEO and affirmative action goals other than diverting resources into selection research that could be used more effectively in such areas as training.

Appendix B

AD HOC COMMITTEE'S REVISION OF THE UNIFORM GUIDELINES ON EMPLOYEE SELECTION PROCEDURES

GENERAL PRINCIPLES

Section 1. Statement of purpose.

A. Need for uniformity—Issuing agencies. The Federal government's need for a uniform set of principles on the question of the use of tests and other selection procedures continues to be recognized. The Equal Employment Opportunity Commission, Office of Personnel Management, the Department of Labor, and the Department of Justice jointly have adopted these uniform guidelines to meet that need, and to apply the same principles to the Federal Government as are applied to other employers.

B. Purpose of guidelines. These guidelines represent a set of recommendations which are intended to assist employers, labor organizations, and employment agencies in understanding the requirements of Federal law prohibiting employment practices which illegally discriminate on grounds of race, color, sex, and national origin as these classifications are defined in section 4B. They are designed to provide a framework for determining the proper use of tests and other selection procedures. These guidelines do not require a user to provide evidence of validity for selection procedures where no adverse impact results. However, all users are encouraged to use selection procedures that are job related.

C. Relation to prior guidelines. These guidelines supersede previously issued guidelines on employee selection procedures.

D. Implementation and interpretation. It is not expected that users will be able to implement completely every recommendation contained in these guidelines. The applicability of specific provisions of the guidelines depends on the particular circumstances of the user. Likewise, these guidelines are not intended to limit or prohibit professional development or innovation. Any interpretation of these guidelines should be made in light of any new and generally accepted professional research findings relevant to any issue in question.

Section 2. Scope

A. Application of guidelines. These guidelines will be applied by the Equal Employment Opportunity Commission in the enforcement of Title VII of the Civil Rights Act of 1964, as amended by the Equal Employment Opportunity Act of 1972 (hereinafter "Title VII"); by the Department of Labor in the administration and enforcement of Executive Order 11246, as amended by Executive Order 11375 (hereinafter "Executive Order 11246"); by the Office of Personnel Management and other Federal agencies subject to section 717 of Title VII; by the Office of Personnel Management in exercising its responsibilities toward State and local governments under section 208(b)(1) of the Intergovernmental-Personnel Act; by the Department of Justice in exercising its responsibilities under Federal law; by the Office of Revenue Sharing of the Department of the Treasury under the State and Local Fiscal Assistance Act of 1972, as amended; and by any other Federal agency which adopts them.

B. Employment decisions. These guidelines apply to selection procedures which are used as a basis for any employment decision. Employment decisions include but are not limited to hiring, promotion, demotion, membership (for example, in a labor organization), referral, and retention. Other selection decisions, such as selection for training or transfer, may also be considered employment decisions if they lead to any of the decisions listed above.

C. Selection procedures. These guidelines apply only to selection procedures which are used as a basis for making employment decisions. Such procedures include the full range of assessment techniques from traditional paper and pencil tests, performance tests, training programs, and physical, educational and work experience requirements through informal or casual interviews and unscored application forms.

Recruitment, activities of college placement offices, and affirmative action practices are not considered by these guidelines to be selection procedures. Similarly, these guidelines do not pertain to the question of the lawfulness of a seniority system within the meaning of section 703(h), Executive Order 11246 or other provisions of Federal law or regulation, except to the extent that such systems utilize selection procedures to determine qualifications or abilities to perform the job. Nothing in these guidelines is intended or should be interpreted as discouraging the use of a job-related selection procedure for the purpose of determining employment qualifications or for the purpose of selection on the basis of relative qualifications.

D. Limitations. These guidelines apply only to Title VII, the nondiscrimination provisions of Executive Order 11246, or other equal employment opportunity requirements of Federal law. These guidelines do not apply to responsibilities under the Age Discrimination in Employment Act of 1967, as amended, not to discriminate on the basis of age, or under sections 501, 503, and 504 of the Rehabilitation Act of 1973, not to discriminate on the basis of handicap, or under section 402 of the Vietnam Era Veterans Readjustment Assistance Act, not to discriminate against Vietnam Era or disabled veterans.

E. Indian preference not affected. These guidelines do not affect any obligation imposed or right granted by Federal law to users to extend a preference in employment to Indians living on or near an Indian reservation in connection with employment opportunities on or near an Indian reservation.

Section 3. Relationship between use of selection procedures and job relatedness.

A. Procedure having adverse impact. The use of any selection procedure which results in an adverse impact as defined in section 4D in the hiring, promotion, or other employment or membership opportunities of members of any race, sex, or ethnic group will be considered to be inconsistent with the recommendations contained in these guidelines, unless the procedure can otherwise be shown to be job related.

B. Consideration of suitable alternative selection procedures. Whenever the user is shown a feasible alternative selection procedure with appropriately documented evidence of at least equal validity and substantially less adverse impact, the user should investigate it to determine the feasibility and appropriateness of using or validating it in accordance with the recommendations of these guidelines. This subsection is not intended to preclude the combination of procedures into a more valid procedure.

Section 4. Information on impact.

A. Records concerning impact. Each user should maintain and have available for inspection records for each race, sex or ethnic group constituting five percent (5%) of the labor force in the relevant labor market. See section 15B. These records will disclose the degree of adverse impact which the user's selection procedures have upon employment opportunities of persons by identifiable race, sex, or ethnic group as set forth in subparagraph B below in order to determine consistency with the recommendations contained in these guidelines. These records should be maintained on the basis of the job or group of jobs for which the particular selection procedure was applied. Where there are large numbers of applicants and procedures are administered frequently, such information may be retained on a sample basis, provided that the sample is appropriate in terms of the applicant population and adequate in size.

B. Applicable race, sex, and ethnic groups for recordkeeping. The records called for by this section are to be maintained by sex, and the following races and ethnic groups: Blacks (Negroes), American Indians (including Alaskan Natives), Asians (including Pacific Islanders), Hispanics (including persons of Mexican, Puerto Rican, Cuban, Central or South American, or other Spanish origin or culture regardless of race), whites (Caucasians) other than Hispanics. The race, sex, and ethnic classifications called for by this section are consistent with the Equal Employment Opportunity Standard Form 100, Employer Information Report EEO-1 series of reports. The user should adopt safeguards to insure that the records recommended by this paragraph are used only for appropriate purposes such as determining adverse impact, or (where required) for developing and monitoring affirmative action programs.

C. Evaluation of selection rates. If the information called for by sections 4A and B above shows that the total selection process for a job has an adverse impact, the individual components of the selection process should be evaluated for adverse impact. If this information shows that the total selection process does not have an adverse impact, the Federal enforcement agencies, in the exercise of their administrative and prosecutorial discretion, in usual circumstances, will not expect a user to evaluate the individual components for adverse impact, or to validate such individual components, and will not take enforcement action based upon adverse impact of any component of that process, including the separate parts of a multipart selection procedure, or any separate procedure that is used as an alternative method of selection. However, in the following circumstances the Federal enforcement agencies will expect a user to evaluate the individual components for adverse impact and may, where appropriate, take enforcement action with respect to the individual components: (1) where the selection procedure is a significant factor in the continuation of patterns of assignments of incumbent employees caused by prior discriminatory employment practices, (2) where the weight of court decisions or administrative interpretations hold that a specific procedure (such as height or weight requirements or no-arrest records) is not job related in the same or similar circumstances. In unusual circumstances, other than those listed in (1) and (2) above, the Federal enforcement agencies may request a user to evaluate the individual components for adverse impact and may, where appropriate, take enforcement action with respect to the individual component.

D. Adverse Impact and the "four-fifths rule." A selection rate for any race, sex, or ethnic group which is less than four-fifths (4/5) (or eighty percent) of the rate for the group with the highest rate merely establishes a numerical basis for the enforcement agencies to seek further information. A less than four-fifths rate may be considered evidence of adverse impact if it is significant in both statistical and practical terms during the relevant time period unless (1) the group's underutilization in the job or group of jobs when compared to their availability in the relevant labor market is not statistically and practically significant, (2) the representation of the group among those selected is not substantially different from the group's representation in the relevant labor market, (3) the pool applicants from the group in question is atypical of the normal pool from the relevant labor market, or (4) the differences are based on small numbers. In the absence of differences which are large enough to meet the four-fifths rate or a test of statistical significance, there is no reason to assume that the differences are reliable, or that they are based upon anything other than chance.

E. Consideration of user's equal employment opportunity posture. In carrying out their obligations, the Federal enforcement agencies will consider the general posture of the user with respect to equal employment opportunity for the job or group of jobs in question. Where a user has adopted an affirmative action program, the Federal enforcement agencies will consider the provisions of that program, including the goals and timetables. Selection procedures under such programs should be based upon the ability or relative ability to do the work.

Section 5. General recommendations for validity evidence.

A. Acceptable types of validity evidence. For the purposes of satisfying the recommendations of these guidelines, users may rely upon criterion-related, both predictive and concurrent, and content or construct validity evidence, in accordance with accepted practices of the psychological profession. It is recognized that the lines of demarcation among these validity strategies are not absolute. Additional strategies for showing the validity of selection procedures may be adopted by users as they become generally accepted by the psychological profession.

B. Criterion-related, content and construct validity evidence. Evidence of the criterion-related validity of a selection procedure typically consists of a demonstration of a statistically significant relationship between the results of the selection procedure (predictor or predictors) and one or more relevant measures of job or training or organizational success (criterion or criteria). Evidence of content validity of a selection procedure consists of a demonstration that a selection procedure samples one or more relevant job or training domains. Evidence of construct validity of a selection procedure should show that the procedure measures the construct (essentially a theoretical concept) and that individual differences on the construct are related to individual differences on the job or training.

C. Guidelines are consistent with accepted professional practices. The recommendations of these guidelines relating to validation of selection procedures are intended to be consistent with generally accepted professional practices for evaluating standardized tests and other selection procedures. Such practices may be set forth in a number of sources including, but not limited to, the *Standards for Educational and Psychological Tests* prepared by a joint committee of the American Psychological Association, the American Educational Research Association and the National Council on Measurement in Education (American Psychological Association, Washington, D.C., 1974), the *Principles for Validation and Use of Personnel Selection Procedures* prepared by the Division of Industrial-Organizational Psychology, American Psychological Association (2d ed. 1980), and standard textbooks and professional journals in the field of personnel selection.

D. Need for documentation of validity. For any selection procedure for which validity evidence is necessary in accord with these guidelines, each user should maintain and have available such documentation as is described in section 15 below.

E. Accuracy and standardization. Selection procedures should be administered and scored under standardized conditions to the extent this is practically possible.

F. Caution against selection on basis of a knowledge, skill, or ability learned in brief orientation period. In general, users should avoid making employment decisions on the basis of measures of a knowledge, skill, or ability that the user expects a person to learn in a brief orientation period.

G. Method of use of selection procedures. Selection standards may be set as high or as low as the purposes of the user require, as long as they are based on job-related procedures. In usual circumstances, the relationship between a predictor and a criterion may be assumed to be linear. Consequently, selecting from the top scorers on down is the most effective procedure for maximizing the utility of the selection procedure providing there is an adequate amount of variance in the predictor.

Selection procedures supported by content or construct validity evidence that differentiate adequately among people usually can be assumed to have a linear relationship to job or training behavior. Consequently, ranking on the basis of scores on a job-related procedure is appropriate.

H. Use of selection procedures for higher level jobs. Use of a selection procedure to evaluate applicants or candidates for a higher level job or job group than that for which candidates are initially selected is appropriate, if (1) the majority of the individuals who remain employed and are available for advancement progress to the higher level within a reasonable period of time, or (2) the user maintains a promotion-from-within policy in which candidates in the lower level job or group are generally the pool from which persons are selected for those higher level jobs. These guidelines recognize that the considerations applicable to the promotion of clerical and hourly employees may vary substantially from those involving managerial and professional employees and therefore a flexible application of this section is necessary.

I. Interim use of selection procedures. Users may continue the use of a selection procedure which is not at the moment fully supported by the evidence of validity recommended in these guidelines, provided that the additional evidence, as recommended by these guidelines, will be gathered and/or examined within a reasonable period of time.

Interim use of a selection procedure is to be differentiated from the transportability of a selection procedure having demonstrated validity. Transportability enables a user to use a selection procedure that has not been validated by the user for a particular job or group of jobs when the user's job or group of jobs and the job or group of jobs for which the validity evidence was examined or gathered include substantially the same major work behavior(s) or substantially the same major knowledge(s), skill(s), or ability(ies) or other worker characteristic(s) as measured by the selection procedure in question. See section 7B. A user may transport such validity evidence without further requirement to provide additional validity evidence, provided that the work behavior(s), relevant knowledge(s), skill(s) or ability(ies), or other worker characteristic(s) involved can be shown to be comparable.

J. Review of validity evidence for currency. Whenever validity has been shown to be in accord with professional practices for the use of a particular selection procedure for a job or group of jobs, additional evidence need not be gathered or examined. There are no absolutes in the area of determining the currency of validity evidence and time in and of itself is not necessarily a factor. The primary factor to be considered is whether major changes in the job or group of jobs make the validity evidence no longer relevant.

Section 6. Use of selection procedures which have not been validated.

There exist circumstances in which a user cannot or need not gather the validation evidence contemplated by these guidelines. In such circumstances, the user should utilize selection procedures which are as job related as possible.

A. Where informal or unscored procedures are used. When an informal or unscored selection procedure which has an adverse impact is utilized, the user may (a) eliminate the adverse impact, (b) modify the procedure, if feasible, to one which is a formal, scored or quantified measure or combination of measures and then validate the procedure in accord with accepted professional practices, (c) adopt a standardized procedure and validate it or support it in accordance with sections 5I and 7B, or (d) otherwise justify continued use of the procedure in accord with Federal law.

B. Where formal and scored procedures are used. When a formal and scored selection procedure is used which has an adverse impact, the validation strategies recommended by these guidelines usually should be followed if technically feasible. Where it is not necessary or feasible to gather the validation evidence anticipated by these guidelines, the user may (a) modify the use of the procedure to eliminate adverse impact, (b) support the procedure in accordance with section 7B, (c) adopt another standardized procedure and validate it or support it in accordance with section 7B, or (d) otherwise justify continued use of the procedure in accord with Federal law.

Section 7. Use of other validity evidence.

A. Validity evidence not gathered by the user. Users may support the use of selection procedures with validity evidence gathered by other users or gathered by test publishers or distributors and described in test manuals provided that evidence meets accepted professional practice. Users obtaining selection procedures from other sources should be careful to determine, in advance of operational use of the procedure, that the information necessary to document validity is available and sufficient in terms of the recommendations of sections 5I, 7B and 15C(5) of these guidelines.

B. Use of validity evidence from other sources. Validity evidence gathered by one user or described in test manuals and the professional literature is appropriate for use by another user when the following conditions exist:

(1) Validity evidence. The validity evidence gathered in accordance with accepted professional practices and the recommendations of these guidelines demonstrates that the selection procedure is valid for the job or group of jobs in question; and

(2) Job similarity. The work performed in the user's job or group of jobs and in the job or group of jobs for which the validity evidence was examined or gathered includes substantially the same major work behavior(s), or involves substantially the same major knowledge(s), skill(s), ability(ies), or worker characteristic(s) as measured by the selection procedure in question.

C. Validity evidence from multiunit study. If validity evidence gathered from more than one unit within an organization satisfies section 7B, evidence of validity specific to each unit will not be required. See also section 8B.

Section 8. Cooperative validation efforts.

A. Encouragement of cooperative validation efforts. The agencies issuing these guidelines encourage users to cooperate in gathering validation evidence.

B. Recommendations for use of cooperative validation efforts. If validity evidence from a cooperative validation effort has been gathered in accordance with accepted professional practices and the recommendations of these guidelines, evidence of validity specific to each user will not be required.

Section 9. No assumption of validity.

A. Unacceptable substitutes for evidence of validity or relationship to job performance. Under no circumstances will the general reputation of a test or other selection procedure, its author or its publisher, or casual reports of its validity be accepted in lieu of evidence of validity or its job relatedness. Specifically ruled out are: assumptions of validity based on a procedure's name or descriptive labels; promotional literature that does not include the information required for users to determine the quality and transportability of the procedures; data bearing on the frequency of a procedure's usage; testimonial statements and credentials of sellers, users, or consultants; and other nonempirical or anecdotal accounts of selection practices or selection outcomes. Similarly, casual reports of test results in other settings, or court or agency findings regarding a procedure in other settings, should not be used as evidence of adverse impact or lack of validity with respect to the selection procedure.

B. Encouragement of professional supervision. Professional supervision of selection activities is encouraged but is not a substitute for documented evidence of validity.

Section 10. Employment agencies and employment services.

A. Where selection procedures are devised by agency. An employment agency, including private employment agencies and

State employment agencies, which agrees to a request by a user to devise and utilize a selection procedure should follow the recommendations in these guidelines. The use of an employment agency does not relieve a user of its responsibilities under Federal law.

B. Where selection procedures are devised elsewhere. Where an employment agency or service is requested to administer a selection procedure which has been devised elsewhere and to make referrals pursuant to the results, the employment agency or service should follow the recommendations in these guidelines. The agency or service may rely on validity evidence or other data in the possession of the employer in accordance with section 7B.

Section 11. Disparate treatment.

The principles of disparate or unequal treatment must be distinguished from the concepts of validation. Disparate treatment occurs where identifiable members of a race, sex, or ethnic group have been intentionally denied the same selection, promotion, membership, or other employment opportunities as have been available to other employees or applicants during the relevant time period. Those specific employees or applicants who have been denied equal treatment must at least be afforded the same opportunities as had existed for other employees or applicants during the relevant time period. This section does not prohibit a user who has not previously followed merit standards from adopting merit standards which are consistent with these guidelines; nor does it preclude a user who has previously used invalid or unvalidated selection procedures from developing and/or using procedures which are in accord with these guidelines.

Section 12. Retesting of applicants.

Users should provide a reasonable opportunity for retesting and reconsideration. Where examinations are administered periodically with public notice, such reasonable opportunity exists, unless persons who have previously been tested are precluded from retesting. The user may, however, take reasonable steps to preserve the security of its procedures. This will often mean limiting the time and frequency of retaking the test.

Section 13. Affirmative action.

The use of selection procedures which have been validated pursuant to these guidelines does not relieve users of any obligations they may have to undertake affirmative action to assure equal employment opportunity.

TECHNICAL RECOMMENDATIONS

Section 14. Technical recommendations for validity evidence.

The following recommendations, as applicable, should be followed in gathering validity evidence. Nothing in these guidelines is intended to preclude the development and use of other professionally acceptable techniques with respect to the validation of selection procedures.

A. *Validity studies should be based on review of information about the job.* Any validity evidence should be based upon a review of information about the job for which the selection procedure is to be used. Any method of job review may be used if it provides the information appropriate to the specific validation strategy used.

B. *Criterion-related strategy.* (1) Users choosing a criterion-related validity strategy should determine whether it is technically feasible (as defined in section 16) to gather such evidence in the particular employment context. For example, the determination of the number of persons necessary to permit the conduct of a meaningful criterion-related study should be made by the user on the basis of all relevant information concerning the selection procedure, the potential sample and the employment situation. These guidelines do not require that a user hire or promote persons for the purpose of making it possible to conduct a criterion-related study.

(2) There should be a review of job or training information to determine measures of work or training behaviors, performance, or organizational outcomes that are relevant to the job in question. These measures or criteria are relevant to the extent that they represent one or more critical or important job duties, work behaviors or work outcomes as developed from the review of job information.

(3) Proper safeguards should be taken to insure that scores on selection procedures do not enter into any judgments of employee adequacy that are to be used as criterion measures. Criteria may consist of measures other than work proficiency including but not limited to length of service, regularity of attendance, work samples, training time or success in job training. Where performance in train-

ing is used as a criterion, the relevance of the training should be shown either through a comparison of the content of the training program with one or more critical or important work behavior(s) of the job(s), or through a demonstration of the relationship between measures of training and job success. Measures of relative success in training may include but are not limited to instructor evaluations, performance samples, or tests.

Whatever criteria are used should represent one or more important or critical work behaviors or work outcomes. Certain job behaviors including but not limited to production rate, error rate, job level achieved, progression rate, evaluation of potential, absenteeism and turnover, may be used as criteria without a full job review. A rating of overall work performance may be utilized where it is based on carefully defined job relevant characteristics. Although it is virtually impossible to identify and quantify bias in subjective evaluation ratings, instructions to raters should be carefully developed so as to minimize that possibility. It should be recognized that group average differences in subjective evaluation ratings are not necessarily indicative of bias.

(4) The sample should be appropriate for the purposes of the researcher's investigation. Race, sex, and ethnic variables should not be assumed to influence the obtained validity in the absence of explicit evidence that they do. Where samples are combined or compared, attention should be given to see that such samples are at least comparable in terms of the most relevant job or training behaviors or associated knowledges, skills and abilities.

(5) The degree of relationship between selection procedure scores and criterion measures should be examined and computed, using professionally acceptable statistical procedures. Generally, a selection procedure is considered related to the criterion, for purposes of these guidelines, when the relationship between the procedure and at least one relevant criterion is statistically significant, *i.e.*, is sufficiently high as to have a probability of no more than one (1) in twenty (20) to have occurred by chance. Absence of a statistically significant relationship between a selection procedure and a criterion should not necessarily discourage other investigations of the validity of the selection procedures or inclusion of that procedure in a combination which is statistically significant. There are no minimum correlation coefficients applicable in an employment situation.

(6) Users should avoid reliance upon techniques that tend to overestimate validity findings as a result of capitalization on chance unless an appropriate safeguard is taken. Use of a large sample is one safeguard; cross-validation is another. Standard statistical cor-

rections for range restriction and unreliability are not considered to be techniques that overestimate validity findings.

(7) *Fairness or differential prediction of the selection procedure.* Differential prediction, unfairness or bias, as typically defined, have not been sufficiently demonstrated for race, sex, and ethnic groups to warrant a guideline recommendation to gather evidence related to these issues. Such evidence is therefore not required by these guidelines.

C. Content-oriented strategy. (1) There should be a definition of a content domain(s) with respect to the job(s) in question. Content domains may be defined through job review of the work or training behaviors or activities, or by the pooled judgments of persons having knowledge of the job. Content domains include one or more critical or important work or training behaviors, work products, work activities, job duties, or the knowledges, skills or abilities or work characteristics shown to be necessary for performance of the duties, behaviors, activities or the production of work. Where a content domain has been defined as a knowledge, skill or ability, that knowledge, skill or ability should be operationally defined. A selection procedure based on inferences about abstract psychological processes cannot be supported by content validity alone, unless the process can be operationally defined. Content validity by itself is not an appropriate validation strategy for intelligence, personality or interest tests. Content validity is also not an appropriate validation strategy when the selection procedure involves knowledges, skills or abilities which an employee will be expected to learn in a brief orientation period on the job.

(2) A selection procedure which is an appropriate sample of a content domain of the job or training as defined in accordance with subsection (1) above is a content valid procedure for that domain. Where the domain or domains measured are critical to the job, or constitute a substantial proportion of the job, the selection procedure will be considered to be content valid for the job. The reliability of selection procedures justified on the basis of content validity should be a matter of concern to the user. Whenever it is feasible to do so, appropriate statistical estimates should be made of the reliability of the selection procedures.

(3) A demonstration of the relationship between the content of the selection procedure and the content domain is critical to content validity. Content validity may be shown if the knowledges, skills or abilities or worker characteristics demonstrated in and measured by the selection procedure substantially correspond to the knowl-

edges, skills, abilities or worker characteristics shown to be necessary for job or training success. The closer the content of the selection procedure is to actual work samples, behaviors, or activities, the stronger is the basis for showing content validity. The need for careful documentation of the relationship between the content domain of the selection procedure and that of the job increases as the content of the selection procedure less resembles that of the content domain.

(4) A requirement for specific prior training or for work experience based on content validity, including a specification of level or amount of training or experience, should be justified on the basis of the relationship between the content of the training or experience and the content domain of the job for which the training or experience is to be required. The critical consideration is the resemblance between the specific behaviors, products, knowledges, skills, or abilities in the experience or training and the specific behaviors, products, knowledges, skills, or abilities required on the job, whether or not there is close resemblance between the experience or training as a whole and the job as a whole.

(5) Under usual circumstances, a content-oriented selection procedure with adequate differentiation can be assumed to have a linear relationship to job or training or organizational behaviors and the results may be used to rank people.

D. Construct Validity. Construct validity is a more complex strategy than either criterion-related or content validity. Accordingly, users choosing to validate a selection procedure by use of this strategy should be careful to follow professionally accepted practices.

(1) There should be a review of information about the job. This job review should result in a determination that the construct of interest is relevant to successful performance of one or more important or critical parts of a job.

(2) A selection procedure should be selected or developed which measures the construct(s) identified in accord with subparagraph (1) above.

(3) A selection procedure may be used operationally if the recommendations of subparagraphs (1) and (2) are met and there is sufficient empirical research evidence showing that the procedure is validly related to one or more critical job duties.

(4) Where a selection procedure satisfies the recommendations of subsections (1), (2) and (3) above, it may be used operationally for other jobs which are shown by an appropriate job review to include the same construct(s) as an essential element in job performance.

DOCUMENTATION OF IMPACT AND VALIDITY EVIDENCE

Section 15. Documentation of impact and validity evidence.

A. Required information. Users of selection procedures other than those users complying with section 15A(1) below should maintain and have available for each job or job group information on the impact of the selection process for that job or job group and, where necessary, validity evidence.

(1) Simplified recordkeeping for users with 250 or fewer employees. In order to minimize recordkeeping burdens on employers with establishments who employ two hundred fifty (250) or fewer employees, and other users not required to file EEO-1, *et seq.*, reports, such users may satisfy the requirements of this section if they maintain and have available records showing, for each year:

(a) The number of persons hired, promoted, and terminated for each job or job group, by race, sex and national origin;

(b) The number of applicants for hire and promotion by race, sex and national origin; and

(c) The selection procedures utilized (either standardized or not standardized).

These records should be maintained for each race or national origin group (see section 4 above) constituting more than five percent (5%) of the labor force in the relevant labor market. However, it is not necessary to maintain records by race and/or national origin (see section 4 above) if one race or national origin group in the relevant labor market constitutes more than ninety-five percent (95%) of the labor force in the relevant labor market. It is advisable to maintain evidence of job relatedness.

B. Information on impact. Users of selection procedures who have more than 250 employees should maintain and have available for each job or group of jobs to which the selection procedure was applied records or other information showing the impact of the total selection process for that job or group of jobs for which records are called for by section 4B above. Adverse impact determinations should be made annually for each such group which constitutes at least 5 percent of the labor force in the relevant labor market. Where a total selection process for a job or job group has an adverse impact, the user should maintain and have available records or other information showing which components have an adverse impact. Where the total selection process for a job or job group does not have an adverse impact, information need not be maintained for individual components.

C. Documentation of validity evidence. (1) For selection procedures having an adverse impact, the user should maintain and have available one of the following types of documentation evidence.

(a) Documentation evidence showing criterion-related validity of the selection procedure.

(b) Documentation evidence showing content validity of the selection procedure.

(c) Documentation evidence showing construct validity of the selection procedure.

(d) Documentation evidence from other studies showing validity of the selection procedure.

(e) Documentation evidence showing why validation is not feasible or not appropriate and why continued use of the procedure is consistent with Federal law.

This evidence should be compiled in a reasonably complete and organized manner to permit direct evaluation of the validity evidence. Previously written employer or consultant reports of validity are acceptable if they are reasonably complete in regard to the following documentation recommendations, or if they are reasonably complete in terms of guidelines which were in effect when the study was completed. If necessary information is not available, the validity report may still be used as documentation, but its adequacy will be evaluated in terms of the recommendations contained in these guidelines.

(2) *Criterion-related validity.* Reports of criterion-related validity of selection procedures should contain the following information:

(a) *Time period(s) of study.* The time period of administration of selection procedures and collection of criterion data and, where appropriate, the time between collection of data on selection procedures and criterion measures should be shown.

(b) *Purpose and setting.* An explicit definition of the purpose(s) and the circumstances in which the validity evidence was gathered should be provided.

(c) *Review of job information.* Where a review of job information results in criteria which are measures other than work proficiency, the basis for the selection of these criteria should be reported. Where a job review is conducted, the report should include either:

(i) the important duties performed on the job and the basis on which such duties were determined to be important; or

(ii) the knowledges, skills, abilities and/or other worker characteristics and bases on which they were determined to be important. Published descriptions from industry sources or the Dictionary of Occupational Titles, Fourth Edition, United States Government Printing Office (1977) are satisfactory if they reasonably describe the job. If appropriate, a brief supplement to the published description should be provided.

(iii) If two or more jobs are grouped for a validity study, a justification for this grouping should be provided.

(d) *Job titles and codes.* It is desirable to provide the user's job title(s) for the job(s) in question and the corresponding job title(s) and code(s) from United States Employment Service's Dictionary of Occupational Titles.

(e) *Criteria.* A full description of all criteria on which data were collected, including a rationale for selection of the final criteria and means by which they were gathered and quantified should be provided. If rating techniques are used as criterion measures, a copy of the appraisal form(s) and instructions to the rater(s) should be included as part of the validation evidence.

(f) *Sample.* A description of how the research sample was selected should be included.

(g) *Selection procedure.* The measure, combination of measures, or procedures studied should be described or attached. If commercially available selection procedures are used, they should be described by title, form and publisher. A rationale for choosing the selection procedures investigated should be included.

(h) *Techniques and results.* Methods used in analyzing data should be described. Measures of central tendency (*e.g.,* means) and measures of dispersion (*e.g.,* standard deviations and ranges) for all selection procedures and all criteria should be reported. Where appropriate, statistical results should be organized and presented in tabular or graphical form. Selection procedure-criterion relationships should be reported. Statements regarding the statistical significance or confidence intervals surrounding results should be made.

Any statistical adjustments, such as for less than perfect predictor reliability or for restriction of score range in the selection procedure or criterion, or both, should be described; and unadjusted correlation coefficients should also be shown. Where the statistical technique used categorizes continuous data, such as biserial correlation, the bases for such categories should be described.

(i) *Uses and applications.* A description of the way in which each selection procedure is used (*e.g.,* as a screening device with a cut-off score or combined with other procedures in a battery) and application of the procedure (*e.g.,* selection, transfer, promotion) should be provided. If weights are assigned to different parts of the selection procedure, these weights and the validity of the weighted composite should be reported.

(j) *Cutoff scores.* Where cutoff scores are to be used, both the cutoff scores and the way in which they were determined should be described.

(k) *Source data.* Each user should maintain records showing all pertinent information about individual sample members in studies involving the validation of selection procedures. These records (exclusive of names and social security number) may be requested by an enforcement agency when it has identifiable questions concerning the adequacy of the report of validity evidence. These data should include selection procedure scores and criterion scores.

(l) *Contact person.* It is desirable for the user to set forth the name, mailing address, and telephone number of the individual who may be contacted for further information about the validity evidence.

(3) *Content validity.* Reports of content validity of selection procedures should contain the following information:

(a) *Definition of content domain.* A full description should be provided for the basis on which a content domain is defined. A complete and comprehensive definition of the content domain should also be provided.

(b) *Job title and code.* It is desirable to provide the user's job title(s) and the corresponding job title(s) and code(s) from the United States Employment Service's Dictionary of Occupational Titles.

(c) *Selection procedures.* Selection procedures including those constructed by or for the user, specific training, education and experience requirements, composites of selection procedures, and any other procedure for which content validity is asserted should be completely and explicitly described or attached. If commercially available selection procedures are used, they should be described by title, form, and publisher. Evidence that the selection procedure measures the content domain should be provided.

(d) *Techniques and results.* The method by which the correspondence between the content of the selection procedure and the job content domain(s) was determined should be described. The adequacy of the sample coverage of the content domain should be described as precisely as possible. Measures of central tendency (*e.g.*, means) and measures of dispersion (*e.g.*, standard deviations) should be reported for all selection procedures as appropriate and feasible.

(e) *Uses and applications.* A description of the way in which each selection procedure is used (*e.g.*, as a screening device with a cutoff score or combined with other procedures in a battery) and the application of the procedure (*e.g.*, selection, transfer, promotion) should be provided. A rationale for the use of the procedure should be provided.

(f) *Contact person.* It is desirable for the employer to set forth the name, mailing address and telephone number of the individual who may be contacted for further information about the validation evidence.

(4) *Construct validity.* Reports of construct validity of selection procedures should contain the following information:

(a) *Construct definition.* A clear definition of the construct should be provided, explained in terms of empirically observable behavior.

(b) *Job review.* The job review should show how the constructs are related to important job or training behaviors.

(c) *Job titles and codes.* It is desirable to provide the selection procedure user's job title(s) for the job(s) in question and the corresponding job title(s) and code(s) from the United States Employment Service's Dictionary of Occupational Titles.

(d) *Selection procedure.* The selection procedure used as a measure of the construct should be completely and explicitly described or attached. If commercially available selection procedures are used, they should be identified by title, form and publisher. The evidence demonstrating that the selection procedure is in fact a proper measure of the construct should be included.

(e) *Anchoring.* The empirical evidence showing that performance on the selection procedure is related to performance of critical job or training behaviors should be included and that individual differences on the construct are related to individual differences on the job or training should be included.

(f) *Uses and applications.* A description of the way in which each selection procedure is used (*e.g.*, as a screening device with a cutoff score or combined with other procedures in a battery) and application of the procedure (*e.g.*, selection, transfer, promotion) should be provided. If weights are assigned to different parts of the selection procedure, these weights (and the validity of the weighted composite) should be reported.

(g) *Cutoff scores.* Where cutoff scores are to be used, both the cutoff scores and the way in which they were determined should be described.

(h) *Source data.* Each user should maintain records showing all pertinent information about individual sample members in studies involving the validation of selection procedures. These records (exclusive of names and social security number) may be requested by an enforcement agency when it has identifiable questions concerning the adequacy of the report of validity evidence. These data should include selection procedure scores and criterion scores.

(i) *Contact person.* It is desirable for the user to set forth the name, mailing address and telephone number of the individual who may be contacted for further information about the validity evidence.

(5) *Evidence of validity from other studies.* When validity of a selection procedure is supported by studies not conducted by the user, the evidence from the original study or studies should be compiled in a manner similar to that required above. See section 7A. In addition, the following evidence should be supplied:

(a) *Evidence from criterion-related validity studies*

(i) *Job information.* A description of the important behaviors or the knowledge(s), skill(s), ability(ies), or worker characteristic(s) of the user's job and the basis on which they were determined to be important should be provided. A full description of the basis for determining that these important job or training behaviors or knowledge(s), skill(s), ability(ies) or worker characteristic(s) are sufficiently similar to those of the job in the original study (or studies) to warrant use of the selection procedure in the new situation should be provided. For purposes of this section, a comparison based on job description in the Dictionary of Occupational Titles, Fourth Edition, 1977, will be satisfactory.

(ii) *Relevance of criteria.* A full description of the basis on which the criteria used in the original studies are determined to be relevant for the user should be provided.

(iii) *Use of the selection procedure.* A full description should be provided showing that the use to be made of the selection procedure is consistent with the original validity evidence.

(iv) *Bibliography.* A bibliography of reports of validity of the selection procedure for the job or jobs in question should be provided. Where a user is relying upon unpublished studies, a reasonable effort should be made to obtain these studies. If these unpublished studies are the sole source of validity evidence they should be described in detail or attached. If these studies are not available, the name and address of the source, an abstract or summary of the validity study and data, and a contact person in the source organization should be provided.

(b) *Evidence from content validity studies—Similarity of content domains.* A full description should be provided of the similarity between the content domain in the user's job and the content domain measured by a selection procedure developed and shown to be content valid by another user.

(c) *Evidence from construct validity studies—Uniformity of construct.* A description should be provided of the basis for determining that the construct identified as underlying successful job or training behavior by the user's job review is the same as the construct measured by the selection procedure.

DEFINITIONS

Section 16. Definitions.

The following definitions shall apply throughout these guidelines:

A. Adverse impact. See section 4D of these guidelines.

B. Content domain. A body of knowledge and/or a set of tasks or other behaviors defined so that given facts or behaviors, as appropriate, may be classified as included or excluded.

C. Employer. Any employer subject to the provisions of the Civil Rights Act of 1964, as amended, including State or local governments and any Federal agency subject to the provisions of section 717 of the Civil Rights Act of 1964, as amended, and any Federal contractor or subcontractor or federally assisted construction contractor or subcontractor covered by Executive Order 11246, as amended.

D. Employment agency. Any employment agency subject to the provisions of the Civil Rights Act of 1964, as amended.

E. Enforcement agency. Any agency of the executive branch of the Federal Government which adopts these guidelines for purposes of the enforcement of the equal employment opportunity laws or which has responsibility for securing compliance with them.

F. Labor organization. Any labor organization subject to the provisions of the Civil Rights Act of 1964, as amended, and any committee subject thereto controlling apprenticeship or other training.

G. Race, sex, or ethnic group. Any group of persons identifiable on the grounds of race, color, sex, or national origin as specified in section 4B.

H. Selection procedure. Any measure, combination of measures, or procedure, other than a bona fide seniority system, used as a basis for any employment decision. Selection procedures include the full range of assessment techniques from traditional paper and pencil tests, performance tests, training programs, or probationary periods and physical, educational, and work experience requirements through informal or casual interviews and unscored application forms.

I. Selection rate. The proportion of applicants or candidates who are hired, promoted, or otherwise selected.

J. Technical feasibility. The existence of conditions permitting the conduct of meaningful criterion-related validity studies. These conditions include: (1) an adequate and appropriate sample of persons available for the study to achieve findings of statistical significance; (2) having or being able to obtain a sufficient range of scores on the selection procedure and job performance measures to produce validity results which can be expected to be representative of the results if the ranges normally expected were utilized; and (3) having or being able to devise unbiased, reliable and relevant measures of job or training performance or other criteria of employee adequacy.

K. User. Any employer, labor organization or employment agency, to the extent it may be covered by Federal equal employment opportunity law, which uses a selection procedure as a basis for any employment decision. Whenever a State employment agency or service does no more than administer or monitor a procedure as permitted by Department of Labor regulations, and does so without making referrals or taking any other action on the basis of the results, the State employment agency will not be deemed to be a user.

Appendix C

UNIFORM GUIDELINES ON EMPLOYEE SELECTION PROCEDURES (1978)

TABLE OF CONTENTS

GENERAL PRINCIPLES

1. Statement of Purpose

    A. Need for Uniformity—Issuing Agencies
    B. Purpose of Guidelines
    C. Relation to Prior Guidelines

2. Scope

    A. Application of Guidelines
    B. Employment Decisions
    C. Selection Procedures
    D. Limitations
    E. Indian Preference Not Affected

3. Discrimination Defined: Relationship Between Use of Selection Procedures and Discrimination

    A. Procedure Having Adverse Impact Constitutes Discrimination Unless Justified
    B. Consideration of Suitable Alternative Selection Procedures

4. Information on Impact

    A. Records Concerning Impact
    B. Applicable Race, Sex and Ethnic Groups For Record Keeping
    C. Evaluation of Selection Rates. The "Bottom Line"
    D. Adverse Impact And The "Four-Fifths Rule"
    E. Consideration of User's Equal Employment Opportunity Posture

5. General Standards for Validity Studies

    A. Acceptable types of Validity Studies

- B. Criterion-Related, Content, and Construct Validity
- C. Guidelines Are Consistent with Professional Standards
- D. Need For Documentation of Validity
- E. Accuracy and Standardization
- F. Caution Against Selection on Basis of Knowledges, Skills or Abilities Learned in Brief Orientation Period
- G. Method of Use of Selection Procedures
- H. Cutoff Scores
- I. Use of Selection Procedures for Higher Level Jobs
- J. Interim Use of Selection Procedures
- K. Review of Validity Studies for Currency

6. Use of Selection Procedures Which Have Not Been Validated

- A. Use of Alternate Selection Procedures to Eliminate Adverse Impact
- B. Where Validity Studies Cannot or Need Not Be Performed
  - (1) Where Informal or Unscored Procedures Are Used
  - (2) Where Formal And Scored Procedures Are Used

7. Use of Other Validity Studies

- A. Validity Studies not Conducted by the User
- B. Use of Criterion-Related Validity Evidence from Other Sources
  - (1) Validity Evidence
  - (2) Job Similarity
  - (3) Fairness Evidence
- C. Validity Evidence from Multi-Unit Study
- D. Other Significant Variables

8. Cooperative Studies

- A. Encouragement of Cooperative Studies
- B. Standards for Use of Cooperative Studies

9. No Assumption of Validity

- A. Unacceptable Substitutes for Evidence of Validity
- B. Encouragement of Professional Supervision

10. Employment Agencies and Employment Services

- A. Where Selection Procedures Are Devised by Agency
- B. Where Selection Procedures Are Devised Elsewhere

11. Disparate Treatment
12. Retesting of Applicants
13. Affirmative Action
    A. Affirmative Action Obligations
    B. Encouragement of Voluntary Affirmative Action Programs

    TECHNICAL STANDARDS

14. Technical Standards for Validity Studies
    A. Validity Studies Should be Based on Review of Information about the Job
    B. Technical Standards for Criterion-Related Validity Studies
        (1) Technical Feasibility
        (2) Analysis of the Job
        (3) Criterion Measures
        (4) Representativeness of the Sample
        (5) Statistical Relationships
        (6) Operational Use of Selection Procedures
        (7) Over-Statement of Validity Findings
        (8) Fairness
            (a) Unfairness Defined
            (b) Investigation of Fairness
            (c) General Considerations in Fairness Investigations
            (d) When Unfairness Is Shown
            (e) Technical Feasibility of Fairness Studies
            (f) Continued Use of Selection Procedures When Fairness Studies not Feasible
    C. Technical Standards for Content Validity Studies
        (1) Appropriateness of Content Validity Studies
        (2) Job Analysis for Content Validity
        (3) Development of Selection Procedure
        (4) Standards For Demonstrating Content Validity
        (5) Reliability
        (6) Prior Training or Experience
        (7) Training Success
        (8) Operational Use
        (9) Ranking Based on Content Validity Studies
    D. Technical Standards For Construct Validity Studies

(1) Appropriateness of Construct Validity Studies
   (2) Job Analysis For Construct Validity Studies
   (3) Relationship to the Job
   (4) Use of Construct Validity Study Without New Criterion-Related Evidence
       (a) Standards for Use
       (b) Determination of Common Work Behaviors

DOCUMENTATION OF IMPACT AND VALIDITY EVIDENCE

15. Documentation of Impact and Validity Evidence
    A. Required Information
       (1) Simplified Recordkeeping for Users With Less Than 100 Employees
       (2) Information on Impact
           (a) Collection of Information on Impact
           (b) When Adverse Impact Has Been Eliminated in The Total Selection Process
           (c) When Data Insufficient to Determine Impact
       (3) Documentation of Validity Evidence
           (a) Type of Evidence
           (b) Form of Report
           (c) Completeness
    B. Criterion-Related Validity Studies
       (1) User(s), Location(s), and Date(s) of Study
       (2) Problem and Setting
       (3) Job Analysis or Review of Job Information
       (4) Job Titles and Codes
       (5) Criterion Measures
       (6) Sample Description
       (7) Description of Selection Procedure
       (8) Techniques and Results
       (9) Alternative Procedures Investigated
       (10) Uses and Applications
       (11) Source Data
       (12) Contact Person
       (13) Accuracy and Completeness
    C. Content Validity Studies
       (1) User(s), Location(s), and Date(s) of Study
       (2) Problem and Setting

      (3) Job Analysis—Content of the Job
      (4) Selection Procedure and its Content
      (5) Relationship Between Selection Procedure and the Job
      (6) Alternative Procedures Investigated
      (7) Uses and Applications
      (8) Contact Person
      (9) Accuracy and Completeness

  D. Construct Validity Studies

      (1) User(s), Location(s), and Date(s) of Study
      (2) Problem and Setting
      (3) Construct Definition
      (4) Job Analysis
      (5) Job Titles and Codes
      (6) Selection Procedure
      (7) Relationship to Job Performance
      (8) Alternative Procedures Investigated
      (9) Uses and Applications
     (10) Accuracy and Completeness
     (11) Source Data
     (12) Contact Person

  E. Evidence of Validity from Other Studies

      (1) Evidence from Criterion-Related Validity Studies

          (a) Job Information
          (b) Relevance of Criteria
          (c) Other Variables
          (d) Use of the Selection Procedure
          (e) Bibliography

      (2) Evidence from Content Validity Studies
      (3) Evidence from Construct Validity Studies

  F. Evidence of Validity from Cooperative Studies
  G. Selection for Higher Level Jobs
  H. Interim Use of Selection Procedures

DEFINITIONS

16. Definitions

APPENDIX

17. Policy Statement on Affirmative Action (see Section 13B)
18. Citations

General Principles

Section 1. *Statement of purpose.*—A. *Need for uniformity—Issuing agencies.* The Federal government's need for a uniform set of principles on the question of the use of tests and other selection procedures has long been recognized. The Equal Employment Opportunity Commission, the Civil Service Commission, the Department of Labor, and the Department of Justice jointly have adopted these uniform guidelines to meet that need, and to apply the same principles to the Federal Government as are applied to other employers.

B. *Purpose of guidelines.* These guidelines incorporate a single set of principles which are designed to assist employers, labor organizations, employment agencies, and licensing and certification boards to comply with requirements of Federal law prohibiting employment practices which discriminate on grounds of race, color, religion, sex, and national origin. They are designed to provide a framework for determining the proper use of tests and other selection procedures. These guidelines do not require a user to conduct validity studies of selection procedures where no adverse impact results. However, all users are encouraged to use selection procedures which are valid, especially users operating under merit principles.

C. *Relation to prior guidelines.* These guidelines are based upon and supersede previously issued guidelines on employee selection procedures. These guidelines have been built upon court decisions, the previously issued guidelines of the agencies, and the practical experience of the agencies, as well as the standards of the psychological profession. These guidelines are intended to be consistent with existing law.

Sec. 2. *Scope.*—A. *Application of guidelines.* These guidelines will be applied by the Equal Employment Opportunity Commission in the enforcement of title VII of the Civil Rights Act of 1964, as amended by the Equal Employment Opportunity Act of 1972 (hereinafter "Title VII"); by the Department of Labor, and the contract compliance agencies until the transfer of authority contemplated by the President's Reorganization Plan No. 1 of 1978, in the administration and enforcement of Executive Order 11246, as amended by Executive Order 11375 (hereinafter "Executive Order 11246"); by the Civil Service Commission and other Federal agencies subject to section 717 of Title VII; by the Civil Service Commission in exercising its responsibilities toward State and local governments under section 208(b)(1) of the

Intergovernmental-Personnel Act; by the Department of Justice in exercising its responsibilities under Federal law; by the Office of Revenue Sharing of the Department of the Treasury under the State and Local Fiscal Assistance Act of 1972, as amended; and by any other Federal agency which adopts them.

B. *Employment decisions.* These guidelines apply to tests and other selection procedures which are used as a basis for any employment decision. Employment decisions include but are not limited to hiring, promotion, demotion, membership (for example, in a labor organization), referral, retention, and licensing and certification, to the extent that licensing and certification may be covered by Federal equal employment opportunity law. Other selection decisions, such as selection for training or transfer, may also be considered employment decisions if they lead to any of the decisions listed above.

C. *Selection procedures.* These guidelines apply only to selection procedures which are used as a basis for making employment decisions. For example, the use of recruiting procedures designed to attract members of a particular race, sex, or ethnic group, which were previously denied employment opportunities or which are currently underutilized, may be necessary to bring an employer into compliance with Federal law, and is frequently an essential element of any effective affirmative action program; but recruitment practices are not considered by these guidelines to be selection procedures. Similarly, these guidelines do not pertain to the question of the lawfulness of a seniority system within the meaning of section 703(h), Executive Order 11246 or other provisions of Federal law or regulation, except to the extent that such systems utilize selection procedures to determine qualifications or abilities to perform the job. Nothing in these guidelines is intended or should be interpreted as discouraging the use of a selection procedure for the purpose of determining qualifications or for the purpose of selection on the basis of relative qualifications, if the selection procedure had been validated in accord with these guidelines for each such purpose for which it is to be used.

D. *Limitations.* These guidelines apply only to persons subject to Title VII, Executive Order 11246, or other equal employment opportunity requirements of Federal law. These guidelines do not apply to responsibilities under the Age Discrimination in Employment Act of 1967, as amended, not to discriminate on the basis of age, or under sections 501, 503, and 504 of the Rehabilitation Act of 1973, not to discriminate on the basis of handicap.

E. *Indian preference not affected.* These guidelines do not restrict any obligation imposed or right granted by Federal law to users to extend a preference in employment to Indians living on or near an Indian reservation in connection with employment opportunities on or near an Indian reservation.

SEC. 3. *Discrimination defined: Relationship between use of selection procedures and discrimination.*—A. *Procedure having adverse impact constitutes discrimination unless justified.* The use of any selection procedure which has an adverse impact on the hiring, promotion, or other employment or membership opportunities of members of any race, sex, or ethnic group will be considered to be discriminatory and inconsistent with these guidelines, unless the procedure has been validated in accordance with these guidelines, or the provisions of section 6 below are satisfied.

B. *Consideration of suitable alternative selection procedures.* Where two or more selection procedures are available which serve the user's legitimate interest in efficient and trustworthy workmanship, and which are substantially equally valid for a given purpose, the user should use the procedure which has been demonstrated to have the lesser adverse impact. Accordingly, whenever a validity study is called for by these guidelines, the user should include, as a part of the validity study, an investigation of suitable alternative selection procedures and suitable alternative methods of using the selection procedure which have as little adverse impact as possible, to determine the appropriateness of using or validating them in accord with these guidelines. If a user has made a reasonable effort to become aware of such alternative procedures and validity has been demonstrated in accord with these guidelines, the use of the test or other selection procedure may continue until such time as it should reasonably be reviewed for currency. Whenever the user is shown an alternative selection procedure with evidence of less adverse impact and substantial evidence of validity for the same job in similar circumstances, the user should investigate it to determine the appropriateness of using or validating it in accord with these guidelines. This subsection is not intended to preclude the combination of procedures into a significantly more valid procedure, if the use of such a combination has been shown to be in compliance with the guidelines.

SEC. 4. *Information on impact.*—A. *Records concerning impact.* Each user should maintain and have available for inspection records or other information which will disclose the impact which its tests and other selection procedures have upon employment opportunities of persons by identifiable race, sex, or ethnic group as set forth in subparagraph B below in order to determine compliance with these guidelines. Where there are large numbers of applicants and procedures are administered frequently, such information may be retained on a sample basis, provided that the sample is appropriate in terms of the applicant population and adequate in size.

B. *Applicable race, sex, and ethnic groups for recordkeeping.* The records called for by this section are to be maintained by sex, and the following races and ethnic groups: Blacks (Negroes), American Indians (including Alaskan Natives), Asians (including Pacific Islanders), Hispanic (including persons of Mexican, Puerto Rican, Cuban, Central or South American, or other Spanish origin or culture regardless of race), whites (Caucasians) other than Hispanic, and totals. The race, sex, and ethnic classifications called for by this section are consistent with the Equal Employment Opportunity Standard Form 100, Employer Information Report EEO-1 series of reports. The user should adopt safeguards to insure that the records required by this paragraph are used for appropriate purposes such as determining adverse impact, or (where required) for developing and monitoring affirmative action programs, and that such records are not used improperly. See sections 4E and 17(4), below.

C. *Evaluation of selection rates. The "bottom line."* If the information called for by sections 4B and B above shows that the total selection process for a job has an adverse impact, the individual components of the selection process should be evaluated for adverse impact. If this information shows that the total selection process does not have an adverse impact, the Federal enforcement agencies, in the exercise of their administrative and prosecutorial discretion, in usual circumstances will not expect a user to evaluate the individual components for adverse impact, or to validate such individual components, and will not take enforcement action based upon adverse impact of any component of that process, including the separate parts of a multipart selection procedure or any separate procedure that is used as an alternative method of selection. However, in the following circumstances the Federal enforcement agencies will expect a user to evaluate the individual components for adverse impact and may, where appropriate, take enforcement action with respect to the individual components: (1) where the selection procedure is a significant factor in the continuation of patterns of assignments of incumbent employees caused by prior discriminatory employment practices, (2) where the weight of court decisions or administrative interpretations hold that a specific procedure (such as height or weight requirements or no-arrest records) is not job related in the same or similar circumstances. In unusual circumstances, other than those listed in (1) and (2) above, the Federal enforcement agencies may request a user to evaluate the individual components for adverse impact and may, where appropriate, take enforcement action with respect to the individual component.

D. *Adverse impact and the "four-fifths rule."* A selection rate for any race, sex, or ethnic group which is less than four-fifths (4/5) (or eighty percent) of the rate for the group with the highest rate will generally be regarded by the Federal enforcement agencies as evidence of adverse impact, while a greater than four-fifths rate will generally not be regarded by Federal enforcement agencies as evidence of adverse impact. Smaller differences in selection rate may nevertheless constitute adverse impact, where they are significant in both statistical and practical terms or where a user's actions have discouraged applicants disproportionately on grounds of race, sex, or ethnic group. Greater differences in selection rate may not constitute adverse impact where the differences are based on small numbers and are not statistically significant, or where special recruiting or other programs cause the pool of minority or female candidates to be atypical of the normal pool of applicants from that group. Where the user's evidence concerning the impact of a selection procedure indicates adverse impact but is based upon numbers which are too small to be reliable, evidence concerning the impact of the procedure over a longer period of time and/or evidence concerning the impact which the selection procedure had when used in the same manner in similar circumstances elsewhere may be considered in determining adverse impact. Where the user has not maintained data on adverse impact as required by the documentation section of applicable guidelines, the Federal enforcement agencies may draw an inference of adverse impact of the selection process from the failure of the user to maintain such data, if the user has an underutilization of a group in the job category, as compared to the group's representation in the relevant labor market or, in the case of jobs filled from within, the applicable work force.

E. *Consideration of user's equal employment opportunity posture.* In carrying out their obligations, the Federal enforcement agencies will consider the general posture of the user with respect to equal employment opportunity for the job or group of jobs in question. Where a user has adopted an affirmative action program, the Federal enforcement agencies will consider the provisions of that program, including the goals and timetables which the user has adopted and the progress which the user has made in carrying out that program and in meeting the goals and timetables. While such affirmative action programs may in design and execution be race, color, sex, or ethnic conscious, selection procedures under such programs should be based upon the ability or relative ability to do the work.

SEC. 5. *General standards for validity studies.*—A. *Acceptable types of validity studies.* For the purposes of satisfying these guidelines, users may rely upon criterion-related validity studies, content validity studies or construct validity studies, in accordance with the standards set forth in the technical standards of these guidelines, section 14 below. New strategies for showing the validity of selection procedures will be evaluated as they become accepted by the psychological profession.

B. *Criterion-related, content, and construct validity.* Evidence of the validity of a test or other selection procedure by a criterion-related validity study should consist of empirical data demonstrating that the selection procedure is predictive of or significantly correlated with important elements of job performance. See section 14B below. Evidence of the validity of a test or other selection procedure by a content validity study should consist of data showing that the content of the selection procedure is representative of important aspects of performance on the job for which the candidates are to be evaluated. See section 14C below. Evidence of the validity of a test or other selection procedure through a construct validity study should consist of data showing that the procedure measures the degree to which candidates have identifiable characteristics which have been determined to be important in successful performance in the job for which the candidates are to be evaluated. See section 14D below.

C. *Guidelines are consistent with professional standards.* The provisions of these guidelines relating to validation of selection procedures are intended to be consistent with generally accepted professional standards for evaluating standardized tests and other selection procedures, such as those described in the Standards for Educational and Psychological Tests prepared by a joint committee of the American Psychological Association, the American Educational Research Association, and the National Council on Measurement in Education (American Psychological Association, Washington, D.C., 1974) (hereinafter "A.P.A. Standards") and standard textbooks and journals in the field of personnel selection.

D. *Need for documentation of validity.* For any selection procedure which is part of a selection process which has an adverse impact and which selection procedure has an adverse impact, each user should maintain and have available such documentation as is described in section 15 below.

E. *Accuracy and standardization.* Validity studies should be carried out under conditions which assure insofar as possible the adequacy and accuracy of the research and the report. Selection procedures should be administered and scored under standardized conditions.

F. *Caution against selection on basis of knowledge skills, or ability learned in brief orientation period.* In general, users should avoid making employment decisions on the basis of measures of knowledges, skills, or abilities which are normally learned in a brief orientation period, and which have an adverse impact.

G. *Method of use of selection procedures.* The evidence of both the validity and utility of a selection procedure should support the method the user chooses for operational use of the procedure, if that method of use has a greater adverse impact than another method of use. Evidence which may be sufficient to support the use of a selection procedure on a pass/fail (screening) basis may be insufficient to support the use of the same procedure on a ranking basis under these guidelines. Thus, if a user decides to use a selection procedure on a ranking basis, and that method of use has a greater adverse impact than use on an appropriate pass/fail basis (see section 5H below), the user should have sufficient evidence of validity and utility to support the use on a ranking basis. See sections 3B, 14B (5) and (6), and 14C (8) and (9).

H. *Cutoff scores.* Where cutoff scores are used, they should normally be set so as to be reasonable and consistent with normal expectations of acceptable proficiency within the work force. Where applicants are ranked on the basis of properly validated selection procedures and those applicants scoring below a higher cutoff score than appropriate in light of such expectations have little or no chance of being selected for employment, the higher cutoff score may be appropriate, but the degree of adverse impact should be considered.

I. *Use of selection procedures for higher level jobs.* If job progression structures are so established that employees will probably, within a reasonable period of time and in a majority of cases, progress to a higher level, it may be considered that the applicants are being evaluated for a job or jobs at the higher level. However, where job progression is not so nearly automatic, or the time span is such that higher level jobs or employees' potential may be expected to change in significant ways, it should be considered that applicants are being evaluated for a job at or near the entry level. A "reasonable period of time" will vary for different jobs and employment situations but will seldom be more than 5 years. Use of selection procedures to evaluate applicants for a higher level job would not be appropriate:

(1) If the majority of those remaining employed do not progress to the higher level job;

(2) If there is a reason to doubt that the higher level job will continue to require essentially similar skills during the progression period; or

(3) If the selection procedures measure knowledges, skills, or abilities required for advancement which would be expected to develop principally from the training or experience on the job.

J. *Interim use of selection procedures.* Users may continue the use of a selection procedure which is not at the moment fully supported by the required evidence of validity, provided: (1) The user has available substantial evidence of validity, and (2) the user has in progress, when technically feasible, a study which is designed to produce the additional evidence required by these guidelines within a reasonable time. If such a study is not technically feasible, see section 6B. If the study does not demonstrate validity, this provision of these guidelines for interim use shall not constitute a defense in any action, nor shall it relieve the user of any obligations arising under Federal law.

K. *Review of validity studies for currency.* Whenever validity has been shown in accord with these guidelines for the use of a particular selection procedure for a job or group of jobs, additional studies need not be performed until such time as the validity study is subject to review as provided in section 3B above. There are no absolutes in the area of determining the currency of a validity study. All circumstances concerning the study, including the validation strategy used, and changes in the relevant labor market and the job should be considered in the determination of when a validity study is outdated.

SEC. 6. *Use of selection procedures which have not been validated.*—A. *Use of alternate selection procedures to eliminate adverse impact.* A user may choose to utilize alternative selection procedures in order to eliminate adverse impact or as part of an affirmative action program. See section 13 below. Such alternative procedures should eliminate the adverse impact in the total selection process, should be lawful and should be as job related as possible.

B. *Where validity studies cannot or need not be performed.* There are circumstances in which a user cannot or need not utilize the validation techniques contemplated by these guidelines. In such circumstances, the user should utilize selection procedures which are as job related as possible and which will minimize or eliminate adverse impact, as set forth below.

(1) *Where informal or unscored procedures are used.* When an informal or unscored selection procedure which has an adverse impact is utilized, the user should eliminate the adverse impact, or modify the procedure to one which is a formal, scored or quantified measure or combination of measures and then validate the procedure in accord with these guidelines, or otherwise justify continued use of the procedure in accord with Federal law.

(2) *Where formal and scored procedures are used.* When a formal and scored selection procedure is used which has an adverse impact, the validation techniques contemplated by these guidelines usually should be followed if technically feasible. Where the user cannot or need not follow the validation techniques anticipated by these guidelines, the user should either modify the procedure to eliminate adverse impact or otherwise justify continued use of the procedure in accord with Federal law.

SEC. 7. *Use of other validity studies.*—A. *Validity studies not conducted by the user.* Users may, under certain circumstances, support the use of selection procedures by validity studies conducted by other users or conducted by test publishers or distributors and described in test manuals. While publishers of selection procedures have a professional obligation to provide evidence of validity which meets generally accepted professional standards (see section 5C above), users are cautioned that they are responsible for compliance with these guidelines. Accordingly, users seeking to obtain selection procedures from publishers and distributors should be careful to determine that, in the event the user becomes subject to the validity requirements of these guidelines, the necessary information to support validity has been determined and will be made available to the user.

B. *Use of criterion-related validity evidence from other sources.* Criterion-related validity studies conducted by one test user, or described in test manuals and the progessional literature, will be considered acceptable for use by another user when the following requirements are met:

(1) *Validity evidence.* Evidence from the available studies meeting the standards of section 14B below clearly demonstrates that the selection procedure is valid;

(2) *Job similarity.* The incumbents in the user's job and the incumbents in the job or group of jobs on which the validity study was conducted perform substantially the same major work behaviors, as shown by appropriate job analyses both on the job or group of jobs on which the validity study was performed and on the job for which the selection procedure is to be used; and

(3) *Fairness evidence.* The studies include a study of test fairness for each race, sex, and ethnic group which constitutes a significant factor in the borrowing user's relevant labor market for the job or jobs in question. If the studies under consideration satisfy (1) and (2) above but do not contain an investigation of test fairness, and it is not technically feasible for the borrowing user to conduct an internal study of test fairness, the borrowing user may utilize the study until studies conducted elsewhere meeting the requirements of these guidelines show test unfairness, or until such time as it becomes technically feasible to conduct an internal study of test fairness and the results of that study can be acted upon. Users obtaining selection procedures from publishers should consider, as one factor in the decision to purchase a particular selection procedure, the availability of evidence concerning test fairness.

C. *Validity evidence from multiunit study.* If validity evidence from a study covering more than one unit within an organization satisfies the requirements of section 14B below, evidence of validity specific to each unit will not be required unless there are variables which are likely to affect validity significantly.

D. *Other significant variables.* If there are variables in the other studies which are likely to affect validity significantly, the user may not rely upon such studies, but will be expected either to conduct an internal validity study or to comply with section 6 above.

SEC. 8. *Cooperative studies.*—A. *Encouragement of cooperative studies.* The agencies issuing these guidelines encourage employers, labor organizations, and employment agencies to cooperate in research, development, search for lawful alternatives, and validity studies in order to achieve procedures which are consistent with these guidelines.

B. *Standards for use of cooperative studies.* If validity evidence from a cooperative study satisfies the requirements of section 14 below, evidence of validity specific to each user will not be required unless there are variables in the user's situation which are likely to affect validity significantly.

SEC. 9. *No assumption of validity.*—A. *Unacceptable substitutes for evidence of validity.* Under no circumstances will the general reputation of a test or other selection procedures, is author or its publisher, or casual reports of it's validity be accepted in lieu of evidence of validity. Specifically ruled out are: assumptions of validity based on a procedure's name or descriptive labels; all forms of promotional literature; data bearing on the frequency of a procedure's usage; testimonial statements and credentials of sellers, users, or consultants; and other nonempirical or anecdotal accounts of selection practices or selection outcomes.

B. *Encouragement of professional supervision.* Professional supervision of selection activities is encouraged but is not a substitute for documented evidence of validity. The enforcement agencies will take into account the fact that a thorough job analysis was conducted and that careful development and use of a selection procedure in accordance with professional standards enhance the probability that the selection procedure is valid for the job.

SEC. 10. *Employment agencies and employment services.*— A. *Where selection procedures are devised by agency.* An employment agency, including private employment agencies and State employment agencies, which agrees to a request by an employer or labor organization to devise and utilize a selection procedure should follow the standards in these guidelines for determining adverse impact. If adverse impact exists the agency should comply with these guidelines. An employment agency is not relieved of its obligation herein because the user did not request such validation or has requested the use of some lesser standard of validation than is provided in these guidelines. The use of an employment agency does not relieve an employer or labor organization or other user of its responsibilities under Federal law to provide equal employment opportunity or its obligations as a user under these guidelines.

B. *Where selection procedures are devised elsewhere.* Where an employment agency or service is requested to administer a selection procedure which has been devised elsewhere and to make referrals pursuant to the results, the employment agency or service should maintain and have available evidence of the impact of the selection and referral procedures which it administers. If adverse impact results the agency or service should comply with these guidelines. If the agency or service seeks to comply with these guidelines by reliance upon validity studies or other data in the possession of the employer, it should obtain and have available such information.

SEC. 11. *Disparate treatment.* The principles of disparate or unequal treatment must be distinguished from the concepts of validation. A selection procedure—even though validated against job performance in accordance with these guidelines— cannot be imposed upon members of a race, sex, or ethnic group where other employees, applicants, or members have not been subjected to that standard. Disparate treatment occurs where members of a race, sex, or ethnic group have been denied the same employment, promotion, membership, or other employment opportunities as have been available to other employees or applicants. Those employees or applicants who have been denied equal treatment, because of prior discriminatory practices or policies, must at least be afforded the same opportunities as had existed for other employees or applicants during the period of discrimination. Thus, the persons who were in the class of persons discriminated against during the period the user followed the discriminatory practices should be allowed the opportunity to qualify under less stringent selection procedures previously followed, unless the user demonstrates that the increased standards are required by business necessity. This section does not prohibit a user who has not previously followed merit standards from adopting merit standards which are in compliance with these guidelines; nor does it preclude a user who has previously used invalid or unvalidated selection procedures from developing and using procedures which are in accord with these guidelines.

SEC. 12. *Retesting of applicants.* Users should provide a reasonable opportunity for retesting and reconsideration. Where examinations are administered periodically with public notice, such reasonable opportunity exists, unless persons who have previously been tested are precluded from retesting. The user may however take reasonable steps to preserve the security of its procedures.

SEC. 13. *Affirmative action.*—A. *Affirmative action obligations.* The use of selection procedures which have been validated pursuant to these guidelines does not relieve users of any obligations they may have to undertake affirmative action to assure equal employment opportunity. Nothing in these guidelines is intended to preclude the use of lawful selection procedures which assist in remedying the effects of prior discriminatory practices, or the achievement of affirmative action objectives.

B. *Encouragement of voluntary affirmative action programs.* These guidelines are also intended to encourage the adoption and implementation of voluntary affirmative action programs by users who have no obligation under Federal law to adopt them; but are not intended to impose any new obligations in that regard. The agencies issuing and endorsing these guidelines endorse for all private employers and reaffirm for all governmental employers the Equal Employment Opportunity Coordinating Council's "Policy Statement on Affirmative Action Programs for State and Local Government Agencies" (41 FR 38814, September 13, 1976). That policy statement is attached hereto as appendix, section 17.

TECHNICAL STANDARDS

SEC. 14. *Technical standards for validity studies.* The following minimum standards, as applicable, should be met in conducting a validity study. Nothing in these guidelines is intended to preclude the development and use of other professionally acceptable techniques with respect to validation of selection procedures. Where it is not technically feasible for a user to conduct a validity study, the user has the obligation otherwise to comply with these guidelines. See sections 6 and 7 above.

A. *Validity studies should be based on review of information about the job.* Any validity study should be based upon a review of information about the job for which the selection procedure is to be used. The review should include a job analysis except as provided in section 14B(3) below with respect to criterion-related validity. Any method of job analysis may be used if it provides the information required for the specific validation strategy used.

B. *Technical standards for criterion-related validity studies.*
—(1) *Technical feasibility.* Users choosing to validate a selection procedure by a criterion-related validity strategy should determine whether it is technically feasible (as defined in section 16) to conduct such a study in the particular employment context. The determination of the number of persons necessary to permit the conduct of a meaningful criterion-related study should be made by the user on the basis of all relevant information concerning the selection procedure, the potential sample and the employment situation. Where appropriate, jobs with substantially the same major work behaviors may be grouped together for validity studies, in order to obtain an adequate sample. These guidelines do not require a user to hire or promote persons for the purpose of making it possible to conduct a criterion-related study.

(2) *Analysis of the job.* There should be a review of job information to determine measures of work behavior(s) or performance that are relevant to the job or group of jobs in question. These measures or criteria are relevant to the extent that they represent critical or important job duties, work behaviors or work outcomes as developed from the review of job information. The possibility of bias should be considered both in selection of the criterion measures and their application. In view of the possibility of bias in subjective evaluations, supervisory rating techniques and instructions to raters should be carefully developed. All criterion measures and the methods for gathering data need to be examined for freedom from factors which would unfairly alter scores of members of any group. The relevance of criteria and their freedom from bias are of particular concern when there are significant differences in measures of job performance for different groups.

(3) *Criterion measures.* Proper safeguards should be taken to insure that scores on selection procedures do not enter into any judgments of employee adequacy that are to be used as criterion measures. Whatever criteria are used should represent important or critical work behavior(s) or work outcomes. Certain criteria may be used without a full job analysis if the user can show the importance of the criteria to the particular employment context. These criteria include but are not limited to production rate, error rate, tardiness, absenteeism, and length of service. A standardized rating of overall work performance may be used where a study of the job shows that it is an appropriate criterion. Where performance in training is used as a criterion, success in training should be properly measured and the relevance of the training should be shown either through a comparison of the content of the training program with the critical or important work behavior(s) of the job(s), or through a demonstration of the relationship between measures of performance in training and measures of job performance. Measures of relative success in training include but are not limited to instructor evaluations, performance samples, or tests. Criterion measures consisting of paper and pencil tests will be closely reviewed for job relevance.

(4) *Representativeness of the sample.* Whether the study is predictive or concurrent, the sample subjects should insofar as feasible be representative of the candidates normally available in the relevant labor market for the job or group of jobs in question, and should insofar as feasible include the races, sexes, and ethnic groups normally available in the relevant job market. In determining the representativeness of the sample in a concurrent validity study, the user should take into account the extent to which the specific knowledges or skills which are the primary focus of the test are those which employees learn on the job.

Where samples are combined or compared, attention should be given to see that such samples are comparable in terms of the actual job they perform, the length of time on the job where time on the job is likely to affect performance, and other relevant factors likely to affect validity differences; or that these factors are included in the design of the study and their effects identified.

(5) *Statistical relationships.* The degree of relationship between selection procedure scores and criterion measures should be examined and computed, using professionally acceptable statis-

tical procedures. Generally, a selection procedure is considered related to the criterion, for the purposes of these guidelines, when the relationship between performance on the procedure and performance on the criterion measure is statistically significant at the 0.05 level of significance, which means that it is sufficiently high as to have a probability of no more than one (1) in twenty (20) to have occurred by chance. Absence of a statistically significant relationship between a selection procedure and job performance should not necessarily discourage other investigations of the validity of that selection procedure.

(6) *Operational use of selection procedures.* Users should evaluate each selection procedure to assure that it is appropriate for operational use, including establishment of cutoff scores or rank ordering. Generally, if other factors remain the same, the greater the magnitude of the relationship (*e.g.*, correlation coefficient) between performance on a selection procedure and one or more criteria of performance on the job, and the greater the importance and number of aspects of job performance covered by the criteria, the more likely it is that the procedure will be appropriate for use. Reliance upon a selection procedure which is significantly related to a criterion measure, but which is based upon a study involving a large number of subjects and has a low correlation coefficient will be subject to close review if it has a large adverse impact. Sole reliance upon a single selection instrument which is related to only one of many job duties or aspects of job performance will also be subject to close review. The appropriateness of a selection procedure is best evaluated in each particular situation and there are no minimum correlation coefficients applicable to all employment situations. In determining whether a selection procedure is appropriate for operational use the following considerations should also be taken into account: The degree of adverse impact of the procedure, the availability of other selection procedures of greater or substantially equal validity.

(7) *Overstatement of validity of findings.* Users should avoid reliance upon techniques which tend to overestimate validity findings as a result of capitalization on chance unless an appropriate safeguard is taken. Reliance upon a few selection procedures or criteria of successful job performance when many selection procedures or criteria of performance have been studied, or the use of optimal statistical weights for selection procedures computed in one sample, are techniques which tend to inflate

validity estimates as a result of chance. Use of a large sample is one safeguard: cross-validation is another.

(8) *Fairness.* This section generally calls for studies of unfairness where technically feasible. The concept of fairness or unfairness of selection procedures is a developing concept. In addition, fairness studies generally require substantial numbers of employees in the job or group of jobs being studied. For these reasons, the Federal enforcement agencies recognize that the obligation to conduct studies of fairness imposed by the guidelines generally will be upon users or groups of users with a large number of persons in a job class, or test developers; and that small users utilizing their own selection procedures will generally not be obligated to conduct such studies because it will be technically infeasible for them to do so.

(a) *Unfairness defined.* When members of one race, sex, or ethnic group characteristically obtain lower scores on a selection procedure than members of another group, and the differences in scores are not reflected in differences in a measure of job performance, use of the selection procedure may unfairly deny opportunities to members of the group that obtain the lower scores.

(b) *Investigation of fairness.* Where a selection procedure results in an adverse impact on a race, sex, or ethnic group identified in accordance with the classifications set forth in section 4 above and that group is a significant factor in the relevant labor market, the user generally should investigate the possible existence of unfairness for that group if it is technically feasible to do so. The greater the severity of the adverse impact on a group, the greater the need to investigate the possible existence of unfairness. Where the weight of evidence from other studies shows that the selection procedure predicts fairly for the group in question and for the same or similar jobs, such evidence may be relied on in connection with the selection procedure at issue.

(c) *General considerations in fairness investigations.* Users conducting a study of fairness should review the A.P.A. Standards regarding investigation of possible bias in testing. An investigation of fairness of a selection procedure depends on both evidence of validity and the manner in which the selection procedure is to be used in a particular employment context. Fairness of a selection procedure cannot necessarily be specified in advance without investigating these factors. Investigation of fairness of a selection procedure in samples where the range of scores on selection procedures or criterion measures is severely restricted for any subgroup sample (as compared to other subgroup samples) may produce misleading evidence of unfairness. That factor should accordingly be taken into account in conducting such studies and before reliance is placed on the results.

(d) *When unfairness is shown.* If unfairness is demonstrated through a showing that members of a particular group perform better or poorer on the job than their scores on the selection procedure would indicate through comparison with how members of other groups perform, the user may either revise or replace the selection instrument in accordance with these guidelines, or may continue to use the selection instrument operationally with appropriate revisions in its use to assure compatibility between the probability of successful job performance and the probability of being selected.

(e) *Technical feasibility of fairness studies.* In addition to the general conditions needed for technical feasibility for the conduct of a criterion-related study (see section 16, below) an investigation of fairness requires the following:

(i) An adequate sample of persons in each group available for the study to achieve findings of statistical significance. Guidelines do not require a user to hire or promote persons on the basis of group classifications for the purpose of making it possible to conduct a study of fairness; but the user has the obligation otherwise to comply with these guidelines.

(ii) The samples for each group should be comparable in terms of the actual job they perform, length of time on the job where time on the job is likely to affect performance, and other relevant factors likely to affect validity differences; or such factors should be included in the design of the study and their effects identified.

(f) *Continued use of selection procedures when fairness studies not feasible.* If a study of fairness should otherwise be performed, but is not technically feasible, a selection procedure may be used which has otherwise met the validity standards of these guidelines, unless the technical infeasibility resulted from discriminatory employment practices which are demonstrated by facts other than past failure to conform with requirements for validation of selection procedures. However, when it becomes technically feasible for the user to perform a study of fairness and such a study is otherwise called for, the user should conduct the study of fairness.

C. *Technical standards for content validity studies.*—(1) *Appropriateness of content validity studies.* Users choosing to validate a selection procedure by a content validity strategy should determine whether it is appropriate to conduct such a study in the particular employment context. A selection procedure can be supported by a content validity strategy to the extent that it is a representative sample of the content of the job. Selection procedures which purport to measure knowledges, skills, or abilities may in certain circumstances be justified by content validity, although they may not be representative samples, if the knowledge, skill, or ability measured by the selection procedure can be operationally defined as provided in section 14C(4) below, and if that knowledge, skill, or ability is a necessary prerequisite to successful job performance.

A selection procedure based upon inferences about mental processes cannot be supported solely or primarily on the basis of content validity. Thus, a content strategy is not appropriate for demonstrating the validity of selection procedures which purport to measure traits or constructs, such as intelligence, **aptitude, personality, commonsense, judgment, leadership, and** spatial ability. Content validity is also not an appropriate strategy when the selection procedure involves knowledges, skills, or abilities which an employee will be expected to learn on the job.

(2) *Job analysis for content validity.* There should be a job analysis which includes an analysis of the important work behavior(s) required for successful performance and their relative importance and, if the behavior results in work product(s), an analysis of the work product(s). Any job analysis should focus on the work behavior(s) and the tasks associated with them. If work behavior(s) are not observable, the job analysis should identify and analyze those aspects of the behavior(s) that can be observed and the observed work products. The work behavior(s) selected for measurement should be critical work behavior(s) and/or important work behavior(s) constituting most of the job.

(3) *Development of selection procedures.* A selection procedure designed to measure the work behavior may be developed specifically from the job and job analysis in question, or may

have been previously developed by the user, or by other users or by a test publisher.

(4) *Standards for demonstrating content validity.* To demonstrate the content validity of a selection procedure, a user should show that the behavior(s) demonstrated in the selection procedure are a representative sample of the behavior(s) of the job in question or that the selection procedure provides a representative sample of the work product of the job. In the case of a selection procedure measuring a knowledge, skill, or ability, the knowledge, skill, or ability being measured should be operationally defined. In the case of a selection procedure measuring a knowledge, the knowledge being measured should be operationally defined as that body of learned information which is used in and is a necessary prerequisite for observable aspects of work behavior of the job. In the case of skills or abilities, the skill or ability being measured should be operationally defined in terms of observable aspects of work behavior of the job. For any selection procedure measuring a knowledge, skill, or ability the user should show that (a) the selection procedure measures and is a representative sample of that knowledge, skill, or ability; and (b) that knowledge, skill, or ability is used in and is a necessary prerequisite to performance of critical or important work behavior(s). In addition, to be content valid, a selection procedure measuring a skill or ability should either closely approximate an observable work behavior, or its product should closely approximate an observable work product. If a test purports to sample a work behavior or to provide a sample of a work product, the manner and setting of the selection procedure and its level and complexity should closely approximate the work situation. The closer the content and the context of the selection procedure are to work samples or work behaviors, the stronger is the basis for showing content validity. As the content of the selection procedure less resembles a work behavior, or the setting and manner of the administration of the selection procedure less resemble the work situation, or the result less resembles a work product, the less likely the selection procedure is to be content valid, and the greater the need for other evidence of validity.

(5) *Reliability.* The reliability of selection procedures justified on the basis of content validity should be a matter of concern to the user. Whenever it is feasible, appropriate statistical estimates should be made of the reliability of the selection procedure.

(6) *Prior training or experience.* A requirement for or evaluation of specific prior training or experience based on content validity, including a specification of level or amount of training or experience, should be justified on the basis of the relationship between the content of the training or experience and the content of the job for which the training or experience is to be required or evaluated. The critical consideration is the resemblance between the specific behaviors, products, knowledges, skills, or abilities in the experience or training and the specific behaviors, products, knowledges, skills, or abilities required on the job, whether or not there is close resemblance between the experience or training as a whole and the job as a whole.

(7) *Content validity of training success.* Where a measure of success in a training program is used as a selection procedure and the content of a training program is justified on the basis of content validity, the use should be justified on the relationship between the content of the training program and the content of the job.

(8) *Operational use.* A selection procedure which is supported on the basis of content validity may be used for a job if it represents a critical work behavior (*i.e.*, a behavior which is necessary for performance of the job) or work behaviors which constitute most of the important parts of the job.

(9) *Ranking based on content validity studies.* If a user can show, by a job analysis or otherwise, that a higher score on a content valid selection procedure is likely to result in better job performance, the results may be used to rank persons who score above minimum levels. Where a selection procedure supported solely or primarily by content validity is used to rank job candidates, the selection procedure should measure those aspects of performance which differentiate among levels of job performance.

D. *Technical standards for construct validity studies.*—(1) *Appropriateness of construct validity studies.* Construct validity is a more complex strategy than either criterion-related or content validity. Construct validation is a relatively new and developing procedure in the employment field, and there is at present a lack of substantial literature extending the concept to employment practices. The user should be aware that the effort to obtain sufficient empirical support for construct validity is both an extensive and arduous effort involving a series of research studies, which include criterion related validity studies and which may include content validity studies. Users choosing to justify use of a selection procedure by this strategy should therefore take particular care to assure that the validity study meets the standards set forth below.

(2) *Job analysis for construct validity studies.* There should be a job analysis. This job analysis should show the work behavior(s) required for successful performance of the job, or the groups of jobs being studied, the critical or important work behavior(s) in the job or group of jobs being studied, and an identification of the construct(s) believed to underlie successful performance of these critical or important work behaviors in the job or jobs in question. Each construct should be named and defined, so as to distinguish it from other constructs. If a group of jobs is being studied the jobs should have in common one or more critical or important work behaviors at a comparable level of complexity.

(3) *Relationship to the job.* A selection procedure should then be identified or developed which measures the construct identified in accord with subparagraph (2) above. The user should show by empirical evidence that the selection procedure is validly related to the construct and that the construct is validly related to the performance of critical or important work behavior(s). The relationship between the construct as measured by the selection procedure and the related work behavior(s) should be supported by empirical evidence from one or more criterion-related studies involving the job or jobs in question which satisfy the provisions of section 14B above.

(4) *Use of construct validity study without new criterion-related evidence.*—(a) *Standards for use.* Until such time as professional literature provides more guidance on the use of construct validity in employment situations, the Federal agencies will accept a claim of construct validity without a criterion-related study which satisfies section 14B above only when the selection procedure has been used elsewhere in a situation in which a criterion-related study has been conducted and the use of a criterion-related validity study in this context meets the standards for transportability of criterion-related validity studies as set forth above in section 7. However, if a study pertains to a number of jobs having common critical or important work behaviors at a comparable level of complexity, and the evidence satisfies subparagraphs 14B(2) and (3) above for those jobs with criterion-related validity evidence for those jobs, the selection procedure may be used for all the jobs to which the study

pertains. If construct validity is to be generalized to other jobs or groups of jobs not in the group studied, the Federal enforcement agencies will expect at a minimum additional empirical research evidence meeting the standards of subparagraphs section 14B(2) and (3) above for the additional jobs or groups of jobs.

(b) *Determination of common work behaviors.* In determining whether two or more jobs have one or more work behavior(s) in common, the user should compare the observed work behavior(s) in each of the jobs and should compare the observed work product(s) in each of the jobs. If neither the observed work behavior(s) in each of the jobs nor the observed work product(s) in each of the jobs are the same, the Federal enforcement agencies will presume that the work behavior(s) in each job are different. If the work behaviors are not observable, then evidence of similarity of work products and any other relevant research evidence will be considered in determining whether the work behavior(s) in the two jobs are the same.

DOCUMENTATION OF IMPACT AND VALIDITY EVIDENCE

SEC. 15. *Documentation of impact and validity evidence.—* A. *Required information.* Users of selection procedures other than those users complying with section 15A(1) below should maintain and have available for each job information on adverse impact of the selection process for that job and, where it is determined a selection process has an adverse impact, evidence of validity as set forth below.

(1) *Simplified recordkeeping for users with less than 100 employees.* In order to minimize recordkeeping burdens on employers who employ one hundred (100) or fewer employees, and other users not required to file EEO-1, et seq., reports, such users may satisfy the requirements of this section 15 if they maintain and have available records showing, for each year:

(a) The number of persons hired, promoted, and terminated for each job, by sex, and where appropriate by race and national origin;

(b) The number of applicants for hire and promotion by sex and where appropriate by race and national origin; and

(c) The selection procedures utilized (either standardized or not standardized).

These records should be maintained for each race or national origin group (see section 4 above) constituting more than two percent (2%) of the labor force in the relevant labor area. However, it is not necessary to maintain records by race and/or national origin (see § 4 above) if one race or national origin group in the relevant labor area constitutes more than ninety-eight percent (98%) of the labor force in the area. If the user has reason to believe that a selection procedure has an adverse impact, the user should maintain any available evidence of validity for that procedure (see sections 7A and 8).

(2) *Information on impact.*—(a) *Collection of information on impact.* Users of selection procedures other than those complying with section 15A(1) above should maintain and have available for each job recors or other information showing whether the total selection process for that job has an adverse impact on any of the groups for which records are called for by sections 4B above. Adverse impact determinations should be made at least annually for each such group which constitutes at least 2 percent of the labor force in the relevant labor area **or 2 percent of the applicable workforce.** Where a total selection process for a job has an adverse impact, the user should maintain and have available records or other information showing which components have an adverse impact. Where the total selection process for a job does not have an adverse impact, information need not be maintained for individual components except in circumstances set forth in subsection 15A(2)(b) below. If the determination of adverse impact is made using a procedure other than the "four-fifths rule," as defined in the first sentence of section 4D above, a justification, consistent with section 4D above, for the procedure used to determine adverse impact should be available.

(b) *When adverse impact has been eliminated in the total selection process.* Whenever the total selection process for a particular job has had an adverse impact, as defined in section 4 above, in any year, but no longer has an adverse impact, the user should maintain and have available the information on individual components of the selection process required in the preceding paragraph for the period in which there was adverse impact. In addition, the user should continue to collect such information for at least two (2) years after the adverse impact has been eliminated.

(c) *When data insufficient to determine impact.* Where there has been an insufficient number of selections to determine whether there is an adverse impact of the total selection process for a particular job, the user should continue to collect, maintain and have available the information on individual components of the selection process required in section 15(A)(2)(a) above until the information is sufficient to determine that the overall selection process does not have an adverse impact as defined in section 4 above, or until the job has changed substantially.

(3) *Documentation of validity evidence.*—(a) *Types of evidence.* Where a total selection process has an adverse impact (see section 4 above) the user should maintain and have available for each component of that process which has an adverse impact, one or more of the following types of documentation evidence:

(i) Documentation evidence showing criterion-related validity of the selection procedure (see section 15B, below).

(ii) Documentation evidence showing content validity of the selection procedure (see section 15C, below).

(iii) Documentation evidence showing construct validity of the selection procedure (see section 15D, below).

(iv) Documentation evidence from other studies showing validity of the selection procedure in the user's facility (see section 15E, below).

(v) Documentation evidence showing why a validity study cannot or need not be performed and why continued use of the procedure is consistent with Federal law.

(b) *Form of report.* This evidence should be compiled in a reasonably complete and organized manner to permit direct evaluation of the validity of the selection procedure. Previously written employer or consultant reports of validity, or reports describing validity studies completed before the issuance of these guidelines are acceptable if they are complete in regard to the documentation requirements contained in this section, or if they satisfied requirements of guidelines which were in effect when the validity study was completed. If they are not complete, the required additional documentation should be appended. If necessary information is not available the report of the validity study may still be used as documentation, but its adequacy will be **evaluated in terms of compliance with the requirements of these** guidelines.

(c) *Completeness.* In the event that evidence of validity is reviewed by an enforcement agency, the validation reports completed after the effective date of these guidelines are expected to contain the information set forth below. Evidence denoted by use of the word "(Essential)" is considered critical. If information denoted essential is not included, the report will be considered incomplete unless the user affirmatively demonstrates either its unavailability due to circumstances beyond the user's control or special circumstances of the user's study which make the information irrelevant. Evidence not so denoted is desirable but its absence will not be a basis for considering a report incomplete. The user should maintain and have available the information called for under the heading "Source Data" in sections 15B(11) and 15D(11). While it is a necessary part of the study, it need not be submitted with the report. All statistical results should be organized and presented in tabular or graphic form to the extent feasible.

B. *Criterion-related validity studies.* Reports of criterion-related validity for a selection procedure should include the following information:

(1) *User(s), location(s), and date(s) of study.* Dates and location(s) of the job analysis or review of job information, the date(s) and location(s) of the administration of the selection procedures and collection of criterion data, and the time between collection of data on selection procedures and criterion measures should be provided (Essential). If the study was conducted at several locations, the address of each location, including city and State, should be shown.

(2) *Problem and setting.* An explicit definition of the purpose(s) of the study and the circumstances in which the study was conducted should be provided. A description of existing selection procedures and cutoff scores, if any, should be provided.

(3) *Job analysis or review of job information.* A description of the procedure used to analyze the job or group of jobs, or to review the job information should be provided (Essential). Where a review of job information results in criteria which may be used without a full job analysis (see section 14B(3)), the basis for the selection of these criteria should be reported (Essential). Where a job analysis is required a complete description of the work behavior(s) or work outcome(s), and measures of their criticality or importance should be provided (Essential). The report should describe the basis on which the behavior(s) or outcome(s) were determined to be critical or

important, such as the proportion of time spent on the respective behaviors, their level of difficulty, their frequency of performance, the consequences of error, or other appropriate factors (Essential). Where two or more jobs are grouped for a validity study, the information called for in this subsection should be provided for each of the jobs, and the justification for the grouping (see section 14B(1)) should be provided (Essential).

(4) *Job titles and codes.* It is desirable to provide the user's job title(s) for the job(s) in question and the corresponding job title(s) and code(s) from U.S. Employment Service's Dictionary of Occupational Titles.

(5) *Criterion measures.* The bases for the selection of the criterion measures should be provided, together with references to the evidence considered in making the selection of criterion measures (essential). A full description of all criteria on which data were collected and means by which they were observed, recorded, evaluated, and quantified, should be provided (essential). If rating techniques are used as criterion measures, the appraisal form(s) and instructions to the rater(s) should be included as part of the validation evidence, or should be explicitly described and available (essential). All steps taken to insure that criterion measures are free from factors which would unfairly alter the scores of members of any group should be described (essential).

(6) *Sample description.* A description of how the research sample was identified and selected should be included (essential). The race, sex, and ethnic composition of the sample, including those groups set forth in section 4A above, should be described (essential). This description should include the size of each subgroup (essential). A description of how the research sample compares with the relevant labor market or work force, the method by which the relevant labor market or work force was defined, and a discussion of the likely effects on validity of differences between the sample and the relevant labor market or work force, are also desirable. Descriptions of educational levels, length of service, and age are also desirable.

(7) *Description of selection procedures.* Any measure, combination of measures, or procedures studied should be completely and explicitly described or attached (essential). If commercially available selection procedures are studied, they should be described by title, form, and publisher (essential). Reports of **reliability** estimates and how they were established are desirable.

(8) *Techniques and results.* Methods used in analyzing data should be described (essential). Measures of central tendency (e.g., means) and measures of dispersion (e.g., standard deviations and ranges) for all selection procedures and all criteria should be reported for each race, sex, and ethnic group which constitutes a significant factor in the relevant labor market (essential). The magnitude and direction of all relationships between selection procedures and criterion measures investigated should be reported for each relevant race, sex, and ethnic group and for the total group (essential). Where groups are too small to obtain reliable evidence of the magnitude of the relationship, need not be reported separately. Statements regarding the statistical significance of results should be made (essential). Any statistical adjustments, such as for less than perfect reliability or for restriction of score range in the selection procedure or criterion should be described and explained; and uncorrected correlation coefficients should also be shown (essential). Where the statistical technique categorizes continuous data, such as biserial correlation and the phi coefficient, the categories and the bases on which they were determined should be described and explained (essential). Studies of test fairness should be included where called for by the requirements of section 14B(8) (essential). These studies should include the rationale by which a selection procedure was determined to be fair to the group(s) in question. Where test fairness or unfairness has been demonstrated on the basis of other studies, a bibliography of the relevant studies should be included (essential). If the bibliography includes unpublished studies, copies of these studies, or adequate abstracts or summaries, should be attached (essential). Where revisions have been made in a selection procedure to assure compatability between successful job performance and the probability of being selected, the studies underlying such revisions should be included (essential). All statistical results should be organized and presented by relevant race, sex, and ethnic group (essential).

(9) *Alternative procedures investigated.* The selection procedures investigated and available evidence of their impact should be identified (essential). The scope, method, and findings of the investigation, and the conclusions reached in light of the findings, should be fully described (essential).

(10) *Uses and applications.* The methods considered for use of the selection procedure (e.g., as a screening device with

a cutoff score, for grouping or ranking, or combined with other procedures in a battery) and available evidence of their impact should be described (essential). This description should include the rationale for choosing the method for operational use, and the evidence of the validity and utility of the procedure as it is to be used (essential). The purpose for which the procedure is to be used (e.g., hiring, transfer, promotion) should be described (essential). If weights are assigned to different parts of the selection procedure, these weights and the validity of the weighted composite should be reported (essential). If the selection procedure is used with a cutoff score, the user should describe the way in which normal expectations of proficiency within the work force were determined and the way in which the cutoff score was determined (essential).

(11) *Source data.* Each user should maintain records showing all pertinent information about individual sample members and raters where they are used, in studies involving the validation of selection procedures. These records should be made available upon request of a compliance agency. In the case of individual sample members these data should include scores on the selection procedure(s), scores on criterion measures, age, sex, race, or ethnic group status, and experience on the specific job on which the validation study was conducted, and may also include such things as education, training, and prior job experience, but should not include names and social security numbers. Records should be maintained which show the ratings given to each sample member by each rater.

(12) *Contact person.* The name, mailing address, and telephone number of the person who may be contacted for further **information about the validity** study should be provided (essential).

(13) *Accuracy and completeness.* The report should **describe the steps taken to assure the accuracy and completeness** of the collection, analysis, and report of data and results.

C. *Content validity studies.* Reports of content validity for a selection procedure should include the following information:

(1) *User(s), location(s) and date(s) of study.* Dates and location(s) of the job analysis should be shown (essential).

(2) *Problem and setting.* An explicit definition of the purpose(s) of the study and the circumstances in which the study was conducted should be provided. A description of existing selection procedures and cutoff scores, if any, should be provided.

(3) *Job analysis—Content of the job.* A description of the method used to analyze the job should be provided (essential). The work behavior(s), the associated tasks, and, if the behavior results in a work product, the work products should be completely described (essential). Measures of criticality and/or importance of the work behavior(s) and the method of determining these measures should be provided (essential). Where the job analysis also identified the knowledges, skills, and abilities used in work behavior(s), an operational definition for each knowledge in terms of a body of learned information and for each skill and ability in terms of observable behaviors and outcomes, and the relationship between each knowledge, skill, or ability and each work behavior, as well as the method used to determine this relationship, should be provided (essential). The work situation should be described, including the setting in which work behavior(s) are performed, and where appropriate, the manner in which knowledges, skills, or abilities are used, and the complexity and difficulty of the knowledge, skill, or ability as used in the work behavior(s).

(4) *Selection procedure and its content.* Selection procedures, including those constructed by or for the user, specific training requirements, composites of selection procedures, and any other procedure supported by content validity, should be completely and explicitly described or attached (essential). If commercially available selection procedures are used, they should be described by title, form, and publisher (essential). The behaviors measured or sampled by the selection procedure should be explicitly described (essential). Where the selection procedure purports to measure a knowledge, skill, or ability, evidence that the selection procedure measures and is a representative sample of the knowledge, skill, or ability should be provided (essential).

(5) *Relationship between the selection procedure and the job.* The evidence demonstrating that the selection procedure is a representative work sample, a representative sample of the work behavior(s), or a representative sample of a knowledge, skill, or ability as used as a part of a work behavior and necessary for that behavior should be provided (essential). The user should identify the work behavior(s) which each item or part of the selection procedure is intended to sample or measure (essential). Where the selection procedure purports to sample a work behavior or to provide a sample of a work product, a com-

parison should be provided of the manner, setting, and the level of complexity of the selection procedure with those of the work situation (essential). If any steps were taken to reduce adverse impact on a race, sex, or ethnic group in the content of the procedure or in its administration, these steps should be described. Establishment of time limits, if any, and how these limits are related to the speed with which duties must be performed on the job, should be explained. Measures of central tend- ency (e.g., means) and measures of dispersion (e.g., standard deviations) and estimates of reliability should be reported for all selection procedures if available. Such reports should be made for relevant race, sex, and ethnic subgroups, at least on a statistically reliable sample basis.

(6) *Alternative procedures investigated.* The alternative selection procedures investigated and available evidence of their impact should be identified (essential). The scope, method, and findings of the investigation, and the conclusions reached in light of the findings, should be fully described (essential).

(7) *Uses and applications.* The methods considered for use of the selection procedure (e.g., as a screening device with a cutoff score, for grouping or ranking, or combined with other procedures in a battery) and available evidence of their impact should be described (essential). This description should include the rationale for choosing the method for operational use, and the evidence of the validity and utility of the procedure as it is to be used (essential). The purpose for which the procedure is to be used (e.g., hiring, transfer, promotion) should be described (essential). If the selection procedure is used with a cutoff score, the user should describe the way in which normal expectations of proficiency within the work force were determined and the way in which the cutoff score was determined (essential). In addition, if the selection procedure is to be used for ranking, the user should specify the evidence showing that a higher score on the selection procedure is likely to result in better job performance.

(8) *Contact person.* The name, mailing address, and telephone number of the person who may be contacted for further information about the validity study should be provided (essential).

(9) *Accuracy and completeness.* The report should describe the steps taken to assure the accuracy and completeness of the collection, analysis, and report of data and results.

D. *Construct validity studies.* Reports of construct validity for a selection procedure should include the following information:

(1) *User(s), location(s), and date(s) of study.* Date(s) and location(s) of the job analysis and the gathering of other evidence called for by these guidelines should be provided (essential).

(2) *Problem and setting.* An explicit definition of the purpose(s) of the study and the circumstances in which the study was conducted should be provided. A description of existing selection procedures and cutoff scores, if any, should be provided.

(3) *Construct definition.* A clear definition of the construct(s) which are believed to underlie successful performance of the critical or important work behavior(s) should be provided (essential). This definition should include the levels of construct performance relevant to the job(s) for which the selection procedure is to be used (essential). There should be a summary of the position of the construct in the psychological literature, or in the absence of such a position, a description of the way in which the definition and measurement of the construct was developed and the psychological theory underlying it (essential). Any quantitative data which identify or define the job constructs, such as factor analyses, should be provided (essential).

(4) *Job analysis.* A description of the method used to analyze the job should be provided (essential). A complete description of the work behavior(s) and, to the extent appropriate, work outcomes and measures of their criticality and/or importance should be provided (essential). The report should also describe the basis on which the behavior(s) or outcomes were determined to be important, such as their level of difficulty, their frequency of performance, the consequences of error or other appropriate factors (essential). Where jobs are grouped or compared for the purposes of generalizing validity evidence, the work behavior(s) and work product(s) for each of the jobs should be described, and conclusions concerning the similarity of the jobs in terms of observable work behaviors or work products should be made (essential).

(5) *Job titles and codes.* It is desirable to provide the selection procedure user's job title(s) for the job(s) in question and the corresponding job title(s) and code(s) from the United States Employment Service's dictionary of occupational titles.

(6) *Selection procedure.* The selection procedure used as a measure of the construct should be completely and explicitly described or attached (essential). If commercially available selection procedures are used, they should be identified by title, form and publisher (essential). The research evidence of the relationship between the selection procedure and the construct, such as factor structure, should be included (essential). Measures of central tendency, variability and reliability of the selection procedure should be provided (essential). Whenever feasible, these measures should be provided separately for each relevant **race, sex and ethnic group.**

(7) *Relationship to job performance.* The criterion-related study(ies) and other empirical evidence of the relationship between the construct measured by the selection procedure and the related work behavior(s) for the job or jobs in question should be provided (essential). Documentation of the criterion-related study(ies) should satisfy the provisions of section 15B above or section 15E(1) below, except for studies conducted prior to the effective date of these guidelines (essential). Where a study pertains to a group of jobs, and, on the basis of the study, validity is asserted for a job in the group, the observed work behaviors and the observed work products for each of the jobs should be described (essential). Any other evidence used in determining whether the work behavior(s) in each of the jobs is the same should be fully described (essential).

(8) *Alternative procedures investigated.* The alternative selection procedures investigated and available evidence of their impact should be identified (essential). The scope, method, and findings of the investigation, and the conclusions reached in light of the findings should be fully described (essential).

(9) *Uses and applications.* The methods considered for use of the selection procedure (e.g., as a screening device with a cutoff score, for grouping or ranking, or combined with other procedures in a battery) and available evidence of their impact should be described (essential). This description should include the rationale for choosing the method for operational use, and the evidence of the validity and utility of the procedure as it is to be used (essential). The purpose for which the procedure is to be used (e.g., hiring, transfer, promotion) should be described (essential). If weights are assigned to different parts of the selection procedure, these weights and the validity of the weighted composite should be reported (essential). If the selec-

tion procedure is used with a cutoff score, the user should describe the way in which normal expectations of proficiency within the work force were determined and the way in which the cutoff score was determined (essential).

(10) *Accuracy and completeness.* The report should describe the steps taken to assure the accuracy and completeness of the collection, analysis, and report of data and results.

(11) *Source data.* Each user should maintain records showing all pertinent information relating to its study of construct validity.

(1) *Contact person.* The name, mailing address, and telephone number of the individual who may be contacted for further information about the validity study should be provided (essential).

E. *Evidence of validity from other studies.* When validity of a selection procedure is supported by studies not done by the user, the evidence from the original study or studies should be compiled in a manner similar to that required in the appropriate section of this section 15 above. In addition, the following evidence should be supplied:

(1) *Evidence from criterion-related validity studies.*—a. *Job information.* A description of the important job behavior(s) of the user's job and the basis on which the behaviors were determined to be important should be provided (essential). A full description of the basis for determining that these important work behaviors are the same as those of the job in the original study (or studies) should be provided (essential).

b. *Relevance of criteria.* A full description of the basis on which the criteria used in the original studies are determined to be relevant for the user should be provided (essential).

c. *Other variables.* The similarity of important applicant pool or sample characteristics reported in the original studies to those of the user should be described (essential). A description of the comparison between the race, sex and ethnic composition of the user's relevant labor market and the sample in the original validity studies should be provided (essential).

d. *Use of the selection procedure.* A full description should be provided showing that the use to be made of the selection procedure is consistent with the findings of the original validity studies (essential).

e. *Bibliography.* A bibliography of reports of validity of the selection procedure for the job or jobs in question should be provided (essential). Where any of the studies included an investigation of test fairness, the results of this investigation should be provided (essential). Copies of reports published in journals that are not commonly available should be described in detail or attached (essential). Where a user is relying upon unpublished studies, a reasonable effort should be made to obtain these studies. If these unpublished studies are the sole source of validity evidence they should be described in detail or attached (essential). If these studies are not available, the name and address of the source, an adequate abstract or summary of the validity study and data, and a contact person in the source organization should be provided (essential).

(2) *Evidence from content validity studies.* See section 14 C(3) and section 15C above.

(3) *Evidence from construct validity studies.* See sections 14D(2) and 15D above.

F. *Evidence of validity from cooperative studies.* Where a selection procedure has been validated through a cooperative study, evidence that the study satisfies the requirements of sections 7, 8 and 15E should be provided (essential).

G. *Selection for higher level job.* If a selection procedure is used to evaluate candidates for jobs at a higher level than those for which they will initially be employed, the validity evidence should satisfy the documentation provisions of this section 15 for the higher level job or jobs, and in addition, the user should provide: (1) a description of the job progression structure, formal or informal; (2) the data showing how many employees progress to the higher level job and the length of time needed to make this progression; and (3) an identification of any anticipated changes in the higher level job. In addition, if the test measures a knowledge, skill or ability, the user should provide evidence that the knowledge, skill or ability is required for the higher level job and the basis for the conclusion that the knowledge, skill or ability is not expected to develop from the training or experience on the job.

H. *Interim use of selection procedures.* If a selection procedure is being used on an interim basis because the procedure is not fully supported by the required evidence of validity, the user should maintain and have available (1) substantial evidence of validity for the procedure, and (2) a report showing the date on which the study to gather the additional evidence commenced, the estimated completion date of the study, and a description of the data to be collected (essential).

Definitions

Sec. 16. *Definitions.* The following definitions shall apply throughout these guidelines:

A. *Ability.* A present competence to perform an observable behavior or a behavior which results in an observable product.

B. *Adverse impact.* A substantially different rate of selection in hiring, promotion, or other employment decision which works to the disadvantage of members of a race, sex, or ethnic group. See section 4 of these guidelines.

C. *Compliance with these guidelines.* Use of a selection procedure is in compliance with these guidelines if such use has been validated in accord with these guidelines (as defined below), or if such use does not result in adverse impact on any race, sex, or ethnic group (see section 4, above), or, in unusual circumstances, if use of the procedure is otherwise justified in accord with Federal law. See section 6B, above.

D. *Content validity.* Demonstrated by data showing that the content of a selection procedure is representative of important aspects of performance on the job. See section 5B and section 14C.

E. *Construct validity.* Demonstrated by data showing that the selection procedure measures the degree to which candidates have identifiable characteristics which have been determined to be important for successful job performance. See section 5B and section 14D.

F. *Criterion-related validity.* Demonstrated by empirical data showing that the selection procedure is predictive of or significantly correlated with important elements of work behavior. See sections 5B and 14B.

G. *Employer.* Any employer subject to the provisions of the Civil Rights Act of 1964, as amended, including State or local governments and any Federal agency subject to the provisions of section 717 of the Civil Rights Act of 1964, as amended, and any Federal contractor or subcontractor or federally assisted construction contractor or subcontractor covered by Executive Order 11246, as amended.

H. *Employment agency.* Any employment agency subject to the provisions of the Civil Rights Act of 1964, as amended.

I. *Enforcement action.* For the purposes of section 4 a proceeding by a Federal enforcement agency such as a lawsuit or an administrative proceeding leading to debarment from or withholding, suspension, or termination of Federal Government contracts or the suspension or withholding of Federal Government funds; but not a finding of reasonable cause or a conciliation process or the issuance of right to sue letters under title VII or under Executive Order 11246 where such finding, conciliation, or issuance of notice of right to sue is based upon an individual complaint.

J. *Enforcement agency.* Any agency of the executive branch of the Federal Government which adopts these guidelines for purposes of the enforcement of the equal employment opportunity laws or which has responsibility for securing compliance with them.

K. *Job analysis.* A detailed statement of work behaviors and other information relevant to the job.

L. *Job description.* A general statement of job duties and responsibilities.

M. *Knowledge.* A body of information applied directly to the performance of a function.

N. *Labor organization.* Any labor organization subject to the provisions of the Civil Rights Act of 1964, as amended, and any committee subject thereto controlling apprenticeship or other training.

O. *Observable.* Able to be seen, heard, or otherwise perceived by a person other than the person performing the action.

P. *Rate, sex, or ethnic group.* Any group of persons identifiable on the grounds of race, color, religion, sex, or national origin.

Q. *Selection procedure.* Any measure, combination of measures, or procedure used as a basis for any employment decision. Selection procedures include the full range of assessment techniques from traditional paper and pencil tests, performance tests, training programs, or probationary periods and physical, educational, and work experience requirements through informal or casual interviews and unscored application forms.

R. *Selection rate.* The proportion of applicants or candidates who are hired, promoted, or otherwise selected.

S. *Should.* The term "should" as used in these guidelines is intended to connote action which is necessary to achieve compliance with the guidelines, while recognizing that there are circumstances where alternative courses of action are open to users.

T. *Skill.* A present, observable competence to perform a learned psychomoter act.

U. *Technical feasibility.* The existence of conditions permitting the conduct of meaningful criterion-related validity studies. These conditions include: (1) An adequate sample of persons available for the study to achieve findings of statistical significance; (2) having or being able to obtain a sufficient range of scores on the selection procedure and job performance measures to produce validity results which can be expected to be representative of the results if the ranges normally expected were utilized; and (3) having or being able to devise unbiased, reliable and relevant measures of job performance or other criteria of employee adequacy. See section 14B(2). With respect to investigation of possible unfairness, the same considerations are applicable to each group for which the study is made. See Section 14B(8).

V. *Unfairness of selection procedure.* A condition in which members of one race, sex, or ethnic group characteristically obtain lower scores on a selection procedure than members of another group, and the differences are not reflected in differences in measures of job performance. See section 14B(7).

W. *User.* Any employer, labor organization, employment agency, or licensing or certification board, to the extent it may be covered by Federal equal employment opportunity law, which uses a selection procedure as a basis for any employment decision. Whenever an employer, labor organization, or employment agency is required by law to restrict recruitment for any occupation to those applicants who have met licensing or certification requirements, the licensing or certifying authority to the extent it may be covered by Federal equal employment opportunity law will be considered the user with respect to those licensing or certification requirements. Whenever a State employment agency or service does no more than administer or monitor a procedure as permitted by Department of Labor regulations, and does so without making referrals or taking any other action on the basis of the results, the State employment agency will not be deemed to be a user.

X. *Validated in accord with these guidelines or properly validated.* A demonstration that one or more validity study or studies meeting the standards of these guidelines has been conducted, including investigation and, where appropriate, use of suitable alternative selection procedures as contemplated by section 3B, and has produced evidence of validity sufficient to warrant use of the procedure for the intended purpose under the standards of these guidelines.

Y. *Work behavior.* An activity performed to achieve the objectives of the job. Work behaviors involve observable (physical) components and unobservable (mental) components. A work behavior consists of the performance of one or more tasks. Knowledges, skills, and abilities are not behaviors, although they may be applied in work behaviors.

APPENDIX

17. *Policy statement on affirmative action* (see section 13B). The Equal Employment Opportunity Coordinating Council was established by act of Congress in 1972, and charged with responsibility for developing and implementing agreements and policies designed, among other things, to eliminate conflict and inconsistency among the agencies of the Federal Government responsible for administering Federal law prohibiting discrimination on grounds of race, color, sex, religion, and national origin. This statement is issued as an initial response to the requests of a number of State and local officials for clarification of the Government's policies concerning the role of affirmative action in the overall equal employment opportunity program. While the Coordinating Council's adoption of this statement expresses only the views of the signatory agencies concerning this important subject, the principles set forth below should serve as policy guidance for other Federal agencies as well.

(1) Equal employment opportunity is the law of the land. In the public sector of our society this means that all persons, regardless of race, color, religion, sex, or national origin shall have equal access to positions in the public service limited only by their ability to do the job. There is ample evidence in all sectors of our society that such equal access frequently has been denied to members of certain groups because of their sex, racial, or ethnic characteristics. The remedy for such past and present discrimination is twofold.

On the one hand, vigorous enforcement of the laws against discrimination is essential. But equally, and perhaps even more important are affirmative, voluntary efforts on the part of public employers to assure that positions in the public service are genuinely and equally accessible to qualified persons, without regard to their sex, racial, or ethnic characteristics. Without such efforts equal employment opportunity is no more than a wish. The importance of voluntary affirmative action on the part of employers is underscored by title VII of the Civil Rights Act of 1964, Executive Order 11246, and related laws and regulations—all of which emphasize voluntary action to achieve equal employment opportunity.

As with most management objectives, a systematic plan based on sound organizational analysis and problem identification is crucial to the accomplishment of affirmative action objectives. For this reason, the Council urges all State and local governments to develop and implement results oriented affirmative action plans which deal with the problems so identified.

The following paragraphs are intended to assist State and local governments by illustrating the kinds of analyses and activities which may be appropriate for a public employer's voluntary affirmative action plan. This statement does not address remedies imposed after a finding of unlawful discrimination.

(2) Voluntary affirmative action to assure equal employment opportunity is appropriate at any stage of the employment process. The first step in the construction of any affirmative action plan should be an analysis of the employer's work force to determine whether percentages of sex, race, or ethnic groups in individual job classifications are substantially similar to the percentages of those groups available in the relevant job market who possess the basic job-related qualifications.

When substantial disparities are found through such analyses, each element of the overall selection process should be examined to determine which elements operate to exclude persons on the basis of sex, race, or ethnic group. Such elements include, but are not limited to, recruitment, testing, ranking certification, interview, recommendations for selection, hiring, promotion, etc. The examination of each element of the selection process should at a minimum include a determination of its validity in predicting job performance.

(3) When an employer has reason to believe that its selection procedures have the exclusionary effect described in paragraph 2 above, it should initiate affirmative steps to remedy the situation. Such steps, which in design and execution may be race, color, sex, or ethnic "conscious," include, but are not limited to, the following:

(a) The establishment of a long-term goal, and short-range, interim goals and timetables for the specific job classifications, all of which should take into account the availability of basically qualified persons in the relevant job market;

(b) A recruitment program designed to attract qualified members of the group in question;

(c) A systematic effort to organize work and redesign jobs in ways that provide opportunities for persons lacking "journeyman" level knowledge or skills to enter and, with appropriate training, to progress in a career field;

(d) Revamping selection instruments or procedures which have not yet been validated in order to reduce or eliminate exclusionary effects on particular groups in particular job classifications;

(e) The initiation of measures designed to assure that members of the affected group who are qualified to perform the job are included within the pool of persons from which the selecting official makes the selection;

(f) A systematic effort to provide career advancement training, both classroom and on-the-job, to employees locked into dead end jobs; and

(g) The establishment of a system for regularly monitoring the effectiveness of the particular affirmative action program, and procedures for making timely adjustments in this program where effectiveness is not demonstrated.

(4) The goal of any affirmative action plan should be achievement of genuine equal employment opportunity for all qualified persons. Selection under such plans should be based upon the ability of the applicant(s) to do the work. Such plans should not require the selection of the unqualified, or the unneeded, nor should they require the selection of persons on the basis of race, color, sex, religion, or national origin. Moreover, while the Council believes that this statement should serve to assist State and local employers, as well as Federal agencies, it recognizes that affirmative action cannot be viewed as a standardized program which must be accomplished in the same way at all times in all places.

Accordingly, the Council has not attempted to set forth here either the minimum or maximum voluntary steps that employers may take to deal with their respective situations. Rather, the Council recognizes that under applicable authorities, State and local employers have flexibility to formulate affirmative action plans that are best suited to their particular situations. In this manner, the Council believes that affirmative action programs will best serve the goal of equal employment opportunity.

Respectfully submitted,

> HAROLD R. TYLER, JR.,
> *Deputy Attorney General and Chairman of the Equal Employment Coordinating Council.*
>
> MICHAEL H. MOSKOW,
> *Under Secretary of Labor.*
>
> ETHEL BENT WALSH,
> *Acting Chairman, Equal Employment Opportunity Commisison.*
>
> ROBERT E. HAMPTON,
> *Chairman, Civil Service Commission.*
>
> ARTHUR E. FLEMMING,
> *Chairman, Commisison on Civil Rights.*

Because of its equal employment opportunity responsibilities under the State and Local Government Fiscal Assistance Act of 1972 (the revenue sharing act), the Department of Treasury was invited to participate in the formulation of this policy statement; and it concurs and joins in the adoption of this policy statement.

Done this 26th day of August 1976.

> RICHARD ALBRECHT,
> *General Counsel,*
> *Department of the Treasury.*

Section 18. *Citations.* The official title of these guidelines is "Uniform Guidelines on Employee Selection Procedures (1978)". The Uniform Guidelines on Employee Selection Procedures (1978) are intended to establish a uniform Federal position in the area of prohibiting discrimination in employment practices on grounds of race, color, religion, sex, or national origin. These guidelines have been adopted by the Equal Employment Opportunity Commission, the Department of Labor, the Department of Justice, and the Civil Service Commission.

The official citation is:

"Section ——, Uniform Guidelines on Employee Selection Procedure (1978); 43 FR —— (August 25, 1978)."

The short form citation is:

"Section ——, U.G.E.S.P. (1978); 43 FR —— (August 25, 1978)."

When the guidelines are cited in connection with the activities of one of the issuing agencies, a specific citation to the regulations of that agency can be added at the end of the above citation. The specific additional citations are as follows:

Equal Employment Opportunity Commission
29 CFR Part 1607

Department of Labor

Office of Federal Contract Compliance Programs
41 CFR Part 60-3

Department of Justice
28 CFR 50.14

Civil Service Commission
5 CFR 300.103(c)

Normally when citing these guidelines, the section number immediately preceding the title of the guidelines will be from these guidelines series 1-18. If a section number from the codification for an individual agency is needed it can also be added at the end of the agency citation. For example, section 6A of these guidelines could be cited for EEOC as follows: "Section 6A, Uniform Guidelines on Employee Selection Procedures (1978); 43 FR ——, (August 25, 1978); 29 CFR Part 1607, Section 6A."

ELEANOR HOLMES NORTON,
Chair, Equal Employment Opportunity Commission.

ALAN K. CAMPBELL,
Chairman,
Civil Service Commission.

RAY MARSHALL,
Secretary of Labor.

GRIFFIN B. BELL,
Attorney General.

Appendix D

federal register

Friday
May 2, 1980

Part IV

Equal Employment Opportunity Commission
Office of Personnel Management
Department of Justice
Department of the Treasury
Department of Labor
Office of Federal Contract Compliance Programs

Adoption of Additional Questions and Answers to Clarify and Provide a Common Interpretation of the Uniform Guidelines on Employee Selection Procedures

[6570-06-M]

Title 29—Labor

CHAPTER XIV—EQUAL EMPLOYMENT OPPORTUNITY COMMISSION

PART 1607—UNIFORM GUIDELINES ON EMPLOYEE SELECTION PROCEDURES (1978)

Title 5—Administrative Personnel

OFFICE OF PERSONNEL MANAGEMENT

PART 300—EMPLOYMENT (GENERAL)

Title 28—Judicial Administration

CHAPTER I—DEPARTMENT OF JUSTICE

PART 50—STATEMENTS OF POLICY

Title 31—Money and Finance: Treasury

CHAPTER I—MONETARY OFFICES: DEPARTMENT OF THE TREASURY

PART 51—FISCAL ASSISTANCE TO STATE AND LOCAL GOVERNMENTS

Title 41—Public Contracts and Property Management

CHAPTER 60—OFFICE OF FEDERAL CONTRACT COMPLIANCE PROGRAMS, DEPARTMENT OF LABOR

PART 60-3—UNIFORM GUIDELINES ON EMPLOYEE SELECTION PROCEDURES (1978)

Adoption of Questions and Answers To Clarify and Provide a Common Interpretation of the Uniform Guidelines on Employee Selection Procedures

AGENCIES: Equal Employment Opportunity Commission, Office of Personnel Management, Department of Justice, Department of Labor and Department of Treasury.

ACTION: Adoption of questions and answers designed to clarify and provide a common interpretation of the Uniform Guidelines on Employee Selection Procedures.

SUMMARY: The Uniform Guidelines on Employee Selection Procedures were issued by the five Federal agencies having primary responsibility for the enforcement of Federal equal employment opportunity laws, to establish a uniform Federal government position. See 43 FR 38290, et seq. (Aug. 25, 1978) and 43 FR 40223 (Sept. 11, 1978). They became effective on September 25, 1978. The issuing agencies recognize the need for a common interpretation of the Uniform Guidelines, as well as the desirability of providing additional guidance to employers and other users, psychologists, and investigators, compliance officers and other Federal enforcement personnel. These Questions and Answers are intended to address that need and to provide such guidance.

EFFECTIVE DATE: March 2, 1979.

FOR FURTHER INFORMATION CONTACT:

A. Diane Graham, Assistant Director, Affirmative Employment Programs, Office of Personnel Management, 1900 E Street, NW., Washington, D.C. 20415, 202/632-4420.

James Hellings, Special Assistant to the Assistant Director, Intergovernmental Personnel Programs, Office of Personnel Management, 1900 E Street, NW., Washington, D.C. 20415, 202/632-6248.

Kenneth A. Millard, Chief, State and Local Section, Personnel Research and Development Center, Office of Personnel Management, 1900 E St., NW., Washington, D.C. 20415, 202-632-6238.

Peter C. Robertson, Director, Office of Policy Implementation, Equal Employment Opportunity Commission, 2401 E Street, NW., Washington, D.C. 20506, 202/634-7060.

David L. Rose, Chief, Employment Section, Civil Rights Division, Department of Justice, 10th Street and Pennsylvania Avenue, NW., Washington, D.C. 20530, 202/633-3831.

Donald J. Schwartz, Psychologist, Office of Federal Contract Compliance Programs, Room C-3324, Department of Labor, 200 Constitution Avenue, NW., Washington, D.C. 20210, 202/523-9426.

Herman Schwartz, Chief Counsel, Office of Revenue Sharing, Department of the Treasury, 2401 E Street, NW., Washington, D.C. 20220, 202/634-5182.

James O. Taylor, Jr., Research Psychologist, Office of Systemic Programs, Equal Employment Opportunity Commission, 2401 E St., NW., Washington, D.C. 20506, 202/254-3036.

INTRODUCTION

The problems addressed by the Uniform Guidelines on Employee Selection Procedures (43 FR 38290 et seq., August 25, 1978) are numerous and important, and some of them are complex. The history of the development of those Guidelines is set forth in the introduction to them (43 FR 38290-95). The experience of the agencies has been that a series of answers to commonly asked questions is helpful in providing guidance not only to employers and other users, but also to psychologists and others who are called upon to conduct validity studies, and to investigators, compliance officers and other Federal personnel who have enforcement responsibilities.

The Federal agencies which issued the Uniform Guidelines—the Departments of Justice and Labor, the Equal Employment Opportunity Commission, the Civil Service Commission (which has been succeeded in relevant part by the Office of Personnel Management), and the Office of Revenue Sharing, Treasury Department—recognize that the goal of a uniform position on these issues can best be achieved through a common interpretation of the same guidelines. The following Questions and Answers are part of such a common interpretation. The material included is intended to interpret and clarify, but not to modify, the provisions of the Uniform Guidelines. The questions selected are commonly asked questions in the field and those suggested by the Uniform Guidelines themselves and by the extensive comments received on the various sets of proposed guidelines prior to their adoption. Terms are used in the questions and answers as they are defined in the Uniform Guidelines.

The agencies recognize that additional questions may be appropriate for similar treatment at a later date, and contemplate working together to provide additional guidance in interpreting the Uniform Guidelines. Users and other interested persons are invited to submit additional questions.

ELEANOR HOLMES NORTON,
Chair, Equal Employment Opportunity Commission.

ALAN K. CAMPBELL,
Director, Office of Personnel Management.

DREW S. DAYS III,
Assistant Attorney General, Civil Rights Division, Department of Justice.

WELDEN ROUGEAU,
Director, Office of Federal Contract Compliance, Department of Labor.

KENT A. PETERSON,
Acting Deputy Director, Office of Revenue Sharing.

I. PURPOSE AND SCOPE

1. Q. What is the purpose of the Guidelines?

A. The guidelines are designed to aid in the achievement of our nation's goal of equal employment opportunity without discrimination on the grounds of race, color, sex, religion or national origin. The Federal agencies have adopted the Guidelines to provide a uniform set of principles governing use of employee selection procedures which is consistent with applicable legal standards and validation standards generally accepted by the psychological profession and which the Government will apply in the discharge of its responsibilities.

2. Q. What is the basic principle of the Guidelines?

A. A selection process which has an adverse impact on the employment opportunities of members of a race, color, religion, sex, or national origin group (referred to as "race, sex, and ethnic group," as defined in Section 16P) and thus disproportionately screens them out is unlawfully discriminatory unless the process or its component procedures have been validated in accord with the Guidelines, or the user otherwise justifies them in accord with Federal law. See Sections 3 and 6.[1] This principle was adopted by the Supreme Court unanimously in *Griggs* v. *Duke Power Co.*, 401 U.S. 424, and was ratified and endorsed by the Congress when it passed the Equal Employment Opportunity Act of 1972, which amended Title VII of the Civil Rights Act of 1964.

3. Q. Who is covered by the Guidelines?

A. The Guidelines apply to private and public employers, labor organizations, employment agencies, apprenticeship committees, licensing and certification boards (see Question 7), and contractors or subcontractors, who are covered by one or more of the following provisions of Federal equal employment opportunity law: Title VII of the Civil Rights Act of 1964, as amended by the Equal Employment Opportunity Act of 1972 (hereinafter Title VII); Executive Order 11246, as amended by Executive Orders 11375 and 12086 (hereinafter Executive Order 11246); the State and Local Fiscal Assistance Act of 1972, as amended; Omnibus Crime Control and Safe Streets Act of 1968, as amended; and the Intergovernmental Personnel Act of 1970, as amended. Thus, under Title VII, the Guidelines apply to the Federal Government with regard to Federal employment. Through Title VII they apply to most private employers who have 15 or more employees for 20 weeks or more a calendar year, and to most employment agencies, labor orgainzations and apprenticeship committees. They apply to state and local governments which employ 15 or more employees, or which receive revenue sharing funds, or which receive funds from the Law Enforcement Assistance Administration to impose and strengthen law enforcement and criminal justice, or which receive grants or other federal assistance under a program which requires maintenance of personnel standards on a merit basis. They apply through Executive Order 11246 to contractors and subcontractors of the Federal Government and to contractors and subcontractors under federally-assisted construction contracts.

4. Q. Are college placement officers and similar organizations considered to be users subject to the Guidelines?

A. Placement offices may or may not be subject to the Guidelines depending on what services they offer. If a placement office uses a selection procedure as a basis for any employment decision, it is covered under the definition of "user". Section 16. For example, if a placement office selects some students for referral to an employer but rejects others, it is covered. However, if the placement office refers all interested students to an employer, it is not covered, even though it may offer office space and provision for informing the students of job openings. The Guidelines are intended to cover all users of employee selection procedures, including employment agencies, who are subject to Federal equal employment opportunity law.

5. Q. Do the Guidelines apply only to written tests?

A. No. They apply to all selection procedures used to make employment

---

[1] Section references throughout these questions and answers are to the sections of the *Uniform Guidelines on Employee Selection Procedures* (herein referred to as "Guidelines") that were published by the Equal Employment Opportunity Commission, the Civil Service Commission, the Department of Labor, and the Department of Justice on Aug. 25, 1978, 43 FR 38290. The Uniform Guidelines were adopted by the Office of Revenue Sharing of the Department of Treasury on September 11, 1978. 43 FR 40223.

decisions, including interviews, review of experience or education from application forms, work samples, physical requirements, and evaluations of performance. Sections 2B and 16Q, and see Question 6.

6. Q. What practices are covered by the Guidelines?

A. The Guidelines apply to employee selection procedures which are used in making employment decisions, such as hiring, retention, promotion, transfer, demotion, dismissal or referral. Section 2B. Employee selection procedures include job requirements (physical, education, experience), and evaluation of applicants or candidates on the basis of application forms, interviews, performance tests, paper and pencil tests, performance in training programs or probationary periods, and any other procedures used to make an employment decision whether administered by the employer or by an employment agency. See Section 2B.

7. Q. Do the Guidelines apply to the licensing and certification functions of state and local governments?

A. The Guidelines apply to such functions to the extent that they are covered by Federal law. Section 2B. The courts are divided on the issue of such coverage. The Government has taken the position that at least some kinds of licensing and certification which deny persons access to employment opportunity may be enjoined in an action brought pursuant to Section 707 of the Civil Rights Act of 1964, as amended.

8. Q. What is the relationship between Federal equal employment opportunity law, embodied in these Guidelines, and State and Local government merit system laws or regulations requiring rank ordering of candidates and selection from a limited number of the top candidates?

A. The Guidelines permit ranking where the evidence of validity is sufficient to support that method of use. State or local laws which compel rank ordering generally do so on the assumption that the selection procedure is valid. Thus, if there is adverse impact and the validity evidence does not adequately support that method of use, proper interpretation of such a state law would require validation prior to ranking. Accordingly, there is no necessary or inherent conflict between Federal law and State or local laws of the kind described.

Under the Supremacy Clause of the Constitution (Art. VI, Cl. 2), however, Federal law or valid regulation overrides any contrary provision of state or local law. Thus, if there is any conflict, Federal equal opportunity law prevails. For example, in *Rosenfeld* v. *So. Pacific Co.*, 444 F. 2d 1219 (9th Cir., 1971), the court held invalid state protective laws which prohibited the employment of women in jobs entailing long hours or heavy labor, because the state laws were in conflict with Title VII. Where a State or local official believes that there is a possible conflict, the official may wish to consult with the State Attorney General, County or City attorney, or other legal official to determine how to comply with the law.

II. ADVERSE IMPACT, THE BOTTOM LINE AND AFFIRMATIVE ACTION

9. Q. Do the Guidelines require that only validated selection procedures be used?

A. No. Although validation of selection procedures is desirable in personnel management, the Uniform Guidelines require users to produce evidence of validity only when the selection procedure adversely affects the opportunities of a race, sex, or ethnic group for hire, transfer, promotion, retention or other employment decision. If there is no adverse impact, there is no validation requirement under the Guidelines. Sections 1B and 3A. See also, Section 6A.

10. Q. What is adverse impact?

A. Under the Guidelines adverse impact is a substantially different rate of selection in hiring, promotion or other employment decision which works to the disadvantage of members of a race, sex or ethnic group. Sections 4D and 16B. See Questions 11 and 12.

11. Q. What is a substantially different rate of selection?

A. The agencies have adopted a rule of thumb under which they will generally consider a selection rate for any race, sex, or ethnic group which is less than four-fifths (4/5ths) or eighty percent (80%) of the selection rate for the group with the highest selection rate as a substantially different rate of selection. See Section 4D. This "4/5ths" or "80%" rule of thumb is not intended as a legal definition, but is a practical means of keeping the attention of the enforcement agencies on serious discrepancies in rates of hiring, promotion and other selection decisions.

For example, if the hiring rate for whites other than Hispanics is 60%, for American Indians 45%, for Hispanics 48%, and for Blacks 51%, and each of these groups constitutes more than 2% of the labor force in the relevant labor area (see Question 16), a comparison should be made of the selection rate for each group with that of the highest group (whites). These comparisons show the following impact ratios: American Indians 45/60 or 75%; Hispanics 48/60 or 80%; and Blacks 51/60 or 85%. Applying the 4/5ths or 80% rule of thumb, on the basis of the above information alone, adverse impact is indicated for American Indians but not for Hispanics or Blacks.

12. Q. How is adverse impact determined?

A. Adverse impact is determined by a four step process.

(1) calculate the rate of selection for each group (divide the number of persons selected from a group by the number of applicants from that group).

(2) observe which group has the highest selection rate.

(3) calculate the impact ratios, by comparing the selection rate for each group with that of the highest group (divide the selection rate for a group by the selection rate for the highest group).

(4) observe whether the selection rate for any group is substantially less (i.e., usually less than 4/5ths or 80%) than the selection rate for the highest group. If it is, adverse impact is indicated in most circumstances. See Section 4D.

For example:

Applicants	Hires	Selection rate Percent hired
80 White	48	48/80 or 60%
40 Black	12	12/40 or 30%

A comparison of the black selection rate (30%) with the white selection rate (60%) shows that the black rate is 30/60, or one-half (or 50%) of the white rate. Since the one-half (50%) is less than 4/5ths (80%) adverse impact is usually indicated.

The determination of adverse impact is not purely arithmetic however; and other factors may be relevant. See, Section 4D.

13. Q. Is adverse impact determined on the basis of the overall selection process or for the components in that process?

A. Adverse impact is determined first for the overall selection process for each job. If the overall selection process has an adverse impact, the adverse impact of the individual selection procedure should be analyzed. For any selection procedures in the process having an adverse impact which the user continues to use in the same manner, the user is expected to have evidence of validity satisfying the Guidelines. Sections 4C and 5D. If there is no adverse impact for the overall selection process, in most circumstances there is no obligation under the Guidelines to investigate adverse impact for the components, or to validate the selection procedures used for that job. Section 4C. But see Question 25.

14. Q. The Guidelines designate the "total selection process" as the initial basis for determining the impact of selection procedures. What is meant by the "total selection process"?

A. The "total selection process" refers to the combined effect of all selection procedures leading to the final employment decision such as hiring or promoting. For example, appraisal of candidates for administrative assistant positions in an organization might include initial screening based upon an application blank and interview, a written test, a medical examination, a background check, and a supervisor's interview. These in combination are the total selection process. Additionally, where there is more than one route to the particular kind of employment decision, the total selection process encompasses the combined results of all routes. For example, an employer may select some applicants for a particular kind of job through appropriate written and performance tests. Others may be selected through an internal upward mobility program, on the basis of successful performance in a directly related trainee type of position. In such a case, the impact of the total selection process would be the combined effect of both avenues of entry.

15. Q. What is meant by the terms "applicant" and "candidate" as they are used in the Uniform Guidelines?

A. The precise definition of the term "applicant" depends upon the user's recruitment and selection procedures. The concept of an applicant is that of a person who has indicated an interest in being considered for hiring, promotion, or other employment opportunities. This interest might be expressed by completing an application form, or might be expressed orally, depending upon the employer's practice.

The term "candidate" has been included to cover those situations where the initial step by the user involves consideration of current employees for promotion, or training, or other employment opportunities, without inviting applications. The procedure by which persons are identified as candidates is itself a selection procedure under the Guidelines.

A person who voluntarily withdraws formally or informally at any stage of the selection process is no longer an applicant or candidate for purposes of computing adverse impact. Employment standards imposed by the user which discourage disproportionately applicants of a race, sex or ethnic group may, however, require justification. Records should be kept for persons who were applicants or candidates at any stage of the process.

16. Q. Should adverse impact determinations be made for all groups regardless of their size?

A. No. Section 15A(2) calls for annual adverse impact determinations to be made for each group which constitutes either 2% or more of the total labor force in the relevant labor area, or 2% or more of the applicable workforce. Thus, impact determinations should be made for any employment decision for each group which constitutes 2% or more of the labor force in the relevant labor area. For hiring, such determination should also be made for groups which constitute more than 2% of the applicants; and for promotions, determinations should also be made for those groups which constitute at least 2% of the user's workforce. There are record keeping obligations for all groups, even those which are less than 2%. See Question 86.

17. Q. In determining adverse impact, do you compare the selection rates for males and females, and blacks and whites, or do you compare selection rates for white males, white females, black males and black females?

A. The selection rates for males and females are compared, and the selection rates for the race and ethnic groups are compared with the selection rate of the race or ethnic group with the highest selection rate. Neutral and objective selection procedures free of adverse impact against any race, sex or ethnic group are unlikely to have an impact against a subgroup. Thus there is no obligation to make comparisons for subgroups (e.g., white male, white female, black male, black female). However, there are obligations to keep records (see Question 87), and any apparent exclusion of a subgroup may suggest the presence of discrimination.

18. Q. Is it usually necessary to calculate the statistical significance of differences in selection rates when investigating the existence of adverse impact?

A. No. Adverse impact is normally indicated when one selection rate is less than 80% of the other. The federal enforcement agencies normally will use only the 80% (⅘ths) rule of thumb, except where large numbers of selections are made. See Questions 20 and 22.

19. Q. Does the ⅘ths rule of thumb mean that the Guidelines will tolerate up to 20% discrimination?

A. No. The ⅘ths rule of thumb speaks only to the question of adverse impact, and is not intended to resolve the ultimate question of unlawful discrimination. Regardless of the amount of difference in selection rates, unlawful discrimination may be present, and may be demonstrated through appropriate evidence. The ⅘ths rule merely establishes a numerical basis for drawing an initial inference and for requiring additional information.

With respect to adverse impact, the Guidelines expressly state (section 4D) that differences in selection rates of less than 20% may still amount to adverse impact where the differences are significant in both statistical and practical terms. See Question 20. In the absence of differences which are large enough to meet the ⅘ths rule of thumb or a test of statistical significance, there is no reason to assume that the differences are reliable, or that they are based upon anything other than chance.

20. Q. Why is the ⅘ths rule called a rule of thumb?

A. Because it is not intended to be controlling in all circumstances. If, for the sake of illustration, we assume that nationwide statistics show that use of an arrest record would disqualify 10% of all Hispanic persons but only 4% of all whites other than Hispanic (hereafter non-Hispanic), the selection rate for that selection procedure is 90% for Hispanics and 96% for non-Hispanics. Therefore, the ⅘ rule of thumb would not indicate the presence of adverse impact (90% is approximately 94% of 96%). But in this example, the information is based upon nationwide statistics, and the sample is large enough to yield statistically significant results, and the difference (Hispanics are 2½ times as likely to be disqualified as non-Hispanics) is large enough to be practically significant. Thus, in this example the enforcement agencies would consider a disqualification based on an arrest record alone as having an adverse impact. Likewise, in *Gregory* v. *Litton Industries*, 472 F. 2d 631 (9th Cir., 1972), the court held that the employer violated Title VII by disqualifying persons from employment solely on the basis of an arrest record, where that disqualification had an adverse impact on blacks and was not shown to be justified by business necessity.

On the other hand, a difference of more than 20% in rates of selection may not provide a basis for finding adverse impact if the number of persons selected is very small. For example, if the employer selected three males and one female from an applicant pool of 20 males and 10 females, the ⅘ths rule would indicate adverse impact (selection rate for women is 10%; for men 15%; ¹⁰⁄₁₅ or 66⅔% is less than 80%), yet the number of selections is too small to warrant a determination of adverse impact. In these circumstances, the enforcement agency would not require validity evidence in the absence of additional information (such as selection rates for a longer period of time) indicating adverse impact. For recordkeeping requirements, see Section 15A(2)(c) and Questions 84 and 85.

21. Q. Is evidence of adverse impact sufficient to warrant a validity study or an enforcement action where the numbers involved are so small that it is more likely than not that the difference could have occurred by chance? For example:

Applicants	Not hired	Hired	Selection rate percent hired
80 White	64	16	20
20 Black	17	3	15

White Selection Rate 20
Black Selection Rate 15
15 divided by 20 = 75% (which is less than 80%).

A. No. If the numbers of persons and the difference in selection rates are so small that it is likely that the difference could have occurred by chance, the Federal agencies will not assume the existence of adverse impact, in the absence of other evidence. In this example, the difference in selection rates is too small, given the small number of black applicants, to constitute adverse impact in the absence of other information (see Section 4D). If only one more black had been hired instead of a white the selection rate for blacks (20%) would be higher than that for whites (18.7%). Generally, it is inappropriate to require validity evidence or to take enforcement action where the number of persons and the difference in selection rates are so small that the selection of one different person for one job would shift the result from adverse impact against one group to a situation in which that group has a higher selection rate than the other group.

On the other hand, if a lower selection rate continued over a period of time, so as to constitute a pattern, then the lower selection rate would constitute adverse impact, warranting the need for validity evidence.

22. Q. Is it ever necessary to calculate the statistical significance of differences in selection rates to determine whether adverse impact exists?

A. Yes. Where large numbers of selections are made, relatively small differences in selection rates may nevertheless constitute adverse impact if they are both statistically and practically significant. See Section 4D and Question 20. For that reason, if there is a small difference in selection rates (one rate is more than 80% of the other), but large numbers of selections are involved, it would be appropriate to calculate the statistical significance of the difference in selection rates.

23. Q. When the ⅘th rule of thumb shows adverse impact, is there adverse impact under the Guidelines?

A. There usually is adverse impact, except where the number of persons selected and the difference in selection rates are very small. See Section 4D and Questions 20 and 21.

24. Q. Why do the Guidelines rely primarily upon the ⅘ths rule of thumb, rather than tests of statistical significance?

A. Where the sample of persons selected is not large, even a large real difference between groups is likely not to be confirmed by a test of statistical significance (at the usual .05 level of significance). For this reason, the Guidelines do not rely primarily upon a test of statistical significance, but use the ⅘ths rule of thumb as a practical and easy-to-administer measure of whether differences in selection rates are substantial. Many decisions in day-to-day life are made without reliance upon a test of statistical significance.

25. Q. Are there any circumstances in which the employer should evaluate components of a selection process, even though the overall selection process results in no adverse impact?

A. Yes, there are such circumstances: (1) Where the selection procedure is a significant factor in the continuation of patterns of assignments of incumbent employees caused by prior discriminatory employment practices. Assume, for example, an employer who traditionally hired blacks as employees for the "laborer" department in a manufacturing plant, and traditionally hired only whites as skilled craftsmen. Assume further that the employer in 1962 began to use a written examination not supported by a validity study to screen incumbent employees who sought to enter the apprenticeship program for skilled craft jobs. The employer stopped making racial assignments in 1972. Assume further that for the last four years, there have been special recruitment efforts aimed at recent black high school graduates and that the selection process, which includes the written examination, has resulted in the selection of black applicants for apprenticeship in approximately the same rates as white applicants.

In those circumstances, if the written examination had an adverse impact, its use would tend to keep incumbent black employees in the laborer department, and deny them entry to apprenticeship programs. For that reason, the enforcement agencies would expect the user to evaluate the impact of the written examination, and to have validity evidence for the use of the written examination if it has an adverse impact.

(2) Where the weight of court deci-

sions or administrative interpretations holds that a specific selection procedure is not job related in similar circumstances.

For example, courts have held that because an arrest is not a determination of guilt, an applicant's arrest record by itself does not indicate inability to perform a job consistent with the trustworthy and efficient operation of a business. Yet a no arrest record requirement has a nationwide adverse impact on some minority groups. Thus, an employer who refuses to hire applicants solely on the basis of an arrest record is on notice that this policy may be found to be discriminatory. *Gregory v. Litton Industries*, 472 F. 2d 631 (9th Cir., 1972) (excluding persons from employment solely on the basis of arrests, which has an adverse impact, held to violate Title VII). Similarly, a minimum height requirement disproportionately disqualifies women and some national origin groups, and has been held not to be job related in a number of cases. For example, in *Dothard v. Rawlinson*, 433 U.S. 321 (1977), the Court held that height and weight requirements not shown to be job related were violative of Title VII. Thus an employer using a minimum height requirement should have evidence of its validity.

(3) In addition, there may be other circumstances in which an enforcement agency may decide to request an employer to evaluate components of a selection process, but such circumstances would clearly be unusual. Any such decision will be made only at a high level in the agency. Investigators and compliance officers are not authorized to make this decision.

26. Q. Does the bottom line concept of Section 4C apply to the administrative processing of charges of discrimination filed with an issuing agency, alleging that a specific selection procedure is discriminatory?

A. No. The bottom line concept applies only to enforcement actions as defined in Section 16 of the Guidelines. Enforcement actions include only court enforcement actions and other similar proceedings as defined in Section 16L. The EEOC administrative processsing of charges of discrimination (investigation, finding of reasonable cause/no cause, and conciliation) required by Section 706(b) of Title VII are specifically exempted from the bottom line concept by the definition of an enforcement action. The bottom line concept is a result of a decision by the various enforcement agencies that, as a matter of prosecutorial discretion, they will devote their limited enforcement resources to the most serious offenders of equal employment opportunity laws. Since the concept is not a rule of law, it does not affect the discharge by the EEOC of its statutory responsibilities to investigate charges of discrimination, render an administrative finding on its investigation, and engage in voluntary conciliation efforts. Similarly, with respect to the other issuing agencies, the bottom line concept applies not to the processing of individual charges, but to the initiation of enforcement action.

27. Q. An employer uses one test or other selection procedure to select persons for a number of different jobs. Applicants are given the test, and the successful applicants are then referred to different departments and positions on the basis of openings available and their interests. The Guidelines appear to require assessment of adverse impact on a job-by-job basis (Section 15A(2)(a)). Is there some way to show that the test as a whole does not have adverse impact even though the proportions of members of each race, sex or ethnic group assigned to different jobs may vary?

A. Yes, in some circumstances. The Guidelines require evidence of validity only for those selection procedures which have an adverse impact, and which are part of a selection process which has an adverse impact. If the test is administered and used in the same fashion for a variety of jobs, the impact of that test can be assessed in the aggregate. The records showing the results of the test, and the total number of persons selected, generally would be sufficient to show the impact of the test. If the test has no adverse impact, it need not be validated.

But the absence of adverse impact of the test in the aggregate does not end the inquiry. For there may be discrimination or adverse impact in the assignment of individuals to, or in the selection of persons for, particular jobs. The Guidelines call for records to be kept and determinations of adverse impact to be made of the overall selection process on a job by job basis. Thus, if there is adverse impact in the assignment or selection procedures for a job even though there is no adverse impact from the test, the user should eliminate the adverse impact from the assignment procedure or justify the assignment procedure.

28. Q. The Uniform Guidelines apply to the requirements of Federal law prohibiting employment practices which discriminate on the grounds of race, color, religion, sex or national origin. However, records are required to be kept only by sex and by specified race and ethnic groups. How can adverse impact be determined for religious groups and for national origin groups other than those specified in Section 4B of the Guidelines?

A. The groups for which records are required to be maintained are the groups for which there is extensive evidence of continuing discriminatory practices. This limitation is designed in part to minimize the burden on employers for recordkeeping which may not be needed.

For groups for which records are not required, the person(s) complaining may obtain information from the employer or others (voluntarily or through legal process) to show that adverse impact has taken place. When that has been done, the various provisions of the Uniform Guidelines are fully applicable.

Whether or not there is adverse impact, Federal equal employment opportunity law prohibits any deliberate discrimination or disparate treatment on grounds of religion or national origin, as well as on grounds of sex, color, or race.

Whenever "ethnic" is used in the Guidelines or in these Questions and Answers, it is intended to include national origin and religion, as set forth in the statutes, executive orders, and regulations prohibiting discrimination. See Section 16P.

29. Q. What is the relationship between affirmative action and the requirements of the Uniform Guidelines?

A. The two subjects are different, although related. Compliance with the Guidelines does not relieve users of their affirmative action obligations, including those of Federal contractors and subcontractors under Executive Order 11246. Section 13.

The Guidelines encourage the development and effective implementation of affirmative action plans or programs in two ways. First, in determining whether to institute action against a user on the basis of a selection procedure which has adverse impact and which has not been validated, the enforcement agency will take into account the general equal employment opportunity posture of the user with respect to the job classifications for which the procedure is used and the progress which has been made in carrying out any affirmative action program. Section 4E. If the user has demonstrated over a substantial period of time that it is in fact appropriately utilizing in the job or group of jobs in question the available race, sex or ethnic groups in the relevant labor force, the enforcement agency will generally exercise its discretion by not initiating enforcement proceedings based on adverse impact in relation to the applicant flow. Second, nothing in the Guidelines is intended to preclude the use of selection procedures, consistent with Federal law, which assist in the achievement of affirmative action objectives. Section 13A. See also, Questions 30 and 31.

30. Q. When may a user be race, sex or ethnic-conscious?

A. The Guidelines recognize that affirmative action programs may be race, sex or ethnic conscious in appropriate circumstances, (See Sections 4E and 13; See also Section 17, Appendix). In addition to obligatory affirmative action programs (See Question 29), the Guidelines encourage the adoption of voluntary affirmative action programs. Users choosing to engage in voluntary affirmative action are referred to

EEOC's Guidelines on Affirmative Action (44 F.R. 4422, January 19, 1979). A user may justifiably be race, sex or ethnic-conscious in circumstances where it has reason to believe that qualified persons of specified race, sex or ethnicity have been or may be subject to the exclusionary effects of its selection procedures or other employment practices in its work force or particular jobs therein. In establishing long and short range goals, the employer may use the race, sex, or ethnic classification as the basis for such goals (Section 17(3) (a)).

In establishing a recruiting program, the employer may direct its recruiting activities to locations or institutions which have a high proportion of the race, sex, or ethnic group which has been excluded or underutilized (section 17(3) (b)). In establishing the pool of qualified persons from which final selections are to be made, the employer may take reasonable steps to assure that members of the excluded or underutilized race, sex, or ethnic group are included in the pool (Section 17(3) (e)).

Similarly, the employer may be race, sex or ethnic-conscious in determining what changes should be implemented if the objectives of the programs are not being met (Section 17(3) (g)).

Even apart from affirmative action programs a user may be race, sex or ethnic-conscious in taking appropriate and lawful measures to eliminate adverse impact from selection procedures (Section 6A).

31. Q. Section 6A authorizes the use of alternative selection procedures to eliminate adverse impact, but does not appear to address the issue of validity. Thus, the use of alternative selection procedures without adverse impact seems to be presented as an option in lieu of validation. Is that its intent?

A. Yes. Under Federal equal employment opportunity law the use of any selection procedure which has an adverse impact on any race, sex or ethnic group is discriminatory unless the procedure has been properly validated, or the use of the procedure is otherwise justified under Federal law. *Griggs v. Duke Power Co.*, 401 U.S. 424 (1971); Section 3A. If a selection procedure has an adverse impact, therefore, Federal equal employment opportunity law authorizes the user to choose lawful alternative procedures which eliminate the adverse impact rather than demonstrating the validity of the original selection procedure.

Many users, while wishing to validate all of their selection procedures, are not able to conduct the validity studies immediately. Such users have the option of choosing alternative techniques which eliminate adverse impact, with a view to providing a basis for determining subsequently which selection procedures are valid and have as little adverse impact as possible.

Apart from Federal equal employment opportunity law, employers have economic incentives to use properly validated selection procedures. Nothing in Section 6A should be interpreted as discouraging the use of properly validated selection procedures; but Federal equal employment opportunity law does not require validity studies to be conducted unless there is adverse impact. See Section 2C.

III. GENERAL QUESTIONS CONCERNING VALIDITY AND THE USE OF SELECTION PROCEDURES

32. Q. What is "validation" according to the Uniform Guidelines?

A. Validation is the demonstration of the job relatedness of a selection procedure. The Uniform Guidelines recognize the same three validity strategies recognized by the American Psychological Association:

(1) Criterion-related validity—a statistical demonstration of a relationship between scores on a selection procedure and job performance of a sample of workers.

(2) Content validity—a demonstration that the content of a selection procedure is representative of important aspects of performance on the job.

(3) Construct validity—a demonstration that (a) a selection procedure measures a construct (something believed to be an underlying human trait

or characteristic, such as honesty) and (b) the construct is important for successful job performance.

33. Q. What is the typical process by which validity studies are reviewed by an enforcement agency?

A. The validity study is normally requested by an enforcement officer during the course of a review. The officer will first determine whether the user's data show that the overall selection process has an adverse impact, and if so, which component selection procedures have an adverse impact. See Section 15A(3). The officer will then ask for the evidence of validity for each procedure which has an adverse impact. See Sections 15B, C, and D. This validity evidence will be referred to appropriate personnel for review. Agency findings will then be communicated to the user.

34. Q. Can a user send its validity evidence to an enforcement agency before a review, so as to assure its validity?

A. No. Enforcement agencies will not review validity reports except in the context of investigations or reviews. Even in those circumstances, validity evidence will not be reviewed without evidence of how the selection procedure is used and what impact its use has on various race, sex, and ethnic groups.

35. Q. May reports of validity prepared by publishers of commercial tests and printed in test manuals or other literature be helpful in meeting the Guidelines?

A. They may be. However, it is the user's responsibility to determine that the validity evidence is adequate to meet the Guidelines. See Section 7, and Questions 43 and 66. Users should not use selection procedures which are likely to have an adverse impact without reviewing the evidence of validity to make sure that the standards of the Guidelines are met.

The following questions and answers (36–81) assume that a selection procedure has an adverse impact and is part of a selection process that has an adverse impact.

36. Q. How can users justify continued use of a procedure on a basis other than validity?

A. Normally, the method of justifying selection procedures with an adverse impact and the method to which the Guidelines are primarily addressed, is validation. The method of justification of a procedure by means other than validity is one to which the Guidelines are not addressed. See Section 6B. In *Griggs* v. *Duke Power Co.*, 401 U.S. 424, the Supreme Court indicated that the burden on the user was a heavy one, but that the selection procedure could be used if there was a "business necessity" for its continued use; therefore, the Federal agencies will consider evidence that a selection procedure is necessary for the safe and efficient operation of a business to justify continued use of a selection procedure.

37. Q. Is the demonstration of a rational relationship (as that term is used in constitutional law) between a selection procedure and the job sufficient to meet the validation requirements of the Guidelines?

A. No. The Supreme Court in *Washington* v. *Davis*, 426 U.S. 229 (1976) stated that different standards would be applied to employment discrimination allegations arising under the Constitution than would be applied to employment discrimination allegations arising under Title VII. The *Davis* case arose under the Constitution, and no Title VII violation was alleged. The Court applied a traditional constitutional law standard of "rational relationship" and said that it would defer to the "seemingly reasonable acts of administrators and executives." However, it went on to point out that under Title VII, the appropriate standard would still be an affirmative demonstration of the relationship between the selection procedure and measures of job performance by means of accepted procedures of validation and it would be an "insufficient response to demonstrate some rational basis" for a selection procedure having an adverse impact. Thus, the mere demonstration of a rational relationship between a selection procedure and the job does not meet the requirement of Title VII of the Civil Rights Act of 1964, or of Executive Order 11246, or the State and Local Fiscal Assistance Act of 1972, as amended (the revenue sharing act) or the Omnibus Crime Control and Safe Streets Act of 1968, as amended, and will not meet the requirements of these Guidelines for a validity study. The three validity strategies called for by these Guidelines all require evidence that the selection procedure is related to successful performance on the job. That evidence may be obtained through local validation or through validity studies done elsewhere.

38. Q. Can a user rely upon written or oral assertions of validity instead of evidence of validity?

A. No. If a user's selection procedures have an adverse impact, the user is expected to produce evidence of the validity of the procedures as they are used. Thus, the unsupported assertion by anyone, including representatives of the Federal government or State Employment Services, that a test battery or other selection procedure has been validated is not sufficient to satisfy the Guidelines.

39. Q. Are there any formal requirements imposed by these Guidelines as to who is allowed to perform a validity study?

A. No. A validity study is judged on its own merits, and may be performed by any person competent to apply the principles of validity research, including a member of the user's staff or a consultant. However, it is the user's responsibility to see that the study meets validity provisions of the Guidelines, which are based upon professionally accepted standards. See Question 42.

40. Q. What is the relationship between the validation provisions of the Guidelines and other statements of psychological principles, such as the *Standards for Educational and Psychological Tests*, published by the American Psychological Association (Wash., D.C., 1974) (hereinafter "American Psychological Association Standards")?

A. The validation provisions of the Guidelines are designed to be consistent with the generally accepted standards of the psychological profession. These Guidelines also interpret Federal equal employment opportunity law, and embody some policy determinations of an administrative nature. To the extent that there may be differences between particular provisions of the Guidelines and expressions of validation principles found elsewhere, the Guidelines will be given precedence by the enforcement agencies.

41. Q. When should a validity study be carried out?

A. When a selection procedure has adverse impact on any race, sex or ethnic group, the Guidelines generally call for a validity study or the elimination of adverse impact. See Sections 3A and 6, and Questions 9, 31, and 36. If a selection procedure has adverse impact, its use in making employment decisions without adequate evidence of validity would be inconsistent with the Guidelines. Users who choose to continue the use of a selection procedure with an adverse impact until the procedure is challenged increase the risk that they will be found to be engaged in discriminatory practices and will be liable for back pay awards, plaintiffs' attorneys' fees, loss of Federal contracts, subcontracts or grants, and the like. Validation studies begun on the eve of litigation have seldom been found to be adequate. Users who choose to validate selection procedures should consider the potential benefit from having a validation study completed or well underway before the procedures are administered for use in employment decisions.

42. Q. Where can a user obtain professional advice concerning validation of selection procedures?

A. Many industrial and personnel psychologists validate selection procedures, review published evidence of validity and make recommendations with respect to the use of selection procedures. Many of these individuals are members or fellows of Division 14 (Industrial and Organizational Psychology) or Division 5 (Evaluation and Measurement) of the American Psychological Association. They can be identified in the membership directory of that organization. A high level of qualification is represented by a diploma in Industrial Psychology awarded by the American Board of Professional Psychology.

Individuals with the necessary competence may come from a variety of backgrounds. The primary qualification is pertinent training and experience in the conduct of validation research.

Industrial psychologists and other persons competent in the field may be found as faculty members in colleges and universities (normally in the departments of psychology or business administration) or working as individual consultants or as members of a consulting organization.

Not all psychologists have the necessary expertise. States have boards which license and certify psychologists, but not generally in a specialty such as industrial psychology. However, State psychological associations may be a source of information as to individuals qualified to conduct validation studies. Addresses of State psychological associations or other sources of information may be obtained from the American Psychological Association, 1200 Seventeenth Street, NW., Washington, D.C. 20036.

43. Q. Can a selection procedure be a valid predictor of performance on a job in a certain location and be invalid for predicting success on a different job or the same job in a different location?

A. Yes. Because of differences in work behaviors, criterion measures, study samples or other factors, a selection procedure found to have validity in one situation does not necessarily have validity in different circumstances. Conversely, a selection procedure not found to have validity in one situation may have validity in different circumstances. For these reasons, the Guidelines requires that certain standards be satisfied before a user may rely upon findings of validity in another situation. Section 7 and Section 14D. See also, Question 66. Cooperative and multi-unit studies are however encouraged, and, when those standards of the Guidelines are satisfied, validity evidence specific to each location is not required. See Section 7C and Section 8.

44. Q. Is the user of a selection procedure required to develop the procedure?

A. No. A selection procedure developed elsewhere may be used. However, the user has the obligation to show that its use for the particular job is consistent with the Guidelines. See Section 7.

45. Q. Do the Guidelines permit users to engage in cooperative efforts to meet the Guidelines?

A. Yes. The Guidelines not only permit but encourage such efforts. Where users have participated in a cooperative study which meets the validation standards of these Guidelines and proper account has been taken of variables which might affect the applicability of the study to specific users, validity evidence specific to each user will not be required. Section 8.

46. Q. Must the same method for validation be used for all parts of a selection process?

A. No. For example, where a selection process includes both a physical performance test and an interview, the physical test might be supported on the basis of content validity, and the interview on the basis of a criterion-related study.

47. Q. Is a showing of validity sufficient to assure the lawfulness of the use of a selection procedure?

A. No. The use of the selection procedure must be consistent with the validity evidence. For example, if a research study shows only that, at a given passing score the test satisfactorily screens out probable failures, the study would not justify the use of substantially different passing scores, or of ranked lists of those who passed. See Section 5G. Similarly, if the research shows that a battery is valid when a particular set of weights is used, the weights actually used must conform to those that were established by the research.

48. Q. Do the Guidelines call for a user to consider and investigate alter-

native selection procedures when conducting a validity study?

A. Yes. The Guidelines call for a user, when conducting a validity study, to make a reasonable effort to become aware of suitable alternative selection procedures and methods of use which have as little adverse impact as possible, and to investigate those which are suitable. Section 3B.

An alternative procedure may not previously have been used by the user for the job in question and may not have been extensively used elsewhere. Accordingly, the preliminary determination of the suitability of the alternative selection procedure for the user and job in question may have to be made on the basis of incomplete information. If on the basis of the evidence available, the user determines that the alternative selection procedure is likely to meet its legitimate needs, and is likely to have less adverse impact than the existing selection procedure, the alternative should be investigated further as a part of the validity study. The extent of the investigation should be reasonable. Thus, the investigation should continue until the user has reasonably concluded that the alternative is not useful or not suitable, or until a study of its validity has been completed. Once the full validity study has been completed, including the evidence concerning the alternative procedure, the user should evaluate the results of the study to determine which procedure should be used. See Section 3B and Question 50.

49. Q. Do the Guidelines call for a user *continually* to investigate "suitable alternative selection procedures and suitable alternative methods of using the selection procedure which have as little adverse impact as possible"?

A. No. There is no requirement for continual investigation. A reasonable investigation of alternatives is called for by the Guidelines as a part of any validity study. Once the study is complete and validity has been found, however, there is generally no obligation to conduct further investigations, until such time as a new study is called for. See, Sections 3B and 5K. If a government agency, complainant, civil rights organization or other person having a legitimate interest shows such a user an alternative procedure with less adverse impact and with substantial evidence of validity for the same job in similar circumstances, the user is obliged to investigate only the particular procedure which has been presented. Section 3B.

50. Q. In what circumstances do the Guidelines call for the use of an alternative selection procedure or an alternative method of using the procedure?

A. The alternative selection procedure (or method of use) should be used when it has less adverse impact and when the evidence shows that its validity is substantially the same or greater for the same job in similar circumstances. Thus, if under the original selection procedure the selection rate for black applicants was only one half (50 percent) that of the selection rate for white applicants, whereas under the alternative selection procedure the selection rate for blacks is two-thirds (67 percent) that of white applicants, the new alternative selection procedure should be used when the evidence shows substantially the same or greater validity for the alternative than for the original procedure. The same principles apply to a new user who is deciding what selection procedure to institute.

51. Q. What are the factors to be considered in determining whether the validity for one procedure is substantially the same as or greater than that of another procedure?

A. In the case of a criterion-related validity study, the factors include the importance of the criteria for which significant relationships are found, the magnitude of the relationship between selection procedure scores and criterion measures, and the size and composition of the samples used. For content validity, the strength of validity evidence would depend upon the proportion of critical and/or important job behaviors measured, and the extent to which the selection procedure resembles actual work samples or work behaviors. Where selection procedures have been validated by different strategies, or by construct validity, the determination should be made on a case by case basis.

52. Q. The Guidelines require consideration of alternative procedures and alternative methods of use, in light of the evidence of validity and utility and the degree of adverse impact of the procedure. How can a user know that any selection procedure with an adverse impact is lawful?

A. The Uniform Guidelines (Section 5G) expressly permit the use of a procedure in a manner supported by the evidence of validity and utility, even if another method of use has a lesser adverse impact. With respect to consideration of alternative selection procedures, if the user made a reasonable effort to become aware of alternative procedures, has considered them and investigated those which appear suitable as a part of the validity study, and has shown validity for a procedure, the user has complied with the Uniform Guidelines. The burden is then on the person challenging the procedure to show that there is another procedure with better or substantially equal validity which will accomplish the same legitimate business purposes with less adverse impact. Section 3B. See also, *Albemarle Paper Co. v. Moody*, 422 U.S. 405.

53. Q. Are the Guidelines consistent with the decision of the Supreme Court in *Furnco Construction Corp. v. Waters*, —— U.S. ——, 98 S. Ct. 2943 (1978) where the Court stated: "Title VII * * * does not impose a duty to adopt a hiring procedure that maximizes hiring of minority employees."

A. Yes. The quoted statement in *Furnco v. Waters* was made on a record where there was no adverse impact in the hiring process, no different treatment, no intentional discrimination, and no contractual obligations under E.O. 11246. Section 3B of the Guidelines is predicated upon a finding of adverse impact. Section 3B indicates that, when two or more selection procedures are available which serve a legitimate business purpose with substantially equal validity, the user should use the one which has been demonstrated to have the lesser adverse impact. Part V of the Overview of the Uniform Guidelines, in elaborating on this principle, states: "Federal equal employment opportunity law has added a requirement to the process of validation. In conducting a validation study, the employer should consider available alternatives which will achieve its legitimate purpose with lesser adverse impact."

Section 3B of the Guidelines is based on the principle enunciated in the Supreme Court decision in *Albermarle Paper Co. v. Moody*, 422 U.S. 405 (1975) that, even where job relatedness has been proven, the availability of other tests or selection devices which would also serve the employer's legitimate interest in "efficient and trustworthy workmanship" without a similarly undesirable racial effect would be evidence that the employer was using its tests merely as a pretext for discrimination.

Where adverse impact still exists, even though the selection procedure has been validated, there continues to be an obligation to consider alternative procedures which reduce or remove that adverse impact if an opportunity presents itself to do so without sacrificing validity. Where there is no adverse impact, the *Furnco* principle rather than the *Albermarle* principle is applicable.

IV. TECHNICAL STANDARDS

54. Q. How does a user choose which validation strategy to use?

A. A user should select a validation strategy or strategies which are (1) appropriate for the type of selection procedure, the job, and the employment situation, and (2) technically and administratively feasible. Whatever method of validation is used, the basic logic is one of prediction; that is, the presumption that level of performance on the selection procedure will, on the average, be indicative of level of performance on the job after selection. Thus, a criterion-related study, particularly a predictive one, is often regarded as the closest to such an ideal.

See American Psychological Association *Standards*, pp. 26-27.

Key conditions for a criterion-related study are a substantial number of individuals for inclusion in the study, and a considerable range of performance on the selection and criterion measures. In addition, reliable and valid measures of job performance should be available, or capable of being developed. Section 14B(1). Where such circumstances exist, a user should consider use of the criterion-related strategy.

Content validity is appropriate where it is technically and administratively feasible to develop work samples or measures of operationally defined skills, knowledges, or abilities which are a necessary prerequisite to observable work behaviors. Content validity is not appropriate for demonstrating the validity of tests of mental processes or aptitudes or characteristics; and is not appropriate for knowledges, skills or abilities which an employee will be expected to learn on the job. Section 14C(1)

The application of a construct validity strategy to support employee selection procedures is newer and less developed than criterion-related or content validity strategies. Continuing research may result in construct validity becoming more widely used. Because construct validity represents a generalization of findings, one situation in which construct validity might hold particular promise is that where it is desirable to use the same selection procedures for a variety of jobs. An overriding consideration in whether or not to consider construct validation is the availability of an individual with a high level of expertise in this field.

In some situations only one kind of validation study is likely to be appropriate. More than one strategy may be possible in other circumstances, in which case administrative considerations such as time and expense may be decisive. A combination of approaches may be feasible and desirable.

55. Q. Why do the Guidelines recognize only content, construct and criterion-related validity?

A. These three validation strategies are recognized in the Guidelines since they represent the current professional consensus. If the professional commmunity recognizes new strategies or substantial modifications of existing strategies, they will be considered and, if necessary, changes will be made in the Guidelines. Section 5A.

56. Q. Why don't the Uniform Guidelines state a preference for criterion-related validity over content or construct validity?

A. Generally accepted principles of the psychological profession support the use of criterion-related, content or construct validity strategies as appropriate. American Psychological Association *Standards*, E, pp. 25-26. This use was recognized by the supreme Court in *Washington* v. *Davis*, 426 U.S. 229, 247, fn. 13. Because the Guidelines describe the conditions under which each validity strategy is inappropriate, there is no reason to state a general preference for any one validity strategy.

57. Q. Are the Guidelines intended to restrict the development of new testing strategies, psychological theories, methods of job analysis or statistical techniques?

A. No. The Guidelines are concerned with the validity and fairness of selection procedures used in making employment decisions, and are not intended to limit research and new developments. See Question 55.

58. Q. Is a full job analysis necessary for all validity studies?

A. It is required for all content and construct studies, but not for all criterion-related studies. See Sections 14A and 14B(2). Measures of the results or outcomes of work behaviors such as production rate or error rate may be used without a full job analysis where a review of information about the job shows that these criteria are important to the employment situation of the user. Similarly, measures such as absenteeism, tardiness or turnover may be used without a full job analysis if these behaviors are shown by a review of information about the job to be important in the specific situation. A rating of overall job performance may be used without a full job analysis only if the user can demonstrate its appropriateness for the specific job and employment situation through a study of the job. The Supreme Court held in *Albemarle Paper Co. v. Moody*, 422 U.S. 405 (1975), that measures of overall job performance should be carefully developed and their use should be standardized and controlled.

59. Q. Section 5J on interim use requires the user to have available substantial evidence of validity. What does this mean?

A. For purposes of compliance with 5J, "substantial evidence" means evidence which may not meet all the validation requirements of the Guidelines but which raises a strong inference that validity pursuant to these standards will soon be shown. Section 5J is based on the proposition that it would not be an appropriate allocation of Federal resources to bring enforcement proceedings against a user who would soon be able to satisfy fully the standards of the Guidelines. For example, a criterion-related study may have produced evidence which meets almost all of the requirements of the Guidelines with the exception that the gathering of the data of test fairness is still in progress and the fairness study has not yet produced results. If the correlation coefficient for the group as a whole permits the strong inference that the selection procedure is valid, then the selection procedure may be used on an interim basis pending the completion of the fairness study.

60. Q. What are the potential consequences to a user when a selection procedure is used on an interm basis?

A. The fact that the Guidelines permit interim use of a selection procedure under some conditions does not immunize the user from liability for back pay, attorney fees and the like, should use of the selection procedure later be found to be in violation of the Guidelines. Section 5J. For this reason, users should take steps to come into full compliance with the Guidelines as soon as possible. It is also appropriate for users to consider ways of minimizing adverse impact during the period of interim use.

61. Q. Must provisions for retesting be allowed for job-knowledge tests, where knowledge of the test content would assist in scoring well on it the second time?

A. The primary intent of the provision for retesting is that an applicant who was not selected should be given another chance. Particularly in the case of job-knowledge tests, security precautions may preclude retesting with the same test after a short time. However, the opportunity for retesting should be provided for the same job at a later time, when the applicant may have acquired more of the relevant job knowledges.

62 Q. Under what circumstances may a selection procedure be used for ranking?

A. Criterion-related and construct validity strategies are essentially empirical, statistical processes showing a relationship between performance on the selection procedure and performance on the job. To justify ranking under such validity strategies, therefore, the user need show mathematical support for the proposition that persons who receive higher scores on the procedure are likely to perform better on the job.

Content validity, on the other hand, is primarily a judgmental process concerned with the adequacy of the selection procedure as a sample of the work behaviors. Use of a selection procedure on a ranking basis may be supported by content validity if there is evidence from job analysis or other empirical data that what is measured by the selection procedure is associated with differences in levels of job performance. Section 14C(9); see also Section 5G.

Any conclusion that a content validated procedure is appropriate for ranking must rest on an inference that higher scores on the procedure are related to better job performance. The more closely and completely the selection procedure approximates the important work behaviors, the easier it is to make such an inference. Evidence that better performance on the procedure is related to greater productivity or to performance of behaviors of greater difficulty may also support such an inference.

Where the content and context of the selection procedure are unlike those of the job, as, for example, in many paper-and-pencil job knowledge tests, it is difficult to infer an association between levels of performance on the procedure and on the job. To support a test of job knowledge on a content validity basis, there must be evidence of a specific tie-in between each item of knowledge tested and one or more work behaviors. See Question 79. To justify use of such a test for ranking, it would also have to be demonstrated from empirical evidence either that mastery of more difficult work behaviors, or that mastery of a greater scope of knowledge corresponds to a greater scope of important work behaviors.

For example, for a particular warehouse worker job, the job analysis may show that lifting a 50-pound object is essential, but the job analysis does not show that lifting heavier objects is essential or would result in significantly better job performance. In this case a test of ability to lift 50 pounds could be justified on a content validity basis for a pass/fail determination. However, ranking of candidates based on relative amount of weight that can be lifted would be inappropriate.

In another instance, a job analysis may reflect that, for the job of machine operator, reading of simple instructions is not a major part of the job but is essential. Thus, reading would be a critical behavior under the Guidelines. See Section 14C(8). since the job analysis in this example did not also show that the ability to read such instructions more quickly or to understand more complex materials would be likely to result in better job performance, a reading test suported by content validity alone should be used on a pass/fail rather than a ranking basis. In such circumstances, use of the test for ranking would have to be supported by evidence from a criterion-related (or construct) validity study.

On the other hand, in the case of a person to be hired for a typing pool, the job analysis may show that the job consists almost entirely of typing from manuscript, and that productivity can be measured directly in terms of finished typed copy. For such a job, typing constitutes not only a critical behavior, but it constitutes most of the job. A higher score on a test which measured words per minute typed, with adjustments for errors, would therefore be likely to predict better job performance than a significantly lower score. Ranking or grouping based on such a typing test would therefore be appropriate under the Guidelines.

63. Q. If selection procedures are administered by an employment agency or a consultant for an employer, is the employer relieved of responsibilities under the Guidelines?

A. No. The employer remains responsible. It is therefore expected that the employer will have sufficient information available to show: (a) What selection procedures are being used on its behalf; (b) the total number of applicants for referral by race, sex and ethnic group; (c) the number of persons, by race, sex and ethnic group, referred to the employer; and (d) the impact of the selection procedures and evidence of the validity of any such procedure having an adverse impact as determined above.

A. CRITERION-RELATED VALIDITY

64. Q. Under what circumstances may success in training be used as a criterion in criterion-related validity studies?

A. Success in training is an appropriate criterion when it is (1) necessary for successful job performance or has been shown to be related to degree of proficiency on the job and (2) properly measured. Section 14B(3). The measure of success in training should be carefully developed to ensure that factors which are not job related do not influence the measure of training success. Section 14B(3).

65. Q. When may concurrent validity be used?

A. A concurrent validity strategy assumes that the findings from a criterion-related validity study of current employees can be applied to applicants for the same job. Therefore, if concurrent validity is to be used, differences between the applicant and employee groups which might affect validity should be taken into account. The user should be particularly concerned with those differences between the applicant group and current employees used in the research sample which are caused by work experience or other work related events or by prior selection of employees and selection of the sample. See Section 14B(4).

66. Q. Under what circumstances can a selection procedure be supported (on other than an interim basis) by a criterion-related validity study done elsewhere?

A. A validity study done elsewhere may provide sufficient evidence if four conditions are met (Sec. 7B):

1. The evidence from the other studies clearly demonstrates that the procedure was valid in its use elsewhere.

2. The job(s) for which the selection procedure will be used closely matches the job(s) in the original study as shown by a comparison of major work behaviors as shown by the job analyses in both contexts.

3. Evidence of fairness from the other studies is considered for those groups constituting a significant factor in the user's labor market. Section 7B(3). Where the evidence is not available the user should conduct an internal study of test fairness, if technically feasible. Section 7B(3).

4. Proper account is taken of variables which might affect the applicability of the study in the new setting, such as performance standards, work methods, representativeness of the sample in terms of experience or other relevant factors, and the currency of the study.

67. Q. What does "unfairness of a selection procedure" mean?

A. When a specific score on a selection procedure has a different meaning in terms of expected job performance for members of one race, sex or ethnic group than the same score does for members of another group, the use of that selection procedure may be unfair for members of one of the groups. See section 16V. For example, if members of one group have an average score of 40 on the selection procedure, but perform on the job as well as another group which has an average score of 50, then some uses of the selection procedure would be unfair to the members of the lower scoring group. See Question 70.

68. Q. When should the user investigate the question of fairness?

A. Fairness should be investigated generally at the same time that a criterion-related validity study is conducted, or as soon thereafter as feasible. Section 14B(8).

69. Q. Why do the Guidelines require that users look for evidence of unfairness?

A. The consequences of using unfair selection procedures are severe in terms of discriminating against applicants on the basis of race, sex or ethnic group membership. Accordingly, these studies should be performed routinely where technically feasible and appropriate, whether or not the probability of finding unfairness is small. Thus, the Supreme Court indicated in *Albemarle Paper Co.* v. *Moody*, 422 U.S. 405, that a validation study was "materially deficient" because, among other reasons, it failed to investigate fairness where it was not shown to be unfeasible to do so. Moreover, the American Psychological Association *Standards* published in 1974 call for the investigation of test fairness in criterion-related studies wherever feasible (pp. 43-44).

70. Q. What should be done if a selection procedure is unfair for one or more groups in the relevant labor market?

A. The Guidelines discuss three options. See Section 14B(8)(d). First, the selection instrument may be replaced by another validated instrument which is fair to all groups. Second, the selection instrument may be revised to eliminate the sources of unfairness. For example, certain items may be found to be the only ones which cause the unfairness to a particular group, and these items may be deleted or replaced by others. Finally, revisions may be made in the method of use of the selection procedure to ensure that the probability of being selected is compatible with the probability of successful job performance.

The Federal enforcement agencies recognize that there is serious debate in the psychological profession on the question of test fairness, and that information on that concept is developing. Accordingly, the enforcement agencies will consider developments in this field in evaluating actions occasioned by a finding of test unfairness.

71. Q. How is test unfairness related to differential validity and to differential prediction?

A. Test unfairness refers to use of selection procedures based on scores when members of one group characteristically obtain lower scores than members of another group, and the differences are not reflected in measures of job performance. See Sections 16V and 14B(8)(a), and Question 67.

Differential validity and test unfairness are conceptually distinct. Differential validity is defined as a situation in which a given instrument has significantly different validity coefficients for different race, sex or ethnic groups. Use of a test may be unfair to some groups even when differential validity is not found.

Differential prediction is a central concept for one definition of test unfairness. Differential prediction occurs when the use of the same set of scores systematically overpredicts or underpredicts job performance for members of one group as compared to members of another group.

Other definitions of test unfairness which do not relate to differential prediction may, however, also be appropriately applied to employment decisions. Thus these Guidelines are not intended to choose between fairness models as long as the model selected is appropriate to the manner in which the selection procedure is used.

72. Q. What options does a user have if a criterion-related study is appropriate but is not feasible because there are not enough persons in the job?

A. There are a number of options the user should consider, depending upon the particular facts and circumstances, such as:

1. Change the procedure so as to eliminate adverse impact (see Section 6A);

2. Validate a procedure through a content validity strategy, if appropriate (see Section 14C and Questions 54 and 74);

3. Use a selection procedure validated elsewhere in conformity with the Guidelines (see Sections 7-8 and Question 66);

4. Engage in a cooperative study with other facilities or users (in cooperation with such users either bilaterally or through industry or trade associations or governmental groups), or participate in research studies conducted by the state employment security system. Where different locations are combined, care is needed to insure that the jobs studied are in fact the same and that the study is adequate and in conformity with the Guidelines (see Sections 8 and 14 and Question 45).

5. Combine essentially similar jobs into a single study sample. See Section 14B(1).

B. CONTENT VALIDITY

73. Q. Must a selection procedure supported by content validity be an actual "on the job" sample of work behaviors?

A. No. The Guidelines emphasize the importance of a close approximation between the content of the selection procedure and the observable behaviors or products of the job, so as to minimize the inferential leap between performance on the selection procedure and job performance. However, the Guidelines also permit justification on the basis of content validity of selection procedures measuring knowledges, skills, or abilities which are not necessarily samples of work behaviors if: (1) The knowledge, skill, or ability being measured is operationally defined in accord with Section 14C(4); and (2) that knowledge, skill, or ability is a prerequisite for critical or important work behaviors. In addition users may justify a requirement for training, or for experience obtained from prior employment or volunteer work, on the basis of content validity, even though the prior training or experience does not duplicate the job. See Section 14B(6).

74. Q. Is the use of a content validity strategy appropriate for a procedure measuring skills or knowledges which are taught in training after initial employment?

A. Usually not. The Guidelines state (Section 14C(1)) that content validity is not appropriate where the selection procedure involves knowledges, skills, or abilities which the employee will be expected to learn "on the job". The phrase "on the job" is intended to apply to training which occurs after hiring, promotion or transfer. However, if an ability, such as speaking and understanding a language, takes a substantial length of time to learn, is required for successful job performance, and is not taught to those initial hires who possess it in advance, a test for that ability may be supported on a content validity basis.

75. Q. Can a measure of a trait or construct be validated on the basis of content validity?

A. No. Traits or constructs are by definition underlying characteristics which are intangible and are not directly observable. They are therefore not appropriate for the sampling approach of content validity. Some selection procedures, while labeled as construct measures, may actually be samples of observable work behaviors. Whatever the label, if the operational definitions are in fact based upon observable work behaviors, a selection procedure measuring those behaviors may be appropriately supported by a content validity strategy. For example, while a measure of the construct "dependability" should not be supported on the basis of content validity, promptness and regularity of attendance in a prior work record are frequently inquired into as a part of a selection procedure, and such measures may be supported on the basis of content validity.

76. Q. May a test which measures what the employee has learned in a training program be justified for use in employment decisions on the basis of content validity?

A. Yes. While the Guidelines (Section 14C(1)) note that content validity is not an appropriate strategy for knowledges, skills or abilities which an employee "will be expected to learn on the job", nothing in the Guidelines suggests that a test supported by content validity is not appropriate for determining what the employee has learned on the job, or in a training program. If the content of the test is relevant to the job, it may be used for employment decisions such as retention or assignment. See Section 14C(7).

77. Q. Is a task analysis necessary to support a selection procedure based on content validity?

A. A description of all tasks is not required by the Guidelines. However, the job analysis should describe all important work behaviors and their relative importance and their level of difficulty. Sections 14C(2) and 15C(3). The job analysis should focus on observable work behaviors and, to the extent appropriate, observable work products, and the tasks associated with the important observable work behaviors and/or work products. The job analysis should identify how the critical or important work behaviors are used in the job, and should support the content of the selection procedure.

78. Q. What is required to show the content validity of a paper-and-pencil test that is intended to approximate work behaviors?

A. Where a test is intended to replicate a work behavior, content validity is established by a demonstration of the similarities between the test and the job with respect to behaviors, products, and the surrounding environmental conditions. Section 14B(4).

Paper-and-pencil tests which are intended to replicate a work behavior are most likely to be appropriate where work behaviors are performed in paper and pencil form (e.g., editing and bookkeeping). Paper-and-pencil tests of effectiveness in interpersonal relations (*e.g.*, sales or supervision), or of physical activities (*e.g.*, automobile repair) or ability to function properly under danger (*e.g.*, firefighters) generally are not close enough approximations of work behaviors to show content validity.

The appropriateness of tests of job knowledge, whether or not in pencil and paper form, is addressed in Question 79.

79. Q. What is required to show the content validity of a test of a job knowledge?

A. There must be a defined, well recognized body of information, and knowledge of the information must be prerequisite to performance of the required work behaviors. The work behavior(s) to which each knowledge is related should be identified on an item by item basis. The test should fairly sample the information that is actually used by the employee on the job, so that the level of difficulty of the test items should correspond to the level of difficulty of the knowledge as used in the work behavior. See Section 14C(1) and (4).

80. Q. Under content validity, may a selection procedure for entry into a job be justified on the grounds that the knowledges, skills or abilities measured by the selection procedure are prerequisites to successful performance in a training program?

A. Yes, but only if the training material and the training program closely approximate the content and level of difficulty of the job and if the knowledges, skills or abilities are not those taught in the training program. For example, if training materials are at a level of reading difficulty substantially in excess of the reading difficulty of materials used on the job, the Guidelines would not permit justification on a content validity basis of a reading test based on those training materials for entry into the job.

Under the Guidelines a training program itself is a selection procedure if passing it is a prerequisite to retention or advancement. See Section 2C and 14C(17). As such, the content of the training program may only be justified by the relationship between the program and critical or important behaviors of the job itself, or through a demonstration of the relationship between measures of performance in training and measures of job performance.

Under the example given above, therefore, where the requirements in the training materials exceed those on the job, the training program itself could not be validated on a content validity basis if passing it is a basis for retention or promotion.

C. CONSTRUCT VALIDITY

81. Q. In Section 5, "General Standards for Validity Studies," construct validity is identified as no less acceptable than criterion-related and content validity. However, the specific requirements for construct validity, in Section 14D, seem to limit the generalizability of construct validity to the rules governing criterion-related validity. Can this apparent inconsistency be reconciled?

A. Yes. In view of the developing nature of construct validation for employment selection procedures, the approach taken concerning the generalizability of construct validity (section 14D) is intended to be a cautious one. However, construct validity may be generalized in circumstances where transportability of tests supported on the basis of criterion-related validity would not be appropriate. In establishing transportability of criterion-related validity, the jobs should have substantially the same major work behaviors. Section 7B(2). Construct validity, on the other hand, allows for situations where only some of the important work behaviors are the same. Thus, well-established measures of the construct which underlie particular work behaviors and which have been shown to be valid for some jobs may be generalized to other jobs which have some of the same work behaviors but which are different with respect to other work behaviors. Section 14D(4).

As further research and professional guidance on construct validity in employment situations emerge, additional extensions of construct validity for employee selection may become generally accepted in the profession. The agencies encourage further research and professional guidance with respect to the appropriate use of construct validity.

V. RECORDS AND DOCUMENTATION

82. Q. Do the Guidelines have simplified recordkeeping for small users (employers who employ one hundred or fewer employees and other users not required to file EEO-1, *et seq.* reports)?

A. Yes. Although small users are fully covered by Federal equal employment opportunity law, the Guidelines have reduced their record-keeping burden. See option in Section 15A(1). Thus, small users need not make adverse impact determinations nor are they required to keep applicant data on a job-by-job basis. The agencies also recognize that a small user may find that some or all validation strategies are not feasible. See Question 54. If a small user has reason to believe that its selection procedures have adverse impact and validation is not feasible, it should consider other options. See Sections 7A and 8 and Questions 31, 36, 45, 66, and 72.

83. Q. Is the requirement in the Guidelines that users maintain records of the race, national origin, and sex of employees and applicants constitutional?

A. Yes. For example, the United States Court of Appeals for the First Circuit rejected a challenge on constitutional and other grounds to the Equal Employment Opportunity Commission regulations requiring State and local governmental units to furnish information as to race, national origin and sex of employees. *United States* v. *New Hampshire,* 539 F. 2d 277 (1st Cir. 1976), *cert. denied,* sub nom. *New Hampshire* v. *United States,* 429 U.S. 1023. The Court held that the recordkeeping and reporting requirements promulgated under Title VII of the Civil Rights Act of 1964, as amended, were reasonably necessary for the Federal agency to determine whether the state was in compliance with Title VII and thus were authorized and constitutional. The same legal principles apply to recordkeeping with respect to applicants.

Under the Supremacy Clause of the Constitution, the Federal law requiring maintenance of records identifying race, sex and national origin overrides any contrary provision of State law. See Question 8.

The agencies recognize, however, that such laws have been enacted to prevent misuse of this information. Thus, employers should take appropriate steps to ensure proper use of all data. See Question #88.

84. Q. Is the user obliged to keep records which show whether its selection processes have an adverse impact on race, sex, or ethnic groups?

A. Yes. Under the Guidelines users are obliged to maintain evidence indicating the impact which their selection processes have on identifiable race, sex or ethnic groups. Sections 4 A and B. If the selection process for a job does have an adverse impact on one or more such groups, the user is expected to maintain records showing the impact for the individual procedures. Section 15A(2).

85. Q. What are the recordkeeping obligations of a user who cannot determine whether a selection process for a job has adverse impact because it makes an insufficient number of selections for that job in a year?

A. In such circumstances the user should collect, maintain, and have available information on the impact of the selection process and the component procedures until it can determine that adverse impact does not exist for the overall process or until the job has changed substantially. Section 15A(2)(c).

86. Q. Should applicant and selection information be maintained for race or ethnic groups constituting less than 2% of the labor force and the applicants?

A. Small employers and other small users are not obliged to keep such records. Section 15A(1). Employers with more than 100 employees and other users required to file EEO-1 et seq. reports should maintain records and other information upon which impact determinations could be made, because section 15A2 requires the maintenance of such information for "any of the groups for which records are called for by section 4B above." See also, Section 4A.

No user, regardless of size, is required to make adverse impact determinations for race or ethnic groups constituting less than 2% of the labor force and the applicants. See Question 16.

87. Q. Should information be maintained which identifies applicants and persons selected both by sex and by race or ethnic group?

A. Yes. Although the Federal agencies have decided not to require computations of adverse impact by subgroups (white males, black males, white females, black females—see Question 17), the Guidelines call for record keeping which allows identification of persons by sex, combined with race or ethnic group, so as to permit the identification of discriminatory practices on any such basis. Section 4A and 4B.

88. Q. How should a user collect data on race, sex or ethnic classifications for purposes of determining the impact of selection procedures?

A. The Guidelines have not specified any particular procedure, and the enforcement agencies will accept different procedures that capture the necessary information. Where applications are made in person, a user may maintain a log or applicant flow chart based upon visual observation, identifying the number of persons expressing an interest, by sex and by race or national origin; may in some circumstances rely upon personal knowledge of the user; or may rely upon self-identification. Where applications are not made in person and the applicants are not personally known to the employer, self-identification may be appropriate. Wherever a self-identification form is used, the employer should advise the applicant that identification by race, sex and national origin is sought, not for employment decisions, but for record-keeping in compliance with Federal law. Such self-identification forms should be kept separately from the application, and should not be a basis for employment decisions; and the applicants should be so advised. See Section 4B.

89. Q. What information should be included in documenting a validity study for purposes of these Guidelines?

A. Generally, reports of validity studies should contain all the information necessary to permit an enforcement agency to conclude whether a selection procedure has been validated. Information that is critical to this determination is denoted in Section 15 of the Guidelines by the word "(essential)".

Any reports completed after September 25, 1978, (the effective date of the Guidelines) which do not contain this information will be considered incomplete by the agencies unless there is good reason for not including the information. Users should therefore prepare validation reports according to the format of Section 15 of the Guidelines, and should carefully document the reasons if any of the information labeled "(essential)" is missing.

The major elements for all types of validation studies include the following:

When and where the study was conducted.

A description of the selection procedure, how it is used, and the results by race, sex, and ethnic group.

How the job was analyzed or reviewed and what information was obtained from this job analysis or review.

The evidence demonstrating that the selection procedure is related to the job. The nature of this evidence varies, depending upon the strategy used.

What alternative selection procedures and alternative methods of using the selection procedure were studied and the results of this study.

The name, address and telephone number of a contact person who can provide further information about the study.

The documentation requirements for each validation strategy are set forth in detail in Section 15 B, C, D, E, F, and G. Among the requirements for each validity strategy are the following:

1. *Criterion-Related Validity*

A description of the criterion measures of job performance, how and why they were selected, and how they were used to evaluate employees.

A description of the sample used in the study, how it was selected, and the size of each race, sex, or ethnic group in it.

A description of the statistical methods used to determine whether scores on the selection procedure are related to scores on the criterion measures of job performance, and the results of these statistical calculations.

2. *Content Validity*

The content of the job, as identified from the job analysis.

The content of the selection procedure.

The evidence demonstrating that the content of the selection procedure is a representative sample of the content of the job.

3. *Construct Validity*

A definition of the construct and how it relates to other constructs in the psychological literature.

The evidence that the selection procedure measures the construct.

The evidence showing that the measure of the construct is related to work behaviors which involve the construct.

90. Q. Although the records called for under "Source Data", Section 15B(11) and section 15D(11), are not listed as "Essential", the Guidelines state that each user should maintain such records, and have them available upon request of a compliance agency. Are these records necessary? Does the absence of complete records preclude the further use of research data compiled prior to the issuance of the Guidelines?

A. The Guidelines require the maintenance of these records in some form "as a necessary part of the study." Section 15A(3)(c). However, such records need not be compiled or maintained in any specific format. The term "Essential" as used in the Guidelines refers to information considered essential to the validity report. Section 15A(3)(b). The Source Data records need not be included with reports of validation or other formal reports until and unless they are specifically requested by a compliance agency. The absence of complete records does not preclude use of research data based on those records that are available. Validation studies submitted to comply with the requirements of the Guidelines may be considered inadequate to the extent that important data are missing or there is evidence that the collected data are inaccurate.

[FR Doc. 79-6323 Filed 3-1-79; 8:45 am]

**FRIDAY, MARCH 2, 1979
PART IV**

EQUAL EMPLOYMENT OPPORTUNITY COMMISSION

OFFICE OF PERSONNEL MANAGEMENT

DEPARTMENT OF JUSTICE

DEPARTMENT OF LABOR

DEPARTMENT OF THE TREASURY

ADOPTION OF QUESTIONS AND ANSWERS TO CLARIFY AND PROVIDE A COMMON INTERPRETATION OF THE UNIFORM GUIDELINES ON EMPLOYEE SELECTION PROCEDURES

EQUAL EMPLOYMENT OPPORTUNITY COMMISSION

29 CFR Part 1607

OFFICE OF PERSONNEL MANAGEMENT

5 CFR Part 300

DEPARTMENT OF JUSTICE

28 CFR Part 50

DEPARTMENT OF THE TREASURY

31 CFR Part 51

DEPARTMENT OF LABOR

Office of Federal Contract Compliance Programs

41 CFR Part 60-3

Adoption of Additional Questions and Answers to Clarify and Provide a Common Interpretation of the Uniform Guidelines on Employee Selection Procedures

AGENCIES: Equal Employment Opportunity Commission, Office of Personnel Management, Department of Justice, Department of Labor and Department of the Treasury.

ACTION: Adoption of additional questions and answers designed to clarify and provide a common interpretation of the Uniform Guidelines on Employee Selection Procedures.

SUMMARY: The agencies which issued the Uniform Guidelines on Employee Selection Procedures (43 FR 38290 et seq., August 25, 1978 and 43 FR 40223, Sept. 11, 1978, 29 CFR Part 1607, 41 CFR Part 60-3, 28 CFR 50.14, 5 CFR 300.103(c), and 31 CFR 51.53) have previously recognized the need for a common interpretation of the Uniform Guidelines, as well as the desirability of providing additional guidance to users, psychologists and enforcement personnel, by publishing Questions and Answer (44 FR 11996, March 2, 1979). These Additional Questions and Answers are intended to provide additional guidance in interpreting the Uniform Guidelines.

EFFECTIVE DATE: May 2, 1980

FOR FURTHER INFORMATION CONTACT:

Pamela Dillon, Chief, Branch of Special Analyses, Room N5718, Office of Federal Contract Compliance Programs, Department of Labor, Washington, D.C. 20210, 202-633-6924.

Frederick Dorsey, Director, Office of Policy Implementation, Equal Employment Opportunity Commission, 2401 E Street, N.W., Washington, D.C. 20506, 202-634-7060.

A. Diane Graham, Assistant Director, Affirmative Employment Programs, Office of Personnel Management, 1900 E Street, N.W., Washington, D.C. 20415, 202-632-4420.

James Hellings, Special Assistant to the Assistant Director, Intergovernmental Personnel Programs, Office of Personnel Management, 1900 E Street, N.W., Washington, D.C. 20415, 202-632-6248.

Arnold Intrater, Chief Counsel, Office of Revenue Sharing, Department of the Treasury, 2401 E Street, N.W., Washington, D.C. 20220, 202-634-5182.

Kenneth A. Millard, Chief, State and Local Branch, Personnel Research and Development Center, Office of Personnel Management, 1900 E Street, N.W., Washington, D.C. 20414, 202-632-6238.

David L. Rose, Chief, Federal Enforcement Section, Civil Rights Division, Department of Justice, 10th Street and Pennsylvania Avenue, N.W. Washington, D.C. 20530, 202-633-3831.

Donald J. Schwartz, Personnel Research Psychologist, Office of Systemic Programs, Equal Employment Opportunity Commission, 2401 E

Street, N.W., Washington, D.C. 20506, 202-634-6960.

Introduction

Because of the number and importance of the issues addressed in the Uniform Guidelines on Employee Selection Procedures (43 FR 38290), and the dual needs of providing a common interpretation and providing guidance to employers and other users, psychologists and others who are called upon to conduct validity studies, and Federal personnel who have enforcement responsibilities, the five issuing Federal agencies adopted and issued Questions and Answers (44 FR 11996, Mar. 2, 1979) to clarify and interpret the Uniform Guidelines. The issuing agencies recognized that it might be appropriate to address additional questions at a later date.

By letter dated October 22, 1979, the American Psychological Association, acting through its Committee on Psychological Tests and Assessment, brought to the attention of the government concerns as to the consistency of the Uniform Guidelines with the "Standards for Educational and Psychological Tests," referred to in the guidelines as the "A.P.A. Standards". The Committee noted in its letter of October 22, 1979, that it had found a high degree of consistency between the proposed Uniform Guidelines and the A.P.A. Standards on February 17, 1978, and that an attempt to resolve remaining inconsistencies was made in the published Uniform Guidelines. Stressing the view that the real impact of the Guidelines can only be fully assessed after agency instructions have been issued and applied, and after court rulings, however the Committee raised areas of possible inconsistency between the Uniform Guidelines, as applied, and the A.P.A. Standards. In particular, the letter raises (among others) three specific concerns: (1) that the Guidelines might call for "a more rigid demand for a search for alternatives than we would deem consistent with acceptable professional practices"; (2) that, with respect to criteria for criterion related validity studies, the Guidelines failed adequately to recognize that "a total absence of bias can never be assured" and that the standards of the profession required only that "there has been a competent professional handling of this problem"; and (3) for criterion related validity studies "in some circumstances there may exist just one or two critical job duties, and that in such cases sole reliance on such a single selection procedure relevant to the critical duties would be entirely appropriate".

Staff of the Federal agencies responded, by letter of January 17, 1980, that "some of the problems discussed in your letter may be due to a lack of a clearly articulated position of the Federal agencies on these matters, rather than to actual differences between the Uniform Guidelines and professional standards." The letter of January 17, 1980, enclosed a draft of three additional Questions and Answers designed to clarify the agencies' interpretation of those three issues, and requested comments on the additional Questions and Answers, and on the consistency of the Uniform Guidelines so interpreted with professional standards. By letter of February 11, 1980, the American Psychological Association, acting through it Committee on Psychological Tests and Assessment, found each of the Questions and Answers to be helpful and has judged, "given the accuracy of our interpretation of these Q's and A's, that these guidelines have attained consistency with the Standards in those areas in which comparisons can now be meaningfully made."

The validation provisions of the Uniform Guidelines are intended to reflect the standards of the psychological profession (Section 5C, Uniform Guidelines). The issuing agencies are of the view that the three additional Questions and Answers accurately reflect the proper interpretation of the Uniform Guidelines with respect to the three areas of concern raised by the A.P.A. Accordingly, the agencies hereby adopt the three Questions and Answers set forth below to clarify and provide a common interpretation of the Uniform Guidelines. These three additional Questions and Answers supplement the original Questions and Answers published on March 2, 1979. (44 FR 11996). As with the originals, these Questions and Answers use terms as they are defined in the Uniform Guidelines, and are intended to interpret and clarify, but not to modify, the provisions of the Uniform Guidelines.

Questions and Answers 91 and 92 are published exactly as written and attached to the letter of January 17, 1980. As the letter from the A.P.A. correctly noted, the Answer to Question 91 implies that the obligation of a user to study unpublished, professionally available research reports is dependent not only on the degree of adverse impact, but also upon the absolute number of persons who might be adversely affected. Where the number of persons affected is likely to be large, a thorough inquiry into unpublished sources is likely to be appropriate, but where the number is small, a cursory review may be sufficient.

The answer to Question 93 has been modified by the addition of an example, as suggested by the letter from A.P.A., and by clarifying language at the end of the last sentence.

The agencies recognize that additional questions may arise at a later date that warrant a formal, uniform response, and contemplate working together to provide additional guidance interpreting the Uniform Guidelines.

Supplemental Questions and Answers

91. Q. What constitutes a "reasonable investigation of alternatives" as that phrase is used in the Answer to Question 49?

A. The Uniform Guidelines call for a reasonable investigation of alternatives for a proposed selection procedure as a part of any validity study. See Section 3B and Questions 48 and 49. A reasonable investigation of alternatives would begin with a search of the published literature (test manuals and journal articles) to develop a list of currently available selection procedures that have in the past been found to be valid for the job in question or for similar jobs. A further review would then be required of all selection procedures at least as valid as the proposed procedure to determine if any offer the probability of lesser adverse impact. Where the information on the proposed selection procedure indicates a low degree of validity and high adverse impact, and where the published literature does not suggest a better alternative, investigation of other sources (for example, professionally-available, unpublished research studies) may also be necessary before continuing use of the proposed procedure can be justified. In any event, a survey of the enforcement agencies alone does not constitute a reasonable investigation of alternatives. Professional reporting of studies of validity and adverse impact is encouraged within the constraints of practicality.

92. Q. Do significant differences between races, sexes, or ethnic groups on criterion measures mean that the criterion measures are biased?

A. Not necessarily. However, criterion instruments should be carefully constructed and data collection procedures should be carefully controlled to minimize the possibility of bias. See Section 14B(2). All steps taken to ensure that criterion measures are free from factors which would unfairly alter the scores of members of any group should be described in the validation report, as required by Section 15B(5) of the Guidelines

93. Q. Can the use of a selection procedure which has been shown to be significantly related to only one or two job duties be justified under the Guidelines?

A. Yes. For example, where one or two work behaviors are the only critical or important ones, the sole use of a selection procedure which is related only to these behaviors may be appropriate. For example, a truck driver has the major duty of driving; and in addition handles customer accounts. Use of a selection procedure related only to truck driving might be acceptable, even if it showed no relationship to the handling of customer accounts. However, one or two significant relationships may occur by chance when many relationships are examined. In addition, in most practical situations, there are many critical and/or important work behaviors or work outcomes. For these reasons, reliance upon one or two significant relationships will be subject to close review, particularly where they are not the only important or critical ones.

Eleanor Holmes Norton,
Chair, Equal Employment Opportunity Commission.

Alan K. Campbell,
Director, Office of Personnel Management.

Drew S. Days III,
Assistant Attorney General, Civil Rights Division, Department of Justice.

Weldon J. Rougeau,
Director, Office of Federal Contract Compliance Programs, Department of Labor.

Kent A. Peterson,
Acting Director, Office of Revenue Sharing.

[FR Doc. 80–13345 Filed 5–1–80; 8:45 am]

BILLING CODE 6570-06-M

Appendix E
SELECTED BIBLIOGRAPHY ON THE UNIFORM GUIDELINES ON EMPLOYEE SELECTION PROCEDURES

Ad Hoc Group on Uniform Selection Guidelines, *A Professional and Legal Analysis of the Uniform Guidelines on Employee Selection Procedures* (1981).

Administrative Law—Weight of EEOC Guidelines in Evaluation of Employment Selection Procedures, 50 Tul. L. Rev. 397 (1976).

American Psychological Association, Division of Industrial-Organizational Psychology, *Principles for the Validation and Use of Personnel Selection Procedures* (2d ed. 1980).

American Psychological Association, *Standards for Educational and Psychological Tests* (1974).

Analyzing Job Analysis: Difficulties in EEOC Compliance, 1977 Ariz. St. L.J. 803.

Application of the EEOC Guidelines to Employment Test Validation: A Uniform Standard for Both Public and Private Employers, 41 Geo. Wash. L. Rev. 505 (1973).

Ashe, *Job-Related Selection Procedures under the Uniform Guidelines in the 1980's*, Proceedings of the Twenty-Sixth Annual Institute on Labor Law, Southwestern Legal Foundation (1981).

Bartholet, *Application of Title VII to Jobs in High Places*, 95 Harv. L. Rev. 945 (1982).

Barrett, *Is the Test Content Valid: Or, Does It Really Measure a Construct?*, 6 Emp. Rel. L.J. 459 (1980).

Bates, *Job Evaluation and Equal Employment Opportunity—a Tool for Compliance, a Weapon for Defense*, 1 Emp. Rel. L.J. 535 (1976).

Benson, *Section 1981 and Employment Testing: Discriminatory Impact Establishes a Prima Facie Case. Davis v. County of Los Angeles, 566 F.2d 1334 (9th Cir. 1977)*, 19 Urb. L. Ann. 268 (1980).

Blumrosen, *Bottom Line Concept in Equal Employment Opportunity Law*, 12 NC Central L.J. 1 (1980).

Boisseau & MacKay, *Job-related Selection Procedures Under the Uniform Guidelines*, 7 EEO Today 301 (1980).

Booth, *Legal Constraints on Employment Testing and Evolving Trends in the Law*, 29 Emory L.J. 121 (1980).

Brown, *Local Policing: A Three Dimensional Task Analysis*, 3 Journal of Criminal Justice 1 (1975).

Cahoon, *Employee Selection Procedures—Uniform Guidelines at Last?*, 5 EEO Today 139 (1978).

Chandler, *The Business Necessity Defense to Disparate Impact Liability under Title VII*, 46 U. Chi. L. Rev. 911 (1979).

Cooper, *Seniority and Testing Under Fair Employment Laws: A General Approach to Objective Criteria of Hiring and Promotion*, 82 Harv. L. Rev. 1603 (1969).

Employment Testing and Proof of Job Relatedness: A Tale of Unreasonable Constraints, 52 Notre Dame Law 95 (1976).

Employment Testing and the Federal Executive Agency Guidelines on Employee Selection Procedures; One Step Forward and Two Steps Backward for Equal Employment Opportunity, 26 Catholic U. L. Rev. 852 (1977).

Employment Testing: The Aftermath of Griggs v. Duke Power Company, 72 Colum. L. Rev. 900 (1972).

Employment Testing Under Title VII of the Civil Rights Act of 1964, 12 B.C. Ind. & Com. L. Rev. 268 (1970).

Feild, *Performance Appraisal and the Law*, 26 Lab. L.J. 423 (1975).

Fossum, *Multiple Dilemmas in Testing: Professional Standards, "Griggs" Requirements, and the Duty to Bargain*, 28 Lab. L.J. 102 (1977).

Francis, *Title VII and the Masters of Reality: Eliminating Credentialism in the American Labor Market*, 64 Geo. L.J. 1213 (1976).

Georgia Power (U.S. v. Georgia Power Co. 474 F.2d 906) Case: Another Federal Agency Comes of Age, or, "My God! Our Employer-Client's Testing Practices Are Being Challenged by the EEOC?", 57 Marq. L. Rev. 515 (1974).

Gorham, *The Uniform Guidelines on Employee Selection Procedures: What New Impact on the Assessment Center Method?*, Journal of Assessment Center Technology (1975).

Hunt, *Civil Rights Testing and Affirmative Action: A Psychologist's Perspective*, 44 U. Cin. L. Rev. 690 (1975).

Intelligence Testing Beyond Griggs v. Duke Power Company, 49 Chi-Kent L. Rev. 82 (1972).

Job-Related Test Rank is Discriminatory, 31 Lab. L.J. 63 (1980).

Johnson, *Albemarle Paper Company v. Moody: The Aftermath of Griggs and the Death of Employee Testing*, 27 Hastings L.J. 1239 (1976).

Kleiman & Foley, *Assessing Content Validity: Standards Set By the Court*, 31 Personnel Psychology 701 (1978).

Koral, *Practical Application of the Uniform Guidelines: What to Do 'til the Agency Comes*, 5 Emp. Rel. L.J. 473 (1980).

Kovarsky, *Some Social and Legal Aspects of Testing Under the Civil Rights Act*, 20 Lab. L.J. 346 (1969).

Kovarsky, *Testing and the Civil Rights Act*, 15 How. L.J. 227 (1969).

Lacy, *EEO Implications of Job Analyses*, 4 Emp. Rel. L.J. 525 (1979).

Landrigan, *True Entrance Qualifications and Objective Performance Measures*, 5 EEO Today 129 (1978).

Ledvinka, *The Statistical Definition of Fairness in the Federal Selection Guidelines and Its Implications for Minority Employment*, 32 Personnel Psychology 551 (1979).

Miner & Miner, *Employee Selection Within the Law* (1978).

Reilly & Chao, *Validity and Fairness of Alternative Employee Selection Procedures*, 35 Personnel Psychology 1 (1982).

Reiter, *Compensating for Race or National Origin in Employment Testing*, 8 Loyola U. L.J. 681 (1977).

Riggins, *Technical Look at the Eighty Percent Rule as Applied to Employee Selection Procedures*, 12 U. Richmond L. Rev. 647 (1978).

Risher, *Job Analysis: A Management Perspective*, 4 Emp. Rel. L.J. 535 (1979).

Rowe, *Employment Testing and Title VII of the Civil Rights Act of 1964: After Albemarle Paper Co. v. Moody*, 38 Ala. Law 357 (1977).

Rubin, *The Uniform Guidelines on Employee Selection Procedures: Compromises and Controversies*, 28 Catholic U. L. Rev. 605 (1979).

Sandman, *Employment Testing and the Law*, 27 Lab. L.J. 38 (1976).

Sculnick, *Guardians and the Uniform Guidelines*, 8 EEO Today 17 (1981).

Sculnick, *The Distinction Between Disparate Impact and Disparate Treatment Theories of Discrimination*, 9 EEO Today 123 (1982).

Section 1981 and Employment Testing: Discriminatory Impact Establishes a Prima Facie Case, 19 Urban L. Ann. 268 (1980).

Seelman, *Employment Testing Law: the Federal Agencies Go Public with the Problems*, 10 Urban Law 1 (1978).

Shoben, *Differential Pass-Fail Rates in Employment Testing: Statistical Proof under Title VII*, 91 Harv. L. Rev. 793 (1978).

Shoben, *Probing the Discriminatory Effects of Employee Selection Procedures with Disparate Impact Analysis under Title VII*, 56 Tex. L. Rev. 1 (1977).

Sloan, *An Analysis of Uniform Guidelines on Employee Selection Procedures*, 4 Emp. Rel. L.J. 346 (1978).

Spradlin, *Additional Comments on the Application of Statistical Analysis to Differential Pass-Fail Rates in Employment Testing*, 17 Duq. L. Rev. 777 (1979).

Stacy, *Subjective Criteria in Employment Decisions under Title VII*, 10 Ga. L. Rev. 737 (1976).

Subjective Employment Criteria and the Future of Title VII in Professional Jobs, 54 U. Det. J. Urb. L. 165 (1976).

Tenopyr & Oeljten, *Personnel Selection and Classification*, 33 Ann. Rev. Psychol. 581 (1982).

Testing for Special Skills in Employment: A New Approach to Judicial Review, 1976 Duke L. J. 596.

Title VII of the Civil Rights Act of 1964—Educational and Testing Requirements Invalid Unless Job-Related, 10 Duquesne L. Rev. 270 (1971).

Validity of Standardized Employment Testing under Title VII and the Equal Protection Clause, 37 Mo. L. Rev. 693 (1972).

Washington v. Davis: Quantity, Quality and Equality in Employment, 1976 Sup. Ct. Rev. 263.

Wigdor & Garner (eds.), *Ability Testing: Uses, Consequences and Controversies* (1982).

Wilson, *Second Look at Griggs v. Duke Power Company: Ruminations on Job Testing, Discrimination, and the Role of the Federal Courts*, 58 Va. L. Rev. 844 (1972).

Zimmer, *Basing Employment Decisions on Tests: Compliance with the New Uniform Guidelines*, 10 Seton Hall L. Rev. 769 (1980).

PUBLICATIONS

AGE DISCRIMINATION IN EMPLOYMENT ACT: A COMPLIANCE AND LITIGATION MANUAL FOR LAWYERS AND PERSONNEL PRACTITIONERS. Edited by Monte B. Lake, Esq. pp. 456, paper (1982). $14.95 members; $19.95 nonmembers.

CONTRACT COMPLIANCE UNDER THE REAGAN ADMINISTRATION—A PRACTITIONER'S GUIDE TO CURRENT USE OF THE OFCCP COMPLIANCE MANUAL. By Jeffrey A. Norris, Esq. pp. 513, paper (1982). $19.95 members; $24.95 nonmembers.

COMPARABLE WORTH: ISSUES AND ALTERNATIVES. Edited by E. Robert Livernash. pp. 270, cloth (1980). $14.95 members; $21.95 nonmembers.

COMPARABLE WORTH: A SYMPOSIUM ON THE ISSUES AND ALTERNATIVES. pp. 100, paper (1980) $9.95 members; $12.95 nonmembers.

COMPARABLE WORTH SET: $21.00 members; $29.95 nonmembers

HUMAN RESOURCES PLANNING: A GUIDE TO DATA (2ND EDITION). Edited by Patricia J. Snider and Renae F. Broderick. pp. 382 paper (1980), $15.00 members; $21.00 nonmembers.

PERSPECTIVES ON AVAILABILITY: A SYMPOSIUM ON DETERMINING PROTECTED GROUP REPRESENTATION IN INTERNAL AND EXTERNAL LABOR MARKETS. Papers by Robert J. Flanagan, George T. Milkovich, Richard B. Freeman, David W. Peterson, Alan E. Bayer and Nathan Glazer. pp. 243 paper (1978). $9.75 members; $12.75 nonmembers.

CURRENT TRENDS IN THE USE (AND MISUSE) OF STATISTICS IN EMPLOYMENT DISCRIMINATION LITIGATION (2ND EDITION). By Frank C. Morris, Jr. pp. 206 paper (1978). $7.75 members; $11.50 nonmembers.

EEAC MONOGRAPH SERIES

No. 1 **PERSONAL LIABILITY OF MANAGERS AND SUPERVISORS FOR CORPORATE EEO POLICIES AND DECISIONS.** By Daniel R. Levinson, Esq. pp. 52, paper (1982). $5.95 members; $6.95 nonmembers.

No. 2 **EMPLOYEE SELECTION: LEGAL AND PRACTICAL ALTERNATIVES TO COMPLIANCE AND LITIGATION.** Edited by Edward E. Potter, Esq. pp. 326, paper (1983). $14.75 members; $19.75 nonmembers.

To order EEAC publications, write the Equal Employment Advisory Council, 1015 Fifteenth Street, N.W., Washington, D.C. 20005. Please include payment with your order.

Equal Employment Advisory Council
1015 Fifteenth Street, Northwest
Washington, D.C. 20005

ISBN 0-937856-07-x